I Remember When I Was Young

I Remember When I Was Young

'A collection of half a century of peoples' personal memories from around Britain and farther afield'

by Rob Horlock

Unlimited Publishing
Bloomington, Indiana

This book is dedicated to my mum and dad
who, sadly, are no longer around
to remember when they were young

Contents

Foreword

Close your eyes and go back in time:

To a time before the Internet and e-mail.
Before TV dinners and juvenile crime.
Before Satellite TV and 'going to the gym.'
Before gap years, heart bypass operations and winter holidays in
    the sun.

Take yourself back to a time . . .

When you walked to school, no matter what the weather. Churches had pews and villages had policemen who knocked on the door if you were caught scrumping. You or your best friend had a pet tortoise, stamp collecting was considered a perfectly normal pursuit and Teddy's best friend in the toybox was a golliwog. Telephones had dials, trainers were called plimsolls and the only time you wore them was at school, for 'PE.' Smith's Crisps packets contained little blue screwed up pouches of salt.

Corners had shops, which closed at 5-30pm and 1pm on Wednesdays and Saturdays. The proud owner's name was painted over the top of the door. They never opened on Sundays.

Your dad checked the oil, water and tyre pressures on the car and made sure the starting handle was in the boot before setting off to drive forty-five miles. You didn't wear seat belts because they weren't fitted.

Things were measured in feet and inches and you paid for everything that you bought in pounds, shillings and pence

Light hearted individuals were often described as 'gay.'

You watched Saturday morning cartoons at the cinema. Commercials for Omo and mild green Fairy Liquid, and children's favourites 'Rag, Tag and Bobtail' and 'Bill and Ben' all appeared on your ten inch black and white TV.

At Christmas, you sat on Santa's knee and your parents weren't at all worried.

You knew everyone who lived in your road—and so did your parents. A shilling was decent pocket money and you'd reach into a muddy gutter for a penny. Nearly everyone's mum was at home when they returned from school.

'Race issue' meant arguing about who ran the fastest. Having a weapon in school meant being caught with a catapult. Taking drugs meant taking an aspirin. Your friends all caught measles, mumps and chicken pox and probably gave them to you. When you were older, you may have had your tonsils out, too. Someone you knew emigrated to Australia.

You or your brother had a hairstyle like the Beatles and tried to learn to play the guitar. The Rolling Stones were considered a threat to public order so you bought all of their singles to play on your Dansette record player. You went to sleep with Radio Luxembourg still playing on your transistor radio.

If all of this reminds you of your childhood, then you grew up in the 1950s and '60s.

How does your decade compare?

Introduction

'I Remember When I Was Young' is a collection of half a century of personal memories. Beginning in the 1920s and ending with the 1960s, each chapter contains stories and recollections from individuals throughout the UK and abroad. A wide range of personal memories from childhood, early adulthood and later life. Some recall humorous or emotional incidents unconnected with the world around them; others describe episodes that have a direct connection to the major events of the day. Written in a variety of styles, all recall a time very different to the present day and all who lived at that time will feel a sense of belonging and possibly a tinge of regret that this time has now passed. Younger readers may be astonished at some of the day to day activities that were taken for granted by their older relatives.

Each chapter covers a decade and begins with an overview of the main historical events of the time. Important discoveries and 'firsts' are highlighted, together with notable anniversaries. The main focus, however, is not on well-documented historical events but on ordinary people's own personal reminiscences. Everyday stories, which will make the reader laugh, cry, ponder and remember.

The memories from each decade paint a picture of life as it was lived by the individuals concerned. Some led similar lives. Some had very different experiences. All are real people sharing their memories with the rest of us. Each decade is distinctly different and the memories captured in this book show how values and lifestyles have changed—perhaps not always for the better . . .

'I Remember When I Was Young' is not a comprehensive view of life in earlier times. It is a series of snapshots of life as it was lived by ordinary (and in some cases, extraordinary) people. People like you and I.

The 1920s

The world at large—the historical context

Recovering from the War

As the decade began, Britain was still recovering from the First World War and the repayment of massive war debts continued throughout the decade. War memorials were built in virtually every town and village throughout Britain to commemorate those from the local community who had not returned from the conflict. The body of 'The Unknown Soldier' was laid to rest on Armistice Day 1920 and hundreds of thousands of people filed past the newly unveiled Cenotaph in the days that followed to pay their respects to those who had given their lives. Poppy Day was introduced in 1921 as a means of both raising money and ensuring that those who had given their lives in the Great War would not be forgotten by future generations. Many ex-servicemen struggled to find work and The British Legion was formed to help them.

Politics

In 1922 the Coalition government led by Lloyd George, which had been in power since the war, broke up and Conservative Andrew Bonar Law became Prime Minister. The following year he resigned after being diagnosed with cancer and Stanley Baldwin became Prime Minister.

In 1924 an election resulted in a Hung parliament and Ramsay MacDonald was appointed as Labour's first Prime Minister heading a minority government which relied on the continued support of the Liberals to keep it in office. This collapsed in October of the same year, largely due to the publication of the 'Zinoviev Letter' (later proved to be a fake) which implied that the Labour government was linked to the rise of communism in Russia. The Tories were returned to power. In the final year of the decade, the general election ended in another Hung parliament. Ramsay MacDonald headed Britain's second Labour government, which included the first female cabinet member—Margaret Bondfield, Minister of Labour.

In 1921, civil war broke out in Ireland following the signing of the Anglo Irish treaty. This conceived the idea of the 26 counties of southern Ireland becoming the Irish Free State, a dominion within the British Empire. Michael Collins, founder of the IRA signed the treaty with the words 'I am signing my own death warrant'; the following year he was assassinated. Civil war raged between the Republicans who wanted full independence and the Free-Staters who accepted the treaty. The Republicans finally accepted the treaty in 1923, under the leadership of Eamon de Valera.

Further afield, world politics were becoming more polarised with Fascist and Communist parties gaining in popularity in countries around the world. In 1922, Italy became the first country in Europe to have a fascist government, under the leadership of Benito Mussolini. At the opposite end of the political spectrum, communists were victorious in the Russian civil war. In China, a communist party was formed in 1921. Following a period of civil war, Pu Yi, the last emperor of China was expelled from Peking and driven into exile.

The General Strike
The miners had been in dispute for years over pay and conditions—thousands of miners died every year in pit accidents and from illnesses caused by the Dickensian working conditions underground. Mines were privately owned and the owners, under threat from cheaper foreign imports, were demanding that the miners accept a cut in wages and work longer hours. In May 1926 the TUC called a general strike in support of the miners and over three million workers joined the strike. This lasted nine days and brought the country to a standstill. Troops were called in to man essential services. Trams and buses, with mesh screens protecting their windows from stone throwing strikers, were manned by students. In the end, the miners were still forced to concede to their employers' demands.

Many men lost their jobs through pit closures and, with no social security payments to help them, life was tough. This was true for all the unemployed, not only the ex-miners. The National Insurance scheme paid a subsistence wage for up to six weeks, after which the unemployed were forced to apply to 'The Parish' for aid. Claimants were means tested and given vouchers for essential foods. Means testing in the Twenties was a severe and humiliating experience—if you had anything of value it had to be pawned before aid could be considered. Destitute people ended up in the workhouse, a hangover from Victorian times. These were finally closed in 1929.

Female Emancipation
Women over thirty years old were now eligible to vote having been granted the right in 1918. This was extended to women over 21 years old in 1928. There will be many of the more senior readers of this book whose mothers were not eligible to vote in their younger years.

Female emancipation was also evident in other ways. Women's hemlines were rising and women's calves were a common sight. Women's fashion dictated that they should emulate men—long hair and bustiers were out, close-cropped hair and flat chests were in. The cloche hat was <u>the</u> female accessory in the middle years of the decade. Even more shockingly, women in large numbers were taking to smoking, drinking, wearing make up and dancing the Charleston—'Flappers' were born! In Paris, twenty-year-old Josephine Baker took the Charleston to extremes, dancing virtually naked and sending audiences wild.

This was also the decade of the cocktail. The martini, a mixture of gin and vermouth became the 'in' drink.

Not all women enjoyed this newfound freedom. With so many men dying in the war, huge numbers of women were resigned to living their lives as spinsters. Many more lost their loved ones in the war and couldn't bring themselves to find love elsewhere. Dances were characterised by an excess of women and the 'wallflowers' standing around the edge of the dance floor without a partner were an ever-present reminder of the after-effects of the war.

Prohibition
In the USA, prohibition was in force throughout the decade. This led to the growth in the 'Speakeasy'—illegal drinking dens. Alcohol smuggled over the border from Canada was on sale together with home brewed 'hooch.' Hundreds of drinkers died every year from the poisonous effects of this illegal bootleg whisky. The more affluent citizens of the US holidayed in the Caribbean where alcohol

Film star Louise Brooks, pictured on the front of a Cuban matchbox

was freely available. Cuba was particularly fashionable with many people discovering the joys of Bacardi for the first time. Prohibition also led to an upsurge in gangsterism, particularly in the big cities. In February 1929, the famous St Valentine's Day massacre took place in Chicago when seven of 'Bugsy' Malone's gang were machine gunned to death on the orders of Al Capone. Capone was defending his virtual monopoly on the sale of bootleg liquor in Chicago.

Prosperity

There was a post-war housing boom, particularly in southern England. This was the era of the suburbs and many acres of fields were turned into fashionable avenues filled mainly with large semi-detached family homes. These houses typically cost under £1,000 and were very affordable for many in the newly emerging middle classes. The houses were spacious but very similar in design. One particular design feature was a small kitchen. It was considered advantageous to be able to stand in the middle of the kitchen and reach any of the cupboards without moving too far.

Even relatively small households often had servants 'to do' for them

In a typical village, prior to the First World War, most people either 'lived in the big house,' worked 'below stairs' or provided services to the upper class landowners. The middle class did not exist until the 1920s when the old order was increasingly threatened as 'office workers' moved in and commuted to the cities.

This housing boom also led to a huge increase in the number of electrical appliances on offer. Electric vacuum cleaners, fires, kettles, cookers and toasters were the labour saving devices at the top of most householders' lists. Electricity itself was a novelty for many of the new homeowners, as was an upstairs toilet (even an indoor toilet at all, for some). During the decade many council houses were also built in the suburbs as city slums were cleared. The social mix of council house tenant and middle class homeowner living in close proximity didn't always result in a happy and tolerant atmosphere. Many council house tenants regretted having to move away from their close knit community and felt that 'more space didn't always mean greater happiness.'

To ease the financial burden on older people, the state pension was introduced during this decade; people over the age of 65 received ten shillings (50p) per week.

Changes in retail prices had been monitored since 1914. The list of items that were monitored remained unchanged in the 1920s. This included mutton, wild rabbit, hard soap, candles, corset lacing, tram fares and lamp oil.

Travel

The decade was a great era of expansion for air travel. In 1919 Alcock and Brown had made the first non-stop flight across the Atlantic. In 1928, Bert Hinkler became the first person to fly solo from Australia to Britain. With a compass and old school atlas to guide him, he successfully completed the journey in 16 days.

Airlines were set up in many countries around the world. In Britain, Imperial Airways was established in 1924 and a large new airport at Croydon was built later in the decade to service the ever-increasing demand for international air travel. Two forms of air travel were available—aeroplanes and airships. The latter were produced in Germany and in Britain. In 1929 the Graf Zeppelin completed a 21-day trip around the world, making only three stops en route. Two months later, the world's biggest airship, the British R101 made her maiden voyage. Many thought that these huge, gas filled, cigar shaped constructions would become the workhorse of the air, transporting freight and people cost effectively around the world. Others put their faith in the development of the aeroplane— noisier and more cramped but faster and more manoeuvrable. It wasn't until the following decade that the appeal of one of these forms of air travel came to an abrupt and tragic end.

The number of cars on Britain's roads grew dramatically during the decade. The introduction of cars such as the Austin Seven and the Morris Minor, both mass-produced in Britain, brought the possibility of car ownership to the middle classes. By the end of the decade more than a million cars were registered, three times the number than at the beginning of the 1920s. At the same time, the price of a basic family car had fallen to about one third of the 1920 price, thanks to mass production. Henry Ford had introduced his Model T earlier in the century and told his prospective customers that 'they could have any colour as long as it was black!' In 1925, Henry Ford's immortal words were overtaken by progress and cars in various colours became available.

In the cities, petrol driven delivery vehicles steadily replaced horse drawn vehicles during the decade. As the volume of traffic increased, congestion in cities, particularly London, became a way of life. This was eased with the introduction of white lines

This Worthington White Shield Bottle Car was one of five purchased by Worthington's brewery in the 1920s. They were used throughout the 1920s and 1930s for promotional purposes

down the middle of the road and traffic lights. These two measures helped to bring some order to the chaos and traffic began to flow in a more ordered manner.

All of this led to more roads being built, garages springing up to service the needs of the more affluent, newly mobile, middle classes and horror of horrors—advertising hoardings! These caused considerable controversy and were seen as a blight on the countryside, though calls to have them banned were ignored. The speed limit at this time was 20 mph though this too, was generally ignored. Anyone over the age of 16 could drive a motor vehicle without the need for any form of test or qualification. The number of fatal accidents increased along with the increase in the volume of traffic. By the end of the decade, more than 5,000 people a year were dying on the roads—many of the fatalities were pedestrians who failed to get out of the way of oncoming speeding cars.

Communication
The telephone became more popular and exchanges began to be automated. Telephones were of the candlestick variety, with a separate earpiece connected to the main handpiece by a short length of electrical cable. In the main, calls were connected by an operator, usually a female who had a bewildering array of electrical plugs and sockets in front of her that she used to connect the caller to his or her destination. The telephone network was not complete during the 1920s and many country dwellers relied on telegrams for urgent messages. This was still a common form of communication and the local telegraph office sent the messages using Morse code. These took a matter of seconds to reach the destination telegraph office, whereupon the message would be written out or typed, put into a pink envelope and delivered by hand to the recipient.

Wireless sets were developed during the decade. In the early twenties, crystal sets were popular which required a set of earphones. By the latter years of the decade, loudspeakers were in general use and the whole family could sit around the wireless listening to the broadcasts of the BBC. The list of programmes was published in the Radio Times, which first appeared in 1923, a year after the BBC was founded. Television was first demonstrated by John Logie Baird in 1926 but TV sets were not available to the general public during the decade.

A Fullers Sparta Crystal Set

World Events

The value of the German Mark collapsed in the early years of the decade. In August 1921, £1 = 340 marks. By October, £1 = 720 marks. In August 1922 after further falls and a brief recovery the mark slid again; £1 = 8,000 marks. In January 1923, £1 bought 112,000 marks. Germany's economic crisis deepened and currency devaluation spiralled out of control. Cash was carried around in wheelbarrows and savings were non existent. The National Socialist Party, led by Adolf Hitler, capitalised on this, blaming the crisis on the crippling level of debt imposed as war reparations after World War One. The rise of Nazism in Germany had begun.

By September 1923, £1 was worth 200,000,000 marks. In November, in an attempt to stabilise the currency a new unit was introduced, the New Mark, worth 1,000,000,000,000 (one trillion) marks.

In the USA, Anastasia Chaikovsky claimed to be the youngest daughter of the murdered Russian Czar. She claimed to have survived the massacre in 1918 and escaped from Russia with the help of citizens loyal to the Czar. This started a mystery which ran throughout the remainder of the century—was she the real Anastasia, or a hoaxer claiming the right to the Czar's lost fortune?

The bones of Australopithecus Africanus were discovered in Africa. This was considered at the time to be an extremely important discovery and the remains became known as 'the missing link'.

Arguably the greatest archaeological discovery of the century was made in Egypt in 1922. Excavating in the Valley of the Kings, near Luxor a team led by Howard Carter uncovered a flight of stone steps. This led to the tomb of the boy king Tutankhamun, which had lain undisturbed since 1337BC. The tomb was not particularly large, but was filled with a fantastic collection of artefacts, many of which were gilded with gold. Unlike most of the other tombs that had been discovered, this one had not been looted and its treasures remained intact. The tomb also contained the mummified body of the boy king, covered by a spectacular golden effigy of the king. The enormous public interest in Tutankhamun and his treasures influenced many designers. Fashions, jewellery, and some new buildings took their lead from ancient Egypt in the later years of the decade.

Sport and Recreation
The Olympic games of 1924 were held in Paris. US swimmer Johnny Weissmuller won three gold medals. Following this success Weissmuller went on to further fame in Hollywood, starring as Tarzan, the man-ape. The Scottish sprinter Eric Liddell was the favourite to win the 100 metres gold medal. However, one of the

heats was run on a Sunday. Liddell refused to compromise his Christian beliefs and declined to compete, thereby disqualifying himself. His colleague in the British team, Harold Abrahams, went on to win the gold. Justice was seen to be done later in the tournament when Eric Liddell triumphed in the 400 metres, a race that he did not expect to win.

The first FA Cup final to be held at Wembley Stadium took place in 1923. Over 200,000 fans crammed in to the ground, many having scaled the walls. A mass pitch invasion before the game threatened to cancel the showpiece event before a lone policeman mounted on a white horse cleared the pitch and restored order, allowing the game to kick off. Bolton Wanderers beat West Ham 2-1.

In the cinema, Rudolf Valentino starred in 'The Four Horsemen of the Apocalypse' and 'The Sheikh'—very popular with women, less so with men! Charlie Chaplin starred in 'Gold Rush.' Other stars included The Keystone Cops, Buster Keaton, Laurel and Hardy and Harold Lloyd. The Hollywood couple of the decade was undoubtedly Douglas Fairbanks and Mary Pickford.

The first 'talking' film, 'The Jazz Singer' starring Al Jolson was released in 1927. Many in the industry thought that sound would be a passing phase. Many others soon found that it was anything but a temporary change and actors and actresses who had been major stars of the silent screen saw their careers in ruins. Some of these found speaking and acting difficult to co-ordinate, some had squeaky voices that didn't match their on screen image and some simply faded away to be replaced by new rising stars. A number of cinemas couldn't afford the new sound equipment and closed down. Many musicians who were employed in the cinema orchestras also found themselves out of work.

Art Deco style was the most significant influence on the decade. Simple geometric shapes—curves, circles and squares, were seen in furniture designs, tableware, buildings and clothes. Many of the new cinemas built during the decade followed Art Deco lines, as did a significant number of office buildings.

An interesting phenomenon of the decade was the huge interest in fairies. This had been sparked off in 1917 when sixteen-year-old Elsie Wright and her ten-year-old cousin Frances Griffiths produced a photograph that showed Frances playing with a group of fairies. These became known as the 'Cottingley Fairies,' named after the village in which the girls lived. Other similar pictures followed and in 1920 Sir Arthur Conan Doyle published two of the photographs in Strand magazine to back up his belief in the existence of fairies. This led to worldwide interest in the subject and arguments between the believers and sceptics continued for several years.

The Crash

The US stock market boomed throughout the decade until 1928 when a slide began.

The 24th October 1929 became known as 'Black Thursday' as the market collapsed.

Mass panic set in and thousands of investors were ruined. Bankrupted stockbrokers and millionaires committed suicide rather than face a penniless future. For many, the optimism that had characterised much of the decade in the USA quickly turned to despair. In Britain, the problems of the US stock market seemed a long way away and life carried on much as normal. At least for a while . . .

Closer to Home—
Personal Memories of the 1920s

Naturally enough, as the decade began the First World War was still fresh in the mind of most people. Several of the personal memories that follow reveal the different ways in which individuals encountered this.

John Rouse in North Yorkshire recalls his exposure to the after-effects of the War

Hilversum and holidays

'As a child in the 1920s I saw something that I never understood until later in life. Groups of men congregated on street corners to chat or watch the world go by. Many of these had a leg, an arm or part of a limb missing. They seemed to be everywhere. Some would shuffle along like a child playing trains. Others would stand on the kerb singing, or selling boxes of matches to earn a few pennies. The Great War lived on in these men, scarred for life.

During the mid '20s wireless was just coming in to its own and what a thrill it was to be able to tune in to the foreign stations such as Hilversum and Radio Luxembourg and sit on the doorstep of your home listening to the records being played. The weather always seemed to be balmy (in my memory, at least) and your neighbours would be doing just the same as you. As we sat on our respective doorsteps, messages passed up the road from house to house and back again; that's how we knew what we were all doing. Personal possessions in the home were only the bare essentials and not worth stealing so we never had to worry about locking a door if you left the house unattended.

In those days before smoke control, one of the biggest hazards to health was smog, a mixture of home and factory generated smoke and fog. Thick and heavy, it would linger for days. This was the cause of many deaths and serious illnesses, often so bad that people took to wearing facemasks to combat it.

Holidays were what other people went on if they were rich enough, usually for a week in the summer. People with high opinions of themselves would boast of going 'down south' to Torquay or Bournemouth. The Isle of Wight was pie in the sky!'

*Hellen Price was born in **Edinburgh.** Her father experienced the horrors of war first hand*

Boys—avoid them (if you can find one)

'My mother, a strict Presbyterian, spoke to me about the dangers of getting involved with boys. 'They're bold, bad and dangerous,' she gravely warned me, 'especially those in uniforms.' The First World War was still fresh in peoples' minds and in day to day life. Young boys played 'killing Germans' and were encouraged to play such games by parents who wanted their sons to grow up 'brave and tough.'

My father had returned to Scotland after the war, following a stay of 2½ years in hospital in Kenilworth suffering from 'gastritis.' This was likely to have been a cover for the real reason that he was there—he was almost certainly suffering from shell shock. Many men suffered from this during and after the war and the condition was eventually recognised as a genuine illness. This came too late for many of the men and boys who had been shot as deserters as they fled the Front in dazed confusion after seeing friends blown apart before their eyes.

Men fought in the war on behalf of 'a land fit for heroes.' They returned as heroes but as the '20s progressed many of these heroes found themselves with no work. They were reduced to begging on the streets with little or no help from the government that had sent them off to war on its behalf.

My father had survived, partly due to the decision that he made in 1915. He was asked to go for officer training. My mother begged him not to accept and he decided against becoming an officer. This decision was based largely on the fact that officers 'led from the front' in those days, leading to an average life expectancy for an officer at the Front of two weeks.

My parents wanted me to train to be a teacher, which was a high level occupation for a woman at that time. I had no intention of becoming a teacher. Nobody liked their teachers and young girls, who could be very catty, said 'Women only went in to teaching if they couldn't get a boyfriend.' Since a large percentage of the available male generation had been wiped out in the previous decade, many women remained without a man throughout their lives and quite a few of these did, in fact, take up teaching. I'm sure that this had nothing to do with their single status, however.

Equal pay did not exist in the 1920s. Men were paid more for the logical reason that they had a family to feed, women only had to look after themselves. Not always true, of course, but it would be many years before equal pay for the sexes became a reality.'

Soldiers recovering from the after-effects of the First World War

*Nellie Lucas in **Birmingham** also remembers
her father coming home from the War*

Horses and men

'Dad came home in 1921. I didn't really know him because he'd been away so long. I was born in 1912 so I'd only seen him when he came home on leave. The First World War finished in 1918 but dad was still out in France for another three years. I was too young to understand at the time, but later I found out that he'd been kept out there on 'jankers.'

Dad was in the gunnery regiment and he looked after the horses that pulled the gun carriages. One night, in 1917, he was on duty guarding the horses when one of his pals asked him to come for a drink. Dad couldn't resist it and went off for an hour or so. When he returned to the stables, he found that one of the horses had got its trace caught around its neck and had hung itself. Horses were considered more valuable than the men at that time—men were easier to replace—and so having a horse kill itself whilst the person guarding it was away, was a serious offence. Dad was court marshalled and sentenced to work on grave duty. He spent the years after the war digging up the dead bodies of soldiers (from both sides) and reburying them in proper war graves.'

*Daisy Woods in **Buckinghamshire** was exposed
to the consequences of the War as a child*

Chalky

'My mother ran a boarding house and we had two men who lived there all the time. Both of these men had fought in the trenches and one of them, who I remember was called 'Chalky,' suffered from shell shock. Sometimes, when the hot water pipes banged and rattled in the early morning he would run round the house with no clothes on shouting 'The Germans are coming, the Germans are coming.' My mother had to calm him down and take him back to his room. He used to cry a lot. I'll never forget Chalky.'

*One of **Joan Barnes** in **Nottingham's** earliest memories was when she was two years old*

Gas lights and Grandy

'I remember walking along the pavement in the early evening winter darkness with my mother when I caught sight of a shadow as we walked under a street lamp. I asked mother what it was and she told me that it was my shadow.

'I don't like it,' I said, 'I don't want it. It's chasing me.'

As I moved along the street the shadow changed position, then faded, then returned when we reached the next lamp. I was very frightened.

When I was few years older I used to wait with my friends for the lamplighter to come on his rounds. The street lamps were gas lit and each one had to be individually lit. As the lamp was lit we stood underneath and made a wish; we believed that any wish made while the lamp was warming up would come true. I don't believe they ever did though. We were very superstitious then—I still am.

I didn't have a favourite food. We ate what we were given and we ate all of it otherwise we'd be in trouble. We always ate at the table. Kids first, then the adults then the kids were called back to wash up.

Mum ran a fish and chip shop in Narrowmarsh in Nottingham, a poor area of the town. Nobody had any money and there were a lot of homeless people. If they had a bit of money they could sleep the night in a hostel for the homeless. I think it was 6d (that's 2½p) for a blanket to sleep on the floor. For 2d (less than 1p), men slept standing up with their arms draped over a line, like a washing line. It was called 'sleeping over the line.' Mum befriended one old man who had no home and who regularly slept 'over the line' in the hostel. He had been brought up in an orphanage and joined the army—the armed forces did a lot of recruiting in orphanages. When he retired from the army he got a pension of 3/6d (about 17.5p) a week so you can see he couldn't afford to sleep in the hostel with a blanket every night. It's true what they say—the government wanted the men during the war to serve their country, then when the war was over the country forgot about them.

Mum used to load him up with fish and lots of chips because she felt sorry for him. It was all he ate most days.

When the hostel was demolished, the old man had nowhere to go and my mum took pity on him and asked him to come and live with us. Us kids slept four to a bed and we had a spare room for visitors that the old man moved in to. He soon settled in and we called him 'Grandy.' He loved playing with us and he really did seem like a granddad. His favourite food was tea with sugar, bread and jam. He drank the tea and put the sugar on the bread and jam!

One day I was walking the quarter of a mile back from school to home with my friend and we saw a funeral hearse. It wasn't unusual to see this so I didn't take much notice. When I turned the corner of our street, though, I saw that the hearse was standing outside of my home. I ran up the road and saw the men carrying a cheap varnished coffin out of the front door. It was Grandy. He had died two days before but nobody had told me. His body had lain in the front room, which was what happened in those days, before funeral parlours were everywhere. There were two bunches of chrysanthemums on the coffin, golden ones from Gran and white ones from Mum. There were no wreaths and I cried because I thought there should have been. It was a pauper's funeral and I was very sad. Poor Grandy.'

John Rice *had a passion for trains during his youth in* **Cheshire**

'Tot'

'I suppose I have had a connection with the railways in some way since the day I was born. I understand I was named after a signalman who worked mainly at Altcar and Hillhouse station on the (now closed) line from Aintree to Southport.

When I was young I lived in a remote farmhouse within walking distance of Hillhouse Junction. My favourite railwayman there was known as 'Tot,' who was quite a character. He made a point of having two or three loaves tucked away and a stockpot on the stove in which he cooked anything suitable he could lay his hands on in the neighbouring woods, undergrowth or waterside. He set traps for rabbits and hares and collected a variety of birds' eggs—coot, peewit, pheasant, partridge and wild duck. In season, there were a few wild mushrooms to be had and lots of blackberries in late summer. The stockpot always put out a tempting aroma and I developed a liking for peewit egg on toast. Tot kept a good fire burning and he liked nothing more than a good long nap in front of this after a hearty meal from the stockpot. I woke him whenever a bell rang to warn that a train was coming.

The line was quiet in winter, except for two weeks. The busy periods were during the Waterloo Cup (hare coursing) meeting that took place at Altcar and the Grand National steeplechase meeting at Aintree. I can still remember the excitement in 1928 when news came through that Tipperary Tim, a rank outsider, had won the National. I didn't know what the fuss was about until in later years the ins and outs of placing a bet were explained to me.

The summer was generally busier, especially at weekends when long holiday trains from Manchester and beyond carried visitors to Ainsdale and Southport.

One day, with Tot deep in the arms of Morpheus, a bell rang, then another. Despite my best efforts to wake him, he remained fast asleep. Soon, I spotted a train coming from the Aintree direction and tried even harder to bring him to consciousness but still to no avail. The train, which was supposed to carry straight on at the signal towards Southport, suddenly veered right along a side branch. Fortunately, the driver soon realised that the points had not been set correctly and applied the brakes. As he reversed back on to the main line, Tot woke and wondered what the fuss was about. The points were duly fixed in their correct position and the train resumed its scheduled journey. There had been a good deal of banter between Tot, the train crew and some of the passengers but everyone promised not to inform the then equivalent of the 'Fat Controller,' or anyone else about the incident. And as far as I know, nobody has—until now!'

Joan Packham who grew up in Sheffield recalls her very early youth

Coats and Flowers

'My parents already had four children when I came along and father was out of work. They found it very hard to feed and clothe their existing family, though mother believed that the children 'bring their own love with them.' It was some time before I realised that we were poor and needed 'school breakfasts' to start the day before classes. My stomach still turns over at the memory of the unvarying menu of one inch thick slices of bread coated in a revolting layer of what they called 'dripping.' I'm sure this had never been near a joint of beef nor anything to give it a flavour; it would have been perfect for greasing an engine. This was followed by a mug of really cheap and nasty cocoa. Is there any wonder that I was often sick afterwards?

It is surprising how one adapts to poverty when that is all one knows. I can distinctly remember feeling cold and asking for another coat on the bed. It was several years before I realised that other people had sheets and blankets.

Nevertheless I was very happy as a child. Among the many pleasures I recall was the Whitsuntide Walk in which the many churches joined together to parade through the streets behind a brass band before congregating in the park for communal hymn singing. Each church had its own banner featuring either a picture or a biblical text which we formed up behind with pride. For children such as us it was the only time that we had a new dress instead of big sister's hand-me-downs. All children carried baskets of brightly coloured flowers. After the Walk the flowers were either taken home or distributed to old people or hospitals; the baskets, though were lovingly put away until the next year. Just once I cried when I realised that during the course of the parade I had lost two of my flowers!'

Bert Triggs grew up near **Bristol**,
sometimes in the 'half light'

Spilling the light

'Our house was lit by gas and we paid by putting 'a penny in the meter.' We often found ourselves suddenly thrown into darkness as the money ran out. If we didn't have any spare pennies, in darkness we stayed. Occasionally the gasman called to empty the meter. Quite often there was a surplus and he would leave the excess coppers. Sixpence or a shilling was quite a bonus at that time.

Another feature of our gas lighting was the inefficiency of the mantles, the fragile pieces of cloth that contained the flame. This was no fault of the mantle manufacturers; it had more to do with my pipe smoking father lighting his 'spill' from the mantle which he then used to light his pipe. In the process he often damaged the mantles, causing them to split and consequently throw out less light.

Once a week, before I went to school my mother sent me to the local butcher's shop to buy '6d beef cuttings' that she used in pies and stews. Every Sunday we sat down to a roast dinner; beef, lamb and occasionally pork but never chicken—this was only eaten at Christmas.'

*Eileen Kelly was born in **Birmingham**. Although not poor herself, she saw many deprived children*

Children and playmates

'At that time, Birmingham was the industrial heart of England. Factories of every sort constantly belched smoke of various colours that mixed with the constant fog throughout the winter. Everyone had coal fires so that smoke was always present. My father, who was in the Navy, wasn't worried by the depressing surroundings because when he wasn't away at sea, he could walk to the library, which was very close. He was extremely knowledgeable and spent his time while at sea studying, particularly Maths and Physics. He was one of the navy's first wireless operators and taught me and my four brothers and sisters Morse code. He even built us little 'tappers' so that we could send messages to each other. There were wireless parts all over the house and my mother exclaimed famously 'How can they call this wireless when I'm tripping over wires everywhere!'

There was a lot of unemployment and real poverty was a way of life for many people. At the primary school there were children with holes in their shoes and clothes and some of them smelt a lot. I felt very sorry for them shivering in their thin clothes during the very cold winters that we seemed to have then. They were also looked down upon as they had free dinners. Everyone knew because they were given a ticket for dinner. I asked a boy what he had for dinner at the school and he replied, 'It's always cheese pie.' As I was going home to meat with vegetables and pudding, that didn't sound like a dinner to me. They were also supplied with free boots, paid for out of the police 'boot fund,' which supplied needy children. I would regularly bring children home with me to my mother to ask her for clothes for them.

Then there were always head lice. The nurse came in regularly to check everyone's hair and the girl who sat next to me had lice. I picked up 'nits,' which I think were eggs. I had to have paraffin put on my hair with a towel round my head for several hours.

Children used to pass our house on the way to the park and in the school holidays whole families of children would trudge up from the back streets; maybe a nine or ten year old girl with a baby, a toddler holding a pushchair and perhaps two or three others. They would have a bottle for the baby, a bottle of 'pop' and some bread and jam and they stayed in the park all day, before trudging back home. I suppose it was almost like a day's holiday for them. I saw one such group and the girl pushing the pushchair was obviously wearing adult's shoes, which were far too big for her. I watched her skipping along, trying to keep the shoes on and finally I went and spoke to her. I told her that my mother would give her some shoes so they all trooped with me into our backyard. My poor mother was confronted with this pathetic group and my explanation of why they were there. As always, she managed to find something for them; shoes for the bigger girl and clothes for the little ones. She also told them to pop in again when they were passing before feeding them with possibly the only decent meal that they'd had all week. Not surprisingly, they came back several times to be fed and pampered.

Christmas was very special. One evening in November we would make the Christmas puddings. We all sat around the large scrubbed table and each had a job—stoning raisins, blanching and chopping almonds, removing lumps of sugar from crystallised orange and lemon peel and chopping it. After the ingredients were mixed in the large bowl we all had a 'stir and a wish.' Next day the puddings would be steamed with a lovely Christmas smell pervading the house. The puddings then had to be stored in a cool place, before the days of refrigerators. Our cool place was in the cellar. The cellar was always cold because of the pattern of holes on the grating, which opened on to the pavement outside and we stored our food on a series of shelves just inside the cellar door. The puddings waited quietly for Christmas Day without being disturbed except every Tuesday when the coalman delivered the coal!

On Christmas Eve, father went to the butchers to collect the turkey. Turkeys had black feathers then; I don't remember us ever having one with white feathers. He brought it home, plucked it, singed it to get rid of the left over wisps of feathers, then removed the insides, putting the tastiest bits to one side. The heart, lungs and neck—the giblets—were boiled and made into soup or fed to the cat who was very appreciative indeed! My mother made sage and onion and parsley and thyme stuffing and the turkey was ready for the oven on Christmas morning.

On Christmas Eve all of us children hung up our stockings, and were as excited as any children before and since when we woke up on Christmas morning. We would usually find a tangerine, an apple, nuts, a bag of sweets and a chocolate shape. Perhaps also a book and a pencil. Not a lot but we were still extremely excited as we came down the stairs on Christmas morning to see a roaring fire and a huge decorated Christmas Tree lit up with real candles. The Christmas dinner was a big event after all the preparation and we particularly looked forward to sharing the puddings that had been maturing in the cellar.

We had a large kitchen with a range. In one corner was the wash boiler underneath which a fire was lit. Every Monday morning, at the crack of dawn, mother would fill the boiler, light the fire and the washing would start. The kitchen sink was earthenware (which is now fashionable again!), very shallow and with one cold tap. Clothes were soaked overnight in a large tin bath. In the morning all white cottons were transferred to the boiler—sheets, pillowcases, shirts, hankies, etc. In the early days there was no soap powder, just Sunlight soap, shaved in to small pieces for the boiler and rubbed into the other items by hand. All the hand washing was well soaked, then thoroughly washed in the very hot water from the boiler. Everything was rinsed in cold water. Shirt collars, tablecloths and various other items had to go through starch. All whites were also rinsed in 'Reckitts Blue,' to keep them white. Everything went through the mangle to get rid of some of the moisture.

Woollens were washed on a different day using 'Lux' and 'Rinso.' It was all hung outside to dry except when it rained, in which case the house looked like a laundry for most of the week.

The visit of the chimney sweep also caused an upheaval. He always came very early in the morning so the room had to be prepared the night before. Curtains and pictures were taken down and all the furniture was covered with old sheets. Newspapers were spread from the front door to the fireplace. We children all stood around watching the sweep fasten the rods of his brushes together and push the brush up the chimney. Eventually he would send us outside to tell him when the brush appeared above the chimney. We felt very important when we rushed in to tell him. He then gathered up his brushes and the bag of soot, collected his fee of 1/- and left. Then the clearing up began. Covers and newspapers gathered up and shaken outside. You could smell the soot and there was a black film over everything. Ceiling and walls had to be brushed and the lino on the floor swept and scrubbed. It took hours to get everything done but the result was a brightly burning fire and a 'new' feeling.

Funerals used to terrify me. Black horses with long black plumed feathers on their heads majestically pulled the horse-drawn carriage slowly along the street. The coachman, dressed from head to toe in black, led the cortege of mourners who were also all dressed in deepest black; the women with veils over their faces. Onlookers respectfully bowed their heads as they passed.

When I was about seven years old, the woman who lived next door to us died in childbirth during the night. In those days we children never knew about babies until they appeared; we thought that the doctor carried them in his bag. So, one morning the three children from next door were in our house in tears. When we asked mum what was wrong she said that their mum had died in the night and they were going to stay with us until after the funeral. I didn't really know what was going on but one of them told me they had a baby brother who was dead and was being buried with their mum. It was just awful. The children had black armbands, which they continued to wear for the next year and more. After the funeral the children all went to live with different relatives. One of them, four year old Kenny, wanted to stay with my mother. She would have had him but he was taken away sobbing, never to be seen again by us. This frightened me so much that I used to run home from school and rush in to the house to make sure that my mum was not dead. One day when I ran in, she wasn't there. My dad was there and he told me that she had gone in to the hospital for an operation. I didn't find out for many years that she had, in fact, had a miscarriage. She was away for three weeks during which my dad looked after us and did all of the cooking. It wasn't too bad at all, but my mother kept a letter, which I had written to her: 'Please come home. Dad cuts the bread too thick.'

I had lots of playmates when I was young. We always played in the street. The traffic was horse-drawn for the most part. If a car appeared it was a sight that brought everyone out to look. The bread van, milkman, dustman and laundryman all had horse-drawn vehicles that called regularly. So we played in the road with no fear of being injured. There was a 'season' for everything. We drew hopscotch 'beds' and played that for a while. Then suddenly it was 'whip and top' time. I think the shopkeepers must have been responsible for the fashions because whips and tops would suddenly appear—a penny each—so everyone had to get them. Then it was hoops. Wooden hoops of many sizes would appear so we all got one and moved on to hoop races. Then 'skipping' was in. Ropes were stretched across the road with two children turning them

Decorative biscuit tins from the 1920s and '30s

while the rest of us skipped. Ball games, marbles and conkers also all had their time.

When I was about nine years old Sir Alan Cobham, the famous aviation pioneer visited Birmingham. Aeroplanes were even rarer than cars and we all looked up when a little bi-plane flew overhead. Sometimes they would write signs in the sky and I can remember asking my Mother what 'Beechams Pills' were after seeing the name spelt out in the sky! Sir Alan Cobham stayed in Birmingham for one week and advertised rides in his aeroplane for half-a-crown. I couldn't afford to have a ride. I couldn't even afford the tram fares to get to the other side of Birmingham. So I walked most of the way and arrived in Castle Bromwich very hot and exhausted. I saw the 'plane take off and land at very close quarters, which for a little girl from the narrow city streets of Birmingham was extremely exciting. I then had to walk home again and arrived late. So not only was I hot and tired, I was also in trouble. It was worth it though.'

Vera Wildig initially recalls the years leading up to the decade

Daisy

'I was fifteen years old in 1920. Before I think about this era, I have two very distinct memories from earlier years that will help to put the time in to perspective. When I was seven years old I went to Southampton docks to see a very large liner depart on its maiden voyage. My father promised me that when it had crossed the Atlantic three or four times we would be going on it to New York. I remember seeing all the people waving as they left the dock. I waved at them then went home to tell my mother that 'the big boat had four chimneys.' We never went to New York on that ship, of course—the Titanic sank a few days later and many of the people that I had seen waving goodbye to their friends and families lost their lives.

My other early memory, from 1918, is of seeing the first car come along our country road. We had never seen a car before and wondered where the horse was!

In the early years of the 1920s my older sister earned 14/- a week working in a shoe shop. She worked from 9am until 8pm most days except Sundays and she had no paid holidays at all. I remember

Sundays as being very quiet. Nothing was open except the Church, which the whole family attended, sometimes twice a day. On other days it was a common sight to see kids playing outside of pubs. They were waiting for their parents to come out of the pub at 10pm after drinking all evening.

I used to go dancing a lot with friends, like young girls do today. We met lots of young men and had a lovely time, though it would all seem very innocent compared to today. My future husband was one of my favourites but I started going out with another young man who was an apprentice engineer. He went off to Canada and left me, though. Some years later, after I was married, he returned and tried to recapture my affections. He even wanted me to divorce my husband! I wouldn't have anything to do with him.

One evening I went to a dance at a social club with friends and we were having a good time, as usual. I noticed a girl sitting on the side who wasn't dancing and looking sad. I went over to her and we started to talk. Her name was Daisy; she was thin and looked very poor. I liked her and she danced with us for the rest of the evening. A few days later we met again. We got on very well and Daisy asked me if she could come and live with me. She told me how her stepfather kicked and whipped her and she lifted her skirt to show me her bruises; she was black and blue from her knees to the top of her legs! I took her home and she asked mother if she could come and live with us. Mother looked at her and I could tell that she was taking pity on poor Daisy. She nodded her head, thinking that Daisy would stay for a few days and then go home. But it didn't turn out like that. Daisy went to the police and complained about her stepfather. She asked the kindly policeman if she would get in to trouble if she came to live with us. He said to her, 'You are sixteen years old so you live where you want.' That was it. Daisy went back to her house to sort herself out, then returned to us on the following Friday. She arrived without any bags and mother asked her where they were.

'I haven't got any.'

My sister Freda and I both gave her some of our spare clothes. Freda slept in the spare room and Daisy slept in the same bed as me. As she lay in the bed she said, 'This bed is lovely, you sink right down.'

I asked her about her bed.

'I didn't have one.'

'Where did you sleep?'

'On a chair in the kitchen.'

The following day, mother took Daisy out and bought her some underclothes, a dress, a coat and a pair of shoes. The following week she bought Daisy a set of Sunday clothes. Very soon Daisy had become one of the family.

About a year after she had moved in with us, Daisy met a wealthy young man called Jimmy and they were soon going out together regularly. They made a lovely couple and we all expected them to get married. That winter, however, a flu epidemic swept across the country and almost every household was affected. Jimmy caught the flu and sadly he died. Daisy, as you can imagine was heartbroken.

Strangely enough, nobody in our house was affected by the epidemic. Mother put it down to the onions that she had bought from 'Johnny Onions' the French onion seller who came over from Brittany every year to sell his strings of onions. That year, the onions that hung in the scullery all went black and rotten—mother said that the onions caught the flu germs, not us.

Daisy's story has a happy ending. Three years later, she met another young man who worked on the railways. They married and lived a long and very happy life together.'

Emily Day in *Devon* has one distinct memory

Goose grease

'During the winter months, our mother regularly smeared goose fat on our chests and backs. Mum said that it would keep out the chill and stop us catching infections. It was sticky horrible stuff but I don't remember that it smelled of much. Some days, when it was very cold, we used to wear paper under our clothes to keep us warmer. Several of the other children were also insulated in the same manner so we didn't feel at all odd.'

Dot Pentelow *recalls her early life in* **Bristol**. *Perhaps she would have benefited from some goose grease and paper*

Zax

'From the age of three, my older sister who was attending school, managed to bring home every infectious disease possible and passed them on to me. After chicken pox, German measles, mumps, impetigo and measles we finally caught whooping cough. That was worse than all the other illnesses put together. I remember dashing across the kitchen to 'whoop' in the chamber pot strategically placed in the grate. Mother was as stressed as we were and father actually stumped up for us to have a fortnight's holiday by the sea at Clevedon to recover. Although it was March and the wind was cold we enjoyed the break! Soon afterwards, I knew I must have looked ill when mother wrapped me in the Paisley shawl, which had been handed down from her great-grandmother. I soon discovered that my tonsil and adenoid removal was to take place the following day! The effect of Syrup of Figs was nothing compared with that lethal dose of castor oil which mother had to administer the day before the operation. No food allowed after that and I was starving! A two-mile tram ride at 8-30 in the morning took us to Lower Maudlin St followed by a short walk to the Bristol Royal Infirmary. The large room which we stepped into off of the street served as an A&E unit as well as a waiting area. Apart from the wooden benches lining the walls it was devoid of furniture, magazines and comics. About twelve children accompanied by their anxious mothers waited in silence. We waited for hours with rumbling stomachs and jangling nerves. The enticing smell of cooked food wafted in to the waiting room and we thought about breakfast. We waited so long that we began to think about lunch. Sometime around 2pm a nurse arrived and announced that operations had begun. My friend Kathleen was led away first and I was next. Sitting on the marble slab of what seemed to be an old larder, I was fitted out with a rubber hat with my hair tucked underneath. The horrible anaesthetic mask gave me nightmares for years.

As we recovered consciousness we were wheeled to a recovery room where our mothers joined us. Most of the children cried about their throats; my cry was different. 'Oh my legs, oh my legs.'

'Hush' said mother, 'it isn't your legs, it's your throat.'

But my persistence made her look; both my legs were cut and bleeding. Kathleen and I had shared a trolley to the operating theatre and her frenzied kicking had damaged my legs, which now hurt more than my throat. By 5pm all of the children had gone home—except me. I could hear the doctor saying that they would keep me in for a night which I was not too keen on. A compromise was reached when mum agreed to a taxi ride rather than taking the tram, a journey which I thoroughly enjoyed. Dad was already home from work and not too pleased that his evening meal wasn't ready. Having to reimburse mother 1/6d for the taxi didn't help either, but after seeing my legs he was more sympathetic.

Seeing the primroses each year always reminds me of Bristol city centre. Let me explain. My mother helped out at an Infant Welfare Centre in a very poor area of Bristol. She was responsible for the care of the youngest babies, in little portable cots, while their mothers had a cup of tea and a biscuit and received advice on their children's welfare from a team of doctors and nurses. Every year on a Saturday afternoon in Spring, we took a tram to the terminus at Filton then walked down a cinder track, across three fields to the village of Charlton—several large farmhouses interspersed with duckponds skirting the road. Across two more fields, over a main road and down another lane to Holly Hill Wood. The wood was carpeted with primroses and violets. We picked some of the buds, not the open flowers and made them in to posies surrounded by leaves, then carefully packed them in to a large basket. When we arrived home my sister and I took some of the posies to sick and elderly neighbours, the rest were placed in bowls in a cool shed. On the following Tuesday, mother took the rest for her city centre mothers and babies. Few had ever seen a primrose, much less smelt one.

The dark cramped conditions that many of these unfortunate people lived in were unbelievable. Inevitably, crime was not unknown. Lady Wills was patron of the centre and helped organise the fund raising jumble sales. On these occasions I was recruited to crawl around beneath the trestle tables containing the clothes. Lady W explained how the thieves worked. Garments would be pulled to the edge of the table and dropped on the floor. The thief would bend down, fill her basket with the articles that she wanted and make a show of putting the others back on the table. My job was to grab the things that dropped on the floor and return them to the other side of the table. At the end of one of these sales there was a huge dictionary which was about to be thrown out. Mother bought it for 3d! It proved very useful in later years, particularly in scrabble games—the word 'Zax' is a particular winner (An instrument for cutting slates, in case you wondered!)

In this poor community lived a tall blind man and his little terrier dog. On Friday afternoons he stood outside of our school gate with an enamel mug tied around his neck and his little dog beside him. Sometimes, if any of us had any pocket money left by Friday we would drop a penny in the cup. The dog would then give a little bark and a wag of the tail before resuming his begging position. When the old man died, we read in the paper that he left over £2,000—a great deal in those days. I have never given to a beggar since!

During my second year at Colston Girls' school, the three forms of that year attended a combined music lesson. Miss Skeet had quite a task controlling ninety of us boisterous children. But she was a 'no nonsense' teacher so we had to behave. On one occasion she was called away, leaving poor Mrs James, the pianist in charge. With her timid manner and nervous voice she soon lost control and there was a near riot going on when Miss Skeet returned. As she crossed the hall she commenced berating us and carried on as she mounted the six shallow steps to the platform, still glaring at us. Alas, in her high state of excitement she missed the top step and sat down heavily then slowly slipped down the six steps one by one. With every jolt a hairpin dropped out of her bun and the hem of her skirt rose another two inches. By the time her bumpy ride had ceased she looked rather like a mermaid, with hair hanging over her shoulders and apart from stockings, very little on her lower half! Mrs James came flapping around.

'Are you hurt?'

Only a bruised backside and loss of dignity, we suspected. Picking up her hairpins she remained seated until her bun was reinstated. Then, adjusting her skirt as she walked, she returned to the platform and announced the next song. Nobody was singing and I could feel her beady eyes on me as I struggled to gain composure. As we reached the last verse I managed to pull myself together and by singing loudly it was easier to concentrate. Hardly had we resumed our seats when Miss Skeet's voice boomed out.

'Stand up Dorothy Pentelow.'

Why was she picking on me when everyone was laughing? I could feel everyone's eyes on me, wondering as I did, why I was being singled out.

'Do you know, you were the only one singing?'

The laughing and giggling returned and the lesson broke up in chaos!'

Doreen Stonebridge *grew up in* South London

Five for 2d

'At the age of five I started at an infants school which was two miles away from home. My mother walked me there in the morning, home again at lunchtime then back in the afternoon—a total of eight miles every day. I must have been fit! The school was situated on a street with a mixture of houses, shops and street stalls. On dark winter afternoons the stallholders lit up naptha lamps which flared alarmingly, or so it seemed to me as a small child. They called out to passers by to encourage them to buy their goods—'Lovely ripe bananas, five for 2d.'

Back in our street, the milkman used to come around every day in his horse and cart and housewives went out with their jugs to collect the measured pints of milk from the churn in the centre of the cart.

We (my mother, brother and myself) lodged in a large house with a very kind lady. I can remember that she had a telephone in the hall, which was a real luxury in those days. It was a tall black 'stick' type with the earpiece hooked on the side. As it was considered to be something of an eyesore, it was always concealed under a cover in the shape of a crinoline dressed lady!'

Eileen Oldridge *grew up in* Birmingham. *She vividly describes her house and family life, which is typical of the period*

Park Road

'The house where I was born was one of two houses linked by a ceilinged entry with gates aslant the top. Coming through the gate you would walk on a blue bricked yard into the large garden, up two steps under a glass roofed open portion with the back kitchen at the end. By the standards at the time, this was a middle class house, made of red brick and bearing a stone lintel over the entry, which declared to all passers by that it was 'Omega Place.'

Three large bedrooms and a box room, a living room, hall and front room, a large cellar. The sidewall of the building away from the doors jutted out onto the pavement, with an iron grating over one side, over an aperture where the coal was dropped to the cellar.

The door had a brass knob and a letterbox and there was a stone step that had to be scrubbed every day as well as the brasses being cleaned. The hall was blue and red quarry tiles, set diagonally, not square. Entering from the road into the hall, the front room was on the left side. This front room was usually kept locked except at Christmas time and the occasions when friends were entertained. It had shutters each side of the flat sash corded window, a musty cupboard, an open grate and a marble mantelpiece—quite large— and the grate was a low four bar, what we now call a basket type. This had to be black-leaded (by courtesy of Ripley's Oval Black Lead—block and water). There was a lovely brass fender, tubular type and an ash guard of cast iron (again this would be black-leaded), and a set of brass fire irons, which were very tall, I remember.

The mantelshelf had a large marble clock with Corinthian pillars. At each end of the shelf stood a bronze figure of a Viking with helmet and sword—which could be lifted from the scabbard, and often was when no one was looking! Each of these was mounted on a plinth. A highly polished Jones tabletop treadle sewing machine held pride of place in front of the window that was home to a large porcelain pot containing some very impressive aspidistras. My mother would wash the leaves of these plants with milk and water and when some flowers appeared around the roots, all were called to view.

In the kitchen, there was at all times a kettle full of water on the hob. Kippers would sometimes be grilled on a wire tray with a handle over it, which could be hung on a hook over the fire. Porridge would be put overnight in the bottom of the oven to cook, in a stone, 2lb jam jar. Sometimes we had toast in the mornings instead. I remember more from my teens about our breakfasts, which changed to cereals; Force (a thin version of cornflakes) and Muffets—compressed wheat in a circular shape like a slice of swiss roll. These were lovely, but did not seem to be very popular. Also, I can recall eating Shredded Wheat.

When we were very young we had 'bubble and squeak' for Monday dinners. On Tuesdays we had stew and on Wednesdays, rabbit. Thursdays was stew again. This consisted of 1lb of stewing beef plus sliced onions, pearl barley, stock, gravy salt (a block similar to a block of jelly but granular black texture; it was called Queens Gravy Salt) and three or four whole cloves. Potatoes accompanied all of this.

On pancake days, we didn't have dinner, only pancakes. On Fridays we had fish; soused herrings or dabs, a small flat fish full of bones. These would be fried. No chips were made in the home. Occasionally, we had what were called scallops, which were really slices of potato, disc shaped and fried.

I've digressed to food when I was talking about the rooms. The living room had a wooden rocking chair in front of the fireplace, a wooden armchair in the corner by the long cupboard (built in). There were at least four ordinary chairs and a settee, which was a two-ended thing with planking for the seat. There were two large photographs of my father and mother when young, on each sidewall of the room and two print type pictures, one of a gamekeeper with his dog, the other a smaller picture. Between these sat a mirror, approximately 12 inches square with a brush and comb box attached at the bottom. There was also a large wooden table with a scrubbed top.

As another child became a wage earner, so the living standards and the furniture improved. We had a walnut piano with a fretwork front and candle holders when I was young, then a pianola, then a Collard & Collard upright, then a modern piano. That gave way to a huge light oak sideboard when my mother could no longer read music; maybe she couldn't bear to have a silent piano in the room, I don't know.

If any of the children were ill, they were taken into the large bed in my parents' room during the day. Dr Duncan was our doctor; he would take the proffered two and sixpence for his visit and when he got to the front door would give it back to one of the young ones.

My mother always had a little bag of fine oatmeal on the washstand which she would dip in the water. She used to have Gibbs coldcream soap or glycerine and cucumber or White Windsor and she always looked immaculate, even when she was black leading the grate. Later, when her sight was denied her, I think that she was really troubled that she could not keep up her appearance to her former standard, though she didn't ask for help.

Discipline was maintained by mutual consent, I think. There was a cane hanging on a large picture; I never remember being caned. My brother Norman was sometimes, but there were never beatings. My mother kept order, my father never interfered. The cane disappeared after Norman put one end in the fire and was trying to smoke through it when my mother was out. Miscreants were sent to bed.

Christmas really began on January 1st. From that date my father placed one penny in a strong wooden moneybox he had made. This was done every day of the year. One part of the box was partitioned off and that was used for money for shoe repairs; he did all our shoe repairs. Sometimes he bought leather soles, cut in the shoe sizes and sometimes he used cycle tyres that he cut and shaped himself. Heels were always of rubber.

At Christmas time the penny a day paid for what was called an 'Aitch bone' of beef and a half of suckling pig. We never had a variant. The earliest Christmas I recall is one when my grandma had bought Elsie and myself matching red velvet smocked dresses. I sat on the fire in mine; there was no fireguard and I leaned back, I was so used to doing this in the living room. I didn't do it again. Another Christmas time we had our black stockings with possibly a few nuts, sweets, some little toy; the boys also had long stockings and we came down early to see what we had—no lighting available to us, only a candlestick which was removed for safety. We did have gas brackets in the bedroom, but too high to be reached quietly. The part to be lit was like a round screw head and it made a fan-like flickering flame. Downstairs, Tom, my brother, climbed on a table to light the gas. This was a double upright fitting with glass shades, inside these a mantle, a very fragile thing. Tom lit the gas with a paper. When it burned his fingers he moved and the paper trimmings caught fire and dropped on our new stockings and burned them. After this, we were not allowed Christmas stockings, but when we were in our teens Tom used to put a pillowslip with gifts in it on the doorknob. He introduced us to rubber hot water bottles in this way, buying us one each; previously it had been crock ones, or the oven plate wrapped in a cloth, but there was only one plate so someone missed out!

One year, I was going out with a boy called Charlie Steele. I was fourteen and a half. At Christmas he not only bought me an iced Christmas cake but also 24 sugar fancies for the tree. These were made of fondant icing and took all shapes—bells and clocks. He was loaded with money but I was not very keen, and I do declare the house resented those decorations! My father had arranged to have a gas conversion done, from upright to inverted; flakestone bowls held by three chains were just becoming fashionable then. The gas fitter had no sense of smell. When he had finished, he put a match to the gas and . . . it went 'poof.' The explosion wrecked the living room and the bedroom and blew out all the windows. No compensation—the job was out of working hours and the man was due for retirement so no mention was made of it. An old composition pipe had fractured. My poor mother was sitting in her chair as she had to do, since her eyelids would not open. It was lunchtime. I had two hours in my lunchtime, 12.30 till 2.30 and was in the habit of calling for the groceries at the Co-op in the 'Flat.' I was almost home when one of the gossips told me there had been an explosion. I asked about my mother and she said she didn't know if she was all right. I dropped my parcel and ran. My mother was covered in plaster pieces from the ceiling. I had the job of cleaning up the mess. Tom plastered the ceiling on Christmas day and we sat on a plank under the covered yard to eat our Christmas dinner. This was the year Frank, my future husband, called to deliver the Christmas meat. I got rid of the sugar fancy man and went with Frank from early the next year.'

George Appelbe in Somerset recalls a shocking experience

A shocking time

'We lived on a farm and I recall my grandfather had an electric pulse generator for arthritis, operated from an accumulator. This was brought out every Sunday evening and the whole family sat round the table linking hands suffering this mild electric shock so that my grandfather could be cured of arthritis. I don't think any of the family suffered from this or arthritis, then or in later years.

I also remember one evening when I had been sent to bed early and my sister had tied a hobbyhorse to a clothes pole, then tapped my window with it to waken me. I did wake with fright and went tearing down the stairs yelling, 'I've just seen a nightmare.'

My favourite food at the time was fried sausages, with a slice of fried bread pudding with sultanas in it!'

Leslie Solomon started work in the city of London in 1928. Today, he might have been a rich man . . .

Rushing about with Russian Imperial Bonds

'I started work in the city office of a firm of importers of grain and seeds, as an office boy, a form of employment that no longer exists. In those days one had to wear a hat and a proper suit to go to the office with a white shirt and stiff collar. Even as a boy of fifteen, I arrived each day in a bowler hat!

My duties included sticking stamps on envelopes and delivering letters by hand around the city. Many of the offices I had to call on had not changed since Victorian times and were often three or four storeys up in old buildings with no lift! So it was quite a tiring job.

At the end of the day we had to make about thirty copies of the day's markets, which were sent to various branches overseas. This was done by pouring a liquid into a metal tray and when the liquid solidified into a jelly the master copy was placed face downwards on the jelly and then removed, leaving a print on the jelly. Then blank papers were placed on the jelly, smoothed by a roller or by hand and the prints obtained. Individual copies of letters, which had been typewritten, were placed in a heavy iron press. A damp cloth was placed over the letter, the press screwed down and the copy obtained. Should the cloth be too wet then the copy would be very smudged.

One day I was called in to the manager's office. He gave me a batch of several Russian Imperial Bonds that were considered valueless now that the communists had taken over in Russia. He told me to tear them up and throw them away. I did this without a second thought. Today, of course, the value of each of these collections would be worth tens of thousands of pounds. I threw away a fortune!'

Mary Cross in Hampshire recalls the paper delivery

The morning paper

'We lived out in the country very near to a train branch line. Us girls used to wait at the bottom of the garden for the train to come. The paper was thrown off as the train steamed past and we tried to catch it. If we weren't there, we had to try to find the paper in all the long grass. Dad wasn't very happy if the paper ended up in the undergrowth when it had been raining! Perhaps he should have trained Monty the dog to fetch his paper!'

Mr G Hubert-White has very different memories of childhood in the 1920s

Single-Parent Boy

I stood, saw door close, heard key turn in lock
Listened to her footsteps down the stairs
Heard street door slam. She was gone

Every day, my mother left me to go to work.
She locked me in—'So I would not wander out—get lost.'

I knew better. I would have no chance to play with other children.
She feared more—my father might come to take me away.
She said this to other women.

Sitting at the table, I opened my reading book
Began to whisper.
I was not reading—untaught
I did not know how to read.
I was making a story. Telling it to myself.

Mr G.E. Hubert-White

David Chapman *was strictly brought up in* **Devon**

The Truth

'At the age of three, my world consisted mainly of the area between the front gate and the back door of the garden outside of our house in Plymouth. Outside that door was a lane, the other side of which consisted of a brick wall with doors similar to ours and belonging to the gardens of the houses in the terrace running parallel to Trematon Terrace. I remember one occasion when Daddy had a new motor scooter—a machine on which the rider stood (there was no seat). He rode it round and round the block past the front door, down the back lane to the front again and so on for what seemed like ages. While this performance was going on, my sister Eunice and I watched from the front gate; rushed through the house and garden and watched from the back door to the lane. At that time I think Daddy was knocking on doors offering to mend watches and clocks and needed the scooter to enlarge his work area.

One of my strongest memories seems to be the sense of taste. The front gate had a strong bitter taste—even stronger at the red parts where the black paint had worn off revealing the red lead undercoating. Varnished wood had a similar taste but was rather less unpleasant. Both Eunice and I had a liking for tomato ketchup; there were times when we were alone in the house and Eunice was able to produce bread and butter with dollops of the red stuff on it—yum yum! The pantry where this kind of stuff was kept was a deep walk-in cupboard in the kitchen. There was no light in there so it was pretty dark even in the daytime.

We were a strictly vegetarian household and so we never tasted meat or its derivatives; nor did we ever taste tea, coffee or any other 'stimulants' which would violate God's temple, our bodies. Our normal beverage was postum which was good because it was produced by an American firm owned and operated by saved individuals who were in the Truth; that is to say that they were Seventh Day Adventists like my father. I think that not being able to have a cup of tea was one of my Mummy's heaviest crosses.

Mummy loved to laugh—everything could be a joke. I shared my third birthday with her when she was thirty but by that age she had lost all her teeth and had to wear plates; by removing these she was able to touch her nose with her tongue and this was a laugh! She played the violin very sweetly and loved to play Irish jigs (the Irish Washerwoman) and Hungarian music but this was only possible when Daddy was out; when he came in it had to be hymn tunes. She was also a skilled piano performer and was able to play a considerable repertoire of Victorian drawing room numbers—The Robin's Return was my favourite—but if she was caught doing so Daddy was able to create a terrifying atmosphere. An example of this atmosphere, which I shall always remember, happened when Mummy was having a cup of tea one day in the kitchen. The inner front door rattled heralding Daddy's return. Mummy picked up the small tray she was using with the tea things on and scuttled into the pantry. She was trembling with fright and was unable to control the rattling of the china so discovery was inevitable. I can still feel the terrifying ambience that prevailed throughout the house for the rest of the day.

Physically Mummy was petite, with light brown hair and always dressed impeccably. She made all her own clothes using a hand operated Singer sewing machine; she also made her own hats being a skilled milliner but these were hidden secrets which had an outing only when it was safe. Her hats had veils, which I remember she would raise so that she could moisten her handkerchief to remove a smut from my face.

I don't remember anything like a pram or pushchair although there must have been some sort of conveyance for me. I doubt whether, when I was young, I could have walked the considerable distance to the Seventh Day Adventist church in Beaumont Road where we invariably went every Sabbath morning.

Perhaps I partly walked and was partly carried; certainly there could have been no other means of progress since anything other than walking would have been taboo for a 'Sabbath day journey.' In the church I could experience the taste of the heavily varnished natural pine pews and see the rest of the familiar congregation. There was Brother Bunker and family consisting of Sister Bunker, sons Wilfred and Glen aged about seventeen and fifteen respectively, and Dora Whiting (an American) who was about the same age as my elder sister Eunice. The Bunkers were American and lived in a timber house raised on stilts and built by Brother Bunker himself with the aid of his sons; it was situated on the Bunker farm at Marsh Mills. Now Marsh Mills was considerably more than a

Sabbath day's journey from Beaumont Road so it was quite permissible for the Bunker family to use their pony and trap for the trip though I doubt whether it would have been permissible to use motor transport. Sometimes the Bunker family would entertain us *en famille* to dinner on a Sabbath, in which case we would all go back to their farm in the trap. This was a bit of a squeeze because it was only about five feet square with rounded corners and a tiny door at the back. If the season were such that the Sabbath went out early enough we would be taken home in the model T Ford.

Other members of the congregation worthy of mention included a pale wraith of a lad aged about eighteen who was dying of 'consumption'—name forgotten. Also, a rather frightening old man suffering from 'delirium tremens' which was the name given to Parkinson's disease at the time (there were no drugs to control the involuntary hand trembling). I can visualise many more Brothers and Sisters whom I can't give a name to, including one who played the zither (and frequently did but only tunes made permissible by inclusion in Moody & Sankey's collection—Juanita was one which I remember). Then there was Sister Coombes, always immaculately dressed in navy blue, genteel, demure and sadly married to a man not in the Truth.

I lived in Plymouth until I was nearly nine, but if I am asked where I come from it never occurs to me to name Plymouth as my hometown. Those first years of my life seem like a quite different world—grey and somehow unreal—dominated by the fact that I was different from people in the real world, the worldly people. The first time I can remember being conscious of this was when I was in the front room one Sabbath, sitting near the window looking out on Trematon Terrace and watching a little girl rolling a hoop. This was a common toy in those days consisting of laminated wood forming a circle about two feet in diameter and a wooden stick to do the rolling. Daddy came in and suggested that I should 'do something edifying'—one of his favourite expressions—like trying to use my new found skill at reading simple words. He explained that I would get better at this and then if I ever was in need of something to do I could always 'take a good book and read'—another favourite expression. I was only interested in going out and playing with the little girl but Daddy explained that even if it wasn't the Sabbath it was better not to mix with people who were not in the Truth. 'We are a very fortunate family,' he said 'to be among the

Saved and that we should be thankful that we are different. At the Second Coming we will be among those that are caught up into the air and go to heaven.'

Of course, the little girl would not be one of those and if I was playing with her I might not be recognised and left behind, to be cast into everlasting darkness. Looking back I think he really believed this and at the time I expect I believed it too. I can remember wondering why all the nice people that I met seemed to be Worldly. I think it was some time before I started to envy the Worldly people and wish to become one of them.

Gradually, my known universe expanded from the ground floor of 2, Trematon Terrace to include the immediate environs—Mutley Plain where the shops were, including Mr Tremlett's dairy. I would regularly be taken here by Eunice when she was sent to buy a newlaid egg (sold singly in individual boxes)—or half a pound of butter which would be cut off a big block weighed and 'patted' on a marble slab into a square or round shape. The final stroke of the pat would mark an appropriate emblem—I think Mr Tremlett's emblem was a thistle.

Opposite the nearby reservoir, off North Hill, was Marlborough Terrace where Uncle Harry and Auntie Bessie lived. Eunice and I would never have dared to visit them on our own because Auntie Bessie was very Worldly. I never knew until years later that Auntie Bessie had been a barmaid—all I knew at the time was that she was rather grand, living in a very large house with a wide staircase and carpeted throughout. Over the fireplace there was a spherical mirror, ormolu framed, which reflected a miniature version of the whole room. A gilded arm from the top of the frame held a gold chain at the end of which was a gilded bird. We would occasionally visit the house as a family. When we did so I could only wonder at the grandeur and at the fact that they had an inside lavatory!'

Aitken Lawrie *grew up in* **Hertfordshire**

Latin and the 1d

'My father, a colonel in the Royal Engineers, built airfields for the RAF. In the early 1920s we lived in Salisbury. We lived in a tall house, where I lived on the top floor with my younger brother under the care of a kind and efficient nanny, who washed us, dressed us, fed us and took us down to see our parents for an hour every evening. I remember my first steps in reading with her. Page one began 'The fat cat sat on the mat.' She stayed with us until I was thirteen.

Bang next door was a prep school, where I enjoyed learning Latin, writing out sentences with a different coloured ink for each part of speech and geography with a map of England on which I stuck bits of wool, coal etc, to show where they came from.

My father retired in 1924 and we moved to Berkhamsted, where he bought a large house, which is now a hotel, for exactly £1000. It had a large garden, croquet lawn and orchard and my mother ran it with an established cook, parlour maid, daily help and gardener, which was considered the absolute minimum. The reason for coming to Berkhamsted was the famous Grammar School, where the fees were £10 a year. The only problem was that it was nearly two miles from our house. My father hated cars and would never own one. He thought bikes were too dangerous, so I had to walk in every morning, come home for lunch and return in the afternoon.

But the teaching was first class. I spent a year in the lower 3rd and another in the Upper 3rd, coming top both times. The system was that the form master took every lesson himself apart from one hour a week with the drawing master. My parents wanted to keep me as a dayboy, but all this walking through the rain brought on colds, and the doctor said I must go to boarding school.

A school in Eastbourne was selected because I had some friends there who had been in Malta. It turned out to be quite useless, with a headmaster who was ninety-three years old. Owing to my good grounding at Berkhamsted I was brought in above top form, but learnt nothing in two years except Greek, which I did with a nice old master, and it got me a scholarship at Wellington.

Now my father had built a new house, designed to his own specification, in two acres of land. He did not have a job, but ran the local Scouts, did a lot for the Conservatives and read the first lesson in Church. He had time to see that I learnt all sorts of extra-curricular activities—golf, tennis, croquet, dancing, riding, fishing, swimming, Bridge, painting etc. I soon gave up golf and fishing but found the others very useful in later life. He also arranged for me to spend a month in Belgium to help to learn French and another in Germany to learn German. Both were immensely useful in school and later.

My mother arranged things so that she never had to shop, cook, wash or iron. Milk and bread were delivered. The gardener brought in fresh vegetables as required by the cook and every Monday she sent a long letter to the Army and Navy stores for everything else, which was delivered on Friday. As for washing, every single item went off in a wicker basket to the laundry and came back a week

Popular Cadbury's chocolate bars of the 1920s

later. She had plenty of time for writing letters and playing the piano.

Neither my prep school nor Wellington went in for half-term holidays. But my parents turned up every term, stayed in local hotels and had long talks with the masters concerned about my future prospects.

I would like to mention the importance of the penny—1d. That was the cost of a letter, in those days, with three deliveries daily. It would also buy a newspaper, ice cream, bar of chocolate, bus ride, pencil and many other small items. I do miss it.'

William Moxham *left school and found work in* **Kent**

Working with George

'I don't know how I came to hear about the job, but here I was at Burrill's Garage in London Road applying for a job as a garage hand. There could surely have been no greater contrast between this and my previous job. I was hoping in a way that I'd be turned down; it was a grubby little place, grease and dirt everywhere. I thought of early summer mornings riding across Hayes and Keston common, with pilots from nearby Biggin Hill up in the clear blue sky. Of a breathless moment when a 'plane flying high started to roll towards the earth with the engine cut out. I waited for the crash, but no, the engine opened out and the manoeuvre was repeated. This I afterwards learnt was known as the 'falling leaf,' a deception used to trick the enemy into thinking you'd had it. I thought of the birds and wildlife. I knew that a very different outlook lay ahead, were I to get the job but there wasn't much I could do about it. Unemployment figures were already beginning to climb, my own trade in the doldrums and my parents and girlfriend expecting me to get on and do something. As it turned out, I was given a month's trial.

The motor trade was then in its infancy, most mechanics were army trained and the majority of these were drivers with just sufficient knowledge to do running repairs. There were only two firms established in the district, Soans and Dunn, Ford agents and Anthony's both in Mason's Hill. It would have been useless for me to apply at either of them as they only took apprentices; this was my first stumbling block. My apprentice years had been wasted, no lad could start his apprenticeship over the age of sixteen, and I was now eighteen, and for years after this was a barrier that kept me out of many a decent job.

George Burrill, the boss at the garage was an ex-coachman. He knew as much about a car as an elephant knows about knitting, yet there was nothing unusual in this, the car was replacing the horse and pair, younger coachmen were drifting into other trades, the older ones just faded out. George's boss had set him up in business. Here was a man of real Victorian vintage; two maids and a butler were a must, dinner at seven on the dot. Often I would have to go over to the Big House nearby with a message of some sort; the only time George sounded an aitch was when he spoke of the House. I watched the butler clean the silver one evening, no messing about with metal polish, he spat on it.

George was full of bright ideas but none of them ever seemed to mature. A classic was when he acquired a small three-wheeled vehicle—I forget the make. The idea was to get this ready for the road, fit a trailer to the rear and polish it so that it looked respectable. The trailer would carry tins of petrol and with me in a smart pair of overalls I would patrol through Bromley ready to go to the aid of any motorist who had run out of petrol. Sort of 'Stop me and buy one.'

The trouble was that the three-wheeler was all in pieces when George bought it and no one knew just how to put it together again! So another great idea fell by the wayside.

Oil was delivered to the garage in beer barrels, at least, that's what they looked like. They were raised off the ground, a beer tap was banged in and empty oil tins stood underneath to fill up ready for sale. It was a slow process, especially in wintertime. The oil trickled out very slowly; there were no winter grades.

Often I would leave a tap running for a couple of hours or so by which time oil would be oozing over the floor. George didn't always see it, I'd manage to clear it up in time, but when he did see it there was always a talk on paying attention to the job and studying the master. A whole barrel ran over the floor once; it had been running from Saturday night 'til Monday morning. I had the job of clearing it up, but I hummed a quiet little tune to myself—George left the tap on that time.

I started driving lessons though they wouldn't be called that nowadays. George and I would go out together in the Studebaker and I would steer through the traffic with George in the driver's seat at the controls. He never let me take over which was understandable as the business depended on the Stude and he didn't like to chance it, but it gave me a bit of road sense. There was no trouble to get a driving licence. You wrote to your County Council enclosing a 5/- postal order asking for a driving licence to be forwarded at their earliest convenience and you were covered for a twelve month.

Not many makes of cars on the road in those days can be seen today. I can name some: The Newton and Bennet, a solid job, quiet and comfortable to ride in. A complete opposite to the Maxwell, an American car. The Calcot a nine hp, two-seater coupe, the Calthorpe a small open tourer. One of the best was the Siddeley Deasy, made by Armstrongs, I believe. The owner of one of these put it up for auction at Goddard and Smiths. He took me with him because everything was laid on for owners to wash their cars before the sale opened; you could either do it yourself or pay to have it done. Paintwork was a big problem, it soon lost its gloss, and no amount of polish would restore it, but they still looked good after they had been cleaned, with the metal work, either plain brass or nickel plating all bright and shiny. I must have made a good job of the Armstrong—the bloke gave me a pound note.

There is one make of car we can never forget, the Ford, or Tin Lizzie. Thousands were used in the Great War. It was easy to handle, the suspension was as near to independent springing as could be got in those days, it put up with any amount of rough treatment, it was cheap, could be driven over rough ground where more expensive cars would break up. Despite the opposition, despite the ridicule, it became, and still is, one of the world's most popular cars.

Just after Christmas I had a bust up with George (he wasn't impressed with my car cleaning skills) and found myself out of a job. I kicked my heels for about six weeks looking for another position without success. There was a chap who lived opposite who I knew slightly who was in the motor trade working for Paige Motors, an American firm in Grosvenor Road along the embankment. I met him one day and he said 'What's the matter with you, you look as if you lost a shilling and found a tanner?'

I said I was browned off hanging around, 'But' he said, 'You were in that garage in London Road, weren't you?' I told him I'd had a bust up. 'Look' he said, 'Why don't you try Maxwell Motors in Lupus Street, they're taking on hands.'

'Well' I said, 'I've only been in the trade about a year.'

'That doesn't matter.' he said, 'Tell them you've been in it for four years.'

'All right, I will.' I felt it would be a waste of time though.

I found Lupus Street in the heart of Pimlico, just off Grosvenor Road, Maxwells were at the top end from Vauxhall Bridge Road, the entrance was through a passage just about wide enough for a car or small lorry to get through. The first thing to catch the eye was a large board with 'Maxwell Motors, Experimental Station.' in gilt lettering. That I thought has just about put the kibosh on it. It was obvious this wasn't just nuts and bolts, but for people with wide experience. However, I got an interview and was started as an improver at 1/5d or 7p per hour, on the following Wednesday.

I bought a tool kit for 30/-, one pair of overalls for 10/-. The flat rate for the job worked out at £3-3s-6d for a 48-hour week. Out of that were the usual stoppages on top of which was 2/6d in fares and about 5/- for dinners at the local Lockharts.

Early morning travel was cheap in those days. A workman's ticket from Bromley to Victoria was 6d return, this applied to any train reaching the terminus before 8am and needless to say it was taken full advantage of.

Lockharts were dining rooms run almost exclusively for working men and women. A board usually hung outside saying 'A good pull-up for car men.' A row of horses and carts stood outside, the horses with their nosebags while the car men were inside tucking into a good dinner. The seats were wooden forms with high backs and with marble topped tables, securely fixed to the floor. You gave your order as you went in and paid as you went out. They were clean and well run, the food was good and cheap, the dinner and pudding and a small tea about 1/-. Tea was served in a thick porcelain mug with a base like a pedestal.

I found this job a big contrast. From a staff of five to one of a hundred or more was like jumping in the deep end but I soon felt completely at ease. But they really were a rough crowd at Maxwells. The main topics of conversation were sex, booze and betting in that order.

Before betting was legalised and we had the betting shop, you put your money with a bookie's runner. He could be anybody. In most workshops there was a runner or it could be a baker, the milkman, the postman, or even the man from the Prudential. He could collect the bets and place them with a bookie. There's many a milkman thought a horse would be left at the post, only to find it in the first three and found himself in financial straits because he hadn't laid the bet. The only way out would be to dip in to the takings.

Maxwells was an American firm under direct control from the United States. Two cars were involved, the Maxwell and the Chalmer. The Maxwell was produced to compete with the Ford. The Chalmer was a classier job that competed with the more expensive American cars. Taking all in all, the Maxwell was a poor job. The two-wheeled brakes with external foot-brake bands that were exposed to mud and grit that would eventually wear the brake drum through so that it came off in two halves. It had a cone clutch, a dyno-starter that wouldn't work if you had the fan belt too tight and a brake cross-shaft on which the operation of the brakes depended. This swung between brackets fitted with wooden brushes, which as soon as they got wet which was often, would swell up and seize the shaft so that you had no brake. I don't think Henry Ford could have found them a serious competitor.

The Chalmer was a different kettle of fish but seemed to fade out altogether soon after I started at Lupus Street. They also produced a Maxwell truck. All vehicles were imported from the United States. They were sent over in large wooden cases held together with thousands of nails. The cases were broken open and the vehicle lifted out. Very little work was needed to prepare them for the road. The four wheels, (tyres were already inflated) steering wheel and side and rear lamps to conform with British road standards was all the assembly that was necessary. There were two departments in Lupus Street. The bottom shop for reception and running repairs, the top shop for machine and experimental work. They were old and dilapidated, particularly the top shop. There was a firm of coachbuilders underneath and there was always rows going on because whenever oil or water spilled over on the floor it would trickle through over their nice new paintwork. Malcolm Campbell had a workshop under ours and I seem to recollect his famous 'Blue Bird' had the body fitted there. One of his mechanics, Jack Davies, came to Maxwells. I worked as his mate, and needless to say learnt quite a lot. He was fully skilled.

Although we came under American control, it wasn't strictly in accordance with American rules. There was no private army, there were no thugs employed to break-up strikes, a common practice in the U.S.A. in those days. At the same time the American employer here was just as ruthless as his counter-part across the Atlantic. If you fell down on the job you were out, there was no quiet removal to another department or finishing up in the House of Lords. If you'd been fiddling you were prosecuted. 'Ding-Dong' Bell the general manager was caught playing tricks and finished up in prison. There was a similar example of this at Lamberts in Kingston, the Ford agents. This was also run on American lines. The general manager got caught and he, too finished up inside. This means of course, that if you wanted to get to the top you had to be as tough and unprincipled as the man at the top, or, as commonly said, the bigger the job, 'the bigger the bastard!'

The Car Yard

Les Kennard has a fascinating extract from a 1920s diary

Duties of a live-in domestic/mothers help

'The following is taken from the diary of a relative and is typical of life as a maid in service in the early decades of the 20th century.'

Wages:
  1920—7/6d per month, plus keep and uniform less cost of any breakages.

Daily Duties:
  Set alarm for 6am

6.30am
  Draw curtains and open windows. Open street door and bring up milk. Put on porridge, clean shoes, do drawing room grate, put on kettle.
7.00am
  Sweep, polish and dust drawing room.
7.15am
  Make cup of tea for mistress and self. Get hot water for mistress.
7.20am
  Sweep, dust and polish dining room, hall and staircase, polish switches, doors and handles etc.
8.15am
  Wash hands and lay table for breakfast. Cook breakfast.
8.40am
  Breakfast
9.00am
  Clear away own breakfast. Help mistress with beds.
9.15am
  Do bedroom and dressing room, put cot ready for baby. Make own bed and do bedroom.
10.00am
  Wash up breakfast things, leave kitchen tidy and gas stove clean. Fill coal scuttles.
10.30am
  Do any washing for baby. Clean both bathroom and lavatory.

11.00am

Prepare anything necessary for dinner.

11.30am

Do extra work—turn out rooms etc.

12.30pm

Wash and tidy up—prepare dinner.

1.00pm

Dinner

1.30pm

Clear away and wash up. Sweep and tidy kitchen, wash over floor—put cloth on table etc.

2.00pm

Change and take baby out.

4.15pm

Bring baby in—prepare tea.

4.30pm

Tea

5.00pm

Clear away and wash up. Dust pram and put away clothes. Draw curtains.

5.30pm

Get baby's bath ready.

5.45pm

Prepare supper, if any to be cooked.

6.30pm

Clean up after baby's bath. Put hot water for master.

6.45pm

Lay supper table.

7.15pm

Supper

7.45pm

Take coffee tray to drawing room.

8.00pm

Clear away, wash up. Own supper. Leave kitchen quite tidy. Take away coffee tray when bell rings.

9.00pm

Fill hot water bottle. Put hot water in bedrooms. Turn down beds.

9.30pm

Bed

Additional Weekly duties:

Monday
  Washing. Clean bathroom. Ironing in evening
Tuesday
  Own bedroom and spare room. Hall and staircase.
  Half day off 2.30pm—9.30pm
Wednesday
  Bedroom and dressing room. Wash white paint alternate
  weeks. Clean brass cans etc.
Thursday
  Drawing room
Friday
  Dining room. Clean silver in the afternoon or evening
Saturday
  Kitchen. Help mistress with sewing or mending and do own
  mending

Jean Hooper *spent her childhood in* **London**

Rough children and the Flasher

'In 1920, school was a very happy time. We started with slates and a slate pencil, the squeaking was horrible to the ears—but most of us learnt pretty well. We were 'mixed infants' and all ran round the playground like mad things. I don't remember any balls, tops and hoops in school. The skipping ropes came later. Being just after the war, we were all intensely patriotic and there was an awful lot of marching round that playground.

When I was seven I was standard IV. We had a teacher who was very fond of the cane. I went home one lunchtime and told my mother I'd had the cane. My mother was aghast and said 'whatever for?' I said I had one whack because I'd got one sum wrong—so headed the queue. The teacher was ages doling out all these whacks. I never understood why she was so furious. Later I was told she'd been dismissed. There wasn't a whimper out of any of us—tears just welled up and our faces went red. I don't remember that we were all that upset—because most mothers walloped their kids.

Dad had come home from five years of war and went back to being a 'Man's man.' He'd been with the Colonel as batman etc. all through the war—Gallipoli, Egypt, Palestine, and finally a horrible year in France, when they were holed up in a village, being shelled. Eventually, when it stopped, they found out the Armistice had been signed and the Germans didn't know either.

Then mummy and daddy decided to branch out on a business of their own. Dad said he was fed up with taking orders. We eventually moved to west London (W2) and we were introduced to life in a big house, which was to be run as a Guest House. The iron railings were not taken for the war—you'd have fallen into the basement and probably broken your neck if they had taken the balcony railings. However, we lived in the kitchen, down the basement steps. It was a large room with red lino. There was a sort of lobby by the back door, leading to the coal hole, the sacks were shot through a round hole in the pavement, protected by a metal circle with a special pattern on it. Next to the coal hole, but outside the back door was a 'lavvy' as my dad called it. That was for the family to use. There was only one other toilet in the bathroom, so people had wash basins and jugs and slop-buckets in their bedrooms. Mummy and daddy had the bedroom next to the guests' dining room. There was a dumb waiter in there and dad would serve the guests (sometimes with the help of the little maid—one who was not so little—a big strong Norfolk girl). Mummy would be down below, filling up the dumb waiter. I believe there was a bell to save shouting.

Going to our new school was a terrible shook. This was our first encounter with cockney and rougher children. They attempted to trip us up and spoil our clothes and shouted out 'you're posh!' There was true poverty in the area. We actually saw children picking up orange peel round the stalls in Norland market and eating it. They had bags to ask for green stuff for their rabbits—but the stallholders knew who the rabbits were! The girls said 'We're not poor—we've got shoes.' We knew they had no knickers—only dresses even in the winter. Sometimes they didn't come to school because their clothes were being washed. Once a girl came to school with an undone hem on her skirt. The teacher asked her to get her mother to do it for her. The skirt remained all droopy and the girl confessed to the teacher 'my mum ain't got no needle to do it with!'

The teachers trod a difficult path. They had to be very diplomatic and dealing with rough girls was very difficult. Sometimes, the mothers would come storming along and attack the teachers. My sister's teacher was a very gentle person with glasses and my sister was very upset when the teacher was shouted at and jostled.

One of the girls of a roughish family appointed herself my friend and minder. She told me that if anyone hurt me, she would tell her sister and she was the best fighter in the school. My sister was also included in this dubious benefit.

The vermin (bugs, fleas, rats and mice) were everywhere. I stood next to a girl and said 'what's that on your shoulder?' 'Oh, just a ladybird!' and she flicked it off. On consultation with my mother, I found that it was a bed bug! The nurse came to look at our hair fairly often. There seemed to be a code. If you were given the number 1 you were okay, 2 meant your mother had to wash your hair and 3 meant you had to go to the dreaded cleansing station, which apart from being a disgrace was horrible because the nurses were rough.

Business went well at the guesthouse—although an occasional unwelcome insect guest would be found. We had a decent class of person—mostly office workers. Also there was a Sir somebody who took us to the circus at Olympia. Dad wasn't so fond of the theatricals who were at the Shepherd Bush Empire. We had a Buffalo Bill man who stayed with us who didn't take off his 'orange' make-up and it was all over the sheets and pillowslips. His boots were thigh boots and that was a lot of polish for dad! Little Tich also stayed.

For recreation, we had the Schoolgirls Own weekly, as we'd grown out of Rainbow. You were not allowed to take 'comics' to school and nothing like Peg's Paper could be passed around.

One day, my sister and her friend and I were walking up to Kensington Gardens when a man in a mac suddenly flashed us! My sister's friend was convulsed with laughter. She'd never seen anything so funny before. It put the man right off and he shuffled quickly away to pester some little nursegirls with babies in the prams.

At the age of 11, I passed my exams and so, in 1924 I was due to start another school. We had to buy our uniform at Harrods, usual white blouse, gymslip, gloves, black stockings, navy felt hat and band for winter and strawyard in summer. I got delayed going there as I caught chicken pox. My sister started it off, with a very bad attack and we were both put in the front drawing room with the balcony. We were truly wretched with delirium. I thought we were both dead and in our coffins. However, all was well and we spent a happy time in quarantine, making lists of names of the General and Thomas Tilling and Pirate buses running up and down Holland Park Avenue.'

A view of the interior of Sainsbury's Chelmsford branch

1920s Discoveries and Developments

- Insulin
- Penicillin
- Vitamins D and F
- Atomic Quantum Theory
- Wireless Broadcasting
- The BBC
- Sound on Film (the 'Talkies')
- Television
- Autopilot
- The Hair Dryer
- Aerosol Sprays
- Frozen Food
- The Aga Cooker
- The Food Mixer
- Helicopter Flight
- Elastoplast

1920s Firsts

- Foxes Glacier Mints
- Chanel No 5
- Max Factor's Kiss Proof Lipstick
- Police Motor Cycles in London
- BCG Vaccination against TB (in France)
- Birth Control Clinic in London
- Labour Government
- The Reader's Digest
- Waterloo Railway Station
- Piccadilly Circus Tube Station
- The Pound note
- Shopping Centre (in the USA)
- London to Brighton Car Rally
- Public Telephone Boxes
- London's Green Belt
- World's first Motel
- Britain's first Diesel Train
- Wembley Stadium
- Winter Olympics
- MGM Studios
- The Monaco Grand Prix Motor Race
- Wimbledon's 'Seeding' System
- Safeways Stores
- Traffic Lights
- Golf's Ryder Cup
- The Irish 'Punt'
- Greyhound Racing in the UK
- Male Stewards on Airlines (Pan Am)
- The Oxford English Dictionary
- The Morris Minor
- Mickey Mouse
- Radio Weather Forecast
- Women Jurors at the Old Bailey
- Tintin
- Harry Ramsden's Fish and Chip Restaurants
- Popeye
- Rupert Bear
- Winnie the Pooh
- The Tyne Bridge
- Teddy Bears first produced in Britain
- Robertson's Gollies
- Thornton's Personalised Easter Eggs
- Cadbury's Creme Eggs
- Cadbury's Flake
- Cadbury's Dairy Milk Chocolate
- Brillo Pads

Robertson's Golly badges were introduced in 1928 and avidly collected for 70 years until they were discontinued

1920s Anniversaries

- 20th of the Death of Queen Victoria (1901)
- 20th of Britain's first Council House Estate (London 1901)
- 30th of the Formation of the Labour Party (1893)
- 50th of the Telephone (1876)
- 80th of the Introduction of the Postage Stamp (1840)
- 100th of the first University Boat Race (1829)
- 100th of the first Photograph (1826)
- 100th of the London Metropolitan Police (1829)

The Future

In 1920, at the beginning of the decade, it would be:

- 19 years before the start of World War II
- 25 years before the first Atomic Bomb was exploded
- 28 years before Israel was established
- 33 years before the coronation of Elizabeth II
- 43 years before the assassination of President John F Kennedy
- 45 years before the abolition of the Death Penalty in Britain
- 57 years before the death of Elvis Presley
- 58 years before the first Test Tube Baby was born

The 1930s

The world at large—the historical context

The Depression

As the decade began, the worst of the Depression had not yet spread to Britain. In the USA, however, people who had lost their jobs were no longer able to buy goods from home or abroad, which in turn led to more bankruptcies and more people losing their jobs. By 1931, the effects of the stock market crash inevitably spread to the rest of the world and by the end of the year over 20% of the workforce in Britain were unemployed. This was particularly acute in the primary industrial areas in the north of England, Wales and Scotland where the output of coal mines, ship builders, textile factories and steel works slumped dramatically due to falling demand. The cotton industry was hit by a 'double whammy.' Falling sales due to the depression was bad enough. The industry was also at the whim of the fashion of the day. Those fashions dictated ever-shorter skirts for women, almost up to the knee with no petticoats—a disaster for the textile industry. In the early years of the decade sales dropped by over 2 million yards of cloth per year.

Protest marches were commonplace but did little to influence London based MPs who, in the main, were shielded from the worst effects of the slump and unsympathetic to the realities of unemployment and trying to make ends meet 'on the dole.' Jarrow in the northeast, one of the worst hit regions, saw two thirds of its workforce unemployed. In 1936, two hundred unemployed men set off on the famous Jarrow Crusade, walking from the northeast to London to draw attention to the plight of the unemployed. This march was the first to be reported sympathetically by the media, though the result was no more positive than previous protests—tea, sympathy but little action. Soup kitchens were set up in many cities to provide basic nourishment for many of the unemployed.

As the depression deepened in the USA, the election of 1932 saw Franklin D Roosevelt move into The White House. He quickly announced a package of measures designed to combat the worst effects of the Depression, which was known as The New Deal. Aid was given to Farmers and Industry and a $3 billion programme of public building works was initiated to create jobs. In the first three months, nearly two million jobs were created, a major step on the long road to recovery.

The rise of the 'Middle Class'
In the Midlands and the south of England, workers felt the effect of the slump but were shielded to an extent by work in the 'new' industries—motor manufacturing, building and white collar jobs. In the southeast in particular, a building boom was led by the development of 'suburbia.' This had started in the previous decade and was in full swing in the south of England as the 1930s began. The boom was given a further boost by a change in the policy of Building Societies. The minimum deposit was reduced from 25% of the price of the house to less than 10% leading to a surge in house purchases in the more affluent areas. Hundreds of thousands of houses were built in the 1930s as the major city suburbs expanded out in to the countryside. The semi-detached house with indoor toilet, running hot water, net curtains and a car in the drive became an affordable reality for many who would previously have lived throughout their lives in rented accommodation. The middle class had really arrived!

Many unemployed workers from the depressed areas moved to the Midlands and south where work in the 'new' industries was more readily available. This increased the demand for affordable housing, adding more fuel to the building boom.

This new lifestyle laid the foundations of the 'consumer' society. Housewives were tempted with adverts for a wide range of labour saving devices, many of which had been introduced in the previous decade—electric cookers, irons, vacuum cleaners, refrigerators and washing machines. At the beginning of the decade only about 1 in 3 houses were connected to the National Grid, which provided electricity. By the end of the decade, more than 2 in 3 houses had access to the Grid.

The new focus on the suburban home led to an increased awareness of the need to manage this new lifestyle. The middle classes couldn't afford servants 'to do' for them so cookery or 'domestic science' lessons became very popular with women. Men, of course, were not expected to venture anywhere near the kitchen unless they kept their pipe tobacco in the kitchen cupboard!

The 'Siemens Neophone' Bakelite telephone was introduced during 1929. This was the first telephone to have a combined receiver and mouthpiece—the 'one-piece handset' and the use of it spread dramatically throughout the 1930s. Direct dialling was becoming the norm and the operator service began to die out as exchanges throughout the country were automated.

Getting Around

The expansion of suburbia led to a corresponding increase in public services, particularly around London. Several of London's Underground lines were extended further out from the city and new bus routes were set up to serve the ever increasing numbers of commuters. The familiar angular map of London's Underground was drawn by Harry Beck in 1933 and simplified the planning of journeys for generations to come.

Car ownership also increased dramatically during the 1930s with the number of cars on the road doubling to two million. The Austin 7 and Morris Minor that had been introduced in the 1920s still dominated the small car market. In 1932, Ford introduced the Model Y. Built in its new factory at Dagenham, it was an instant success.

As Britain's roads became busier, casualty rates increased. The Road Traffic Act of 1930 introduced compulsory Third Party insurance and an initial version of the Highway Code. Traffic lights, traffic signs and pedestrian crossings were all standardised. A compulsory driving test was introduced in 1934 together with a 30mph speed limit in built up areas. Perhaps the most significant contribution towards reducing driving related accidents was the introduction of cats-eyes on Britain's roads in 1935. Percy Shaw developed these after watching a cat cross the road and seeing the light reflected in the cat's eyes. Like many inventions, it was simple, yet incredibly effective.

The 'by-pass' became a familiar term during the 1930s as planners built road systems that routed the traffic around a town or city rather than through the centre in order to ease congestion. This, though, set off a cycle of building more roads, providing easier access, building more houses, more local residents, more cars, more congestion and so on. A cycle which still continues today.

The Quest for Speed

Off road, the pursuit of speed became a new sport. Malcolm Campbell in his high powered car Blue Bird, set a new world land speed record of 245 mph on Daytona Beach in 1931, successively increasing this until he topped 300mph in 1935.

Rival shipping companies competed for the 'Blue Riband' to see which liner could cross the Atlantic in the fastest time. The French liner Normandie held the trophy for a time before the Queen Mary, which made her maiden voyage in 1936, regained the Blue Riband for Britain with a record breaking crossing of less than 4 days.

The cruise liner was still the only way to cross the Atlantic in style

On the railways, the Cheltenham Flyer achieved a record speed of 81 mph in 1932. This was superseded in 1934 by the Flying Scotsman, which attained a top speed of 97 mph, only to be topped the following year by the Silver Jubilee at a speed of 112 mph. Even this was bettered in 1938 by the famous Mallard, which travelled at a top speed of 126 mph.

In the air, the competition between 'planes and airships became an unequal struggle. Doubts about the safety of airships were cast in the minds of many when the R101, the world's largest airship, hit a French hillside and burst in to flames. Over five million cubic feet of hydrogen, which was used to keep the ship airborne, exploded in a massive sheet of yellow flame. Forty-four lives were lost with only eight people surviving the catastrophe. Later in the decade, a similar disaster effectively ended the days of the airship. The Hindenburgh, having safely crossed the Atlantic, exploded at New Jersey as it came towards its mooring mast. Static electricity was blamed for the explosion, which killed thirty-three people and the hopes of an entire industry. The skies were left free for the development of the aeroplane to go unchallenged.

The Royal Family

King George V made the first Christmas broadcast to the nation, in 1932. His speech was written by 'the voice of the Empire,' Rudyard Kipling, though this was a well guarded secret for many years. He was also the first monarch to take to the air and began the King's Flight.

Three years later, the King and Queen Mary celebrated their Silver Jubilee. The following year, in January 1936, King George V died. His passing was mourned throughout the country; his subjects feeling particularly close to him, thanks to his broadcasts to the nation in their homes, via the wireless.

He was succeeded by Prince Edward, who became Edward VIII, Defender of the Faith and the Head of the Church of England. Prince Edward had a reputation as a playboy and enjoyed the company of rich friends on extended holidays in glamorous locations around the world. In the early years of the decade he had met the American divorcee Mrs Wallis Simpson and fallen in love with her. Reports of their dalliances were openly reported in newspapers and magazines in the United States and on the continent. In Britain, however, nothing appeared in the press and imported magazines even had articles snipped out of them to stop the news reaching the British public. The British populace first learned of the liaison soon after Edward became King. When news leaked out, hate mail poured in to Buckingham Palace. Mrs Simpson was threatened with having acid thrown in her face and she left England for her house in the south of France. She offered to leave Edward and this divided public opinion. By this time Edward had declared that he would marry his lover. The Church opposed divorce so King Edward was forced to choose between his crown and his love for Mrs Simpson. He chose to marry and in December 1936, after only ten months on the throne, Edward became the only British monarch to voluntarily abdicate, to be succeeded by his brother who became George VI.

George had far less charisma than his brother and stammered when nervous. He had less appeal then his fascinating brother and the Royal family focussed publicity on George's glamorous wife, Elizabeth. Edward became the Duke of Windsor, married Wallis in 1937 and lived the rest of his life in exile abroad, mainly in Paris.

Overseas

During the early years of the decade, Japanese troops invaded and occupied a vast area of northern China, known as Manchuria. In 1932 a Manchurian puppet state was set up with Pu-Yi, 'The Last Emperor,' installed as the notional head of state. The Japanese occupying forces were unsympathetic to the needs of Chinese civilians and stories of atrocities were common.

In Japan itself, western influences were increasing and Japanese men and women were keen to adopt the latest western hairstyles, fashions and dances. The increasingly militaristic government frowned upon this; dance halls were closed and a more traditional Japanese approach to life was overtly encouraged.

In Russia, Stalin's grip on the country increased. He introduced compulsory 'collectives,' in which all farms were turned in to peasant co-operatives. Their produce was sold to the state with the peasants' only additional income coming from the sale of their garden vegetables, the proceeds of which they were allowed to keep in full. Many of the richer peasants, or kulaks, refused to co-operate, killing their cattle and burning their crops. Tens of thousands of kulaks were murdered or sent to Siberia.

India's Nationalist Movement, led by Mahatma Gandhi demonstrated against British occupation and agitated for independence. In 1930, Gandhi led a 125-mile march to the sea to collect salt. This was a symbolic protest against government monopoly, which resulted in Gandhi's arrest. Peace was declared and Gandhi led a Nationalist delegation to London to discuss constitutional reform, the first steps along the road to Independence in the following decade.

In the USA, the infant son of US flying hero Charles Lindberg was kidnapped in 1932 sparking a national manhunt. The baby's body was found two months later, beaten to death even though a $50,000 ransom had been paid.

Prohibition ended in 1933, after fourteen years with President Roosevelt calling for the nation to drink in moderation. Al Capone, legendary gangster, general miscreant and a prime beneficiary of the restrictions during the prohibition era through his bootlegging operations, was jailed for 11 years for tax evasion in 1931. This was the longest term ever given in the USA for tax evasion.

Entertainment and Leisure

The cinema became the most popular form of entertainment during the decade. Cinemas opened in every town throughout Great Britain and most people lived within easy reach of this recently developed form of mass escapism. Westerns, Comedies, Thrillers and Horror films were all lapped up with equal enthusiasm. Actors and actresses became the new heroes and heroines. Hollywood was a land filled with milk and honey for everyone looking to escape from the drudgery of their day to day lives.

Marlene Dietrich starred in 'The Blue Angel,' the Marx Brothers and Charlie Chaplin were at the heights of their careers and John Wayne got his big break in 'Stagecoach'.

Slimming was very fashionable with women trying to emulate the 'film star' look. Pills were available containing tapeworms for the more determined slimmer. Many relied on smoking cigarettes and some also chose to use cocaine in an attempt to lose weight. The quest for the slimmer figure also led to a marked drop in potato consumption.

Pierced ears became fashionable among young women during the middle years of the decade. Previously, only older women had their ears pierced.

The cinema moved in to the 'Talkie' era and fans avidly followed
the news of their favourite stars

The principle of Birth control was cautiously welcomed by the Church of England, though not for purposes of 'selfishness, luxury or convenience.' However, the Roman Catholic Pope Pius XI condemned the rising tide of sexual liberation and reconfirmed the Catholic position on divorce and birth control (i.e. no, you can't do it.)

The first football World Cup was staged in Uruguay in 1930. Several European teams including England, Scotland, Wales and Ireland did not participate, mainly due to an ongoing dispute relating to payments to amateurs. The final was eventually won by the home team.

The 'Ovaltinies' advertised Ovaltine, a nourishing healthy drink. Five million children joined the Ovaltinie Club and the brand became the most popular hot drink of the decade.

Politics

As the economic situation grew worse a run on the pound left Britain's economy teetering on the verge of bankruptcy. In 1931, foreign currency speculators forced Britain to abandon the Gold standard, severing the link between the value of the pound and the value of gold. This had the effect of dramatically devaluing the pound against foreign currencies, particularly the US dollar. Servicemen's pay was cut to help the government balance its budget, leading to a riot by sailors in Scotland.

Confidence in the Labour government evaporated and an all party National government was formed to counter the economic crisis, led by Ramsay MacDonald. In the election of 1931, the electorate gave this government a massive mandate, though Labour's support was severely reduced. In 1935, Stanley Baldwin became Prime Minister, heading the National government following Ramsay MacDonald's resignation due to ill health. The election in November of the same year confirmed the electorate's faith in the government but with a massive Tory majority. Neville Chamberlain took over as Prime Minister when Stanley Baldwin retired in 1937, but the thrust of the National government remained the same—to tackle the economic crisis and counter the growing threat of war in Europe.

The appeal of Fascism in Britain grew, led by Oswald Mosley's British Union of Fascists. Their rallies were often marred by violence as rival supporters protested against Mosley's support for the Fascist cause in Europe.

Towards World War II

Fascism became popular in many European countries as well as Britain. Mussolini rose to power in Italy and the Fascists in Spain, under General Franco, were victorious in the Civil War. In 1933 Germany, the Nazi party under Adolf Hitler was declared the only political party, starting the slide towards the Second World War. In 1936, Hitler's forces occupied the Rhineland, territory that had been taken from Germany at the end of World War One. When Germany occupied Czechoslovakia in 1938, Hitler stated that his territorial aggression was at an end. This was accepted by the British Prime Minister, Neville Chamberlain and the Munich agreement was signed with Chamberlain making the famous 'Peace in our time' speech. The following year, in September 1939, Hitler invaded Poland. Britain and France declared war on Germany two days later, on September 3rd and launched in to the century's bloodiest conflict.

Immediately, Britain's cities were 'blacked out.' Street lights were turned off, thick curtains put over all windows and cars drove with their headlights masked, save for small slits which allowed a glimmer of light to give some indication of the state of the road ahead. The television service that was broadcast to the 2000 owners of TV sets was switched off on September 1st and not resumed until 1946.

Many children were evacuated from major cities, as the threat of aerial bombardment was ever present. When the threat failed to materialise in the first few months of the war, large numbers returned home for Christmas. Perhaps it wasn't going to be quite so bad after all.

Closer to Home—
Personal Memories of the 1930s

Whilst the 1920s began with the painful after-effects of World War I, the 1930s ended with the outbreak of World War II. Some of the later memories in this chapter are poignant reminders of the slow build up to another major conflict. Firstly, though, schooldays are recalled.

Edward Foxwell in Norfolk recalls his early swimming days

Sink or swim?

'I learnt to swim in the sea, near our school. One of the masters, Mr Whitlock (I've changed his name) took us down to the beach for swimming lessons. There was a wooden raft moored about fifty yards out from the beach and Mr Whitlock told us to swim out to this raft, whether we could swim or not. The raft seemed hopelessly far out as we all set off in a group. I was surprised that I managed to reach the raft with the others and climb up on top to catch my breath. All the boys that swam out of their depth climbed up on that raft. Only two gave up in the shallows and walked back to the beach. Mr Whitlock didn't seem to mind this, which also surprised me. Then we all jumped back in the water and swam back to the beach.

I was exhausted but elated. I went home that night and ran into my parents shouting gleefully 'I can swim, I can swim.' I was very excited.

Next day was Saturday and I couldn't wait to make my way down to the river near our house, to practice my new skills. I stripped off down to my swimming trunks and jumped confidently in to the river. At this point in my life my scientific knowledge was not as developed as it was in later years. In particular, I wasn't aware that salty seawater was more buoyant than fresh river water! So when I cockily jumped in to the river, I didn't really understand why I had difficulty in keeping my head above the waterline. I spluttered and coughed and choked and only managed to stay afloat by clinging on to a clump of reeds that was drifting downstream in the current.

In retrospect, I'm sure that Mr Whitlock was testing our confidence when he 'threw us in at the deep end.' He wouldn't really have allowed any of us to drown, would he?'

Basil Marcuson attended school in London and has very different memories of his schooldays

Eccentrics in the classroom

'My recollections of earlier years are dominated by encounters with a number of quite extraordinary eccentrics.

Mr Van der Kiste, who seemed to be Dutch only in name, had a florid complexion that clashed alarmingly with the thick 'pepper and salt' suit which he wore in all seasons. He ran a masculine version of a dame school in a small house in Golders Green, with two schoolrooms on the ground floor, and his living quarters upstairs. The total number of pupils could not have exceeded fifty, and with fees of four guineas per term his cash flow must have been a trickle.

However, it seemed to suffice to enable him to climb up the hill past Prince's Park to the 'Royal Oak' pub each lunchtime; imbibe enough to make his face even more puce than usual, and then roll back down the hill in time for afternoon lessons. Needless to say the quality of his teaching was better in the mornings than in the afternoons, the latter being spent in filling up our exercise books with tables, spellings and lists of dates and places.

When these were full and we demanded new books, we were told to fill up every margin with our writings, because new books were not to be made available 'until the financial crisis is over!' My parents naively thought that he was referring to the Economic Depression of 1929-33 that covered those formative years. It was only later that I understood that the 'crisis' he referred to was a personal one.

Dear Mr Van der Kiste imposed discipline merely by having a terrifying exterior, but as we came to discover, he was a kindly man, and totally adept at instilling a grounding in the 'three Rs'. He gave me a great skill in speedy mental arithmetic (largely irrelevant since the invention of the pocket calculator), and the knowledge (vouchsafed to only a few these days) of the exact position on the map occupied by the County of Westmorland.

Mr Sturgeon, our history teacher at Haberdashers' School (in West Hampstead before its move to Elstree) taught by rote. History was a poem, a liturgical chant in which he took the leading part and the class had the roles of the chorus.

'At the beginning of the Nineteenth Century,' he would intone, 'England entered the period of the Industrial Revo . . .' and the chorus would joyously respond 'looshun!'

We had a limited interest in the solo passage, but waited impatiently for the familiar key phrase which was the cue for our entry 'The Battle of Water . . . . . . loo!'

As a result my awareness of history as a continuous interplay of complex political, social and economic forces, only came much later in life. History rather seemed to consist of an apparently unconnected series of personages and events, whose meaning was obscure but whose names evoked a half-forgotten schoolboy chant.'

Denys Harvey in Somerset recalls another aspect from his formative years

Take your partner

'Ballroom dancing was introduced which as you can imagine was not universally popular. We didn't have regular partners. At the beginning of each lesson all of the girls threw one of their shoes in to the middle of the dance floor and we boys had to choose a shoe and hence our partner. I was a reluctant participant for several weeks until I drew the shoe of Miss Ashworth, the senior mistress who taught Maths with a passion. The experience was so nerve racking that I never went back!

My most embarrassing moment at school though was when my father visited. He was a local church soloist and he came to teach us a new school song 'Forty Years On.' I think that my efforts at harmony were so poor that he wished I was forty miles away!'

Enid Pratt attended a private school near **Brighton**

Coronets and the Empire

'Many of the girls at the school were 'young ladies' from various European countries, who were over here to perfect their English. I remember Winifred Cleare one of my friends, telling me that one pupil had coronets embroidered on all her underwear!

In 1935, the school moved to new premises in Shoreham-by-Sea and this prompted a reunion of old pupils complete with dinner and speeches. One of these speeches, by Alderman Franklin, was reported in the local paper. Here is an excerpt:

. . . referring to the fact that private schools were less under the domination of examinations than the State schools—a point in their favour—the Alderman Franklin added:

'The education of girls today tends towards the careers that are open to them. Not more than six per cent go on to university. Academic education in itself is not a real need for a great many

Multicultural Young Ladies

girls. Far more valuable is an education which provides the girl with an appreciation and love of literature, art and music and the duties of citizenship. In the attempt to make education wider in its scope, the private schools did not forget the real problems girls had to face when they grew up—those of self-government, cultural knowledge and homecraft. They did not forget the value of physical training in providing mental and physical balance and they did not overlook the importance to giving to young girls an appreciation of their duty to their country and to their Empire.'

When war broke out, the school had a very panicky time trying to get all of the girls safely back to their homes. I have often wondered how many of them were actually safe throughout the war.'

Brenda Hall's schooldays were postponed for several months as she experienced illness before the days of the National Health Service

Under the weather

'I was aged four and my sister was a year younger when we were struck down with the illnesses all families dreaded; I had scarlet fever and my sister had diphtheria. I remember the ride in the ambulance to the fever hospital. Despite my illness, I was entranced by the streetlights as we went through the town—there were no lights where we lived. The hospital was a single story building on a hill on the outskirts of the town.

We were not allowed visitors in to see us. My grandma came one day and I was carried on to the veranda to wave to her through the glass doors. She brought me six eggs as a gift; I expect she thought they might help me to recover.

I was kept in isolation. I had an iron cot instead of a bed, which I wasn't pleased about. The walls were plain and painted white with small windows high up near the ceiling. It was rather like I imagined a prison cell might be.

There was an iron stove in the centre of the room. I cooked two of my eggs on this which I soon realised I was not supposed to do. The rest were confiscated.

My sister left hospital before me—whilst recovering from scarlet fever I caught diphtheria. I have no memory of anything else until I returned home three months later.

I had to learn to walk again.'

*A E Thomas also had experience of eggs in hospital in **London***

Hot water and Hops

'When I was ten years old I was diagnosed with scarlet fever. The ambulance came and I was carried in to it wrapped in a scarlet blanket and conveyed to the fever hospital, not far from home. Visitors were not welcomed but families were expected to pro-

Hop Pickers

vide fresh eggs with the patient's name written on them. I always felt that the nurses dispensed the medicines in the rice pudding because it tasted so horrible!

At home, like most people we had no bathroom; not even a hot water tap. My two sisters and myself were bathed in a stone copper when small but when we were old enough we trekked up to the local baths once a week. Here, you entered a cubicle and the bath was filled from some central point. When you wanted more hot or cold water, you called out the number of your cubicle and an unseen hand turned the tap on to answer your command.

Holidays were spent in the hop fields of Kent. A mattress filled with faggots (branches) spread on the floor of a barn was our bed. The sun always seemed to shine and I can still feel the many scratches on my arms as the long vines were pulled down and laid across the bin ready for our nimble fingers to strip the fragrant hops from the stiff stalks.

On my fourteenth birthday, much against my wishes, I was told that there was a job for me at the Metal Box Company; twelve shillings a week for working from 8-30am until 6pm. Ten shillings for my mother and two shillings for me. I had been attending the Central School, doing very well and should have stayed until I was sixteen. I really never forgave my mother.'

George Appelbe also recalls an episode from his early life

Words of Wordsworth

'I was born in Somerset and although my family moved when I was six, I still have a distinct Somerset accent. During my second year at the Grammar School when I was in an English grammar class each person had to read a passage from a particular book. I can recall my passage was from Wordsworth. *I wandered lonely as a cloud, that floats on high o'er vales and hills, when all at once I saw a crowd, a host of golden daffodils.* So I started to read . . . 'oi' wandered lonely as a cloud, when all at once 'oi' saw a crowd . . . The next thing I knew was that my English teacher grasped me by the ear and twisted it saying 'Say I, Say I.' Of course I said 'oi' and 'oi' again until he gave up and pushed my face into the book.

Isn't it strange how these things stick in one's mind!'

Nancy Hornsby *(nee Greene), spent her childhood years in* ***India*** *during the days of the British Empire.*

Passage from India

'In some ways I had an unusual childhood, growing up in India in the 1930s. I survived without outings, parties or concerts; I mostly stayed at home and played by myself in the garden and I managed to get along without friends of my own age. I was not aware of the cinema, shops, toys or holidays. I just ate what was on my plate, went to school in the army lorry, tried to learn my lessons and didn't ask questions.

I can remember one big adventure. My parents and some of their friends had planned a day trip to northwest India in the area that is now covered by Pakistan. We had an army escort and set off along the two parallel roads that wind their way along the contours leading to the Khyber Pass. One road was for motor vehicles the other was for animals, mostly camels and donkeys. After a few hours we reached what was considered to be the furthest safe place. My mother said to me 'You'll not come back here again; just remember this place.' I looked over from our vantage point to the mountains of Afghanistan—bare, solid and awe inspiring. I thought about the wars that had been fought in the area and how the Afghans had beaten the British army in the previous century. Even today I can remember the Khyber Pass.

My brother Peter and I returned to England to attend school. The following is an account of our journey, which I wrote as a child and was published in the school magazine of 1938.'

My Voyage from India

When we got on board the Neuralia we met lots of friends who had come to see us off. We met the Methodist Padre who had come to see another Padre off. After the boat started we waved to Daddy as long as we could see him. As we neared Colaba we waved again. Daddy also would be waving a jaran (which is a tea towel). We could see a white thing fluttering about, so we thought that was Daddy waving.

We did not stop at any port except Port Said. I went out twice in the morning with mummy and in the afternoon with Mrs Lewis, who took care of my little brother Peter. Mummy didn't buy anything but took a walk to the beach where we collected shells for Peter who is fond of stones and shells and sand. Mrs Lewis bought a big bag and three necklaces; one for her daughter, one for Mary (my big sister) and one for me.

The Red Sea was not at all hot, if anything cold and the Mediterranean was very rough and nearly everyone was seasick.

Every day I watched the map. Somebody must have been in charge of it because every morning it told roughly where we were at 8pm. The day we arrived at Southampton was rainy but it cleared later in the day. We waited about an hour for my sister, then we had something to eat. She did not come and we decided something had happened so we caught a train. We had rather a difficult time finding the boarding house where we were going to stay. Mary came in during dinner. We stayed here for a few days and soon found a house for a future home.

Nancy Greene (aged 8 years)

Fred Bishop *now lives in South Africa but grew up in* **Dorset.**
Here he recalls his early life, both in and out of school

Breaking the rules

'I was born in a three-storey house with four large bedrooms, a sitting room, a living room with a kitchen range where all the cooking was done and a lean-to containing a scullery, washroom and toilet. Bathroom there was not! All bedrooms contained a washstand with a marble top on which stood a large china bowl containing a large china jug. Alongside this sat a china soap dish and all of these china items were elaborately decorated with either birds or flowers. My favourite had blue irises on it. Under the marble slab was a cupboard containing a pair of matching china chamber pots decorated to match the rest of the set. Under the cupboard stood a large enamel bucket with a vented lid called a slop pail, in which all dirty water was taken to the toilet for disposal. Cold water was kept in the jug and hot water was brought to the bedrooms in enamel jugs. Here, we washed ourselves daily from top to toe. Bathing was a weekly ordeal carried out in a portable galvanised tin bath, usually in front of the fire. Parents carried out their bath time ritual in relative privacy after the children had gone to bed.

We had no electricity or gas in the house and oil lamps and candles provided lighting. It was a regular weekly task for my father to keep the lamps full, the wicks trimmed and the glasses polished. The oil lamps were often very ornate things and they gave off a remarkable amount of light considering the primitive contraptions that they were. Some households had large numbers of these lamps in one room, my grandfather's front room being one of these.

During the winter we slept in the bedrooms on the first floor. In the summer we moved to the third floor. My mother took in summer visitors who stayed in 'our' rooms on holiday. The tax laws were different then and no tax was levied on 'paying guests' so that's what we had!

What always struck me about our bedrooms were the pure white counterpanes, bed sheets and pillow cases that adorned each bed. Always pristine, as was the table linen. How my mother managed to wash all this by hand, starch it to varying degrees of stiffness, dry it in our enclosed yard, iron it with flat-irons heated on the range and still keep it white, always amazed me.

My own white bed was less than pristine one night when I was ill. In fact, I was very ill and the doctor told my mother that I would probably not survive the night. A Cresoline lamp was kept burning through the night to aid my breathing and my mother sat up with me. At 1-30am she gave me my medicine. Immediately I shrieked and blew it out all over my lovely white bedding. In her tired state, mother had given me a spoonful of Cresoline instead of medicine. While my weeping mother held me, father ran nearly a mile in his bare feet to fetch the doctor. They arrived back together to find me with my throat burning and my mother still sobbing. The doctor quickly examined me and declared that my parents should not worry any longer. The shock of the burning Cresoline on my throat had brought me round and I would survive, after all. An effective treatment, apparently, but not one that I would recommend!

My Uncle Frank married a 'foreigner,' a girl from London! She remained a 'foreigner' to many of the locals until she died aged eighty-seven. They had two daughters and all three women spent their adult years working in a steam laundry as ironers. They stood all day at a large table and ironed everything from handkerchiefs to bed sheets using gas irons.

At school, we were taught the alphabet using a phonetic system. I had already learned the alphabet forwards and backwards before I started school so this did not make much sense to me. I enlightened the teacher of this fact one day and received a whack on my head with a wooden ruler. I stood up and told her that she should know better than to hit children over the head in this way. For my trouble, she placed a traditional pointed dunce's cap on my head and made me stand in the corner. While I was undergoing this punishment, the head teacher came into the class and asked me why I was a dunce. I told her the whole story, uncensored. When asked, the rest of the class corroborated my story. Our teacher left the class with the head teacher and after returning never used the ruler again.

In conjunction with the alphabet lessons, we were also taught to count using small brown beans. Once again, I already knew how to count and in my boredom, pushed the beans up my nose. Whilst trying to recover her beans, the teacher made my nose bleed and I ended up at the doctors having my beans removed. Thankfully, no lasting damage was done.

When I was about nine years old, one of my classmates, a boy called Patrick caused something of a stir. Toys were not allowed in class and any that were found were confiscated, put on top of a cupboard and not returned until the end of term. During a lesson that was being delivered by our rather strict Headmistress, Patrick began playing with something under his desk. The hawk-like Head soon noticed the disturbance, not least because several of the pupils sitting close to the miscreant were giggling. 'Patrick, bring whatever you are playing with under your desk and put it on the table. You can't have it back until the end of term.' This caused the level of mirth to rise audibly as Patrick's near neighbours could see what he was playing with. As a precocious nine-year-old, he had already learned one of life's lessons—stroking your juvenile penis causes it to grow larger and is a very pleasurable experience! On hearing the headmistress's stern voice, Patrick quickly hid the evidence and protested his innocence. When asked, nobody would admit to knowing what Patrick had been playing with.

We also attended Sunday school which was quite usual for children and particularly so for me. Our family was very religious; my grandfather, who was a farmer was particularly strict over Sunday observance and only the duties that were absolutely necessary were carried out. No work was done and the farm animals were rested. Cows were milked and all of the animals were fed as a necessity but that was all. Only books of a religious nature were read and no games were played. Knitting and sewing weren't allowed; not even a button could be sewn on. Food for Sunday was cooked on Saturday and eaten cold. Sunday newspapers were delivered but neither read nor paid for until Monday. Walking and visiting relatives were permitted. Listening to the radio was banned except for religious programmes. I wasn't even allowed to ride my bicycle on a Sunday. However, the rules against bicycle riding came to a strange end. One of the cows had the temerity to ignore the Sunday rules and fell ill, requiring the vet to be called. He didn't have the necessary medicine, which was only available from a town ten miles away. There were no trains or buses (they all observed the Sunday rules in those days) and cars were still few and far between. The answer to my suggestion 'If I was allowed to, I could go on my bike' was an unequivocal 'Yes.' I fetched the medicine, the cow survived and nothing was ever said again about Sunday cycling.

Farm work continued at a hectic pace on the other six days of the week. Grandad bought a Fordson tractor in the early '30s to replace the carthorses. As a young boy, I was taught to drive it and I spent whole days ploughing and harrowing until the sun set. In the dairy I washed bottles and utensils in very hot water. These were never wiped but placed in racks to dry. The bottles were then filled by hand with full cream milk from a large jug and waxed card tops were fitted to the top of each bottle to seal them. Sometimes the cream was separated from the milk in a Separator. Milk was poured in to the top of the machine and turned using a crank handle. Cream came out of one spout and skimmed milk from the other. The cream was put in to cartons to be sold in local shops. In those days before diets and 'healthy lifestyles' became a fashionable way of life, the skimmed milk was fed to the pigs!

The Sunday observance regime held firm until the onset of World War II, when it soon became clear that war didn't observe the Sunday day of rest. In particular, close friends of my Grandfather's were killed when a bomb dropped on their house while they were enjoying their Sunday lunch.

The day before war broke out is fixed firmly in my memory. I was allowed to go to the cinema to see John Wayne in 'Stagecoach.' I enjoyed it so much that I remained in my seat and watched it a second time! Soon after the film started, people sitting near the front of the cinema began to move farther back. I noticed this but didn't realise the significance until the film ended and I walked down the steps outside of the cinema into three feet of water. It was the first night of the blackout that would last for five years, so I couldn't see where I was going. A very heavy period of rain coincided with high tide to produce a flood. I managed to get to higher ground and eventually to my grandmother's house. My aunt went out in the storm and passed a message to my father across the flood waters that I was safe.

War was declared the following day and we all wondered what was going to happen. In fact, very little happened to us for several months with minimal changes to our lives—apart from food shortages and the gas masks that we were required to carry.'

Joe North in *London* *found his education cut short due to family circumstances*

Choir practice

'At the age of eleven years I sat the 11+ exam for a place at 'Churchless College.' I was the only one in the school that passed the written exam but had to attend an interview because there was only one vacancy at the college. That interview was one of the most frightening experiences of my life. Standing in the Big Hall in front of the Board of Directors—twelve in all, mostly retired military personnel, I was asked two questions. The first was about oranges in a barrel; if so many were rotten, what was the percentage of good ones? The second was about my father; what work did he do? That was the end of the interview. Needless to say, two days later my headmaster was told to tell me and my parents that I had failed. That two-minute interview ended my academic career. The headmaster told me that they couldn't teach me any more at my current school so I spent the next three years looking after the school sports equipment, doing the milk monitoring and book binding until I left at fourteen years of age. For the next three and a half years I did a number of menial jobs simply to earn a living but most of my energies were directed towards my other interests.

I joined the church choir when I was eight years old, practising three evenings a week and singing in church twice on Sundays, for which we were paid 1/6d every quarter. After two years I was promoted to Leading Choirboy and had a raise to 2/6d.

Being in the choir led to other experiences. In 1936 we formed part of a massed choir singing in Crystal Palace which was broadcast on radio; I was extremely honoured to be asked to sing a solo. Two months later the Crystal Palace burned to the ground, an experience that was particularly moving for me, for obvious reasons. My solo didn't go unnoticed and I was offered a place in the Winchester Cathedral Choir. Unfortunately, once again, I was unable to take up this offer due to my family circumstances; coming from a large family, my parents couldn't afford to pay for my board and uniform, even though the tuition was free. My situation was not uncommon at that time and many young people from working class families were unable to accept the opportunities that their wealthier contemporaries took for granted. At this time, our choir was also asked to sing at Windsor Castle. We performed for the King and Queen in St George's Chapel, the highlight of my singing career.

At ten years of age I also joined the Scout movement, learning many useful things which stood me in good stead later in life. Apart from the usual knot tying, cooking over the campfire and first aid, we learned semaphore signalling, Morse code, including building our own Morse keyboard and how to build an oscillator from a radio valve and transformer. Communication soon became my favourite subject and I became very proficient at the areas that we studied. I became patrol leader after two years and then troop leader soon afterwards. Unfortunately, our 'skipper' who was a Lt Commander in the RN Reserve was called up for action when war broke out and was replaced by one of our local school teachers. Within weeks, he too was called up and at the tender age of fourteen, I was left in charge of the scout troop!'

Geoff Saunders *recalls school in* **Ealing**

Pearls before swine

'When I was about six years old we moved to Ealing and it was decided to send me to Ealing College, one of about half a dozen private schools in the borough although there were some excellent elementary schools nearer home. The establishment was run and owned by a 'Dr' McKay, a gentleman with very parsimonious ideas when it came to schoolbooks and accommodation but very handy with the cane. I spent three years in what we called the 'Cowshed'—a large corrugated iron structure with three internal wooden partitions situated in a gravel yard.

In spite of the spartan surroundings the standard of education was very good. I still have a table of the annual examination results—for some reason G Saunders was in top position. I also still have a school prize inscribed by a Mr D K Armstrong, a very earnest young man who was a dedicated teacher and a zealous disciplinarian which I found to my cost on a number of occasions. Needless to say, like most schools in those days it was boys only so there were few distractions in class apart from those young rotters who put carbide from their bicycle lamps into the inkwells. There was a fair amount of bullying so one had to stand up for oneself even if you came home with a torn blazer or muddy short trousers—the latter being the norm for the uniform at the time.

Having passed the entrance exam, I was accepted into Ealing County School, run by the local education authority. The school day was 9am to 12.30pm and 2pm to 4pm with a half day for sports. Discipline was strict but fair—not wearing your school cap merited a detention, as did chewing toffee in class! On one occasion I shot at the bus conductor with my peashooter from the open upper deck and was unfortunate enough to travel with the same conductor going to the sports ground. He reported me to the accompanying teacher, a Dr Harris, who sent me back to school and to report to the Head which resulted in six of the best, hardly merited I feel—after all none of the peas hit the man! (The Head, Mr W.J. Dudman, was killed with all his family during the blitz in 1940).

There was only one staff change during the six years I was there. Those teachers who remain in my mind, all in their black gowns in class, were a mixed bunch but managed to knock us into shape whatever our background. (Later one lad known as Fishy Gibson, the son of an itinerant fishmonger and a right tearaway was awarded the D.F.C. and married one of the Coleman girls from the mustard family).

There was Nobby Clarke, the deputy Head, who rarely appeared to take a class but seemed to spend most of his time prowling around the corridors. My favourite, Ben Booker whose subject was chemistry was an ex Dulwich Hamlet footballer who limped from a war injury. 'Pansy' Barrett, well turned out, taught French and was alleged to have a soft spot for Miss Elton, the Head's secretary,—a well endowed young lady. Tubby Vaughan, rotund and country tweeds, geography, rather boring we thought. Father Gleed, a tall cadaverous figure with an incisive tongue whose sarcastic comments included 'pearls before swine' as we struggled with the Golden Treasury or Henry IV Part One. Then there was Bill Mathers who joined the staff from Manchester in my fourth year. He was brilliant in history, an excellent bat at cricket and adept at boxing ears—quite acceptable in those days! His predecessor, Bob Roberts, was a lovely man but the only teacher who could not keep discipline—hence his replacement.

Mr Tew, a dry north countryman with an odd accent who in physics referred to Hoyt, Light and Sound! A character was Algy Holding, the maths master who frightened me to death but taught me more in one year than the four previously—his favourite expression to us dullards was 'rabbits.' Finally there was a rather mysterious character named Herr Baswitz—I was never in his class as he taught German which I later regretted not taking. There was also our PT instructor and choirmaster, ex Sergeant Major Potts, a typical ex WW1 regular soldier whose voice carried across the playground over the yells of six hundred boys. To complete the school's personnel was our caretaker and his wife, the latter running the 'tuck shop' which was a table in front of the kitchen, and who cooked school dinners which were so revolting I was happy to go home by train or bus to have mine.

Nevertheless those dedicated teachers achieved results. The year I took the General Schools Exams in 1935—of the seventy-five boys who sat, twelve matriculated with honours, forty gained matric standard, twenty reached general schools level and only three failed—not a bad result.'

The smell of burning wood reminds **Gil Haines** of his boyhood in **Reading**

Mmmm . . .

'Every Monday morning as I lay in bed I heard the sound of mother chopping wood in order to light the fire in the brick copper which was in one corner of the scullery. This was the start of her 'Big Wash' as she called it. She would be up at 6am picking up the rugs and mats from the floor of the scullery to hang them over the washing line and give them a good beating. She then rolled them up and put them to one side before lighting the fire. Whilst the water was heating up she cooked the breakfast.

I lay in bed, listening to the wood crackling as the fire caught hold. My nostrils caught the smells of the burning wood mingling with the mouth-wateringly delicious aroma of cooking bacon. It was heaven for me. At least it was until I heard mother's voice shouting up the stairs, 'breakfast is on the table.' In other words, 'get up now'!'

Arthur Featherstone from Kent recalls an early advertising campaign

Bisto given the boot

'We tend to think that advertising aimed at children is a recent development. But this has been the case for years. I can vividly remember getting my mother to buy something that she had never bought before because of advertising in the newspapers. Mum always bought Bisto gravy powder when I was young. The advert was for Oxo. If you sent in one hundred Oxo wrappers you would receive a full-size leather football! Me being football mad, this was obviously too good an opportunity to let pass by. So, for the next weeks and months mum used Oxo instead of Bisto and I got my football. This despite the fact that, at the time, nobody in our

ANTIRRHINUM
(Presumption.)

"Soon shall we have gold-dusted
Snapdragon,
Sweet-William with his homely
cottage smell,
And Stocks in fragrant blow."
Matthew Arnold

The old name of this flower is
Snapdragon. When the bloom is
pressed between the thumb and
forefinger, a mouth opens which was
supposed to resemble that of a
dragon. Other names were Calf's
Snout, Toad's Mouth, Dog's Mouth,
etc. The modern name Antirrhinum
means "snout-like."

In the olden days the Snapdragon when carried was considered
a potent charm against the evil-eye
and witchcraft. This belief still
survives in many Continental and
Eastern countries.

The Antirrhinum flowers from
July to October.

Cigarette card collecting was very popular. Kensitas cigarette packs all included
an embroidered silk flower held within a printed card

household particularly liked Oxo! It was back to Bisto as soon as I had my football but an early lesson in the power of advertising.'

*Jane Woods has always lived in **Norwich**.*
Everything was on the doorstep

Empire Day

'I was brought up in Union Street. We had every type of shop in the street. There was a barbers, a bakers where everyone had their Christmas cakes decorated, a wet fish shop, a dairy, a newsagent, an outdoor shoe shop where all of the shoes and plimsolls were hung up outside, a cobbler who mended the shoes when they were worn out, Dunhams, which sold bacon at one end and wool at the other, two pubs—everything that you needed was there. International Stores was the largest shop, which had a counter running all down one side of the shop and the staff—men and women—all stood behind, ready to serve the customers. They always looked smart. We didn't have a Fish and Chip shop though—we had to walk round the corner for that!

We played in the street all the time, there weren't many cars in those days. We also used to hire bikes from Mr Kerrison and his brother—'dodgers' we called them—in Chapel Street. They cost 2d for an hour. I didn't have much money so I'd run anywhere for ½d. I was always running errands.

Our family had a tradition on Valentine's Day of leaving the children a present on the doorstep. Every year there would be a knock on the door; I would open it to find a paint set, a book or a whipping top sitting on the doorstep. I never knew how they got there; my mum said it was the fairies.

My grandma lived in the next street, near my school and I often walked round to see her in the evenings. I was never afraid of the dark; there was no need to. My mum didn't worry about me and never came to look for me. I also used to visit my Grandma most days for my meal instead of having school dinners. This saved us money and also allowed me to see my Gran, which I liked.

I remember my schooldays at Crook's Place with fondness. The teachers were friendly and I learned to read and write with enthusiasm. I started school at the age of 3½ and for the first few years we all had a little nap in the afternoon. May 24th was Empire Day. Every year at school we all dressed in costumes from different countries belonging to the British Empire—India, Canada, Australia, Rhodesia, South Africa and others from all over the world; it was very colourful and lots of fun. I learned a lot of my geography because of those Empire days. The Sheriff of Norwich visited our school and 'inspected' us, then gave us all an extra half-day's holiday. He was very popular.

In the summer holidays we spent our time in Chapel Fields, a park near our house. Mum gave us a bottle of lemonade and sometimes a picnic and she didn't see us again until late in the evening. We also went to the pictures—the Globe in Northumberland Street—and queued up for ages to pay our 2d entrance fee. Everybody's hero was Charlie Chaplin. One young man even dressed like him and often stood on Boundary Bridge impersonating his hero, complete with bowler hat and cane.

I remember those days as being very happy. I look back now and think that they were magical days. Sometimes I still dream about going to Chapel Fields or dressing up at school. It was all like a fairy tale!'

Muriel Stirling also remembers life in **Norwich**.

Three in a bed

'I can recall when the first council estate was built near our home and school. Children came to school with newspaper in their shoes that had holes in the soles. When mother made a large bread and butter pudding for us all (I was one of seven children) another one would also be made for a family not as well off as us.

Sleeping arrangements for the family would be frowned upon today. My eldest brother, who was slightly retarded, slept in a single bed. In the same room slept the next two boys in a double bed, with my youngest brother keeping them company but with his head at the other end of the bed. My elder sister and myself slept in the small back bedroom in a single bed. Our youngest sister slept with mum and dad. We didn't have duvets or eiderdowns; bedclothes consisted of a sheet, a blanket and anything else that could be used to keep us warm.

I don't know where the idea came from but we never had a Christmas Tree. A pole was slid in to the chimney pot of a wooden doll's house. Three hoops were then fastened to the pole and presents hung from the hoops. We didn't know any different and apart from the hoops, all decorations were hand made. Toys were equally simple. Apart from tops, hoops and conkers we also used acorns as ammunition in our pop guns.

Our dad died in 1939 just before the war broke out. He died from the after-effects of the previous war; he had been gassed in the trenches and returned home in 1919 suffering from shell shock. Life was hard for our mum; she was always working, cleaning, cooking, washing and ironing. Stiff collars had to be starched and the iron was heated on the open coal fire. But she always seemed to be happy. I don't know if she was actually happy or if she pretended to be, in front of us. I hope she was pleased with the way that we all turned out—she brought us all up to be good to each other and she should be proud of that.'

Deana Whine lived in **Bow, East London.** *She recalls the original 'home delivery' service*

The ice delivery

'In the 1930s there was no such thing as a refrigerator for the ordinary person so shopping had to be done every day otherwise the food would spoil. We at least had an icebox, which was only used in the summer. This was a massive wooden chest with a zinc-lined well in the top with a lift up lid in which a block of ice was placed. I can see the iceman now—he came twice a week, with a sack on his shoulder heaving this enormous block of ice. If it was too big he chipped away with an ice pick until the block slipped into place. We children stood around ready to catch the chips of ice which flew off and we sucked them like ice-lollies.

The ice-cream man came round every day in the summer. I still remember the name, Assenheims. He had a pushcart painted in garish fairground colours, and he called out 'hokey, pokey, penny a lump.' A 'lump' was a waxed paper packet about four inches by two inches and an inch thick. For a halfpenny a child could have half, which the man cut diagonally. I've never tasted ice-cream like it since! Later on Walls started coming. They had a contraption like a square box on wheels, one in front and two behind, which the man rode like a bicycle, but I didn't think their ice-cream was nearly so good; commercially made as against a family concern.

Because of the lack of refrigeration, it was necessary to shop every day and many trades people brought their wares to the door. The milkman, of course and the coalman. The muffin man also called, with a tray of goodies on his head. He rang a bell to let us know he was there. So did the catmeat man who had pieces of horsemeat on wooden skewers. The greengrocer also came along every week with a cart full of fruit and vegetables, pulled by a horse.

On Thursday evenings regular as clockwork a blind man came down the street playing an accordion accompanied by a dog called Nell who must have been a forerunner of today's Seeing Eye dogs. When I heard him I used to run out with my penny for the man and piece of sugar for the dog. We also had a troupe of tumblers who, I realise now were men in drag though to me in those days they appeared like very large ladies. They performed right there, in the middle of the road, there being very little traffic other than the occasional horse-drawn carriage. They danced and did acrobatics much to the delight of we children who danced with them, and they then passed round the hat. We also had a barrel organ man with a monkey on top who wore a little jacket and tiny red fez.

Buses in those days had open tops—no roof. If it rained, as it very often did, passengers on the top deck could pull a leather apron over their legs to keep dry. And put up their umbrellas. Hospitals in those days were run by charities—no NHS—and outside the London Hospital in Whitechapel Road there stood a chute just the height of a doubledecker bus. As the bus went past people would throw money in. As a child it was a great thrill for me to go on a bus with a lid on.

I left school just before the start of World War II. As a fully-fledged shorthand typist I earned the magnificent sum of twenty-five shillings a week—about £1-25p in today's money. No photocopiers then and I used to bruise my fingers banging out six carbon copies, so that the last one was legible. This was on a manual typewriter that incidentally I still use—I prefer it to my electronic one. If a lot of copies were needed a stencil had to be cut. This was done by immobilising the ribbon on the machine and typing on a special stencil sheet with a backing, so that you could see that the letters had been cleanly cut—very hard on the fingers. This was then fixed to the drum of a duplicating machine, the roller inked from a tube of thick gunge and the handle turned by hand, very arm-aching if you needed a couple of hundred copies!'

The sausage filling lines at Sainsbury's Blackfriars factory

*Jack Ramsey's first experience of earning a living, off the **East Coast** nearly came to a premature end*

Shrimping

'As a lad, I lived in Harwich where my parents kept a small hotel. I grew up practically living for fishing and small boats. I often used to go out with the fishing boats to catch the famous Harwich Shrimps (sadly no more due to overfishing). We left very early in the morning and returned in the afternoon, landing sacks of these pink shrimps on the pier to be put on the train to London, destined for some of the best restaurants in town. I cooked these shrimps in a copper on the boat as soon as they were caught and then sacked them up—I can taste them now, after all these years! My last fishing trip was at the end of 1939. The old skipper of the boat went to investigate a large red buoy, which was several hundred yards away in a position that seemed unusual. Yes, you've guessed it—it was a mine, with large metal horns sticking out all around it. The skipper was quite unperturbed by this and circled around

Mitchells and Butlers advertising posters
and a Tadcaster Tower Brewery bar price list

the buoy—all this while the shrimp trawl net was still down! I and the other seaman were both in a state of near panic as we swept around the deadly red device; we were both convinced that the mine would get caught up in the net. I remember praying until I was convinced that the boat and the net were well out of range of potential disaster.

That evening, the skipper had a pint of beer with my dad down the pub and told him all about it.

'I don't know why he was so scared,' said the skipper, 'it was one of ours!' Needless to say that was the end of fishing trips for me.'

Eileen Kelly left a promising academic career at sixteen years old to earn money for the family

Telephone House

'My older brothers and sisters had all left home apart from my brother Nick, who was apprenticed to an engineering firm. Apprentices didn't get paid, so money was short and I had to leave school to start work. I got a job in a nasty office in a dirty back street that smelled of fish. I was a general runabout from 9am until whenever they closed; an early night was 6pm. I worked Saturdays as well for 10/- (50p) per week that I gave to my mother in exchange for my bus fares. So I didn't get very rich. I got out of this in 1937 when they opened 'Telephone House' in Birmingham, a large modern telephone exchange. To get in to this required three months training at telephone school, run by the nastiest woman, then we were given a telephone, a locker and a schedule of shift work. It was like being back at a girl's school. The whole thing was run by women, men only covered the night shift. A large number of girls coped with local calls, toll calls (a thirty mile radius) and trunk calls. The switchboards were placed all round a huge room and calls could be taken by any of the operators. There was one supervisor for every ten girls and she sat on a stool watching to make sure that nobody spoke to anyone else. We had to record every call on a pad with date, time and length of call. So we communicated by writing notes to each other on our pads and passing them down the line. In this way we collected for birthdays and engagement presents, arranged get-togethers where we could moan to each other and make arrangements to swap shifts. The supervisor poked us if we weren't working fast enough and we could not leave our post until we were relieved. Most girls stayed there until they got married. After I had been there for two years (it seemed like ten) the war started. My job was a reserved occupation, which meant that I wouldn't be called up. Since I didn't want to spend the war on the telephone, I handed in my notice, got a job with British Oxygen and waited for my call up. I was going to be a WREN!

Looking back now and not being a financial expert, I often wonder why we could have such small wages, with food, rents and everything correspondingly cheaper, yet now everyone has to have more because the goods are so much dearer. The man next door to us worked in a factory and earned 10/- per week in 1930. He had a wife and child; the wife didn't work and there was no child allowance, yet they moved to the outskirts of Birmingham and bought a house. In 1931, that house cost £450. At the turn of the century it was worth over £100,000. Everything was so much simpler then and people didn't seem to get depressive illnesses. People had to be very ill before the doctor was called. There was no free Health Service and a visit from the doctor cost 2/6d, or half a crown; over a day's wages for many people. If you were well enough to go to the surgery you were given a 'bottle,' which cost two shillings (10p). It was certainly cheaper to stay healthy. Most workers paid 1d per week to the 'Hospital Saturday Fund.' I think that entitled you to hospital treatment followed by convalescence if necessary, so it was a form of insurance'.

Stephen Wright in Worcestershire, a farmer's son, was put to work at an early age on the farm

Prince and Duke

'In the summer we went haymaking. The grass was cut by a mower, which had a long blade moving back and forth inside metal points called 'fingers.' This was drawn by two carthorses which were driven by Old Bill, who sat on a metal seat at the rear of the machine. I can remember two of these horses were called Prince and Duke. They looked enormous to me at the time and I expect they were pretty big in anyone's language. The grass dried in the sun over a couple of days and another horse-drawn machine turned the grass over. After about four days the grass had dried and become hay, ready to be collected. A horse drawn cart moved slowly through the field and dad and his workers used large hay-forks to pick up forkfuls of dry hay and throw them up on to the cart. Another man on the cart arranged the long swathes of hay quickly and efficiently around the cart to even the load and ensure that as much as possible was collected on the cart. When the cart was full, it was pulled to the hayrick where one of the men forked the hay off of the cart on to a wooden elevator which moved the hay up to the top of the hayrick. Two men layered the hay expertly around the rick, gradually building it up to its full height with a

Haymaking

Old Bill with Prince and Duke cutting the corn

'pitched roof' type top. It looked very easy to me as a ten-year-old boy. In fact, it was quite a skilled job, which I gradually picked up in the following years. Finally, the hayrick was thatched, to keep out the rain, much in the same way that a cottage is thatched. Even to my young eyes, this looked complicated and I never learned the rudiments of thatching.

In the autumn, the harvest was 'gathered in'. This term accurately describes what happened to the corn before the days of combine harvesters. When the corn was ripe Prince and Duke were hitched up to a 'Binding' machine. Again, Old Bill was in charge. This had a mower, similar to the hay mower but it also had a wide canvas belt that took the cut corn up to the top of the Binder. Here, it was collected in to a 'sheaf,' tied with string and ejected off of the side of the Binder to fall on the ground. Men walked behind, collecting the sheaves and stacking them up in groups of four or six. This gave the corn some small protection against the weather until it was gathered in, which could be several days later.

Like the hay, the corn was collected on to a cart and transported to large corn stacks where it was covered, either with thatch or more loosely with some of the previous year's old straw. These stacks were about twenty feet square and built up to about twelve feet high and were temporary structures to keep the corn dry until later in the year, when the 'Thrasher' would arrive (more formally known as a Thresher). The Thrashing machine was used to separate the corn from the straw and was a vast contraption, which few farmers could afford. It was usual for a Thrasher to be owned by a contractor (although they weren't known by that term in those days) who travelled from farm to farm. The corn stacks were gradually dismantled and the sheaves cut loose and fed in to the top of the Thrasher. After a great deal of noisy 'winnowing' inside the machine, which created clouds of itchy dust, the corn appeared and was funnelled in to large one hundredweight sack bags. These were sold off, either for bread making, cattle food or seed corn for the following year. Where they ended up depended on the quality of the corn and the price varied accordingly.

The separated straw appeared at the back of the Thrasher and a great pile built up if it wasn't moved away swiftly enough. This was stacked up again and a more permanent straw rick constructed in a similar manner to the hayrick. This too, was thatched when the strawrick was completed.

By the time the Thrasher arrived, the harvest had probably been completed three months previously so the corn stacks had become part of the scenery in the barnyard. The corn attracted large numbers of birds and rodents who did their best to reduce the yield of the harvest. Rats and mice also made their nests in the base of the corn stack—it was warm, dry and provided a ready supply of nutritious food. What could go wrong? Unfortunately for the rodents, they had chosen to make their home in a temporary construction, so when the Thrasher appeared, their days were numbered. As Thrashing got under way, the corn stack gradually shrank in size. The bottom three feet or so housed all of the rodents' nests. The adults attempted to run away before they were uncovered but the very alert terriers that patrolled the surroundings of each corn stack killed most of them. Their young in the nests fared even worse as they were either killed or left to die. It was not unusual to see twenty rodents' nests in one corn stack.'

The 1930s

Joyce Wood enjoyed watching films,
in her home town of Nottingham

The movies come to town

'One of my earliest memories, when I was about four years old, is of a big lorry coming to the end of our street in the evening, stopping and rolling down a large white sheet. A crowd quickly gathered and waited in eager anticipation. All at once, a projector was switched on (though, of course, I didn't realise that at the time) and the sheet was illuminated with a bright light, which soon turned in to moving pictures. The whole area was crowded with people from the surrounding streets watching the black and white film. I can't remember much about the film but a do recall a lot of people were crying at the end; it must have been very sad.'

Colin Holloway had an early introduction
to public transport in Coventry

Trams

'One of the earliest things that sticks in my mind is my dad coming home in his tram conductor's uniform when I was three years old. I can still see my dad with his ticket machine and pads of different coloured punch tickets, which he issued to the passengers—different colours for different journeys. The smell of those tickets is with me still. I became tram mad. My mother would often take me to town to see the trams in the city centre. At the age of four I had a mastoid operation at Coventry hospital and during this period the Coventry carnival was held, which passed by the hospital. All the children that were confined to bed, like me, were taken outside in their beds to witness the fun and once again, trams played their part. All the traffic was halted to make way for the carnival and two trams stopped just up the road. Some of the passengers climbed on to the roof of the trams to get a better view; I wished that I was with them. I can still point out the exact spot where those beds were placed even though the hospital was destroyed and redevelopment has taken place.

In April of the following year, I started school and the first day included an air raid drill, even though war had not been declared.

Two months later, in June, I was again in hospital, this time with ear problems. My mother took me to Maplethorpe to recover. She told me that we wouldn't be able to go back there because of the war. This was still three months before the war started but I recall mum and dad having lots of conversations about the war, as if it had already started. When war was declared, in September, the first thing I remember was that the street lights didn't come on, even on the night that war was declared.'

*Entertainment for **Frank Salter** in **Yorkshire**
was somewhat different*

The Severn Bore

'Our toilet was down the bottom of the garden and it shared a back wall with the toilet of the house in the next street whose garden backed on to ours. The toilet had a wooden seat over a hole which opened in to a large sewer pipe running the length of the road. I remember it was very smelly. Every so often, I can't remember how often, a surge of water ran down the pipe from one end of the road to the other, carrying all before it and cleaning the toilets.

One summer evening, a group of us lads opened the manhole cover at the top of our road and waited for the water surge. As the water started, we set light to pieces of rolled up newspaper that had been doused in paraffin and threw them down on to the rushing torrent. The flames were carried right along the street and several screams could be heard as people who were leisurely going about their business suddenly had their bums singed! Whenever I see the Severn Bore, I think about our old toilet.'

*__Gwen Hatchard__ grew up in **Dorset***

Drink Up

'My father ran a grocery cum off licence store, which was open from 8am–10pm. The locals came in with quart jugs for their draught bitter and most of them emptied their jugs on the premises (out of sight of their wives) before refilling them again to take home. When the Weights and Measures man was in the area it was my job to run down the street warning the other shopkeepers. The quarrymen used to come in for their Digger Shag tobacco with stone dust on their boots and leather straps on their wrists.

I often sat under the counter drawing on the cheese paper and pinching the odd chocolate drop—old ladies offered to buy me, which filled me with dread! One of the more memorable customers, who my father called 'The Missing Link,' had long dark hair, even longer flowing white garments and earned his living carrying sandwich boards around the town advertising local businesses.'

Gordon Barlow *grew up in the* **Black Country** *and helped his father at work*

Blowing the Steam Bull

'My father worked for a firm called Isaiah Oldbury in West Bromwich. This particular firm made axles for railway wagons and other similar vehicles. It was father's job to fix the bearings and brake drums on to the axles after my Uncle Fred had worked the roughly drop forged axles in to shining smooth accurately machined parts. At the age of eleven I was attending the Cronehills Central Boy's school and the midday break ran from 12 until 2pm. During this time I had to catch the bus home, pick up father's dinner and take it to Isaiah Oldbury's before 1pm; father only had thirty minutes for his break. If I managed to arrive at the factory before 1pm and the Boilerman was in a good mood he would allow me to blow the 'Steam Bull,' to let everyone know that it was dinnertime. The Boilerman and I walked up the steps at the side of the boiler and he handed me the piece of rope attached to the whistle that was known as the 'Bull.' He took out his pocket watch and at the precise moment, instructed me to give it a good pull. I felt very important as I opened the valve, setting off the dinnertime whistle.

The factory was driven by steam power from a stationary engine that had a very large flywheel. A leather belt ran around this driving a massive shaft that ran the length of the factory. Various pulleys were attached to this at regular intervals and these were used to drive all of the machinery throughout the factory. So the Boilerman's job was an important role; if the boiler stopped, so did the factory.'

The staff at Isaiah Oldbury

John Garland *spent his youth in* Ebbw Vale

The Church(es)

'My father, mother and grandfather were all very involved in the life and work of James Street Wesleyan Methodist Church, near our home. The founder of Methodism was John Wesley. That is well known, but what is not so well known is that he never intended to be the founder of the Methodist Church or any other church. He was a clergyman of the Church of England until the day he died, and he tried to keep the Methodists within the established Church. All the same, things were happening and in fact John Wesley himself was doing things which made it inevitable that a break would come. Soon after he died, it happened. And not only did the Methodists break away from the Church of England, they split among themselves. There were the Wesleyan Methodists and the Primitive Methodists. And there were a number of other bodies who came together in 1907 to form the United Methodist Church.

There were no United Methodists in Ebbw Vale, but there were Wesleyan Methodists and Primitive Methodists. The Primitive Methodists were called 'Prims' for short, or nicknamed 'The Ranters.' They were more informal and evangelical than the Wesleyans, whom they thought much too prim and proper. My Aunt Ethel told me that the 'Prims' used to say, 'You might as well go to church as go to the Wesleyans' (Church meaning Church of England).

In 1932 the three main branches of Methodism—the Wesleyans, the Primitive Methodists and the United Methodists—joined together to form the Methodist Church. This was known as Methodist Union. So the James Street Wesleyan Methodist Church became the James Street Methodist Church without the 'Wesleyan,' but it was still popularly known as 'Wesleyans.' 'You go to Wesleyans, don't you?' people would say.

Nonconformity was strong in South Wales, and there were a good many churches and chapels in Ebbw Vale. To the best of my recollection, in the main body of the town there was one Wesleyan Methodist church and one Welsh Wesleyan, two Primitive Methodist, four Congregational, four Baptist and three Presbyterian churches (also known as Apostolics). There was also the Brethren (popularly called the Plymouth Brethren, but I think they prefer simply to go by the name of 'The Brethren'), and the Holiness Mission. These four latter bodies were fundamentalists and evangelistic. They would hold open-air evangelistic meetings from time to time. There were also two Anglican churches and one Roman Catholic.

One part of the town called Briery Hill (popularly known as 'The Tump') was noted for the number of pubs and chapels which it contained. Those who frequented the one did not usually frequent the other! (Incidentally, there was a street in Briery Hill called 'Drysiog Street,' pronounced 'dru-see-og' with the accent on the second syllable. The story goes that a policeman found a dead horse in Drysiog Street. He got out his notebook to make a report, but then realised that he did now know how to spell 'Drysiog,' so he dragged the horse to Hart Street!)

Nonconformist places of worship were usually known as 'Chapels.' 'Are you church or chapel?' people would say.

One of the reasons there was more than one church of the same denomination, sometimes in fairly close proximity to one another, was that one had originally been English and the other Welsh speaking. But by my time, the use of Welsh had been abandoned in most of them. Another reason was that sometimes there had been a dispute within the church, as a result of which part of the congregation has broken away and formed their own church. But sometimes the reason was simply geographical; the two churches were in different parts of town.

The nonconformist's churches co-operated in the Free Church Council. But there was no co-operation, so far as I am aware, between the Non-conformists and the Anglicans, and certainly none between the Protestants and the Roman Catholics. In those days, if you were a Roman Catholic you regarded a Protestant as a heretic. He might not be absolutely debarred from any chance of getting into heaven, but it would take an exceptional measure of the grace of God to get him there. And if you were a Protestant, you very likely had similar views about the Roman Catholics. My Aunt Edith once said to me, 'It doesn't matter what denomination you are, so long as you are not a Roman Catholic.'

But although local Catholics and Protestants might criticise each other's religions, there was no sectarian bitterness. I had no personal animosity against anyone simply because they were a Roman Catholic, nor was I aware that any Roman Catholic had anything against me simply because I was a Protestant.

In the sixth form at school, there was a fellow in the class who was preparing to go into the Church. He gave me to understand that the Church of England was the only true Church. I asked him why, in that case, the apostle Paul had written letters to the Romans, the Ephesians, the Philippians etc. but there was no epistle to the Anglicans, the true Church! He replied that the Churches to which Paul had written were weak in the faith! (Thereby showing an abysmal lack of acquaintance with what Paul had said).

Most people went to a place of worship. Many went to both morning and evening services, but the evening services had a larger congregation. Shortly before service time the place would be full of people walking to the various churches. Sunday School (now called Junior Church) was in the afternoon.

In my upbringing, Chapel was three times a Sunday. As a small boy, I was not at all devout. The morning and evening services were beyond my childhood comprehension, and the sermon might as well have been preached in a foreign language. There was no distraction. I just had to sit through it. Nowadays the communion is celebrated as part of the normal service, in many churches at least, but at that time it was something extra, following the evening service, once a month. And sometimes there would be a prayer meeting after Sunday School. My Father told me once that people used to be punished for going to church. 'Why did they go then?' I said. 'Because they believed it was right to go,' he replied. I could not make this out. I thought it was punishment to go to church, without being punished for going!

The inter-war period during which I grew up was a kind of half-way house between the Victorian age and the present day. This was so as regards standards of personal conduct. There was a fair amount of Puritanism or semi-puritanism, and a disapproval of what was regarded as 'worldliness.' In mainstream nonconformist circles, the cinema and the theatre were not absolutely forbidden, but to some people, at least, they were suspect. The more fundamentalist churches regarded them as sinful. The Pentecostals and, I dare say, some of the others even considered it a sin to attend a football match.

Sunday was pretty strictly observed as the Lord's Day. The cinemas were closed, and there would have been strong opposition from the churches to attempt to open them. I once mentioned to my Aunt Edith that I had been doing some drawing on a Sunday. This was not disapproved of at home, but she made it clear to me that she thought I was breaking the Sabbath.

At one time a Congregational Church in the town started holding services for children on a Sunday evening. The services were pitched at the children's level, and the children were encouraged to take an active part, even by giving the address. I started going along, and there was no objection at home, so long as I went somewhere. But my Aunt Edith (the one who disapproved of drawing on Sunday, and said it did not matter what you were, so long as you were not a Roman Catholic) told me that I should not go away from my own church. 'James Street is your church, and that is where you should go,' she said. I said that they ought to introduce the same sort of thing in James Street, but she said that it did not make any difference, I should stick to my own church. It did not occur to me to reply that if everyone went to the church in which they were brought up, James Street church would never have come into existence.

My father and grandfather were very much involved in the temperance movement. Actually the term 'temperance' is not quite accurate. 'Temperance' means 'moderation,' but the emphasis was on total abstinence from all alcoholic drinks. The idea was that if you never drank any alcohol, you would never be in danger of drinking too much. However, as this is generally known as the temperance movement, I will use that term here.

My grandfather was such a strict teetotaller that I am not sure he would have taken anything alcoholic even to save his life. My father was not quite as strict as that. When in the army, he would not draw his rum ration for himself but if someone else came in who was in a bad way, he would draw it and give it to him to revive him.

Bands of Hope carried on the temperance movement. Every chapel had its Band of Hope, in which children were taught the evils of drink. In our own Band of Hope we used to repeat at the end of every meeting the pledge, 'I promise by the help of God to abstain from all intoxicating drinks as beverages, and to get others to do the same.'

Sometimes at home my grandfather would sing a temperance song and I remember two in particular:

> 'My drink is water bright, water bright, water bright,
> My drink is water bright from the crystal spring.'

> 'Break the pledge never, no, no, no!
> Not while the streams of the valley shall flow.
> Drunkards can never attain to the prize.
> We must be abstainers, for we all want to rise'.

During the early months of the war, I went down to Cardiff one day and saw my Aunt Sukie. She had been a Baptist, but had joined the Brethren, and was by this time a strong fundamentalist. She believed that the Bible was infallible, every word of it. Something I said indicated to her that I was not a fundamentalist, but she would not tell me what it was. During the ensuing conversation, I said that I did not believe that Adam and Eve had actually lived. She said 'If you do not believe in Adam and Eve, you do not believe in

Christ and I have no hope for eternity for you.' She was not judgmental. She did not condemn me. But she said that God would condemn me, for not believing His word. She and my Uncle Fred (her husband) believed that the Second Coming of Christ was imminent, and so they would not have a gas mask in wartime, because they believed that God would take them out of the situation. My Aunt said to me 'If we have a gas mask, that would show that we have no faith.' Thankfully poison gas was never used during the Second World War. Otherwise, the consequences for them might have been disastrous.'

Alastair Dunn lives in the *Scottish Isles.*
Here, he remembers life in the big city

No Mean Memories?

'In death, it is not the one who dies who is diminished, but those who are left. That part of them which lives in the memory of the one who died has been lost forever, and by that amount they are lessened; the personal and individual view of their habits, foibles, mannerisms, their good and their bad, all gone with the dead.

So it is, with the dirty, warm, kindly, violent, beautiful, ugly, fog-and-soot-ridden town in which I was born and spent my youth and which I left with regretful relief how many years ago? How has it been diminished? How many memories have already been lost in the slow sideslip of time? How many years between the remembering now and the remembering then? Judge by the fading pictures on the walls of my recollection.

I remember . . .

The shipyards, with giant Meccano-set cranes and gantries dwarfing the tenements in their shadows, their sirens calling the workers to daily labour.

Beardmore and Browns, Harland and Wolff, Lobnitz, Connel, Fairfield and Son, Yarrow, Barclay Curl and Company, MacKay and Thomson, Napier and Miller.

Names as well known as the players in the football teams: Glasgow Rangers, Celtic, Clyde, The Jags, Queens Park.

I remember . . .

The huge, hissing, living steam engines in the echoing vastness of the railway stations, and the porter calling out in raucous breath:

'Charingcrosspatrickannieslandwestertondrumchapelsingerd almuiroldkilpatrickdumbartoncardrosscraigendorranandhelensburghtrain'

There were compartments then, with long cushioned seats holding five a side, leather straps embossed LNER to raise and lower the windows, mesh luggage racks overhead, and sepia tinted photographs of strange unknown places:—Morecambe, Cardiff, York, Harrogate and more.

In the tunnels the trapped steam turned the windows a soft grey-white, filling the compartments with a faint moist smell. From the outside, the doors were opened by solid brass propeller-shaped handles which needed two boyish hands to turn, and inside, the ashtrays were brass chocolate-bar-sized cups set in plates of brass.

I remember . . .

The cold, killing, freezing fogs, filling the town with magical mystery, muffling the roar of invisible traffic only a few feet away. Every step was an adventure, each road or lane blocked by a grey-green blanket, each building transformed, the known made unknown, the everyday made excitingly, frightening alien.

I remember . . .

Clydesdale horses waiting in passive, massive dignity to be hitched in pairs to laden iron-tyred four-wheeled carts, heaving them over clattering whinstone causies to the top of the hill. Here, they were unhitched and galloped back down the hill, the tiny boys in charge bouncing joyously on their mattress-wide rumps.

Irish bullocks coming up from Broomielaw, filling Bath Street with their sweet breath mist and stirring, like a half-forgotten song, memories of moor and heather in the ladies sipping tea sitting in the windows of Wendy's Tea Rooms, watching the swaying, steaming, horn-tossing mass pass slowly by.

I remember . . .

The warm darkness of the rococo, art deco, Byzantine, Egyptian, Indian, gilded classic of the picture houses, beautiful in their tawdry tastelessness, where you could watch a double feature twice round. The Regal, Coliseum, Paramount, Grand Central, A.E. Pickford's strangely named Elephant, with its double seats for lovers. At La Scala you could sit at a table and eat a meal by the dim light of a table lamp while you watched the screen. Green's Playhouse had golden divans, and the topmost gallery was so high that only half the screen could be seen. Up there, no one watched the film, and the lights were only slightly dimmed. Unemployed men read their papers and filled in their football pools, young lovers cuddled in the back rows, and old men could sleep away the long empty days in warmth and comfort for sixpence, waiting patiently for the long empty endless sleep that lay waiting for them.

I remember . . .

The jigging at the Locarno, the Astoria, the Plaza, to the music of Delroy Summers, Joe Loss, Harry Parry and Mrs Elrick's wee boy, George. The theatres; the Royal, Kings, Pavilion and Metropole, with Rene Houston and Donald Stewart; Nat Mills and Bobby; Wilson Kepple and Betty—and Wilson Narret, the last of the actor-managers.

I remember . . .

Leerie with his magic wand, always with a gaggle of children in tow, lighting the hissing gas lamps. The children's games; peever, moashie, ringy, peeries and gurdies—and the songs they chanted to the bounce of a ball or the swish of a skipping rope. The glow of Dixon's Blazes, a pillar of smoke by day and fire by night, where tramps slept and sometimes died on the warm ashes. The great ships, funnels towering over the buildings, returning to the places of their birth, some to die in the breakers' yards. The endless desert of depression years with men huddled without hope, hunched against the cold at street corners. Women, bolster breasts resting on mottled folded forearms, leaning from windows and shouting conversations with their mirror images across the street.

I remember, I remember.

But even now the pictures are fading. When I and others of my age have gone, the town will have diminished by the sum of our recollections. The good, the bad, the loved and hated, the squalor and opulence, beauty and ugliness. In thirty, forty years time the memories will not be of the town that I knew. New memories will paint different pictures of a different town.

Will it, I wonder, this new town, be remembered with the same mixture of emotions? The love and loathing which those of my generation hold for the old, sprawling, dirty town of Glasgow, which will soon, with our passing, be gone forever, all memory gone.'

Dorothy Hornby grew up in the *Lake District*

Curing and Napping

'I was born in 1927 on a small farm about three miles north of Kendal on the Appleby Road, in the county of Westmoreland as it then was (now Cumbria, alas). We went to school in Mealbank, a small village about a mile away and walked there and back, of course. It was a pleasant walk through a wood for part of the way, which in the spring was filled with wood anemones, bluebells, celandines, wood sorrel and mayflowers.

There were two classrooms at the school, one for infants and one for juniors, divided by a partition, and heated by a large iron stove. We wore wooden clogs in the winter and when it was snowy all the snow collected into a ball on the bottom of the clogs and we had to keep knocking it off. These clogs were hard and stiff especially when new and we carved pieces out of them around the anklebone to stop our ankles being rubbed raw. Our house was two fields from the main Euston to Glasgow railway line and we always set off for school when the goods train with a wagon advertising 'Palethorpe's sausages' went up! So it must have been the same time every day.

At home we had no electricity, just candles and oil-lamps and no hot water except for the fireside boiler and a big boiler (called a 'sett-pot') in the adjoining lean-to washhouse. The sett-pot was also used for boiling water for clothes washing, cooking black puddings and baking 'laverbread' (a thin oatcake) on the up-turned lid. Baths were taken in a long bath in front of the fire. The loo was in the stick-yard, and was an earth-closet—a double-seater for adult and child! The stick-yard was a small, enclosed space where the tree branches and hedge-trimmings were stored; these were used for the fire. This was a little way from the house and when you needed to go to the loo, you had to set off before you were ready! The cold water came from a spring and really was cold and tasted wonderful. It ran out of the pipe opposite the back door and down a channel and under the dairy, which was a step down from our parlour. So you had to go through the parlour to churn the butter. We had a big end-over-end churn and sometimes I would help with this job. The milk stood in big enamel bowls on stone slabs round the walls of the dairy, and the floor was stone 'flags.' Very cold in the winter. The kitchen floor was also flagged, but had several pegged rugs spread on it. We had a big frame to make these rugs on, which took up nearly the whole of the kitchen when a rug was being made. The rugs were made out of lengths of waste material (old coats, skirts etc) pegged on a strong sacking base; some were looped and cut, and others just looped. All the cooking was done on the cast-iron range and in the fireside oven. We kept and killed our own pigs and the hams and 'flitches' (sides) of bacon hung on hooks from the kitchen ceiling. My grandmother, who was a widow, and lived with us, did most of the curing of the bacon as she was better at it than my father and took more pains rubbing in the salt. The bacon was kept in an old 'kist' (chest) until cured.

We used to 'stand the market' (have a stall) in Kendall and sell our produce—butter, eggs, poultry. Sometimes flowers and plants in the summer, dyed eggs at Easter (Pace or Pasche eggs) and holly wreaths at Christmas. These were made on a base of hazel stems, strong, but flexible, bent into a circle and covered with moss and then decorated with sprigs of holly (some variegated if possible) tied on with raffia. After the market finished we would go to the shops for essentials like wicks and glasses for oil-lamps from Baillie and Hargreaves (Ironmongers) in Finkle Street, or tea and sugar from the Co-op or Daish's or the Maypole in Stricklandgate. All these shops had wooden floors and lovely polished wooden counters, and goods were weighed out into strong bags for you while you waited. Brunshall's, on the corner of the Market Place, was a special favourite which sold haberdashery, material, household linens, and clothes. Shopping done, we would go to Thackery's on the Market Place for fish and chips, or the Cocoa Rooms in Stranmongate for pie and peas. The Cocoa Rooms belonged to my Auntie's parents and her father and brother made the pies in their bakehouse at the bottom of Kent Street and carried them along the New Road (which was quite a way) in big wooden trays covered with tea-towels, on their heads.

We never had holidays as such. A day out to Morecambe between haytime and harvest was the height of excitement! I was never told beforehand when we were going, as if it rained and we didn't go, I threw a tantrum! We went on the bus and took the train—an exhilarating experience, even a bit frightening!

My parents' relaxations in the winter months were 'napping parties' (card parties—the game being Nap). They both gave these and went to others, travelling by bicycle with carbide lamps. When we had a card party, we were allowed to stay up a bit later to watch proceedings, and there was always a great meal halfway through the evening—cold meats and pickles, trifle and cakes.'

Dave Mitchell spent the pre-war years in *London*

Basques and gas masks

'At the age of five or six I went to the Ideal cinema in New Cross, SE14 on my own and saw 'King Kong!' Two or three years later the film was reissued and when I tried to get in again I was stopped. The film category system was now in force and I was considered too young to watch the antics of the giant ape! Cinemas were the most popular entertainment in the '30s. Seats ranged from 4d, 6d or 9d for front seats to 1/-, 1/6d or 2/- at the back or up in the circle. Seats at the children's Saturday show cost 2d. Each show would normally contain two full-length films, a newsreel, a documentary and a cartoon. There were no advertisements apart from the 'coming attractions' trailers. The bigger cinemas might have their resident organist playing before and at intervals during the performance (the opportunity for the usherettes to sell ice creams and sweets). He would rise from the orchestra pit on a hydraulic lift, seated at a giant Wurlitzer or Hammond organ big as a car. On certain days of the week they may have a live stage show or a live dance-band performance. The programme showing was normally continuous (one could enter at 1pm and stay in one's seats through to 11pm or so). The show ended with the national anthem. Most of the audience stood still for this, though some would try to get out before it.

My parents were careful, caring and responsible. Nevertheless, on occasions I would walk the quarter of a mile or so to the New Cross Gate Tram Depot. Trams ending their journey there would disgorge their passengers who, if they had 'all day' or evening tickets no longer wanted, might hand them to an appreciative kid waiting there. One would then climb on a suitable tram and take off to the end of the line. Perhaps a number 38 or 40 through

Deptford, Greenwich and Woolwich. Getting off at the Free Ferry for a return trip or two across the Thames. Back home, perhaps a ticking-off for being late, but a child was much safer then at night than today during the day.

The tram was less comfortable than the bus but more reliable and could carry many more passengers. They ran in fog and all night. They were noisy but rarely broke down. If one did, the tram behind had little trouble pushing it along.

In the summer of 1937, my school took a day off for a friendly visit to the Basque refugees who were living somewhere in Kent. They had escaped from the civil war that was raging in Spain at that time. The idea was to show our friendship by playing them at football and enjoying a tea party together afterwards. As a show of friendship it was a waste of time—little contact because of language and little interest in football! It was a nice day though, for all concerned.

In 1939, well before war was declared, my father worked for Harvey Engineering in Charlton. A section of the works was made over to nightwork, manned by voluntary employees who assembled domestic or civilian gas masks. I worked for two or three nights with him and saw what was going on. This is one small example of the quiet preparation for war that was going on which few people realised.

Examples of prices from the 1930s prices, as I remember them:

- *Tram Fares in London*: From 1d off peak, 2d all the way. 1/- all day anywhere. Half fare for kids under fourteen.
- *Sweets*: Usually about 2d for ¼ lb.
- *School dinners*: 7d. Not subsidised in any way.
- *Unemployment benefit*: for the whole family, about 12/6d a week.
- *Woolworths:* (in most shopping areas) sold nothing over 6d including most household items, clothing, spectacles, tools, pipes and tobacco, toys etc.
- *Marks and Spencer*s: sold more upmarket stuff but still nothing over 2/-.
- *The Fifty-Shilling-Tailors:* sold an excellent range of made-to-measure three piece suits for £2.10.0d. *Burtons:* charged from about £2.19.6d

- Ownership of *Cars* was restricted in towns by lack of garage space (on street parking was not allowed overnight until the late '50s). The horsepower of the engine governed the taxation of cars. An 8hp car would pay 25/- x 8hp = £10 per year.
- *New Houses:* A 3 bedroom, freehold, house in an average suburb of London with modern plumbing etc would cost less than £450.'

John Lucas also grew up in *London*

The Entertainers

'In the early days, in Bermondsey, we were a very close family with relatives living in the neighbouring streets. We lived in rooms upstairs in my grandparents' house, which were lit by gaslight. Our entertainment was a radio that worked off of an accumulator, which had to be regularly recharged. We would sit for hours listening to the stars of that era—my favourites were ITMA (It's That Man Again), Variety BandBox, Gert and Daisy and the Al Read show.

My father was employed at the Peek Frean's biscuit factory as a chief electrician. Once a week, each employee was allowed to purchase a bag of broken biscuits, which we all looked forward to when father came home.

I liked going to the cinema and as a special treat, I would be taken to the Astoria cinema on the Old Kent Road to see George Formby, Laurel and Hardy, Will Hay and others in glorious black and white. Occasionally, on a Saturday evening the whole family took the tram to the New Cross Empire to see stars such as Max Miller and Old Mother Riley in the Variety shows.

Maybe once a year during the summer we travelled by train to Hastings; how lovely it was to feel the sea breeze on our faces as we sat on the pebble beach. Like so many families back then, each was limited to what they could afford; you were rich if you had a shilling in your pocket.'

A Ferranti Nova Radio—the popularity of the 'wireless'
was at its peak during the '30s and '40s'

Aitken Lawrie *saw active service during the 1930s*

Empire Reminiscences

Afghanistan

'I was commissioned in the Royal Engineers on 1st Feb 1934. In those days we still had an Empire and I was asked to choose one out of ten possible postings from Jamaica to Hong Kong. I chose India and never regretted it.

I was ordered to Wana one mile from the Afghan border and sixty miles from the nearest railhead to Manzai. My first posting was nearly my last. I arrived there the day after a terrible tragedy. Four thousand tribesmen had spread out on a hillside in their filthy clothes, indistinguishable from the earth around them and had not been spotted by RAF patrols. When a convoy of fifty lorries protected by armoured cars had set out from Manzai, the tribesmen cut loose a string of camels, which blocked the road and brought the convoy to a halt. Four thousand tribesmen poured volleys into the convoy at point blank range, causing heavy casualties. As night fell they escaped across the border with hundreds of rifles and boxes of ammunition.

Next day I was taken up to Wana in an armoured car. We stopped at the battlefield and tipped still smouldering trucks down the hillside. The road was completely closed to British traffic for the next two years.

I learnt that Wana had twice been overrun in the past by recalcitrant Afghans. Now we were building an impregnable stronghold with a high stone wall, surrounded by thick barbed wire entanglements and floodlit at night. We could look out across the plain dotted with prosperous villages each guarded by its own watchtower. Anyone leaving the camp was regarded as a legitimate target for local snipers, except on Sundays. This was when the Wana 'drag' set out in the early morning with its own pack of hounds chasing the smell of a jackal for miles across country, while the locals watched and waved. They realised that the sahibs had to have their exercise!

After I had become fluent in Urdu and Punjabi, the languages of my men, I decided to learn Pushtu. We encouraged the locals to bring in provisions for sale in the camp. They were searched and disarmed half a mile from the camp and came in to set up their stalls. My teacher would grab some of these and sit them down on the floor of my room and make them talk to me in various dialects. In this way I learnt about their way of life and customs.

In those days there was a notorious terrorist called the Faqir of Ipi, who was being paid by Hitler to stir up trouble. Sixty thousand troops of the Indian army spent two years trying to catch him with no success. He always managed to slip away into some cave. Every few months my brigade would sweep out to join up with other brigades and try to catch him, with no success.

One of my jobs was to make roads where there were none at all. Wana lay at about five thousand feet, higher than hills all around, so I got used to moving about in this very difficult terrain which was exactly the same as Afghanistan itself. It was very tough going. British troops were hopeless. The only ones who found it easy were the Scouts and the Gurkhas who were at home in the mountains. Apart from making roads I also had to fix up water points for the five thousand horses and mules that accompanied the brigade and needed to drink twice a day, and to blow up watch towers of villages who had refused to hand over arms.

After two years of marching and counter-marching both sides had had enough and peace was agreed. I watched a hundred tribal chieftains with long white beards being searched and led into the camp. The Governor of the North West Frontier Province made a brilliant speech in Pushtu and accepted a gift of a flock of beautifully washed white sheep, handing out bags of gold in return, and the war was over. The road was declared open and we could return to India.

The Himalayas

I belonged to King George V's Own Bengal Sappers and Miners, which laid down some tough rules. Anyone who married before the age of thirty must resign and no one could take leave to England unless he had shot a tiger, played polo for the Corps or been on a long trek in the hills. I had no wish to kill a beautiful animal, and was only a beginner at polo, which left me with only one option.

I poured over maps and decided on taking the age-old route to Tibet. The place names were pure magic—Fagu, Matiana, Bali, Narkanda, Taklech, Daranghati, Wangtu and finally Chini on the Frontier. I went up to Simla with my bearer Palman, himself a Gurkha, and stocked up with all that we would need for two months. Then we hired a man with five mules and sent them on ahead. I followed with Palman after two days on bikes and caught them up in Narkanda. The road was now too steep for cycles so we left the bikes beside the road and picked them up again on the way back.

The road was just earth, and wide enough for one mule or bike, but it went through gorgeous scenery, climbing up 10,000 feet and down again 2,000 feet, crossing and recrossing the Sutlej River. Every ten miles or so was a Government Inspection bungalow, sparsely furnished, but provided with a man to open it up and supply water and firewood. However, each of them was sited opposite a breathtaking view of the mountains.

The road went through fragrant, sighing woods of deodar to emerge among sunlit strips of flower covered pasture. Deep ravines plunged to valleys so far below the road that there was hardly a murmur from the rushing torrent dashing from rock to rock in its headlong descent to the plains. Beyond the nearby hills one could glimpse the jagged peaks of the 'Roof of the World' on the distant skyline with their perpetual covering of snow.

There was a steady stream of traffic with groups of skinny peasants, whose frail legs had carried them for many miles from their villages perched high on distant hillsides. Skull-capped Kashmiri coolies staggered along, carrying on their shoulders huge balks of timber so long that no one could get past until they turned sideways. Then there were charcoal burners, black from head to foot, singing as they went, brightly dressed gypsies, and Tibetans bringing jade and antiques to sell in India. Sometimes there was a string of mules, and I shall always remember the sound of their bells jangling down the hillside.

I was intrigued by the entries I saw in the Visitor's book of Miss Ball and Miss Gunn, who were a few days ahead of me. But when I met them on the road, they turned out to be missionaries in long skirts, who bowed politely as they passed, wishing me Good Morning. One other officer turned up, having crossed Tibet from East to West with a team of Yaks. When he told me how bleak and boring he found the country, I decided to stay in Chini, the last bungalow in India.

This was where Lord Dalhousie had stayed in 1854, when he was Governor General, and there had been few visitors since then.

I was amused to come across an old Tatler of 1908 with pictures of my parents, announcing their engagement.

There were no schools or hospitals in Chini, and of course no shops, so I had to rely mostly on what I had brought with me. However, every morning the caretaker would appear with a huge basket of produce from his garden—peas, lettuces, strawberries, raspberries and apricots, for which he charged the equivalent of 2p. That was also the price of a chicken. Palman never claimed to be a cook, but he managed pretty well, making scones every day instead of bread.

At the time I was working hard at Urdu, preparing for the Interpretership exam. My teacher used to send me newspapers in English and Urdu and make me translate passages from one to the other. I was amazed to find that my post came out from Simla in three days by means of relays of runners.

I was sad at having to return to the real world when my leave was up.'

*Back in **London, George Green** recalls the outbreak of the Second World War*

Heavy Gates

'After school, all of us kids would play in the streets, usually kicking a ball about. Our parents often came out with us and chatted with the neighbours at the garden gate. When war broke out the chatting continued but not over the garden gates; they were taken away, along with the iron railings next to them, to be melted down and turned in to tanks or armaments. I often imagined our garden gate landing on some unsuspecting German's head!

I left Trinity School and I'm sure Adolf Hitler got to hear about it because war was declared shortly afterwards. I well remember that Sunday morning of September 3rd 1939. We were 'over the rec' playing football, a gang of teenagers without too much to worry about. All of a sudden, Mrs Selby complete with pinafore came rushing over to us. 'Listen boys. Come over at once and listen to the radio.' We heard Neville Chamberlain confirm that 'We are now at war with Nazi Germany.' We looked at each other and went back to our game of football. Within minutes, the sirens sounded and we decided that war had really started; we had better go home. I spent the rest of the day helping dad and 'Paddy' Rice, our next-door-neighbour, dig earth and erect our Anderson shelters in the gardens.'

***Eric Pringle** was evacuated from **London** at the outbreak of the war*

The Morris 12

'I was born in 1930 in a long since disappeared London County Council estate of flats known as East Hill Estate, in Wandsworth. We were not well off but the times we had were generally happy and we had very neighbourly people around us. At the outbreak of war all of the pupils in our school were evacuated. We marched along in file to Wandsworth Town railway station each with gas mask and identity label attached to our clothing. We all carried some sort of bag in which were stowed our worldly possessions. I was eight and my brother was twelve years old and we each had a rucksack fashioned by mother from a 'Bagwash' sack. My brother had strict instructions not to lose sight of me.

Of course, our destination was a secret, even our parents had no idea where we were going and they looked extremely concerned as they waved us off on the train.

After what seemed like a long ride we disembarked at a place called Reading. We were assured that it was pronounced 'Redding' and this is where we would be staying—it seemed to us as if it was on the other side of the world, not just in Berkshire.

We formed up outside of the station and boarded buses to a school called Redlands where we were all herded in to the assembly hall and each given a bottle of milk and the biggest bar of chocolate I had ever seen. I thought, 'If this is war, I like it!' Somewhat like the slaves of yesteryear we were offered to matronly women who proceeded to inspect us like goods for sale. My brother, obeying instructions, refused to be parted from me. Consequently, as no one wanted to take responsibility for two poor waifs, we were the only children left when all potential 'carers' had departed. In desperation the good lady organiser of the event was forced to take us home herself. We arrived at a sweet little semi-detached, which actually had a back garden. Imagine, a real garden for playing, just outside of the back door. That was not all. To my great fascination I found a bathroom with hot running water! I was beginning to like war even more!

My brother and I shared a double bed in the second bedroom, which was an improvement on the three boys in a bed to which we were usually accustomed. Our host parents had no children of their own, they were middle-aged and middle class and wonders will never cease they had a motor car too! We had never even been in a car before and certainly knew no one who owned one and here we were riding around Reading in a magnificent Morris 12. We really were the envy of the other evacuees. We were given so much love and affection and introduced in to the world of the middle classes, a whole new way of life for us. I thought it was wonderful and I am sure that the whole experience inspired me to be ambitious with a great desire to improve my lot.

We stayed in Reading until Christmas 1939, when our parents decided that, as not a single bomb had been dropped on London, we could return home and join the rest of the family for the festivities.

We never returned to Reading and our wonderful foster parents, staying in London for the duration of the war.'

Jean Hooper recalls her relationship with a German in the years leading up to the war

Parties in Bloomsbury and Stormtroopers

'My friend Trixie found out about the International Friendship League. Meetings were held in a very ordinary upper room, holding about thirty people. Talks were held on different 'world' subjects and plays were put on, mostly in aid of 'Leftish' causes. Communist dances, in aid of the people of Spain fighting against the Fascists, were also held in the National Portrait Gallery. If you were not enamoured with your partner you could always look at the paintings while whirling around! These dances had Russian tea and lemon in the interval. Various decent bands came and did an hour. On a couple of occasions the Coconut Grove boys came and livened us all up. (Later we heard that they'd all been killed by a direct hit during an air raid.)

Some of these dances resulted in odd 'dates' for gallery visits and concerts. The International Friendship League also resulted in a German friendship for me—leading to engagement—until I realised that I loved my dad more. My other big friendship was with an actor from the Abbey theatre. This lasted a fair time and there was never a dull moment. This included a 'party' at Bloomsbury, which I attended with the actor and his friend. The three of us arrived late (we'd been dancing) and we missed out on the drinking. We walked in to find a semi-comatose lot there. It was almost bedtime so we tidied up as best we could and went to bed, sharing a room. I stayed more or less fully dressed all night. It did not ease matters when the hostess came in with some man, put on the light and said, 'Est'ce que vous n'avez pas honte?' The actor fellow answered, 'Et toi?' We three got up early, borrowed someone's toothpaste and sloshed water on ourselves. The lads prepared breakfast for anyone who could face it then they came home with me on the tram to apologise to my dad for keeping me out all night. He was prepared to forgive them, but was horri-fied that I was arriving home on a Sunday morning in my dance dress—which by then did look a bit bedraggled!

We were keen walkers at this time and joined the Southern Railway Ramble. These were beautifully arranged. You caught the train at Waterloo, Croydon, Victoria or Clapham Junction to the designated area. Once on the train, quite full with jolly walk-ing types, you were given the choice of walks—short, medium or long, with varying degrees of difficulty. You chose your walk and got out at the appropriate station. The first one that I went on with my sister was to see the sunrise. We had prudently had a two-hour nap the previous afternoon. There was a bit of a moon, but it was cold and at 4am, when there was a hint of dawn we looked around at a number of rather mauvish faces! The ultimate destination of this particular trip was Hastings and we played leapfrog on the pebbly beach. Some of the other stalwarts continued the walk after breakfast. We all caught the train back in the late afternoon. The great thing about these walks was that it was a special train and took different branch lines to reach the destinations.

At Easter 1936, the German that I'd met at the League came over on business. I recall attending a dance at the German em-bassy—luckily there was not a swastika in sight. In the same year my sister and a girlfriend went to Germany on holiday. They were rather upset to see agricultural workers marching and using their spades as guns over their shoulders. They were chirpily drilling up and down and called out to the girls, 'We are not soldiers, only workers on the land.' We talked this over at home after my sister returned and even wondered if we should contact someone. Dad said, 'Don't worry, this country knows what's going on!'

Later that year, I went with Trixie to Germany to meet my German friend. We stayed at the flat where he lived with his brother. Their parents were dead and there was a general shift round of rooms so that Trixie and I could share the room that overlooked the gardens. We went sightseeing and had a lovely time. I was a bit surprised, however, to find that our host had become a stormtrooper! He explained that every tenth man was called up. Gradually, we saw the signs of repression; at the swimming baths for example, Jews were 'verbotten.'

In 1937, Trixie and I returned to Germany, via Luxembourg. The stormtrooper was away on manoeuvres or attending rallies. He was a flag bearer at one of the parades and I always felt that I saw him later on film, in the cinema news, but it was probably wishful thinking. When he returned I didn't see him immediately as he said that he was too dirty. The next day he'd spruced up and we had some nice little outings in parks and the country. We also went to one of those posh restaurants where you can 'phone a table to talk. The boys that we were with were livid that there was a 'phone call for their sister who had accompanied us!

On my return to England, the stormtrooper wrote one of his long letters and proposed. I sort of accepted, but could see troubles ahead and had a faint hope that he could get to England before the troubles started. They even registered me at the town hall in Germany! Later, he suggested that I go to him in Germany for Christmas, but the idea was not on as I realised that I loved my dad more!

I never heard from my stormtrooper again'

In the early years of the decade, **Barry Brown** *in* **Kent**
recalls the vulnerability of youth

Remembered Walk

What path is it that I must follow
between the tide and the rising cliff?
Was it never over virgin sand
or is that a painting in my mind?

Sometimes the sand was unbroken crust,
white cut the cliffs and smooth the sea,
whose reflected light could blind and steal
small fragments of my memory.

There were the daunting rocks to climb,
seaweed covered, cragged, unsafe, which
I clambered over to watch
the disappearing outline of the older man.

No, the sea was not always smooth.
Relentless waves in angry curves
crashed, disintegrated at my feet
and I grasped for finger holds.

Greyness at times, cliff overhang,
shadows that hid but could not prevent
sight of the sand, footsteps and rocks,
the landmarks of remembered walks.

There were four miles to travel from
grey castle to the broken cliff,
but not far enough for time to catch
the disappearing outline of the older man.

Barry Brown

'My father took me when I was five years old (1932) along the shore-
line from St. Margaret's Bay to Dover. He walked relentlessly ahead
saying very little as if he was pre-occupied. It was all I could do

to keep up and I remember being afraid that he would disappear before I caught up with him'.

*Towards the end of the decade, **Barry** has further memories of human vulnerability, this time not his own*

Refugees

'It was in York in 1938 while I was home on holidays from my Catholic boarding school that I met my first Jewish family. I was eleven years old.

The Irish parish priest of our local church had asked members of his congregation to offer hospitality to Jewish refugees who had recently come from Germany. My mother invited one of these unfortunate families round for Sunday lunch. It was a very special occasion, as I never remember my parents entertaining strangers, yet alone foreigners who spoke English very slowly and with a strange accent. The father, whom I judged to be in his mid forties, did most of the talking.

He said that he had been imprisoned because he was a Jew. I was bewildered having been brought up with the idea that in our times people didn't get put into prison for their religion. There must surely be another reason why he was imprisoned, but he assured us that he had done nothing illegal. He was an innocent man. I couldn't make it out. He and his family were so obviously well educated and what my mother would call 'respectable.'

After we had eaten, our family and the Jewish family continued to sit round the table and I listened to the father in disbelief. He told us of the abominable conditions in which he and his fellow prisoners had to live in the prison. There was a single bucket that was used for everything: for carrying water, their food and as a toilet. It was disgusting to hear and unbelievable that people could be treated in this way. It was the first time, too, that I heard the term 'concentration camp.' Only at the end of the Second World War in 1945 when Buchenwald, Belsen, Aushwitz and Dachau were discovered, did I begin to appreciate the full extent of the horror the father of the German refugee family had experienced.

The father said he had been able to buy his way out of prison on condition that he and his family left Germany immediately. It was a new idea to me that prisoners could buy their way to freedom. The family paid the government under Hitler to release him and bought a passage on a train for them all to leave Germany.

I was astonished when war was declared in 1939 how this Jewish family, who had suffered so much at the hands of the Germans under Hitler and whom we had welcomed and entertained as friends was treated by the British government. They were now classed as German aliens and enemies, not to be trusted and were confined to a temporary gaol on York racecourse. It all seemed so cruel and unreasonable. They were eventually freed.

I never saw them again.'

Ruth Sheridan also experienced the build up to the war from the Jewish perspective, but from another direction—in Berlin

Brownshirts and smuggling

'I was born Jewish but from an early age I decided that I was an atheist. On my sixteenth birthday I was queuing up at the doors of the Berlin Town Hall when they opened at 8am. I registered out of the Jewish faith and have been an atheist ever since. However, my birth certificate still stated that I had been born as a Jew and this was good enough for Hitler.

Three years later I attended law lectures at the Berlin University. We were the first year law students and therefore occupied one of the largest auditoria on the top floor. In the middle of a lecture, the extremely heavy oak doors were pushed open and a troop of Brownshirts with the crooked cross band on their arms marched in to the auditorium. The professor, dumbfounded, said in a very polite manner, 'Gentlemen, we are in the middle of a lecture. Please be kind enough to go out and shut the doors.'

He was told in no uncertain manner to 'shut his trap' or he would be treated in the same way as some of his students. Brusquely, they then ordered us to stand, so that our seats lifted in the same way as theatre seats and there was room to walk along each row in front of us. The Brownshirts took a row each and moved slowly along facing each of us in turn. They stopped in front of each student for what seemed like an eternity, studying his or her face. They were not interested in identity papers (luckily for me). These uneducated men, many of whom had criminal records, were, of course, 'experts' at identifying the Jews amongst us by carefully looking at each face. Those who they decreed to be Jewish were pushed roughly to the side gangway. The feeling that I had when the Brownshirt stood in front of me, knowing that I was a Jew in Hitler's view because of my four Jewish grandparents (One was enough to condemn me) is difficult to describe. There was this overwhelming fear, but I was conscious of the fact that he must not detect that fear, that I must try to look completely unconcerned, even amused. I managed it with the help of my very short straight nose and blond hair. The relief when he took a step sideways to face the student next to me was absolutely overwhelming. The collection of Jews, as decreed by these 'experts' were then pushed out of the open window into the cobblestoned orchard a long way below.

We never saw them again.

Later in the same year, when I came home on the underground from University, I met my father at the exit of our station. He was white as a sheet and trembling all over. 'What have you done?' he asked, 'Hitler's Stormtroopers are at the flat, in your room to be precise and waiting for you.'

I assured him I had done nothing that I knew of which would have caused this distressing situation. Yes, I had written a short story about the persecutions led by Hitler but that had been taken to London by my future mother-in-law when she had returned home from her recent visit to Berlin and she had already confirmed that it was safely there. So I really had no idea what they wanted. When I entered my room, it seemed as if we had experienced a heavy earthquake. My large wardrobe was on the floor, its contents strewn all over. The mattress of my bed had been slashed open, everything stored in my desk drawers was on the floor. The carpet was rolled up in case I had hidden anything underneath. The Nazis would not answer me when I asked them what they wanted; they told me that I would be taken to the Alexanderplatz—the main police station. There were three Nazis escorting me to the underground station, one on each side and one in front to prevent me escaping! When we arrived at the Alexanderplatz station we had to walk up a long flight of steps to reach street level. I vividly recall looking up at the sky and the sun, thinking that this could be the last time that I might ever see them. They marched me in to the building, along a narrow corridor and in to an interrogation room where about ten people sat behind a long table. I was asked to sit on the single chair placed on the opposite side of the table, near the far wall. The interrogation began and I tried hard to make sense of the questions, which seemed completely unconnected. I also tried to use my limited legal knowledge to understand what was happening but failed from that angle too. After one and a half hours, they finally told me why I was there.

Two years previously I had come home from school with my friend Gisella, to find the flags flying outside of the apartment block, a very common site in Germany. Standing in front of our house we studied the various designs. From my friend's balcony the red, white and black Nazi flag fluttered in the breeze. From our balcony, the gold, red and black flag of the Democracy competed for attention. I said to Gisella, not thinking of the political background, that I thought the gold, red and black colour combination was much softer than the sharp red, white and black.

This remark had been overheard by the porter's wife, who denounced me when Hitler came to power two years later!

I was allowed to leave the Alexanderplatz and walked out without a backward glance, once again keeping my feelings hidden deep within myself.

One year later, in 1934 I was barred from attending university because of my Jewish birth. By this time I had met and married my husband, an Englishman who was studying in Berlin. We decided to move to England to escape the growing mood of resentment towards the Jews that was being fuelled by Hitler and we set off in my father's big old Buick. My husband couldn't drive so I drove all the way, a journey that was not without its problems. The car broke down several times which used up all of our money. We went without food and drink for twenty-four hours until we reached the Dutch/Belgian border. Here, we discovered that holders of German passports needed a visa to enter Belgium. We had been issued with the incorrect tickets in Berlin and we had no money to buy a visa so took the decision to drive through the barrier. I put my foot down and drove past the border guards at high speed. Within minutes a police car appeared in the distance behind us. I drove into a small town and by doubling back several times, managed to lose our pursuers. It was with a massive sigh of relief that we arrived at the coast some time later and boarded the last boat of the day bound for Dover.

Through unforeseen circumstances, I had to return to Germany twice before war broke out.

The first time, I had become ill with an internal gynaecological problem. Since this was in the days before the NHS, my father decided to send me the money for a return rail fare back to Berlin and obtain treatment from the family physician. The journey took twenty-four hours and I was in constant pain throughout. I arrived in Berlin and was taken straight to the home of the doctor who examined me and performed a minor operation to cure me. I was soon feeling much better and looked forward to returning to my husband in England. Many of my old friends visited me. These were either Jewish or married to Jews and knew that their possessions would soon be confiscated. They asked me to take their most treasured pieces of jewellery with me back to England, which I agreed to do, though with a certain degree of apprehension.

On the day that I boarded the train I was wearing several necklaces, concealed under my dress. Under my gloves, I also wore six bracelets and rings on each finger and thumb. As we arrived at the German frontier, a ticket inspector entered the carriage. He asked to look inside my case and noticed a book written by a Jewish writer. This raised his suspicions and he ordered me off the train for a full body examination. I was led in to a cold room with very little furniture and brusquely ordered to strip. The male guard left the room. My heart was exploding as I slowly took off my clothes under the stern gaze of the female medical examiner. I ripped off the gold necklaces with the dress as I pulled it over my head and dropped it carefully on the floor. In my underclothes and gloves, I was ordered to face the wall with my arms outstretched. The examination began and in order to try to divert the woman's attention I spoke to her in German about my love for my mother country, how Hitler was such a wonderful man and how much I was looking forward to returning to Germany after my trip to England. I continued talking as she prodded and probed my body hoping that she wouldn't notice that I was sweating profusely. Finally (and incredibly) she told me to put my clothes back on and rejoin the train. She left the room and my legs almost gave way with the release of tension. My gloves never left my hands until I arrived in England.

My second trip back to Berlin took place in November 1938. By this time, my father's flat had been confiscated and my grandfather was on the point of losing his house. They were moving into a rented flat together and as a result, had a large quantity of spare household items; bed linen, cutlery, towels and much more. We had very little money in England and these would help us enormously. My father sent me another ticket and against my husband's wishes, I set off once again to return to Berlin. I arrived on the morning of the 10th November to find a scene of dreadful devastation. Unbeknown to me at the time, I was witnessing the aftermath of the infamous 'Kristallnacht,' when Jewish owned shops throughout Germany were systematically looted and destroyed and Jews were subjected to an orgy of violence.

I saw Jewish owned shop fronts all smashed in, their contents looted and the counters and shelves broken up and left on the pavement outside. As I walked along I passed an Etam shop which was being looted. Clothes were thrown randomly to the crowd. I caught a pair of tights, though I left them on the ground as I walked away, disgusted at the actions of my fellow countrymen.

The rioting was all reported on the radio news back in Britain and my husband was frantically trying to contact me to tell me to return to England straightaway. Instead, I visited the British Consulate in Berlin and asked for protection, which I received in the form of official papers stating that I was a British subject.

I caught a bus back from the Embassy to my father's flat. It was crowded and I sat next to a tall very Aryan looking German.

'Isn't that a lovely sight, Miss' he said, looking out of the window at the devastated Jewish businesses which lined the street.

I did not want him to know that I was Jewish, neither did I want to show my agreement, so I decided to pretend that I was an English girl.

In broken German, I replied, 'Lovely sight? In my country, in England we would be ashamed.'

The man looked shocked and quickly stood up. Addressing the other passengers on the bus he said, 'This is an English girl. She said we should be ashamed. Shall we throw her out?'

Fortunately no one agreed. There was total silence. The man sat down and I got off at the next stop without uttering another word.

The household effects that I was taking back to England took five days to pack. An official visited the house to inspect everything and give me authorisation to take the items out of the country. I left the next day and journeyed back to England once again, the last time that I would make this trip until after the war.

Ten months later, war was declared and I wondered whether I would ever see my family again.'

1930s Discoveries and Developments

- The Planet Pluto
- Vitamin C
- Vitamin E
- The Influenza Virus
- Halogen
- RADAR
- The Jet Engine
- Nylon
- Nuclear Fission
- Perspex
- Polythene
- Teflon
- Catseyes

1930s Firsts

- The Sydney Harbour Bridge
- New York's Empire State Building
- San Francisco Golden Gate Bridge
- Whipsnade Zoo
- Xerox Copy
- EMI was formed
- Frozen Peas
- Sliced Bread
- Kangol Berets
- The Highway Code
- Instant Coffee
- The Spitfire Aircraft
- Nylon Stockings
- The Electric Razor
- The Anglepoise Lamp
- Automatic Electric Blanket
- Pop-up Toaster
- Stereo Sound
- Scotch Tape
- Monopoly
- The Youth Hostel Association
- 30mph Speed Limit
- The Driving Test
- Volkswagen Beetle
- Gatwick Airport opened
- Penguin Paperback Books
- Butlin's Holiday Camps
- The AOC Wine Classification in France
- The 999 Emergency Telephone Number
- Superman
- Donald Duck
- Milky Way
- The Mars Bar
- Maltesers
- Rolo
- Smarties
- Extra Strong Mints
- Cadbury's Roses
- Live TV Soccer Match
- The Parking Meter
- Pinewood Studios
- Book Tokens

1930s Anniversaries

- 50th of the Motor Car (1885)
- 50th of the first Photographic Picture Postcard (1889, in Germany)
- 50th of the Gunfight at the OK Corral (1881)
- 50th of the Education Act making school compulsory for children aged 5-10 (1880)
- 100th of the Monarchy moving to Buckingham Palace (1837)
- 100th of the deportation of the Tolpuddle Martyrs (1834)
- 100th of the Grand National Horse Race (1839)
- 150th of the Mongolfier Brothers first flight, in a Hot Air Balloon (1783)
- 200th of 10 Downing St becoming the Prime Minister's residence (1735)

The Future

In 1930, at the beginning of the decade, it would be:

- 27 years before the European Common Market was created
- 29 years before the launch of the Mini car
- 29 years before the advent of the Car Phone
- 31 years before the Berlin Wall was erected
- 39 years before 18 year olds were given the right to vote
- 45 years before the discovery of the Terracotta Warriors in Xian, China
- 50 years before The Humber Bridge was built
- 59 years before the Berlin Wall was demolished
- 64 years before the Channel Tunnel was opened

The 1940s

The world at large—the historical context

The decade was, of course, dominated by World War II, the world's bloodiest conflict.

World War II

As the decade began, Britain had been at war for four months. At home, apart from the blackouts and the general climate of fear and apprehension, life carried on for many, much as normal. This changed in May 1940 when the British forces that had been active in France were pushed back to Dunkirk by the superior German forces. Large quantities of precious equipment were lost in France but over three hundred thousand men were saved by an armada of small boats that criss-crossed the Channel, making the evacuation possible. The Nazi army was now massing its troops in northern France and an invasion of England's south coast seemed inevitable. The 'Local Defence Volunteers,' later renamed 'The Home Guard' was formed to help in the country's defence. World War I veterans and men in reserved occupations volunteered their services, keen to 'do their bit' for the war effort. The courage of the 'Battle of Britain' pilots during the summer of 1940, who stopped the Luftwaffe gaining air supremacy, staved off the expected invasion. Hitler changed his strategy and in September, the bombing of Britain began with the 'Blitz' on London and other British cities which resulted in nightly bombing raids until the middle of the following year.

From 1941 until 1943, the land war was fought mainly on the Eastern Front following Hitler's invasion of Russia, in North Africa and the Far East. The North Atlantic was another major battleground where German U-boats attempted to prevent the convoys of much needed supplies from the USA reaching Europe.

The Japanese precipitated the US entry into the war with the surprise attack on the US Pacific fleet in Pearl Harbour, Hawaii in December 1941. Two thousand five hundred men and all of the US destroyers were sunk but crucially the aircraft carriers were at sea and remained untouched. The US declared war on Japan, bringing both nations into the World War. Japan invaded Thailand and Malaya and overran the British garrison at Singapore. They also invaded many of the islands in the Pacific in an attempt to dominate the Eastern Pacific. Allied forces fought back with the tide turning in late 1942. The allies regained territory but at a high cost as the Japanese fought to the last man rather than surrender.

At the end of 1942, the Germans were defeated in Africa and the following year the battle to regain control of Europe began with the invasion of Italy by allied troops. On June 6th 1944, the French living on the coast of Normandy were woken by the explosive sounds of the D-Day invasion. In one of the greatest achievements of modern warfare, tens of thousands of allied troops were landed on five beaches along the coast and beachheads were established despite stiff German resistance. The allies fought their way out over the course of the following six weeks and after the breakthrough, made rapid advances across France. Paris was liberated on August 25th and by September allied troops were entering Germany. At the same time the Russians were advancing in the east and Hitler's forces were forced back towards Berlin. Although heavy allied bombing had extensively damaged most major German cities and industrial centres, Hitler was still not beaten and ordered the launch of his V1 rocket propelled flying bombs, nicknamed 'Doodlebugs,' aimed at London. These were followed shortly afterwards by the V2, an even bigger threat. Hitler finally admitted defeat in April 1945 and committed suicide in his bunker under the streets of Berlin.

The war in the Far East ended following the first use of the recently developed atomic bomb. The bomb that decimated Hiroshima on August 6th 1945 was dropped from the US aeroplane named Enola Gay. The second atomic bomb devastated Nagasaki three days later, killing over seventy thousand people outright. On August 15th, Emperor Hirohito announced the Japanese surrender on the radio, the first time that his voice had ever been heard in public. The war in the East was finally over. However, the effects on many of the combatants, particularly those who had been incarcerated in prison camps, remained with them for many years.

300,000 British servicemen and women were killed during the war. The four million that returned were demobbed. Men were issued with a full set of clothes, including the famous 'demob' suit to help them to begin their lives back in 'civvy street.' Women were given the option of a demob suit or £12-10s and fifty-six coupons instead.

The role of women

During the war, the role of women in the workplace changed dramatically. The men who were called-up to fight had been replaced in the workplace, whether that was in the factory or on the farm. In December 1941, the conscription of women aged 18-30 was introduced. When called-up, women were given the choice between the women's services, civil defence or working in industry. In factories of all types, women proved themselves to be the equal of men in almost all respects. The Land Army was formed and women joined to work on farms, carrying out all but the heaviest of tasks as well as the farm workers that they had replaced.

Many of these women left domestic service to serve their country and never returned to their former lives when the war ended. During the war, women also learned that they didn't have to listen to their menfolk and could make their own decisions; a development that wasn't universally popular with every returning war hero.

Rationing

Rationing of basic foodstuffs began in 1940. Other items followed and coupons were introduced to provide a system of allocation for scarce resources. Each person in the country was given a monthly ration of basic food items and sixty-six coupons per year to spend on other goods including clothes. Many luxury goods disappeared or became prohibitively expensive. Most things were still available for a price though, and 'Spivs' could always get hold of the items that were in short supply.

Cheaper foodstuffs were introduced to help to stretch resources. Horsemeat was eaten by many and Supply Pressed American Meat (Spam) became very popular as it could be served in a number of ways. Egg powder was less popular.

People were urged to 'Dig for Victory' and gardens and areas of public parks were given over to vegetable growing.

After the US entered the war, hundreds of thousands of American troops were stationed in Britain, particularly in the months leading up to D-Day. Airmen and soldiers were popular with women and children, as they brought with them Hershey bars, nylon stockings and ice cream. They were not so popular with British servicemen who accused them of being 'over paid, over sexed and over here.'

In spite of (or perhaps, because of) the restrictions, the general health of the average person was better after the war than it had been at the start of the decade.

The Royal Family

At the beginning of the war, it was suggested by the government that members of the Royal Family should be evacuated to Canada. King George VI refused and he and his wife Queen Elizabeth and family remained in London throughout the war, sharing the austerity measures with the rest of the population. Their visits to bombed areas of cities throughout the country were much appreciated and brought hope to everyone they met. The king's eldest daughter, Princess Elizabeth, reached the age of conscription a few months before the end of the war and joined the ATS as a Second Subaltern. After the war, in 1947, she married Philip Mountbatten, the nephew of Lord Mountbatten. The wedding was a welcome break from post-war austerity and amongst the wedding presents was a gift from the Cabinet—all of their combined food coupons.

Britain after the war

In Britain during the war, the coalition government led by Winston Churchill enjoyed almost universal support. After the war, however, the electorate chose a socialist government and Churchill was defeated in the election of 1945. People looked forward to a better life. The National Health Service was launched and Social Security was introduced. Working class children with ability were given the chance to improve themselves with the introduction of the 11+ exam, the gateway to a Grammar School education. The Bank of England, utilities and transport industries were all nationalised. Rationing continued throughout the decade though, and the latter half of the decade became known as 'the austerity years.'

The winter of 1947 was the worst of the century. The River Thames froze, industry was crippled and there were regular electricity cuts. Coal deliveries were stopped and water pipes froze for several weeks. The inevitable thaw arrived during March leading to widespread flooding, which affected wide areas of Britain. On top of rationing, the cold weather which dragged on for almost two months, did nothing to lift the feeling that the end of the war had not brought with it the hoped for return to prosperity.

In 1948 the British Nationality Act confirmed the right of Commonwealth subjects to settle in Britain. This led to a steady influx of British subjects from the Caribbean and the Indian sub-continent, which would have far reaching effects in the decades to follow.

The Interim Index of Retail Prices was set up in 1947. This updated the original list of items that had been used to monitor changes in retail pricing since 1914. The index included corned beef, streaky bacon, turnips, boiled sweets, Derby tweed raincoats, shirts (each with two separate collars), the hair mattress, distemper, wireless licences and 78 rpm records.

After the war—overseas

At the end of the war, the territory occupied by the Soviet forces became communist states. Stalin installed communist leaders in Poland, Bulgaria, Romania, Hungary and Czechoslovakia as well as the eastern part of Germany. In 1946, Winston Churchill declared that an 'Iron Curtain' had descended over Europe, separating the capitalist West from the communist East.

When hostilities ceased, an estimated fifteen million displaced and homeless people began to rebuild their lives. The majority of these returned to their homelands but many more began a new life in North and South America, Australia and New Zealand. Many of these chose the New World rather than return to life under a communist regime within the newly defined borders of Eastern Europe. For the Jewish people, the destination of choice for many was the state of Israel, controversially founded on the 14th May 1948 under the leadership of David Ben-Gurion.

The United Nations was formed in late 1945 with both of the superpowers, the Soviet Union and the USA, being founder members. Its aim: 'To save succeeding generations from the scourge of war.' The reconstruction of Europe was helped by the Marshall Plan; monetary aid was provided by the USA to regenerate the economies of countries that had been devastated during the war.

In 1948, the Russians closed off the city of Berlin and allied aircraft flew food and fuel in to the city to prevent the population from starving. This continued until May 1949 when the Russians withdrew the blockade and Germany was split into two countries— East (the German Democratic Republic) and West Germany.

In China, the communists successfully took over the country and declared the People's Republic, led by Chairman Mao, in 1949. The Republic declared that peasant management of village economies would lead the country's prosperity and there would be equality for all. Like their counterparts in Russia, the peasants soon realised that some citizens were more equal than others. It was an extremely authoritarian regime however, and merciless towards the many dissidents who disagreed with Mao's policies.

India became Independent in August 1947. The country was partitioned along religious lines; India for the Hindus and the Independent State of Pakistan was created for the Muslims. Religious unrest continued, however, climaxing in the assassination of Mahatma Gandhi by a Hindu extremist in January 1948.

Decade developments

Two massive world-shaping developments took place during the decade, one of which was the direct result of the War. The splitting of the atom led to the development of the atomic bomb and nuclear power. The development of ENIAC (Electronic Numerical Integrator and Computer) laid the foundations of the modern computer industry.

Other notable developments included the jet-propelled aircraft, the electric guitar and the first attempts at organic farming.

Closer to Home—
Personal Memories of the 1940s

Memories of the 1940s are dominated by the Second World War, which raged for half of the decade. The personal recollections which follow in this chapter paint many pictures of the varying effects that this had on individuals' lives, both indirectly and directly.

*Malcolm Batt from **Oxfordshire** grew up*
in the immediate post war period

Brown Windsor soup

'I lived in a middle class family, my father worked at Harwell. I remember going shopping with my mother as a young child and seeing the ration coupons cut out of the ration book each time a purchase was made. We always ordered our groceries from the same grocer who delivered once a week. Milk and bread were also delivered by horse drawn transport and fresh vegetables came from a local nursery.

Holidays were taken once a year when we usually went to the Isle of Wight. Before my father had a car, we would travel by train to Portsmouth and then by paddle steamer to Ryde—it was quite an adventure. I fondly remember my father taking me to see the engines that were always on show in such boats. The gleaming brass, hot oil, hissing steam and the splendour of the massive connecting rods turning the paddle cranks always impressed a youngster. At the end of the pier in Ryde we transferred to a little train for the trip to Shanklin and Miss Bleu's boarding house.

I guess the boarding house catered for four or five families and three meals a day were taken in the dining room (unless you were late, in which case you went without). It's funny but this room even now conjures up images of badly hung floral wallpaper. I think Miss Bleu papered the walls herself during the winter months. I remember having to leave the beach each day at noon and walk back up a long steep path to Miss Bleu's for lunch, we daren't be late. Evening meal was taken at 6pm prompt every day and it was my first experience of eating a three-course meal. The Brown Windsor soup stands out in my memory as the usual starter.

We went to the beach most mornings, weather permitting then after lunch we walked somewhere or took a bus further afield. We saw the donkey wind up the bucket from the well at Carisbrooke Castle and we excitedly collected sands of various colours from the cliffs of Alum Bay, near the Needles. These days, the deliberate undermining of the cliff to collect sand is forbidden, not surprisingly. You could also go to the shop and choose a hollow, clear glass shape—a test tube, milk bottle, vase or something more ornate like a fish, I think. You then went around various troughs full of coloured sand and put a layer of each colour in to your shape, so that you ended up with a multi-layered, coloured sand ornament to take home and hopefully not smash too quickly.'

Horace Gamble lived in *Leicester*
during the early years of the decade

Not so Much a Hobby: More a Way of Life

'Trainwatching! Now, there's a noble pursuit if ever there was one. A totally acceptable title rather than the new fangled 'Trainspotting,' with its derisory implication, which was unknown until after World War II.

Those schoolboys who would gather late afternoon, at weekends and during holidays, on the elevated alleyway overlooking Leicester LMS shed yard became, in the weeks leading up to the outbreak of hostilities, the nucleus of the fledgling Leicester Railway Society (still thriving) and about whom some of this is told.

But first two personal memories, which perhaps ought to be best forgotten! Soon after the commencement of the war the government issued leaflets listing the areas of photography which were banned for security reasons; railway installations—but not locomotives—included. At the same time the supply of films to the civilian population dried up. Somehow I had managed to secure one, before they went off the market, for the sole purpose of snapping a few engine record shots locally. After being warned by the Leicester station inspector that my behaviour was illegal, the camera was put away for the remainder of that evening. Having one exposure left I was determined not to sully the film with anything unconnected with railways and so a day or two later I took the camera to my place of employment, outside the city, which adjoined a small railway yard. Ideal fodder. The deed done I returned to my desk smugly satisfied that the film could be developed and the results collected from the chemist's shop a few days later. It did not turn out quite like that. Just before lunchtime a large, stolid, police constable, obviously not versed in the niceties of trainwatching, was ushered into the office intent on making an arrest. Had I not taken a photograph in the vicinity of an army barracks? Well, yes, but my back turned towards it and anyway it was out of sight at the top of an embankment on the other side of the railway line. Here followed an hour long interrogation over notebooks containing engine names and numbers uncovered in my desk drawer, the contents of which convinced him that it was the secret code of an enemy spy ring. On seeing that I was never going to make a full confession of being a traitor he took the precious camera away to the police station, for the film to be developed, with the parting shot that if anything incriminating should be discovered I would be for the 'high jump.' A week later the empty camera was returned with the stern warning not to be seen near a railway line again!

Among the many restrictions imposed upon the populace during those dark years was that the south and east coasts, with their well loved holiday resorts, were out of bounds to all but the indigenous natives together with members of the armed forces. France had fallen, the amazing exodus of the British Expeditionary Force from Dunkirk accomplished, the Battle of Britain just getting into its stride and my own call-up into the forces looming ever nearer decided me to take a trainwatching holiday away from Leicester.

Grandmother had relatives living in a mining village, not far from Staveley, where there was not one railway company but three—the Midland Railway, the Great Central and the Lancashire, Derbyshire and East Coast Railway. It would be an ideal place to sleep and eat, from whence I could, and did, ride my bicycle to Sheffield, Wath and Huddersfield in search of unfamiliar locomotive classes. One afternoon a local jaunt was envisaged necessitating a visit to an alleged good vantage point at a nearby junction. Clad in shirt, khaki shorts and sandals, with obligatory gas mask box in saddlebag, I pedalled away in determined mood towards the goal. However, the lane gave way to a cart track dwindling to a footpath which eventually petered out in the middle of a field—and nary a railway in sight! Frustrated I turned back, then, approaching the village espied a signal in the 'off' position on the Great Central embankment. Members of the Auxiliary Fire Service were engaged in some hose-pipe water related exercise in an adjacent meadow so I leaned myself and bike up against a fence to enjoy some free entertainment whilst keeping a weather eye upon any rail traffic which might perchance to come along.

What did come along was unexpected and unwelcome. A large black Wolseley saloon car drew up alongside disgorging two uniformed officers, one rather ominously carrying a pair of handcuffs. My compulsory ID card was studied carefully, scrutinising name, address and National Registration Number with questions as to why I was so far from home. Railway hobby connections, thankfully, did not enter the equation this time and I think they were led to be convinced of my innocence by the official stamp of the Leicestershire Home Guard B Company in the ID card. What, I ventured to enquire, was the cause of this sudden interest in my welfare? A farmer, through whose fields I had cycled, reported seeing a German parachutist armed with a collapsible bicycle acting suspiciously thus spurring into action the County Constabulary!

I had now been transposed from a potential secret agent to, ostensibly, a member of the Wermacht. However, just to be doubly sure, they drove off to the house where I was staying in order to corroborate my explanation but when I arrived, shortly afterwards, there was worse to come. Hadn't I brought shame upon this clean living, honest, God-fearing family that had never seen such a thing as 'the Police' darken their door in the past!

One cannot blame the constables for investigating a possible national emergency but to check up at the house was beyond the call of duty. Still, I suppose they had to while away the time somehow given that, then, there would be more policemen, numerically than lawbreakers in the country.'

Liz Rosenberg recalls her early schooldays

Spinsters and ink wells

'I was four and a half years old when I started school. All these other children were sitting at little tables and chairs. I remember all the things in the room had labels on like 'door,' 'window,' etc. We learnt to write on slates with chalk. I remember when I was about five, having my slate held up for all the others to see as I had got all my sums right. Later on we graduated to nibbed pens with inkwells. (My parents always wrote with fountain pens. We had bottles of Blue Quink Ink in a special place so that they could be filled.) The primary school I went to was a small private one, run by two spinster ladies, I think their prospective partners had been killed in the First World War. But they were very progressive. They were very up to date with their maths teaching as I remember many years later when I was at Uni discussing with some of the other maths students how they had been taught and some had been taught incorrectly and had to unlearn some methods.

The school was for both boys and girls and we played sports as well as lessons. I was never very good at sports and only when I went to Boarding School and had my eyes tested did I discover that I was very short sighted in one eye, so no wonder I couldn't see the ball. I always used to sit at the front of the class at Primary School, as I couldn't see the blackboard.

But I wasn't the only one in the class with this problem, so I didn't think anything of it. Those two ladies gave me a love of learning, which has lasted all my life. It was a real vocation for them to teach their pupils, not just a job.'

Heather Copeman grew up in *Norwich*

Mod cons?

'We lived in Bolingbroke Road and had few mod cons. In the kitchen, we had a gas copper, an oven, a pantry and a meat-safe. In the living room were two armchairs, one for Dad and one for Gran. The other chairs were hard wooden ones. We did, though also have a piano, which everyone in our family of seven could play and we were always having family singsongs. The radio, with its valves and winding tuning dial was only really turned on to hear the BBC news. The floors were all covered in lino with six home made rugs in various rooms.

In the war us kids all got used to carrying our gas masks around, it was just part of daily life. I never got used to going in to the air raid shelter, though; it was always so cold and damp.

Our meals were usually stodgy but we never got fed up with them. They were very filling and warming and we didn't know anything else. There was nothing fancy then, no choice.'

Miss Patterson in Edinburgh was born in 1938

The Broons

'We had 4oz of sweet rations a week and we saved them up and went to a wee 'tablet' shop in Morrison Street. Tablet is like fudge only harder. It's made from sugar, condensed milk and flavouring. Nowadays, I think it only comes in vanilla flavour but back when I was young we could get chocolate, orange, lemon, peppermint and cinnamon flavours. Others as well that I've forgotten; orange was my favourite. We also went to another shop run by an old lady that sold home-made 'toffee doddles.' These were hard boiled sweets and they lasted for ages.

During the war when we were at school we sometimes used to get apples from Canada; Mackintosh Reds they were called. We were given one each and the extra ones were used as prizes for those with the best handwriting or the most correct spellings. Those of us with brothers and sisters took the apple home and shared it. We always shared.

We had porridge for breakfast and porridge for supper every day. Mother used to make soups and stews and 'mince and tatties' so she made the best of what she had. On birthdays we had a special treat which wasn't a birthday cake. It was 'Clouttie Dumpling.' This was made from suet, water and flavouring and wrapped in a cloth. Mum also hid threepences in it. After it was unwrapped you could cut it in slices and eat it cold or fry it with sugar on top. It was delicious.

At Christmas we each hung up a pillowcase. On Christmas morning we might each have a mandarin orange and an Annual— Boys Own or Hotspur for the boys or Bunty for the girls. One of us always got 'The Broons' annual. We all got something different so that we could share.

We always shared.

If we were lucky we also had some chocolate and perhaps a shilling in the bottom of the pillowcase.

My Aunt Patsy was a tailoress and that was very lucky for our family. Clothing coupons went farther if you bought material rather than ready-made clothes. So we could buy material and Aunt Patsy made up the clothes for us. I was tall and lanky and my sister was too fat but we both had clothes that fitted us perfectly thanks to Aunty Patsy.

In those days too, everyone passed on their clothes to younger brothers, sisters or cousins. Toys were also passed on as well as prams and cots; everything that could be passed on was reused.

We always shared. Except shoes. Shoes were always scuffed and worn out before they could be passed on!

When rationing ended, in the 1950s, food became more plentiful and varied. I must have been fifteen or sixteen before I ever saw a banana, let alone eat one!

My father's parents lived in an Edinburgh tenement building. Four families to each floor and one toilet between them, no bath-room. They had gas lighting and a bed in every room because of the size of the family. We lived in Dundee Terrace and had electricity in the flat but gas lighting on the stairs. We also had a bathroom.

An elderly lady lived downstairs and she taught me to crochet. She couldn't read a pattern and neither can I but she showed me how to make doll's clothes by just measuring the doll. She was a lovely old lady.

It was safe for kids then. We used to meet up in hordes and go to the park and play rounders or swim in the Portobello open-air pool. The big ones looked after the little ones. We had a packed lunch and stayed out all day long, then caught the bus home. Nobody ever came to any harm.'

Jeff Jacobs from **Birmingham** *is Jewish*

Not wanted here

'Before World War II my brother had the opportunity to enter business life in Blackpool. A family decision was made to move and we settled in Cannock Avenue, Blackpool. I was not happy leaving the Birmingham Hebrew School for my first experience in a non-Jewish school. I remember being a six-year-old boy attending assembly first thing in the morning. The Headmaster boomed out in a loud voice, 'Jacobs, leave the hall as we say prayers; you do not believe in Jesus.' Over two hundred pair of eyes glared at me. Can you imagine that happening today?

War was declared in September 1939. Our family decided to return to Birmingham. We now resided in Willows Crescent, Cannon Hill. When the air raids commenced the family routine was down in the cellar by 6pm. It was dark, damp, musty and full of coal dust; the bombs dropping every night shaking the house to the foundation. Very scary for a young child. The all clear did not happen until 6am. One morning I walked to school (no school buses) to find the Hebrew School had received a direct hit the previous night. We were told to go home until further notice. The majority of the school students had been evacuated. I asked my parents to allow me to stay which they did. During one heavy night of bombing, windows shattered in our home as a stick of bombs all chained together fell around the corner in Jakeman Road, killing many local families.

Life was very tough; no water on many days due to mains being bombed, no electric, shortage of food, what you could find was rationed. As far as school was concerned a number of months went by until we were called to meet at a teachers home for a few hours schooling. That lack of educational time and the following months with a shortage of schoolbooks and materials left a gaping hole in the kids' education of that era.

When a group of boys asked the headmaster Mark Harris if we could form a School cricket team he answered, 'By all means but we have no equipment and no budget for same.' I was advised to approach a big time businessman in the city centre of Birmingham for help. As I was ushered into his office my knees were shaking. I presented my case. Little did I understand that this was the first selling job of my lifetime. He kindly took his chequebook out and gave me £5. In those days that was sufficient to purchase the basics and so was born the Birmingham Hebrew School Cricket team of 1941/1942.'

David Lowe was evacuated from London during the war

Chocolate bars and pianos

'In 1940, along with numerous other children, my brother and I were evacuated from our bombed out part of London. I was six at the time, my brother was only five, and we eventually arrived at a church hall in what was expected to be a fairly safe place in the country. The idea was we would all sit there while the local population came in to choose which children they would look after. This was a government requirement at the time, so doubtless they weren't all doing it out of choice. We were not exactly angelic looking at the best of times and the long train journey for two as young as us had clearly taken its toll. The result was that we were still left 'unchosen' in the hall after every 'chooser' had left. The person in charge was clearly at a loss what to do with us when suddenly a large Rolls Royce pulled up outside and a wealthy looking couple entered the hall. They looked around in case there was a better choice than us but seeing that we were the only ones left, took us back to their home. And what a home! I still think of it as more like a castle, with scores of rooms, its own church in the grounds and lots of space in which to play.

The couple turned out to be Mr and Mrs Fry, owners of the famous chocolate firm. Mrs Fry also wrote novels under the name of Sheila Kaye Smith. Needless to say we spent most of the war in absolute luxury. Mr and Mrs Fry took to us immensely, having no children of their own. Although we had our own quarters, Mr Fry would sometimes take me to his study and teach me the rudiments of playing piano. This paid off in later years as I became quite an accomplished semi-pro pianist playing with the very top musicians in the country. Music also introduced me to my wife, with the consequent birth of our daughter and then granddaughter. I sometimes wonder if they would ever have been born if someone else had chosen my brother and me in that church hall.'

***John Lucas** was also evacuated from **East London**
during the war*

An evacuee in Wales

'Along with a lot of other children, my brother, sister, myself and our mother were evacuated to somewhere safer; in our case this was to Ferndale in the Rhondda Valley, in South Wales. The family was billeted with a family called Phillips, in Taff Street. They treated us as one of the family but we did feel out of place—cockneys in a Welsh mining village. We did become part of the local community, attending Sunday school and church, where I sang in the choir. After a while, I attended a 'London' school—Clydach Court—at Trealow, which was a school for evacuees. I don't know why we had a separate school but I think that we still managed to get on well with the children of the Welsh families. We went to the local cinemas—Workman's Hall and The Tudor Picture House—and paid our 3d entrance fee. After the show, we usually bought 1d worth of chips and strolled down Station Road with our friends talking about the film that we had just seen; the war seemed a long way away. I'm still in touch with my best friends from those days, so we must have made some sort of impression! We remained there for four years until peace was declared and we could return to our homes. We were shocked by the devastation that had been caused in London while we were away.

After the war, I started to collect movie stars' autographs. This was a very popular hobby at the time and most of my friends were busy writing letters to their favourite Hollywood stars. I will always remember the thrill that I felt when I received my first letter with a Californian postmark. It was from Bette Davis and I was hooked from that day on.'

***Mrs Self** was a young child in **Guernsey** when war broke out*

Evacuated to the mainland

'In September 1939, mum and dad told my sister Mavis and I to be very quiet. It was a Sunday morning—the 3rd of September—and

**The cinema was the main form of escapism and the actors and actresses
were the idols of their day**

dad had brought a friend to the house to listen to the wireless as
the Prime Minister, Mr Neville Chamberlain, was going to make an
important announcement. Mavis was four years old, I was eleven.
We listened to the stern voice on the radio, which said that we
had declared war on Germany. We didn't really know what war
was. Mavis was too young to understand but I knew that mum
and dad both had brothers who had been killed or wounded in
the Great War.

At school we learnt about the countries involved in the war and
sang their national anthems. However, life went on much as usual
except that mum was hoarding extra food in the cupboard.

The following summer we broke up for the school holidays in
June which was unusual. However, the weather was lovely, so we
went to the beach most days. On the 19th of June mum took us to
see grandmother at L' Ancresse but the visit was brief. At 4pm dad
came out in the car to collect us and we hurried home. Mum and
dad went off to attend a meeting at the school at which the States
Education Council briefed everyone on the plans for evacuating
the children. I was left in charge of Mavis, a thing unheard of before. The 'phone kept ringing and I had to answer it, which I didn't
normally do as telephones were still not common in 1940. When
our parents returned home they told us that we would be leaving
at 4am the following morning—not much time to pack!

We arrived at school and said our tearful goodbyes to mum and
dad. They said that we shouldn't worry, that we were going to stay

with an aunt in Derbyshire and that they would come and fetch us after a week or two. With heavy hearts, Mavis and I and all of our fellow evacuees were taken by bus to the White Rock where we waited for our boat. We waited for several hours while other schools were taken away in an array of boats. We finally embarked on the 'Antwerp' at 10am. 1,154 of us set off for Weymouth. I can't remember much about the trip; we weren't seasick but we were hungry and thirsty—we had eaten our sandwiches and chocolate while we were waiting in Guernsey. Mum had made me promise never to leave Mavis and to look after her. I looked after her so well that I wouldn't let her go to the toilet by herself!

We landed at Weymouth, tired and grubby and were taken to a local cinema where we were fed and had our heads checked for nits, I think. We then boarded a train; we didn't know where we were going. Many hours later we arrived in Glasgow, not the most direct route to Derbyshire, I later realised. We ended up in a Church Hall sleeping on camp beds. The Scottish ladies met us and we had difficulty in understanding them at first (and them us, probably). They were very kind to us. They washed our clothes and took us to the public baths to have a bath—we had never heard of public baths before. Mavis and I shared a bath and made sure that each other was clean. We also had our heads inspected again and I was so ashamed because my sister had nits; had she caught them since Weymouth? She must have caught them from some of the other children because mum would be very upset if she had known about it.

On the 30th June, ten days after we had left home, we heard the news that the Germans had occupied Guernsey and we were very concerned about our family and older friends.

Most of the children were billeted with Scottish families but we were going back south to Derbyshire, to granddad's stepsister, so we stayed in the Church Hall except for the last week when we stayed with two schoolteachers. One month after we arrived in Glasgow we set off for Chesterfield supervised by Miss Dear, a Guernsey St John's lady who was on her way back to England.

We arrived in Sheffield to be met by our aunt, a lady who was old enough to be our grandmother. Straightaway we joined the local school. Mavis was in the infant section and I was in the 'Big school.' It was all so different from what we had been used to in Guernsey; we didn't have boys in the same class there! And all the children spoke differently—they had two languages—one for school, which wasn't too difficult to understand and one for the playground and friends, which was unintelligible to me.

That winter was very, very cold with lots of snow. Mavis and I weren't used to this weather and we had no wellington boots—they had been left at home in the rush to leave. There wasn't enough money to buy us new ones, but we survived. Home was a miner's cottage, a two up two down with an outside lavatory. My aunt kept it very nicely, which wasn't easy, as Chesterfield is a mining town (or was) and there was a lot of coal dust in the air.

We occasionally had twenty-five word messages from mum and dad which the Red Cross organised through Switzerland but they seemed to take months to arrive. We were allowed to send similar messages back. This cost 2/6d, a lot of money for us to save up.

One day, our aunt asked us to come and listen to the radio. We all cried as we heard Mr Winston Churchill make his famous speech, uttering the words 'Our dear Channel Islands would be freed today.' We cried again when, a week later, we received our first letter from mum and dad from a newly liberated Guernsey.

Mavis and I returned to Guernsey on the 3rd of August 1945 and mum and dad were at the top of the White Rock to meet us as the harbour was still covered with barbed wire and people couldn't walk down to the boats. As we walked towards our parents, the first thing that we noticed was how thin they had become; they had been virtually starving for several months until the Red Cross had managed to deliver food parcels.

We soon settled back in to life on Guernsey. In the mornings, mum would poke her head around our bedroom door to make sure that we were really there and it wasn't just a dream that we were home'

Charles de Carteret *was also evacuated from* Guernsey

Gas masks and the SS Isle of Jersey

'My entire family was evacuated from Guernsey in 1940 as the threat of a German invasion grew. In the chaos, the family was initially dispersed throughout Britain, or so it seemed; two sisters in Scotland, one sister was initially lost en route and finally ended up in Cheshire, mother, brother and myself in Blackburn and father and my other two brothers in Yorkshire. Eventually we all ended up in the small Yorkshire town of Brighouse (latterly of 'Brass Band' fame, with neighbours Rastrick) where we lived, safe and sound until September 1945.

During the long summer holidays of 1940 the builders moved in to my school at Brighouse. When we returned for the new term we were astonished to see eight red brick 'air raid shelters' in the schoolyard. These were single brick structures, about thirty feet long by ten feet wide. They seemed to us to be little better than cosmetic reassurances!

At this time my parents were notified that they were to report to an issuing depot to be given the family's supply of gas masks. They set off and reappeared about two hours later with a supply of boxes. Father, having been gassed twice in the trenches of World War I, was keen to ensure that we were properly briefed and he gave us a grim lesson in the use of these peculiar gadgets. Within minutes the house was the scene of a grotesque pantomime as seven hideous faces ran through the house laughing and playing the fool. My younger brother was given a 'Mickey Mouse' mask, which had painted eyepieces, and a nose protruding at the front—a red piece of rubber, which produced a wonderful rasping noise during respiration. The hilarity was soon ended, however, when the last gas mask was unboxed. My youngest brother was a baby of only a few weeks old and this was to be his defence against the dreaded gas. David was placed inside so that only his tiny legs protruded at the base and his little face could be seen through the glass front. Filtered air was supplied by hand pumping. When mother saw David inside she said that she was 'damned if she was going to use it' and consigned it to the top of the wardrobe. This scene was, I believe, repeated throughout wartime Britain.

Next day we set off for school with our gas masks slung over our shoulders. We were introduced to a new lesson—'gas mask drill,' a daily ritual. Every day after early morning assembly we practised using the gas masks. It was funny and scary at first but we soon got used to them. Then we moved to the next phase of school defence, the Air Raid shelter. We filed out in to the playground and halted outside the new air raid shelters. Our teacher, Miss Thornton unlocked the door and told us what to do. We were to file quietly inside and not to be afraid of the dark. She held up a paraffin hurricane lamp which she lit with a match to show us we would at least have some sort of light inside the windowless, airless structure. Inside, we found that there were wooden benches running down both sides of the room with another running down the centre. We sat as instructed very quietly and waited for the next 'happening.' Today, however, was a dry run and we soon filed out, satisfied that this was easy. However, over the next few weeks we progressed to the first 'terror.' We all held hands and the teacher treacherously blew out the lamp leaving us all sitting in the claustrophobic darkness for several minutes; a traumatic event for some of the children including my brother who has suffered from claustrophobia ever since. However, since I was holding the hand of my pretty deskmate, I was a 'big boy' outwardly and full of bravado. Inwardly, I strove to control my fright and rapid heartbeat!

The second 'terror' was the same procedure but with the added complication that we had to wear our gas masks. It was not repeated. Everyone cried very loudly. Sitting in the dark wearing a gas mask is very spooky. Cheeks and underclothes were severely stained that morning.

Later, drills were relegated to once a week until, with great relief we handed in our gas masks in 1944.

By this time, I was a proper 'Yorkshire Lad' with almost unintelligible accent to match. One day, we received a letter informing us that all Channel Islanders could return to their homes. My memory is of being totally bemused and excited at this break from routine. I remember the shock I delivered to my classmates when I rose from my desk to announce to the teacher that I wouldn't be coming to school next week as I was going back home to Guernsey.

Preparations to return began with a heated row between my parents. Mother didn't want to go, father didn't want to stay. Father won! The local rag and bone man, the only one in town to deal in second hand goods, duly arrived with his horse and cart to inspect the furniture. What really impressed me was the enormous roll of £5 notes that he carried in his trouser pocket. To me, it was like a miniature roll of wallpaper (but a lot more valuable!). Only mother and I were home that morning as the potential buyer of our home inspected the furniture with a shake of his head as he inspected each item. Five bob here, two and six there; my poor mother was almost in tears as her precious furniture was knocked down to a mere pittance. It was a buyer's market and he took advantage. As soon as the price had been agreed, the man's assistant removed the item and placed it on the cart outside and the cash was placed in mother's hand. The last item was the roll of lino on the sitting room floor. Only purchased a few weeks previously, mother had planned to take it back to Guernsey. But he was insistent and the amount of money in mother's hand was so small, she gave in with great reluctance. It was his last comment that decided her. 'It'll only tear missus, when I take it up. Not much good to you then.' She agreed and he paid up. With a triumphant flourish, he grabbed a corner of the nice shiny bright red lino and 'Oh dear,' it tore from corner to corner. The rag and bone man cursed. Mother hid her grin of delight behind her hand, which, of course, already held the money. So he had to take away the torn lino and some measure of justice was realised.

The following day we departed on the train with mixed emotions; tears of regret and excitement for the future. We arrived in London and headed for the reception centre in Cromwell Road. For the second time in my life I was an official refugee ('returning'). It was also about this time that a family mystery was cleared up which had baffled my father since 1940. At that time, in a spirit of fervent patriotism he had volunteered for the RAF. But he had never received his call-up papers. In the heat of a discussion, mother let slip that when the postman had delivered his 'Notice to Report to his Unit' in late 1940, she had promptly thrown the call-up papers into the fire! The old man went up in the air! Actually, I think that he was secretly pleased at mother's initiative—he had survived a second war.

We remained at the reception centre for four days, in very crowded conditions, due to gales in the channel. We occupied what must have been an annex to the Union Jack Club next door; a wartime transit camp for servicemen moving through London en route for wherever. At last, we boarded a train for Southampton, which took us in smoky splendour to the embarkation point for the SS Isle of Jersey. By this time, it was pitch dark, raining and the sea looked very rough. Most uncomfortable, particularly for those who had to travel on deck huddled in blankets on deckchairs. But everyone was in high spirits.

During the night there was a problem in the Ladies lavatory. An elderly lady was thought to have been taken ill in a locked toilet. No one could see clearly below the door or over the top and the lady didn't respond to repeated questions. Someone would have to unlock the door from the inside and since the only possible access was the narrow opening above the door, someone very small would have to climb through the gap and release the lock. I was volunteered, being skinny and only four foot six. I suspect that my father put my name forward. However, my mother objected and my older brother, equally skinny but taller by two inches and a former miner was pushed over the top in my place. I remember an icy chill running down my spine as I heard my brother's voice on the other side of the door—'She's dead.' Eighty years old and longing to return to her beloved home in Jersey, she had passed away so close to realising her dream. It was very sad.

Early the next morning, the 'Isle of Jersey' entered St Peter Port harbour. It was still dark, still wet and the sea had remained rough. I couldn't see my feet! Not a light could be seen; wartime blackout conditions had not been readjusted, except for a dim light from somewhere in the region of Elizabeth College. Father organised us to all hold hands in a long line and led us like the blind down the harbour and up the Pollet to the Hotel de Normandy. For the next two years, this was the reception centre for returning refugees with no home to go to. My immediate observation was the overpowering smell; the sea air, seaweed and a strange smell that I only recognised many years later when I worked on building sites. It was the smell of drying concrete. All of those bunkers that the Germans had built were still drying out!

Later that day we had another surprise. As my father bluntly observed, 'The bloody Jerries are still here.' Under armed guard they spent a long time clearing up the wartime munitions and storing them safely out of harm's way.

All good things come to an end and we had to return to school. My first day at Cauvert Boys School was amazing. I joined a class of foreigners! They were all Guernsey boys, but having returned recently from England they all spoke in different regional accents. Every county of England seemed to be represented, as well as Wales and Scotland. I later found that some boys retained their newly acquired accents for years, particularly those who spent the war years in Wales and Scotland. Within a few months, more boys joined us. These boys were the sons of English parentage who had been sent to German detention camps for the duration of the war. I thought that I was skinny but these boys resembled the survivors from concentration camps. Even now I feel great sorrow for them but at the time we looked away in confused grief. They, of course, behaved like the rest of us—noisy, boisterous boys! Our teachers were as mixed as we were. Mostly ex-servicemen who were recently demobbed, they usually wore part of their old uniforms to school; the trousers and shirts. I wonder who was teaching who at that time—them or us. But, of course, to skip out of a boring lesson we could always divert them in to reminiscing about their wartime escapades . . .'

Brenda Allen lived in *Birmingham*

Cod liver oil

'During the war I was evacuated from Birmingham to Rugeley in Staffordshire. As a young evacuee, I don't remember any kindness, only being very thin when my mother fetched me home.

When I was seven years old, my father died of TB, aged thirty-two. We had free school dinners, which extended throughout the holidays because my mother was poor. I can still recall the smell of cabbage, which wafted down the stairs. This must have helped her a little. She took in sewing to earn some money and we used to cut up old coats in to strips for mother to make nice rag rugs.

Mother collected free orange juice and cod liver oil for us from the welfare clinic. We didn't mind the orange juice but the cod liver oil . . . ugh!

For recreation we spent all day at the park with a sandwich and a bottle of squash. If we found empty pop bottles we rushed off to the shop to collect the 2d deposit. We could buy various sweets and sticks of liquorice for 2d!'

Derick Johnson lived in *London*

Nine Lives

'It seems crazy now but we were much affected by the belligerent attitude encouraged by the rousing speeches of Winston Churchill. We kids felt we could take on the Germans if they came and we called ourselves 'The Parachute Gang.' We had our Molotov

Cocktails all lined up ready for use and arrow head pokers fixed to hardwood shafts, which we used as javelins. This probably spawned my interest in becoming an AAA coach at the throwing events in later life. We also embarrassingly had a ready supply of sharpened sticks to put in the ground in the event of an invasion by airborne troops. In the words of Dad's Army, 'They don't like it up 'em.' I'm rather surprised we were not taken away to a mental hospital but there we are.

My friend Michael's father was an officer in the Home Guard and told us he was having trouble with potential recruits filling in the forms. His answer was to use a blackboard at the recruitment centre stating—

Name: John Smith,

Address: The Cottages, Anytown, Anywhere,

Date of Birth: 10.10.1910

etc. etc.

The method worked quite well but two forms that he received back were actually exactly what he had written on the blackboard!

Sainsbury's East Grinstead branch was badly damaged during a bombing raid and business was transferred to a nearby disused church until 1951

On one occasion when I was at Michael's cottage where he lived with his parents and his Aunt Miss Skeffington who was a teacher at Turnham Road School, he said he was doing an experiment. Thinking it was a chemistry set sort of experiment I made to go to his garden shed but he asked me to go upstairs where he had his cat. A harness had been attached to the cat, the other end of which had been tied to a large handkerchief. He then opened the window and dropped the cat. Obviously the handkerchief did not perform the same way as a parachute and the cat fell into the flower border. It was incredible to watch the indifference of the cat as it strode with due decorum to the back of the house. Minutes later we saw the cat finishing off its dinner by the back door as if it hadn't had to use one of its nine lives.

It is worth mentioning that Michael had a narrow escape one morning when German aircraft strafed the gasworks near his home. He had been asleep in his bed and he showed me a line of large holes in the wall made by cannon-shells just above where he was sleeping. It was sheer luck that he didn't sit up when the attack took place. This brought home the reality of war like nothing else.'

Maureen Redko recalls growing up during the war

Missing in action and the Twins

'When the war started, my younger brother and I were sent away to live with a maiden aunt in Oxfordshire, away from the coast. She was very strict and we hated it. At one point my brother threw a hand written note out of the bedroom window which read 'Help. Come and save us!'

We were 'saved' after a few months and returned to life at home.

My elder brother had a paper round and enemy 'planes often flew overhead while he was out in the early morning. One morning he didn't come home and we went looking for him. Very soon we found his bicycle, riddled with bullets, lying by the side of the road. Of Tony, there was no sign. With beating hearts, we ran to the local First Aid station but no luck. Where was he? The question was answered at our next stop—the hospital. He was lying in a bed covered with pristine white sheets, his head on a spotless starched white pillow but with his hair completely covered in red brick dust. Apparently, the enemy 'plane had appeared and started firing at random. Tony jumped off of the bike and took cover in a shop doorway sitting on a step and covering his head with his un-delivered papers. The doorway was blown away from around him but miraculously he wasn't badly injured. He was hit by pieces of flying shrapnel, though and covered in the aforementioned brick dust. The dust came off when he had a bath, the shrapnel is still coming out, piece by piece, all these years later.

We knew the sound of the engines of all of the 'planes, the enemy's and ours. If the machine gunning started when I was in bed I always pulled the bedclothes up over my head. I'm not sure how I thought that I would be protected, but I did feel safer! During the day, I was particularly fearful of bright sunny days with puffy cumulus clouds floating along. The enemy 'planes hid behind the clouds and suddenly appeared, engine screaming and guns blazing, causing us to run for cover until they had passed over. Every time that I heard machine gun fire I took cover. On one famous occasion, while I was watching a war film at the cinema, the machine guns started and I shot under my seat, much to the amusement of the people around me.

My mother was often not in the house at night as she took her turn on fire watch. She was usually out all night. When her shift finished, she had to go and wake up one of the neighbours to take over from her. As she arrived at the house, the routine was for mum to give a healthy yank on a piece of string, which dangled out of a bedroom window. The other end of the string was attached to her friend's big toe! Mum said that she was always afraid that one day she would pull the string too hard and a toe would drop on her head!

Towards the end of the war, my mother worked in the local food and registration office. One day a woman came in to register the birth of her new twins, a birth that had caused quite a lot of excite-ment. The lady was married to a US airman, who was white. The twins were both black! Accusations flew, divorce was threatened and the local gossips lost their voices spreading the news far and wide. After some time the dust settled and the husband found that he had a black ancestor of whom he had previously been blissfully unaware. So the situation was resolved, much to the relief of the twins' mother who was as surprised as everyone else when the two boys made their dusky entrance in to the world.'

John Dymock lived on a farm near *Aylesbury*

Home made pies and cream cakes

'We regularly used to slaughter a pig, which we shared with another farmer, Uncle Walt. Then, later in the year, he would share his pig with us. This was a necessary arrangement with no deep freeze to store the meat. Some joints were eaten fresh, others were used as presents for neighbours who also returned the compliment when their pigs were killed.

Mother made what she called Walter Rose pies. These consisted of cubed pork inside a long pastry case with a pastry plait down the centre. It was so called because Walter Rose describes them in one of his books. The pig's fat was rendered down and stored in a large crock. The crispy bits that were left were the 'crinklings,' which were eaten with bread for supper.

The sides of bacon were salted in brine in a salting lead, a table with 45° sloping sides that formed a sort of large tray and which was lined with lead. This was kept in Uncle Fred's back kitchen next door. We had to 'do the pig' before we went to school, which involved basting the meat with the brine, using an old cup. Hams were pickled in a large crock; one of these was always saved for Christmas.

Mother also made bacon clangers. This was a suet pastry spread with bacon bits and sage, then rolled up like a swiss roll and boiled in a cloth. Delicious!

Lambs' tails were another treat. These were dipped in boiling water then the wool was pulled off. The tails were cut up and fried, usually eaten for supper.

Thinking of pigmeat reminds me of the time when two landmines came down in the village. One landed in a muckheap at Manor Farm in the centre of the village and didn't explode. Will Orchard, from the Home Guard came to investigate and seeing a parachute, thought that a German was hiding beneath. Not the most likely hiding place but perhaps Will thought that was the point! The second landmine did explode in a field and left a large crater. Fortunately the blast went away from the village. The crater became known as the bomb-hole and became the village rubbish tip; very useful, as there was no council refuse collection in the village.

At this time I was a member of the church choir, until my voice broke. After that I pumped the organ. There was a gauge to show how much air was in the bellows and one soon got to know how much effort was needed to keep it full according to the tune that was being played. At the end of the service, the Reverend Wigg gave the final blessing and I could see the congregation starting to fidget. They would be thinking about Sunday lunch and how far the meat ration would stretch while adjusting a fox fur stole or looking for their gloves. On regular occasions at this point, Mrs Bernard, the organist would suddenly start pulling out all the organ stops and I would start pumping with great gusto. I knew then that the National Anthem would be played with the congregation standing to attention and singing loudly and patriotically. The reason for this? Any advance by the Allies that Mrs Bernard felt worthy of celebration!

After I left school I had a year before my National Service, so I went 'into service' as a manservant to Lord and Lady Corrington— butler would have been too grand a word! There was a resident cook and nanny, daily nurserymaid and housemaid. I enjoyed that time, in spite of having quarrels with the cook from time to time.

The china was decorated with a coronet and a letter C, as was the bed linen. Tables always had to be laid in the prescribed fashion and to this day I always make sure that the pattern on a plate is the 'right' way for the person using it.

At this time, although food rationing was still in force, cream cakes were on sale again and one day Lady C brought two chocolate cream gateaux back from Fortnums. As she usually had tea in the nursery, one cake was eaten there. Joyce, the cook and I arrived back one evening from the cinema and both being hungry looked at each other and thought of the other cake. One slice perhaps? We ended up eating the lot. There was a nervous cook and a nervous manservant who presented themselves for work the next day in front of Lady C. Relief all around when Lady C told us to finish off the other cake—perhaps she was psychic!

My 'gap year' was soon ended and National Service loomed. After enduring the rigours of basic training I was posted to an army unit in north Wales, in a place with a name that I found difficult to pronounce at first—Trawsfynydd. I was the only one of my intake going there and as the train rattled through the mountains, for hours on end it seemed, I wondered if I would ever get out again.

The camp, an explosives unit, was certainly remote. On arrival, I couldn't believe my good fortune when I was sent to work in the officers' mess. Although I had training in running army stores, the Captain who interviewed me thought I would be of more use in the mess, so that's where I went. Within weeks, I had two stripes up and was put in charge. It was a proud moment for me when, on my first leave, I happened to meet a lance corporal who had given me hell in basic training. He couldn't believe his eyes when he saw my stripes.

One of my duties back at camp was to wake the Colonel every morning at five minutes to six. Not six minutes to six, or four minutes to six, but five minutes to six. The Colonel's breakfast consisted of tea and one thin slice of bread and marmalade. This was the routine every day and woe betide me if anything was not exact.

The Colonel kept chickens and geese, which were looked after by we mess staff. One morning as I poured the tea he said to me, 'If you kill and pluck a goose for me to take away on my leave at the weekend, you can have an extra day on your next 48 (hours of leave). I'll also give you a lift to London.' As a farmer's son I set about the task. I took half the night to pluck and 'dress' the goose. That favour was hard earned and no-one else would help me, but he was true to his word and I got my extra day and my lift to London.'

Betty Longden *grew up in* Yorkshire *during the war*

Hilda's ashes

'As I was only five when the war started my first memory of holidays is spending a week each summer with relatives in Darlington. I remember during one of these holidays going to Redcar, which was deserted and the beach covered in rolls of barbed wire. My favourite holidays were the Girl Guide Camps that I went on each summer. I was very much a tomboy and loved the countryside and the 'roughing it' element of camping. I had a brother ten years older than me, my parents having been nearly in their forties when I was born. My father had fought in the First World War, which probably explained his remoteness—I never felt I knew him. He and my mother either quarrelled ceaselessly or spent weeks in silence, due to his 'other woman' at the munitions factory where he worked. My father had not wanted any more children and I was always aware of being the odd one out, also I think my brother resented losing his 'only child' place, and I became something of a loner. I think I was the only Girl Guide in Britain who was never homesick during Summer Camp.

I also spent a lot of time during school holidays helping out at the farm in the village. At the age of ten I could single-handedly yoke a horse to the milk float, take a herd of cows down the road to the pasture, muck out the cowsheds and loved every minute of it. The family across the road had a large garden and we would collect manure from the farm in their home-made cart. We would sit the youngest of our 'gang', a sickly boy of about six, who died not long afterwards from rheumatic fever, in the cart, wheel him to the farm, fill the cart to overflowing with fresh horse manure, then sit him back on top and push him home again!

Although we were very working class and my father gave my mother very little money, my mother was a great snob. She'd call me in for tea when playing out with the other children, calling so they'd hear—'Tea's ready, Betty—come and get your strawberries and cream' and it would be jam and bread, if that. When I passed the scholarship to go to the Grammar School (this being 1944, I was one of the first working class children to get in on the scholarship rather than through the usual route of paying school fees) she made me give up the farm.

I've always regretted not being a bit older so I could have joined the Women's Land Army.

Mother worked sometimes in the kitchen at a nearby college. This was used to educate young ladies that had been evacuated from London and she often brought home leftovers as a treat. I can remember large enamel dishes with something brown and dry that had been warmed up in our fire oven and served up with gravy that she would tell me was 'roast duck and green peas.' We also had warmed up rissoles that she said were 'turkey and stuffing' (neither of which I'd ever seen). I was a great reader of the Just William books and for a long time could never understand why he went overboard about duck, turkey and the like when describing their Christmas dinner. I suppose it's not the same when it's warmed up.

We should have been better off than we were as my father worked from 7am to 7pm every day at the munitions factory, but only ever gave my mother £2 per week to cover everything. I learned only recently from my brother that when he left us in 1950 to marry his other woman he took with him savings of £1000! Imagine what that was worth in those days!

However, as children we weren't aware of being under-privileged as everybody around was the same. There was an area of the village where the 'posh' children lived, but we never played with them.

We all suffered the ailments of poverty such as scabies, head lice, impetigo, boils, tonsillitis etc. which were treated with old wives' remedies as we couldn't afford the doctor. I must have stunk to high heaven, as I was made to wear around my neck under my clothes a small Bakelite box containing a block of camphor to ward off germs, colds etc. You could smell me coming up the road! Added to this was the regular ritual of soaking my long hair in sassafras oil and small-tooth combing it over a newspaper to catch the lice. Even more aromatic was the dosing with sulphur tablets to 'cleanse the blood' at the first signs of listlessness or pallor. The gaseous escapes resulting from this cleansing I remember to this day! I dread to think what effect the combined odour had on my schoolmates in the classroom, although we probably all smelled the same.

Headaches were treated with vinegar and brown paper;—yes, really, like Jack and Jill. Swollen glands with a hot boiled onion squashed up in a sock and wrapped round the neck; boils with an application of soap mixed with sugar 'to draw it out' and tonsillitis with a piece of raw bacon fat (saved from the ration) tied to a piece of cotton. We were made to swallow this then it was drawn back again 'to grease the throat.'

Bear in mind also, that baths were a rare treat as we had only one cold tap in the kitchen. Water had to be carried into the cellar to be boiled in a copper then carried back up to be poured into the tin bath that had been brought in from the garden to be placed on the rug in front of the fire. Changes of clothes were equally rare as they were also boiled up in the copper, put through the mangle, carried back upstairs and hung out in the garden to dry. We had only gas lighting and one gas ring in the kitchen, so ironing was by means of flat irons that were heated up on the fire, where all the cooking was done also. The lavatory was two doors away down the street. It would freeze up in winter and I remember my mother picking her way through the snow, sprinkling hot ashes from a shovel in front of her so she wouldn't slip on the pavement, carrying a bucket of hot water to try to flush the pan. All this was done with great hilarity and shrieks of laughter.

My father had a battery-run radio and he would make me carry the accumulator that it required down to the garage once a fortnight to have it charged up, which cost 4d. He also had an old piano as he had taught himself to play from a correspondence course. When he went off for weekends or on holiday with his fancy woman he would hide the battery for the radio and lock up the piano keyboard in his bedroom! (My mother had moved out into the attic by this time).

In spite of being skinny waifs, the rations must have sufficed as few of the children I knew suffered serious illness (except the child across the road who was forced to sit on the manure). We had no sweets and ate apples we pinched off trees or bought a carrot for a ½d from the allotment on the way home from school. Hilda, my mother, was not a very organised housewife and when she collected the rations from the Co-op on Friday we would have a blow-out over the weekend. We finished off the meat ration, the bacon and dried eggs and the cheese. For the rest of the week we ate her homemade bread (which was one thing she was good at) and lard, or 'scallops'—thick slices of potato dipped in batter and fried in dripping. She'd also buy a sheep's head for about 6d and boil it whole in a pot on the gas ring with onions and carrots. We'd have it doled out into bowls—bones, eyes, brains, teeth and all—the tongue was a special delicacy—and pick the meat off, mopping it up with chunks of her homemade flat cakes. And that would keep us going until the next ration . . .'

Brenda Hall *lived in the country during the war*

'Good for the rhubarb'

'My father was in the Territorial Army so was one of the first to be called up when war broke out. My maternal grandparents were concerned that we were in danger because we lived in Birmingham and they persuaded my mother to move to rural Shropshire. An uncle found us a cottage that belonged to the farm that he managed. It was a shock to move from a modern council house with modern facilities to a cottage that was without the most basic of amenities. It was a one up, one down building. Our toilet was a wooden plank with a hole in the middle over a bucket in a shed, which was halfway up a very long garden. Worse, two other households shared this 'amenity.' The contents were emptied by the menfolk, in to a trench in the garden with much talk of how good the rhubarb would be. I still have a feeling of revulsion when I think of that all these years later.

Water for all of our needs was supplied by a spring in the woods, up a hill behind the cottages. It was piped down to a tap by the gate. One tap for three cottages.

Because of wartime petrol rationing we children were allowed to walk to school through the fields and woods and up the long drive of Walcott Hall instead of using road transport. We were supposed to keep to the pathways and not trespass on any of the fields. However, in one field, up against the boundary of a wood was a building that intrigued us. It was a brick-built open-fronted place with a tiled roof held up by brick pillars.

Eventually, curiosity overcame our fear of the gamekeeper and we climbed over the fence and went to investigate. It was an awful, frightening sight. There were heads of cattle and sheep on a big slab. They were covered with flies, big blue bottles and crawling with maggots. It was the maggot house, where bait was obtained for fishing in the lake of the Hall grounds.

At the time, Walcott Hall was a convalescent home for wounded soldiers. We often saw them in their blue uniforms sitting at the lakeside fishing. I remember seeing one of the soldiers catching a large eel. He bashed it against a tree to kill it.

At the local school we did our bit for the war effort. Part of our day was taken up with knitting socks and balaclava helmets for the soldiers at the front line. I could turn a very good heel at the age of eight.

Farm workers were exempt from call-up, as they were needed for food production. As they were no longer allowed to use guns to control vermin, the men became experts with catapults. At harvest time, we children went in to the fields on rabbit patrol. As the standing crop became a smaller and smaller square, the rabbits that were trying to find shelter would panic and make a run for the hedges. Out would come the men's catapults and we children would give chase and try to kill the rabbits with long sticks that we carried for the purpose. I don't ever remember bagging a rabbit myself but I know that the men did.

Country children ate a lot of rabbit during the war!'

Joan Horlock recalls the opening months of the war in Kent

Hot flasks and hens

'My sister and I were sitting on the back doorstep of our house in Downham, Kent when war was declared, and I can well remember the particular time when Chamberlain was broadcasting that we were at war with Germany. From memory, it was a fine clear day with cloudless sky and as the broadcast finished a lone 'plane flew over. From then on, memories become a bit dim, but where we lived was on a flight path into London and when the blitz started we used to see the bombers flying overhead on their way to bomb a specific target in London. We also used to watch many a dog fight overhead during the day, never realising the danger or loss of lives involved, and as kids, we used to come out of the shelter each morning and gather up the pieces of shrapnel that had dropped during the night.

When we had the Anderson shelter put in, the nightly ritual was to go down into the shelter with warm clothes on. My mother used to have a tray with a flask of hot water and the inevitable teapot and tea (no tea bags in those days!) plus something to eat—you never knew if you would be trapped in that shelter should a bomb explode nearby. Before we had our own shelter, we used to share a shelter with three other families across the road and we used to sit head to tail along the shelter floor, with hardly any room to lie down.

As the blitz became worse, our parents decided we needed to be evacuated, and we were sent up north to our grandparents. I can remember the panic on Kings Cross station. Everyone was pushing and shoving to get tickets. My sister and I were put on the train, together with our suitcases, and left in the care of two servicemen in the carriage while my mother went to 'fight' for the rail tickets (—no way would you leave children like that these days!).

During the time before we were evacuated, life was pretty difficult around the London area. There were many days when no gas or electric power was available and my mother used to have a little sort of tiny burner with a 6" flame and a pan of potatoes used to be put on this about 4pm and take about two hours to cook! Rationing made things difficult and my mother used to 'trade' her sugar ration for a neighbour's tea ration. If there happened to be oranges or bananas in the shop, word went round pretty quickly. Everyone dashed round to the queue—many's the time the last two or three pieces of fruit were sold to someone just in front of us, and we went home empty-handed.

Eggs were at a premium and we did have two hens, which supplemented the rations a bit, although I think there was some ruling that if you kept hens, your weekly ration from the shop was stopped—I'm not sure about that. We did have tins of dried egg (which was pretty awful) and it is amazing the ingenuity of house-wives in those days to make something out of nothing, plus using ingredients which were 'not the real thing.'

My sister and I came back to London when the blitz quietened down, but not long after that the 'doodle bugs' started and I can remember the first night they came over (again on the flight path to London) and the awful din they made. Little did we know at that time that when the noise stopped, it meant they were coming down to explode. As the raids got worse, we were again sent north to get away from the bombing. I often think about those days and all the children separated from their parents, plus husbands and sons etc separated from their families and many of them killed. There were no counsellors around in those days—we just got on with our lives and I don't think we were any the worse for it in many ways, apart from the sorrow at losing a loved one of course.'

John Murison in *Newport* *had a strange experience thirty years after his childhood.*

The family jewels

'As a young boy in the 1940s, I remember the 'Sally Walkers' pub at the entrance to Newport Docks but never realised its personal significance. Years later, I worked for the company that demolished the pub, still ignorant of any family ties. It was only later that I found that my great great grandmother had run Sally Walkers. Her husband was a sea captain and was away for long stretches at a

An example of the famous 'Bill Sticker' advertising campaign for Draught Bass,
Britain's favourite draught ale

time, returning to much celebration and bearing gifts and more from far off countries around the world.

If I had known when we demolished the pub that my great, great grandfather had lived there I'd have paid more attention to what was hidden under the floors. He must have hidden his fortune somewhere!

As a small boy during the Second World War, I can remember the air raids over Newport. We had a bomb shelter joined to the side of our house. When the siren went off, mum took me in to the shelter. Dad never came with us. He used to say 'If the bomb's going to land on us it'll kill us all so I'll carry on with my dinner.' And he did!'

Mike Guy lives in Dorset

A child's war in Swanage

'My earliest recollections of the war are of the Battle of Britain being fought in the skies over Swanage. At first, these encounters seemed very exciting to a five-year-old. However, after spending night after night in a Morrison Shelter with my mother and grandmother, I realised that this was not a game and that these aeroplanes and their pilots were trying to destroy our homes and our way of life.

During the first year of the war my father and my uncle became Home Guards. Later they were both called up; my father served with the Royal Engineers and my uncle joined the Royal Navy. Sadly my uncle was killed whilst on active service on D Day, whilst landing troops on the Normandy Beaches from his landing craft.

In the early days of the war my family looked after two evacuees, but these two individuals became so home sick that they returned to Southampton to be with their own families. I often wondered if they survived the bombing. Little did I know then that our small town would have more than its fair share of German bombs.

It was hard to understand why such a small seaside town as Swanage should have been bombed as much as it was. Apart from the radar station at Worth Matravers, and until the Americans were stationed there, there was nothing of strategic value in the town. Situated on the south coast, we were the victims of hit and run raids.

By 21st January 1944 air raid alerts in Swanage had totalled 929 compared to 700 in London.

During 1943 my pals and I had made friends with a crew of artillerymen, who were manning a Bofors ack-ack gun at Belle Vue, which was my uncle's farm. The gunners supplied us with steaming hot tea and allowed my friends and I to raise and lower the gun's barrel. Whilst doing this I chipped one of my front teeth, a reminder to this day of that Bofors gun. December 1943 saw the arrival in Swanage of our American cousins, and countless goodies that I had never seen before. It was a good Christmas that year with parcels from America filled with sweets, candy bars, toothpaste, soap, and letters from American children of our own age. The parcels were distributed to the children in Burt's Corner House, now the White Horse Inn.

The Americans were very kind to all us youngsters and soon they had supplied us with all manner of things. They gave us mess tins, steel helmets, bullet bandoliers (no bullets!), small picks and shovels. We were ready to go to war; our hideouts were in and around the quarries that abounded around my uncle's farm. At that time we gave little thought that our new found friends who were billeted in all the large hotels in Swanage would soon be in action in France and Germany. The Americans that had become

US soldiers in the weeks leading up to D-Day

our friends, were part of the 5th U.S. Corps 1st Division. On D-Day they were to lead the assault on Omaha Beach, which proved to be the bloodiest assault beach of the entire operation.

Before the invasion of mainland Europe there was a need to carry out mock invasions. The main exercise took place on the 18th April 1944 at Studland, Dorset. I remember this well because my mother and I were on our way to visit my grandmother at Parkstone. When we arrived at Swanage railway station a porter informed us that we could not travel that day because the trains had been cancelled.

We later learned that the Royal Train was in the station, and that H.M. King George VI accompanied by Prime Minister Winston Churchill and General Sir Bernard Montgomery had arrived to witness the exercise 'Smash Assault' at Studland. General Dwight D Eisenhower and his staff later joined them. They watched the exercise from a concrete bunker named Fort Henry.

June 6th 1944 and D Day had arrived. My mother was taking me to school; countless aircraft towing gliders were passing overhead on their way to France. When we looked out into Swanage Bay all we could see was an armada of ships of all descriptions ready to cross the channel, taking our troops and our American friends across the channel to assault the Normandy Beaches.

The assault on Omaha Beach took its toll and there were many casualties. The people of Swanage had lost many friends. The town, which had bustled with thousands of troops, reverted back to the quiet seaside town it was.

On looking back, time has dimmed the horrors of the war, but I have always been grateful that I was born in Swanage and to have spent my childhood during such momentous times in such a lovely part of the country.'

Les Shergold grew up in London

Scouts and jellied eels

'At the age of eight I joined the cubs, the 10th Fulham. One Sunday each month we went on church parade in the morning and an outing in the afternoon; no church parade, no outing. In 1939 we went to camp on the Isle of Wight for a fortnight. The fare by train and ferry cost £1-1s-0d; we saved all year for the annual camp. When we returned to the mainland my parents met the ferry at Lymington and we headed off towards Hereford to stay with my grandparents. I stayed on after my parents returned to London and while I was there, war was declared. On that day, in deepest Herefordshire I planned to go for a walk along the river with three friends that I had made. Grandmother was horrified. 'You are not going down by the river,' she said gravely 'the Germans might come up it!' She was not joking.

I stayed on in Hereford and was not allowed to listen to the radio as London was being bombed.

Soon afterwards my parents left London and moved down to Hereford. At the same time my father was called up and joined the RAF. I stayed in Hereford until the end of the war.

During this time, I had one interesting encounter whilst at an Army Cadet camp. I had recently joined and as I didn't have a cadet uniform I was allowed to wear my scout uniform. After a few days at camp a cadet officer called me into his tent and told me that I had been invited out to tea at Eastnor Castle. This puzzled me particularly when he told me that I would be going alone. It transpired that I was being entertained by Lord Somers, the then 'Chief Scout!' He had apparently enquired after me when he saw me at the camp in my scout uniform.

After the war I returned to London with my mother and life returned more or less to normality. I knew that I was back home when I caught the smell of the Pie and Eel shop in Hammersmith. The aroma of that place was out of this world. People would take their basins to get some mushy peas, jellied eels or meat pies. Dad sometimes cycled to the shop, a distance of about two miles each way to buy pies for our tea. Wrapped in newspaper, they were still piping hot when he returned home; they tasted lovely!'

*Roy Kenny recalls **The West Country** during the war*

Dorniers and Alcohol

'I was born in Bristol. I think we learned to cope with death at an early age even if we didn't quite understand it. For example, at school the register would be called and there would be thirty-six in the class. A week later, only thirty-two. A further week on, only twenty-nine. Eventually, I arrived at school one morning and Adolf had interfered with my education—the school was a pile of rubble, having been bombed overnight. This happened three times and by the time I went on to Grammar school I had been to fifteen different schools in the space of six years!

Of course, aircraft were being shot down all the time and it used to be a race between the kids, the police and the military to get there first. We kids were looking for souvenirs. I always envied a friend who had collected the tail fin of a Dornier 17 and had it proudly displayed in his bedroom! It took up half the wall.

I was evacuated from Bristol to Bude, in 1944. There was a large contingent of US soldiers based there, both black and white. The theory was that they should never be allowed in town together. This worked quite well until one night something went wrong and both groups were in town together. It was a bloody night, with quite a few stabbings and fights—my first contact with racial prejudice. And they were supposed to be on our side! If you have friends like them you did not need any enemies! However, we did have a terrible tragedy that turned out to be a kid's delight and a customs officer's nightmare. One night, an American ship was torpedoed off the coast. I went down to the beach in the morning as usual and lo and behold, there were tins of peanuts, sweets, fruit etc. washed in on the tide line. We had not seen this stuff for years! Also wines and spirits, which is where the Customs come in. They set up a post to try and catch the grown ups that were taking the stuff away. So the grown ups paid us kids to grab the stuff for them, because there was also plenty of tobacco and cigarettes coming in. So began and ended my life of crime in the space of one month, when supplies, as it were, dried up. Trouble is that the aftermath also caused a lot of tragedy to the local bird population; what followed the palatable delicacies was oil! We spent much of our time cleaning birds that were still alive or actually taking them home to look after them. In fact, we had a pet guillemot (a sort of penguin-like creature) that used to wander around the house as if he owned it! We eventually returned him to the wild when the oil stopped coming in with the tide and he left us none the worse for his adventure!'

Gordon Carter *lived in* **London** *throughout the war*

Head choirboy collects apples

'My family was very poor as my father had been badly wounded in World War One and was disabled for the remainder of his life. I joined the church choir and as most of my friends were evacuated during the war, I was in great demand as a soloist at weddings and sadly but inevitably, many funerals. I travelled all over London singing at society weddings. I belonged to a choir that was set up to sing at St Pauls and Westminster Abbey. After one service, several of us were invited to tea with the Lord Mayor of London; we sang for him and he thanked us for being so brave and keeping up people's morale. I was very excited about my final service at Westminster Abbey; I was Head Boy and Princess Elizabeth, our future Queen, was in the congregation. The church magazine reported that my face was as red as my cassock!

Although my singing life was sometimes glamorous, the family was still struggling to make ends meet. Two regular incidents stick in my mind.

My mother sometimes allowed me to buy one penny's worth of broken biscuits; the sales lady knew me and she would usually pick out my favourite bits!

The other memory took place every autumn. After a windy night, my father would wake me and we walked together to the local park, a distance of about a mile. We waited impatiently until the park keeper arrived to unlock the gates at 6am at which time we entered the park and I ran from fruit tree to fruit tree collecting the windfalls. For the next ten days or so we feasted on stewed pears and apple pies; it wasn't so bad being poor!'

Joan Donnelly *in* **Manchester** *was born in 1938 and her early memories are of the war years.*

The sky at night

'Our father was in the 8th Army which was known as 'Monty's Lot.' My sister and I saw very little of him during those early years so we were brought up by our mother. Life must have been very hard. As young as I was I can clearly remember the friendly neighbours and how everyone pulled together and even managed to laugh quite a lot. I can vividly remember one night during the war being taken from my warm bed when the siren went off. My sister was about three years old at the time and as she was being carried to the shelter she looked up the stars in the clear night sky. She began to sing 'The stars at night are big and bright, deep in the heart of Texas . . .' Even through all the ugliness of war, the stars still shine bright.

From time to time a group of mothers would take their children and others up to Bootal Woods. They pushed old prams and wheelbarrows and collected logs and twigs to keep the fires burning—coal was in very short supply.

Of course, the really happy time was when the war was over and we had a street party. The grown-ups managed to come up with quite a good spread for us children. My mother gave me, my sister and my cousin Georgie a dining room chair each to sit on to listen to the band. A man in the band thought they were for the band to use and took them away. I was a bit put out about that!'

*John Williams, in **Dorset**, was a farmer and recalls the war years on the farm*

The Home Guard

'As farming was a reserved occupation, I was never called up. I did, though, join the Home Guard. We started off, in 1940 I think it was, with two guns between thirty of us. The rest of us practised with pitchforks, broom handles and twelve-bore shotguns. It was just like 'Dad's Army' only worse, I reckon. We had to stay up on the cliff all night between Swanage and Lulworth, looking out on the black English Channel, keeping watch for an invasion. If Hitler's army had come over then, they'd have walked straight in. I wouldn't have been hanging around on the cliff with my twelve-bore, that's for sure.

One day the platoon had a practice march from Swanage to Kingston and back, about five miles each way. When we arrived in Kingston, tired and thirsty, we all marched straight in to the pub for a quick drink before starting the return journey. All, that is, with the exception of Old Bill, an ex World War One veteran and a man who enjoyed a drink or two.

'Aren't you coming in for a pint?' I asked, somewhat surprised that he wasn't at the front of the queue at the bar.

'No,' came the immediate response, 'Bugger the marchin' an' bugger the quick drink. I'm goin' to catch the bus back to Swanage and have several pints in the Anchor while you're all marchin' back down the 'ill.'

You couldn't really argue with that, though our CO wasn't very impressed!

We had a field on the farm which became known as Shellhole. This field in particular was heavily bombed during the war. The field adjoined what was then a private house called Leeson. This was one of the locations in which the development of radar took place and the Germans bombed it several times. Most of the shells fell in Shellhole, though. Also, I can remember several times when German bombers were returning from raids in the Midlands and had a few bombs left. They dropped them on the last piece of British soil before they crossed the channel so coastal farms like ours were bombed indiscriminately. I can also remember one day I was standing on a straw-rick when a German Stuka came over. He strafed the farmyard and we had to jump off of the rick as the

Pest Control

bullets cut a line through the farmyard. It was the nearest I came to seeing action in the war, thank God.

I met the woman who became my wife during the war. I was working on the farm and she came round to gas the rabbits and badgers that were damaging the wheat crop. She was in the Land Army. We weren't used to seeing attractive young women on the farm and as soon as I saw her I knew she was the one for me. It took me a long time to win her over but we did finally get together and married in 1951.'

Eileen Kelly also joined the Land Army

The sting

'My dreams of becoming a Wren were shattered when I got my call-up papers. They had enough Wrens so I was offered factory work, the fire service or the Land Army. I had always wanted to live in the country so I opted for the Land Army and work on the farm.

Before I left Birmingham the city was bombed every night for six weeks with one night off—the night that Coventry was flat-tened. The Germans always dropped firebombs first, which lit up the city then the high explosive bombs followed. My Dad was the local air-raid warden and he had to go out with his stirrup pump and help to put out the fires. Every morning there were smoking gaps where houses had once stood. Friends and colleagues were killed or called up and when my turn came to leave, it was with mixed emotions that I set off for the country. After several months of being sent to work on different farms as the need arose, I was offered a permanent position on a farm in Warwickshire. Those were great days and I learned to milk the cows, feed the animals, drive the horse drawn implements and also the tractor. I made hay and harvested corn. It was idyllic and the war seemed a long way away. Until you looked over the hedge and saw the American Army camp full of young exuberant GIs who seemed to have noth-ing better to do than to watch me working in the fields, or so it seemed to me at the time. One particular sunny day I remember I was sitting on a hay-turner, being pulled by a single horse. All I had to do was drive the horse round and round the field. Watched by our local GIs, I was casually progressing round the field when suddenly, the horse was stung on the rear by a wasp. The startled horse took off at full pelt. All I had was an iron seat on the machine and the reins to try and control the excited horse. I think we did three laps of the field before we came to a halt much to the amusement of my audience!

Land Army girls 'off duty'

I returned to Birmingham towards the end of the war and found it more depressing than I had remembered it. I went back to office work where everyone seemed to be eating all day and I had no appetite. My dad was dying, I felt shut in and when the war finally finished the shortages of food and everything else was making life very grim. The winter of 1947 was particularly severe with snow from January until April and we couldn't get any coal to heat the house. The doctor gave us a medical note to get coal for my dad but the coal never came. We had to sit in the kitchen at the gas oven to keep warm and just wrap dad in blankets with hot water bottles around him. Winter finally passed and my dad died the following August. I couldn't leave my mother so I was stuck with my office work. After a time I moved to Foster Brothers' head office. This was a men's outfitters with branches all over the country. We kept the books, working in a Dickensian office called 'The Counting House,' where we sat on high backless stools at huge tables. The books were, in fact, very large ledgers, which had to balance every month. Everything was totted up in our heads and added across and down the page. They had to balance to the nearest penny and if they were out, the missing pennies had to be found. We checked each other's additions and just had to stay on until the books balanced—sometimes this was late in to the night.'

Eileen Kelly's brother Dennis, a wartime dispatch rider

Brian King *grew up in* Wales

Lobelias and Furry Feet

'Looking back, all appears a drab sepia colour against modern technicolor. As children we were oblivious to the meaning of those military maps in the newspapers regaling yet another disaster; we simply drew in like mother's milk the invisible camaraderie of the moment. I should say that it was the Second World War to which I was oblivious at that time, in a military sense, that coloured most vividly the day to day existence. People then, as opposed to now, had a greater dynamism. I have now a suspicion that they used time better, whether it was by their own discovery or simply the constraints of war. In one month during the blitz, Londoners were averaging two hundred bombers a night—and they still kept planting their lobelias!

The 1940s introduced me to the cinema. The streets were darkened by the wartime blackout, it was dark in the cinema, surely it was divine providence that no new Jack the Ripper emerged.

My father had been born in 1880 and could hardly read and write his name when he died. He had to leave the little farm in County Tipperary in his early teens and catch the cattle boat to Wales to the valleys and their coalmines. Here he met my mother. By the time I was growing up, she was worn out with eleven kids, a Welsh terrier, and a greyhound—all having to be fed and administered to. She took in washing over at the 'Big House,' the house of the doctor of medicine and his family. I shall never forget until my dying day the almost daily admonition during World War Two to 'Eat bread with it.' Even if a little luxury came our way it was quickly swamped by 'Eat more bread with it.' Rich we were not!

The Post Office made three deliveries a day, and we looked forward to receiving two dead rabbits with our address wrapped round their furry waists, sent by my brother who worked for the Forestry Commission in west Wales. It was a chance to have a bowl of vegetable soup with a rabbit's leg sticking out of it.

Sometimes, my mother with mock seriousness told me to inspect my feet before I climbed in to bed to see if they were becoming webbed like a duck or clawed like a chicken because of all the American powdered egg I was eating. Spam was another American product that was served to us in many varied ways.

At Secondary Modern School we never had a soccer ball or cricket bat in the school for our use. Rugby was never played there. All we had, two years after the end of the war, was a tennis ball owned by one or other of the boys. It was the poorest schooling imaginable. The war had made standards lax, and they carried on after the war when rationing of food did not end for many years. I was born, we all were, in the wrong place at the wrong time. One looks back at the teachers and it is difficult not to castigate them.

My eyesight, hearing and speech were not all that good, and I well remember my parents sleeping out in the kitchen of the modest terraced house. They were out to the world when I answered the door and found that it was the insurance agent I had specifically asked to call. I showed him into the front room, then always called the parlour, and he explained various policies to me. After about twenty minutes he suggested that he call back next week by which time I would have made a choice of policy I wanted. I agreed to this and he departed. I was twelve years old and I wanted an insurance policy. So you can just imagine how much love and security I was getting in that family!'

Mrs Kennard recalls here teenage years in the North East

A British Teenager 1940s Style

'As I was born in 1930 and so all my teenage years were in the '40s, I must be considered to be the typical example of the breed!

My home was in Sunderland, the largest county borough in England and at that time, the biggest shipbuilding town in the world. The chief employers of labour in my hometown were the shipyards, engine works, and the coalmines. During the '20s and '30s, in common with most of the rest of the world, we had suffered from the trade recession and the unemployment rate in our area was very high. The outbreak of war changed that situation and, as my generation reached school leaving age, there were jobs to spare.

I started at the local Grammar School in September 1941. So, unlike the majority of my contemporaries, I was not expected to leave school at the age of fourteen but to continue in education for at least a further two years and sit the School Certificate Examination. Afterwards I would have the choice of leaving school to enter the Civil Service, a commercial office or some similar job, or remaining at school for a further two years to study for the Higher School Certificate. Gaining H.S.C. meant it was possible to go on to college or university. Only a small proportion of young people did this; those going to university were still predominantly the offspring of the more wealthy members of the community.

I continued in education and eventually qualified as a teacher. Inevitably, most of my later teens were spent in the penury of student life so, in that sense I am less typical of my generation. Many of my friends who were working were earning comparatively good wages in the post war years. Many of the boys in our group became apprentices in the shipbuilding or engineering trades and most joined the Merchant Navy at the age of eighteen. National Service was compulsory for all young men at this time and they were required to join the armed services for eighteen months at the age of eighteen, or if they were apprentices, when their apprenticeship ended at twenty-one. Those joining the Merchant Navy were deemed to have fulfilled this obligation and many found that preferable to the army. A number of young men I knew remained in the navy, did in-service training, and built a very good career. Courses of Further Study were freely available to boys wanting technical training, many at our local Technical School and College. Opportunities for girls to study were more limited though office skills were taught at evening classes.

The outbreak of war in 1939 had brought many restrictions for everyone and these continued to some degree right through the '40s. My father had been injured in a mining accident during the 1914-18 war and had found it impossible to find work during the depression. When the war came he was unfit for military service but was very soon trained in the skills needed for ship repair work. As a consequence our standard of living rose but rationing then restricted us!

It seemed as though everything was rationed, or in short supply, or quite simply totally unobtainable. For mothers trying to provide for a growing family it must have been a nightmare and teenagers like me needing ingredients for our cookery classes can only have added to the problems. One soon learned to be a reasonable cook when the precious food ration was at stake. By the time I was sixteen and preparing for domestic science exams there was a small amount of rationed food available for our use, but in the early years, when we were more likely to make mistakes, it was the family food ration that suffered.

One could choose to forgo the family egg ration and have an allocation of corn for poultry food. We had an allotment garden and kept half a dozen chickens. We did not give up the egg ration but fed the hens on table scraps collected round the other members of the family and food grown on the allotment. Nominally the hens were going to augment the meat ration but those birds were my personal friends and I never could bring myself to eat them! The allotment was a boon as it kept us in fresh vegetables at a time when they were hard to get and fruit was almost unobtainable except for a short period in the Autumn when English apples, pears and plums were ripe. Shipping space could not be spared for fruit and throughout the war years oranges were only for young children under five; we did not even see bananas and the more exotic fruits. I think there were people who fared better. Venison was not subject to rationing nor pheasant or grouse—provided one had access to it. Most people got by on the ration and we were surprisingly healthy. I have a sweet tooth so, like most youngsters, I found 2oz of sweets a week a bit hard to bear. Great was the joy when we received a parcel from my aunt in Canada with fruit drops, chocolate, chewing gum and such goodies. She would also send dried fruit, fruitcake, toilet-soap and for me best of all, items of clothing.

Clothes were rationed from 1940 on a kind of points system. Each person had a set number of coupons to last six months and every garment had a value. We had between thirty-two and forty coupons and even towels, sheets and knitting wool had a value. A pair of shoes needed five coupons, a skirt seven, and a coat twelve.

During the early '40s fashion was about saving fabric as you may imagine. The garments in the shops were cut with the idea of saving every scrap of fabric. Skirts were short and slim and jackets very fitted. In the late '40s, when the fashion industry was again operating without constraints we saw skirts dip to mid calf length and the full circle skirt also became fashionable. Hats went crazy with swathes of chiffon tied under the chin. Men were wearing the Edwardian look which had them dubbed Teddy Boys and clothes altogether were more lavish. I'm afraid I did not take any great part in the fashion scene. As a schoolgirl and then a student my budget was limited and I had to have practical clothing for college and for my leisure interests. At that time teachers—and even aspiring teachers—were expected to dress quite formally in smart suits or dresses. To dress in casual clothing would have been frowned on by the headteacher and then goodbye to any prospect of promotion.

Leisure time as a teenager was spent in a variety of ways with some variation according to age and one's interests. A higher percentage of young people attended some form of worship than is the case today, and there were many church based activities in which we took part.

As a thirteen to fourteen-year-old I was a member of the school Guide Company and stayed after school for meetings. This kept my mother happy as it meant I did not need to go out after dark to go to a Guide meeting. At the time we had blackout restrictions which were very strictly enforced because of the danger of air raids. I was a member of the church youth group, which met in the clergy-house and as this was only a few hundred yards from home my mother saw no problem in me going there.

Though we lived within walking distance of lovely beaches and cliffs they were closed to everyone and barricaded with barbed wire and reinforced concrete. One of the great joys of the years just after the war was being able to walk the cliffs freely and enjoy the beach and the sea.

It was as a guide that I was able to have my first 'grown-up' holiday. We often went on hikes in the country near Sunderland, taking the bus for a short distance to get out of town and then spending the rest of the day walking in lanes or along the riverbank. In the early months of 1943 our Guider suggested that we might like to go Youth Hostelling, walking in Northumberland and sleeping at night in a different hostel each night. We went by bus to Hexham, a market town about thirty miles from home, and from there followed a circular route, walking between ten and fifteen miles each day and returning to Hexham after five days. Not very exciting by the standards of today but a great adventure for me. It was not until five years later that I had the thrill of visiting London, and again it was through my involvement with the Guide movement. It was the twenty-fifth anniversary of the Rangers and a rally and parade were planned for a Spring weekend. As accommodation was hard to get in London, especially at a price young people would be able to afford, it was decided to make the deep air-raid shelters available to us. These were tunnels which had been dug pre-war with a view to extending the underground train system and they were used all through the war as shelters against the blitz. They had been equipped with very utilitarian bunks and at the height of the bombing some Londoners slept there for weeks on end. There were very basic toilet facilities and areas where hot drinks could be prepared but they were very deep underground and the stairs had to be climbed as the escalators had not been fitted. It was another great adventure for us. We held a rally and performed a pageant on the Saturday evening in the Albert Hall, slept in the shelters and on the Sunday there was a great parade in Hyde Park at which Princess Elizabeth took the salute. On the great day the sun was shining and we were instructed to wear only our white shirts and navy skirts (I was a Sea Ranger) together with our hats.

We wore the flat caps issued to Wrens and bought at the Army Surplus store, and we carried navy blue Jerkins of the kind issued to Air Raid Wardens, again from the surplus store as they did not require clothing coupons. All was fine until it began to rain and we put on those navy jerkins. The dye soon washed out and into our smart white shirts. It took more than a drop of rain to dampen our spirits though. After the parade our group of about sixteen girls, looking like drowned rats I must admit, adjourned to the Hyde Park Hotel, an extremely up-market place, and ordered tea and cream cakes. To our amazement the very generous cakes were filled with lashings of fresh cream! We had not seen such luxury since 1939 but it seemed not everyone was in the same position; some were more equal than others! Back home on the night train from King's Cross and so ended that adventure.'

*Mr Spencer from **Blackpool** spent his early years in Lytham St Annes*

Life in the country

'One of my earliest memories was seeing King George VI and his mother, Queen Mary parade down Blackpool's Church Street in an open horse-drawn carriage. As war broke out both of my parents joined the forces and I moved to Catforth to live with my grandparents. The country school that I attended was very different from the one that I'd been used to. We had Gardening lessons and Woodworking classes at Woodplumpton Tec. As the war progressed, the local farmers would come and take us lads over eleven years old to work on the farms. We did stone picking, potato planting, weeding and picking Turnips and Mangels amongst other things. At autumn time we helped with the harvest. A threshing machine would arrive at the farm and 'thrash' the corn from the straw, or chaff. We bagged up the chaff, which was used for bedding for the cows. In winter we went 'Turnip snagging'—harvesting them.

My grandparents' house was fairly new. However, there was no gas, no electricity and no running water. Drinking water was from a hand pump in the yard which was shared with next door. The fire was coal with a hot-water boiler on one side and an oven on the other. Once a week my grandmother baked bread and enormous great muffins. All the cooking was done on the fire or paraffin stove and on Saturdays we took turns to churn the butter. We had no radio, no TV and used an oil lamp in the centre of the table for light in the dark evenings.'

Stan Shurey grew up in Hounslow

Bombs and Biscuit tins

'During the war, a number of bombs dropped around the house with unpleasant but not disastrous consequences. One day an incendiary bomb landed on the path at the side of the house. Mum pushed me out of the front door to 'put it out.' I saw the glow within a large concrete slab that we had placed on the corner of the path to stop people taking a short cut across our front flowerbed. Knowing that the bomb was likely to 'go up' I rushed back indoors. Almost immediately we heard a loud 'bang,' then a splintering of glass as parts of the concrete slab crashed through the bathroom window. I had a lucky escape there!

One evening we 'retired' to our Anderson shelter when the siren sounded. I pulled the wooden top of our old mangle across the top of the shelter. As I lay on my bunk, there was an enormous 'bang'; a German bomb dropped near the house. The top of the mangle hit me, I fell off of the bunk on to my mother who was knitting at the time and my throat became impaled on one of her knitting needles. I pulled it out without any apparent damage, although mum complained that she had dropped a few stitches!

After the war, I spent a lovely summer holiday camping near Littlehampton with my future wife. Her mother wouldn't allow us to go on our own, so we had her cousin for company. At that time, everyone on the campsite cooked using a paraffin Primus stove and fried eggs and bacon were the staple diet. I found a square Smith's Crisps tin and decided to cook a special Sunday lunch for the three of us. We went off to Woolworth's and bought a 6d baking tin, then to the butcher to purchase a small leg of lamb and some potatoes. Back at the campsite, I dug a hole slightly bigger than the Smith's tin, put the Primus stove in it with a brick on either side. The Smith's crisp tin sat on this with the baking tin containing the lamb and potatoes inside. The lid sealed the Smith's 'oven.' I lit the

Primus and the tin began to heat up. Soon, the unusual aroma of roasting lamb wafted across the campsite carried by the breeze. Campers came over to see what we were doing and I was beginning to worry that we would have a dinner for three feeding twenty people. I hoped for a miracle! That came in an unusual way. The lamb cooked very slowly, taking over six hours to cook through. By this time our new friends had dispersed back to their own tents and the smell of bacon and eggs filled the air, competing with our own roasting lamb. Sunday lunchtime came and went and it was a hungry trio that eventually tucked in to roast lamb for their late afternoon meal.'

Eileen Wills lived in Surrey

Limited resources

'Prior to the war my father had worked at the Army and Navy Stores in Victoria which necessitated him cycling some ten miles each way every day. When war broke out he transferred to a factory helping to produce munitions. Perversely, this resulted in him working locally and earning better pay, which made things a little easier financially. Even so, my mother still checked to see when the gasman was coming along the road. He would come to empty the gas meter, which usually resulted in a refund, something that was all-important to many households at the time.

We had electricity, but only one wall socket that I can remember, which provided the power to the radio (previously this was powered by an enormous battery, that had to be taken to the radio shop to be recharged). As a young teenager it was a great thrill to tune the radio to Radio Luxembourg in the evenings despite the erratic signal and endless interference!

The other main electric appliance, the iron, was plugged in to the ceiling light socket—I shudder to think of it now.

Apart from all the obvious effects of the war—bombs, death, air raid shelters, blackouts, V1 and V2 rockets—I suppose the shortage that had the most effect on my young life was sweets. Even though one's parents would give up their sweet ration coupons to the children, sweets were in very short supply. This continued almost until the end of the decade, several years after the war had ended. My mother often bought jelly tablets and broke them up as extra sweets for us children.

Another shortage at the time was paper—paper to draw on. The paper available was of awful quality (not a pure white or cream and it had black/brown specks in it). To help us out, my mother would carefully unwrap the large sheets of white paper which covered the greaseproof paper protecting the weekend joint of meat. When flattened out, this paper was ideal for drawing.

Speaking of weekend joints, however short money was, we still managed to have a roast lunch on Sundays (cold for Monday, of course). One of us children would be sent to the local grocer's on a Monday, with a cup, to purchase some mustard pickle (I don't know how this was sold, by weight or by the cup.) One of our mid-week meals would be to go to the local Co-op and buy 'Bits and Pieces'—off cuts of ham and bacon, which mother would put into a pie. Then we would call at the baker's to buy stale cakes, which were always cheaper.

I started work in 1947, at the age of fourteen, with a film company in London. My starting salary was £2 per week. After paying 5/- a week for fares, buying lunches and giving mother something for my keep, there wasn't a lot left! In the post war period when most things were still hard to come by (or very expensive) I remember how hard it was to obtain fresh stationery from the person in charge. We had to produce a worn out piece of carbon paper or typewriter ribbon before being allowed a replacement!

Typewriters at the time were of the 'steam' variety (i.e. manual) rather than electric. One machine that I used had a twenty-four inch carriage to cope with accounting schedules. Imagine pushing the carriage return back after every line on that one!'

Arthur Featherstone worked as a teenager
at a mill when the war began

Bugs and White Feathers

'There is a lot said today about food poisoning. Whilst I worked at the mill, mum spent Sunday morning baking pies and tarts for our dinners at work the following week. The pies were of beef and very tasty. In the rest room at the mill we had an old range with an oven.

This served two purposes—it kept the room warm and provided the means for us to heat our food. Come Friday, the pies were five days old and with no refrigeration, they had been kept cool in a meat-safe. These pies were heated through for about a quarter of an hour before our break. They were only just warmed through and tasted delicious—I can never remember anyone going down with food poisoning; there's a lesson there somewhere.

At this time, all available men were being called to the colours and I knew it would not be long before it would be my turn. This didn't particularly worry me, but it did worry mum and dad. I knew dad was very bitter about the whole affair; he thought that the First World War was enough for any family. He had spent time in the trenches and was dead against me going to fight. So much so, that when Bert, a family friend came to visit, dad asked him to persuade me to sign up for a course which would set me up for a 'reserved occupation.' With mum, dad and Bert all persuading me, I agreed to apply for a course as a fitter which would lead to a job in a government research centre.

In early 1941, I reported to Redbridge Government Training Centre near Southampton and began the course. The city had been heavily bombed before I arrived but no bombing occurred while I was there. I settled in to the course and generally enjoyed learning the new skills. However, as the weeks went by it became increasingly apparent that we people at the Centre were looked upon by the majority of the rest of society as something that had crawled out of dung! I found this hard to swallow, but in my soul of souls I had to agree with them. We were 'dodgers,' nothing more, nothing less. The last straw came when we finished our shift one afternoon and walked out on to the street to find several ladies handing out white feathers (I can understand their feelings as most of them had men folk in the services). This really got to me. So much so that when I went in the following day I spoke about it to my mate, a lad called Jimmy Angel, the son of the Southampton Football Club manager. I told him that I'd had enough and was going to sign up for the RAF. As I expected, Jimmy agreed to join me.

That afternoon we went to the Recruitment Office and were eagerly accepted in to the RAF Volunteer Reserve. We had a medical (which basically proved that we were breathing, could see a bus coming and hear a bomb exploding), signed some papers and we were in. Next, we were issued with railway tickets for Penarth in

South Wales where we attended our 'Attestation Ceremony.' This was carried out en masse, at the end of which we were all sworn in, given one shilling and a number—mine was 1299514. That was it, we were in and all we had to do was wait for the call to start our training.

Jimmy and I travelled back to Southampton the next day and reported back to the Training Centre. When we told the foreman what we had done he took us to the manager's office where we were almost treated as criminals. Accused of wasting the government's time and money, the manager even tried to stop us from leaving. He 'phoned the Recruitment Office but to no avail. They told him that as volunteers, we had to be accepted. He could have stopped us being called-up whilst on the course, but not now that we had volunteered.

So that's how I joined the RAF against the wishes of my family and my manager! Thankfully, unlike many of my comrades, I lived to tell the tale.'

Barbara Staton trained as a nurse in *Nottingham*

Antibiotics

'I commenced my nursing training in 1940. The nurses' home, in which every nurse was supposed to live, was full at the time and several of us were housed on the Ropewalk. On May 9th and 10th of the following year, Nottingham was extensively bombed. I was eighteen years old at the time and on the evening of the 9th I went with a group of friends to the Palais. We left at about 10pm and on the way home to the Ropewalk, called at a fish and chip shop on Shakespeare St. Hours later it was flattened.

Two days previously two of the hospital wards had been cleared for spring cleaning—what a God send! All day staff were called at 5-30am on the morning of the 10th and were on duty for many hours. The two wards were quickly filled with the casualties and camp beds were put up in most of the other wards. We saw some horrendous sights but worked throughout the day and in to the night without any breaks. Nobody grumbled; it was accepted.

As the war progressed we regularly received troop trains carrying casualties from several nations—English, German, Russian and many others. Several wards in the hospital were reserved for them. I was on one such ward when the first treatment of penicillin was administered—the results were truly miraculous!'

Peter Denzil Edwards witnessed an interesting episode from WWII in Wales

The Day They Bombed the Railway

'During the Second World War, I was living at home on a farm on the Preseli Mountains in Pembrokeshire. A quiet railway line, which had closed except for one goods train a day, passed through our farm.

One day in 1942, two high ranking Royal Air Force officers called at our home, and told my father that our family would have to move out for two days. When he asked why, he was told it was top secret and no questions to be asked, as there was a war on. When he asked about the milking times for the cows, he was told he would be able to go back for those specified times.

On the first day appointed, everyone within a mile distance had to clear out. We noticed that on the railway embankment, some-one or other had placed a huge cross, made of white material that could be seen from a long distance. During the morning, a wave of Typhoon fighter-bombers swept in from the south-east at ter-rific speed and dropped their bombs, one under each wing, onto the railway track where the white cross was situated. Surprisingly, there were no explosions, so they must have been using dummy bombs.

The following day, the Typhoon fighter-bombers again flew in low from the south-east and dropped their bombs. This time, however, they used high explosive bombs and the railway and embankment was blown to smithereens.

Almost immediately, a gang of workmen appeared and went in to repair the damage done to the railway. Within forty-eight hours, the goods train was able to travel past as normal!

The reason for this experiment was as follows:

The RAF had been bombing railway lines in northern France for some time but were unable to have an accurate account of the damage they had caused. They knew that they had disrupted the railways, but they were fairly sure that the Germans were able to repair the damage in a very short time. If this was true, it did not warrant the RAF risking the loss of life and planes on these missions. So they decided to see for themselves how soon the railways could be made usable again. This was the background to the scenes played out in front of us in rural Pembrokeshire. It clearly had results. After this experiment, the bombing of railways in northern France was reviewed and subsequently scaled back.'

John Parsons left school and started work in **London**

My Free Pass

'I hope that Keith survived the war. He had received his call-up papers and was about to enter the Army. The company, of course, had no option other than to release him and advertise for a replacement. This appeared in the Kentish Mercury just at the right time, as I had left school and was looking for a position. After an interview with the General Manager, it was left to Keith to show me over the place and he was impressed with my typing skills, which resulted in my getting the job there and then. A week or so later Keith left to go to the war. His misfortune was my good luck.

So I commenced my time as a Production Assistant with Downtons who, at that time, were the big name in film and theatre advertising. My luck was certainly in, as I was put to work with a man who apart from being my boss, later became a very good friend. Reg Hillier controlled the prestige account in the firm; all the advertising for the Rank Group, which meant that before long I had a free pass to all the Odeon Cinemas. This was a great perk for a 'lad about town.' I soon found that I was never short of girlfriends.

By November 1944 I was well into the job. Most Saturday mornings I would go into the office for a couple of hours to finalise the last bits and pieces for the advertisements due to appear in the Sunday papers (including Reynolds News, The Sunday Dispatch and others which are now defunct). I would then make my way home arriving at New Cross Gate Station around half past midday. Ruth, about my age and working in the art department, was a regular enjoyer of my free pass and as both of us had nothing special on that afternoon we decided to see the film at the Odeon Leicester Square (Abbot and Costello in 'In Society'). Telephones in private houses being virtually non-existent prevented me from letting anyone know what I was doing. Apart from which young lads have always been uncaring to one's parents' concerns. So after seeing the film, having a spot of tea in Joe Lyons and then taking Ruth home to Bromley, it was well after 10pm when I arrived back at New Cross Station, the Gate Station being closed for some reason or other.

Making my way through the back street to Clifton Rise, I missed the kerfuffle that was taking place along New Cross Road, but as soon as I entered the house I was made aware of the situation. My Mother was beside herself with grief. Having expected me home about the time that the V2 fell and as the hours passed without word, she assumed the worst and had gone to the Casualty Clearing Station to look for me. Some of the victims were badly mutilated and not easily recognisable, my Mother unfortunately was convinced that one lad was me and so my name was added to the casualty list. As you may well guess, Mother's grief soon turned to anger as she lambasted me for not letting her know what I had been up to.

The following morning I spent almost two hours convincing the authorities that my name should be removed from their records. Ever since I have had a soft spot for the Odeon Leicester Square, its free pass may well have saved my life!'

Gil Haines also started his working life during the war

The Black Market

'A year before I left school I found myself a Saturday morning job at our butcher's shop as an errand boy delivering customers' orders. My hours were 8am to 1pm for which I was paid 5/- plus any tips that I might be lucky enough to get. I also had to collect money from some of the customers. At this time, 1944, meat was still rationed. The people that were having a hard time were the pensioners, more so if they lived on their own as the meat ration was very small; a week's ration would be what we would call a good meal today.

Where and when I could, I tried to give them a little extra. Sometimes, when there was an order for a large family, I would sneak a slice of corned beef or a sausage or two and put it in with the pensioner's meat order.

My last errand of the day was always the same—to a Public House, to the butcher's girlfriend and to the butcher's mother. I changed bikes for this, to one with a deeper basket and it was always packed waiting for me by the time I returned from my other errands. The butcher told me not to go poking around in the parcels, just hand the orders over. The first layer, some five or six parcels, went to the pub for which the landlord gave me a 2/6d tip. In the summer, I got a glass of lemonade as well. The next layer was for the girlfriend, about the same amount of parcels for which I received a 6d tip. The final delivery was for the butcher's mother and I had to hand over the whole basket to her, for which I received no tip!

After a few weeks I began to get a bit nosy and I looked inside the parcels. Well, I soon saw that there was a lot more meat going to these people than there should have been and I decided to even things up a bit. Each week I cycled away from the shop until I was out of sight. Then I opened up some of the parcels and took out a chop here, a sausage there or a bit of liver, even a steak if I felt brave. I made up a couple of extra parcels with these extras and delivered them to two different pensioners each week—I told them it had fallen off of their joint ration in the basket.

I got away with this for over a year, though I did have one or two narrow escapes. One day I heard the butcher telling the lady cashier that one of the customers had not received their full ration. When she asked the name of the customer, he named a person that the cashier and I both knew had actually received their full quota. Some of the old dears would come in to the shop to thank the butcher for the little extras that they'd received, which he obviously knew nothing about. He never did twig what was going on and because he was giving extra to his friends, nothing was ever said.

The actual owner of the shop was in the army fighting in the desert in North Africa. When he came home after the war it wasn't very long before the butcher's fiddles were discovered and he found himself looking for another job.

The days of rationing, though they were hard at the time, at least taught me to appreciate what I have today. We often ate horsemeat and whale meat steaks, which were smothered in onions to cover the fishy taste. It was better than nothing at all. Fruits such as oranges, bananas and grapes disappeared from the shops and sweets were very scarce too. One day at school the word went round that the shop across the road had two tins of ice cream wafers selling at five for a ½d. Pupils were asking to go to the toilet so that they could nip out to buy the wafers. Very soon, nearly half of the school was queued up outside of the shop and the noise of the shop doorbell constantly ringing alerted the headmaster to the situation. Needless to say, everyone was soon back in their classrooms and the shop was out of bounds until after school.'

Trudy Lazarus *grew up in* East London

Shrapnel and Sunbeam Talbots

'My father had a shoe shop on the Whitechapel Road. He was also an ARP warden during the war, spending his nights attending fires and ensuring that the shelters were occupied when the air raid warnings sounded. A third career also beckoned as a dealer on the Black Market. I don't know if he had cash that he wanted to 'get rid of' or simply played the system but he always seemed to have something to sell. At the end of the war when the ARP post was closing he bought all of the contents, including the billiards table and the dartboard and none of it ever saw the inside of our house.

During the war my mother adopted an American Jewish guy who was quartered in Peterborough. He visited us regularly and brought us chewing gum and nylons for mother. I have no idea where she met him and I have wondered since if she was having an affair with him while father was away on his black market dealings.

One day, mother told us that we would not be able to buy any more bananas because of the war. I kept a 'Fyffes' label and stuck it on one of the doors to remind me of the taste of the fruit. It stayed on the door until the room was decorated—several years after the end of the war!

As children we enjoyed the war years. Bombsites were ideal playgrounds and I built up an impressive collection of shrapnel in varying shapes and sizes. It was just a game to us and we were blissfully unaware of the dangers of unexploded bombs and piles of rubble. At the other extreme my mother was extremely protective. If anything unsuitable came on the radio she would put her hands over my ears. The attitude of the time was one of total parental control. I'm sure that it was too strict and led to many repressed children rebelling in later years. As an eleven-year-old I recall seeing the first films of the survivors of Belsen, all Jews like myself and having no idea of the significance. To me it was like watching a scene in a doll factory; my parents never spoke to us of the tragedy.

1940s style

In 1949, my father became the proud owner of a pale green Sunbeam Talbot, complete with starting handle. At that time it was very difficult to buy a car as petrol was still rationed, unless you had a defined need. Doctors were in the 'defined need' category and were able to purchase a car. My father was very friendly with one of our local doctors (who probably owed him a favour from his 'black market' days) and the doctor gave father his allowance. The doctor was content to walk on his rounds and father was more then happy to allow him to continue to do so!'

Keith Levoir spent the war years in Surrey

Cider apples

'I attended school at Lingfield during the war and Canadian troops were in the area in great numbers. I have only recently learnt that there was a whole Division, and it was the only fully equipped Division in the south of England during the threatened German invasion. These troops, having recently arrived, were most friendly. I remember helping at the apple orchard, and some of these fellows also came in to help. We had jobs in the packing warehouses, with huge great aluminium containers twenty or thirty feet square, which had to be packed from the bottom up, until the cap was sealed and then filled with ammonia. There were conveyor belts at which the local women sat packing boxes. And there was a great deal of 'chatting up' with the Canadians, also a lot of very bad language, which meant very little to us twelve-year-olds. At lunchtime I remember the old local men selecting a rotten apple, one that was completely brown with a touch of white mould on the outside and yet solid. They would put it between their hands and squeeze the juice into a cup. It was a very lethal concoction, being virtually cider fermented in the apple.

The Canadians were stationed in force at Felcourt, and some of their armoured vehicles were in the trees on the opposite side of the road to the Felcourt Stores. The concrete roads still remain in the undergrowth. Just before Dieppe, not that we knew it at the time, they were arming up for the raid and I remember going down with friends to watch. We ended up helping to pass shells up into the turrets on a hand to hand principle. What excitement for boys of our age. The next day they moved out. Much later we heard how they had been virtually wiped out in the ill-fated mission. They were great guys and treated us so well. I suppose we reminded them of their own families back in Canada. Families that most of them never saw again.'

Many wartime weddings were organised at short notice
before loved ones were sent overseas

Ken Hansford grew up in *Street, Somerset.*

Here today . . .

'During 1943 the Yanks arrived in my home village. I was about ten years old and along with my pal Sammy, we would make our way to one of the camps after school. Lots of camouflaged tin huts, surrounded by high wire fencing and guarded by soldiers with guns. Camouflaged tanks covered in netting lined the roads leading to the camp.

Being young and eager to scrounge anything, we would chat up any of the Yanks who might be interested. We got to know some of them well while they were there.

After a while, as the atmosphere became more relaxed, we were allowed to enter the camp to watch them play baseball or visit the camp cinema. I remember at Christmas being given a 7lb tin of butter to take home along with three large red apples and some of the famous American Hershey bars. On arriving home, I was severely questioned about how I came by these items, as they were not readily available to civilians.

As the months sped by, Sammy and myself spent much of our time at the camp, particularly during school holidays. We ran errands for some of the lads that we befriended. One day I went to White's fish and chip shop with a 10/- note. On my return I was given 2/6d for my efforts; a fortune to me. The most that I had ever had in my pocket was three or four pennies—2/6d was thirty pennies! My usual meagre pocket money was earned by collecting returnable beer and lemonade bottles (they were all returnable) and taking them back to the pub. We also collected blackberries and wild hips that we took to Framptons for weighing. The heavier the fruit, the more pennies we earned.

One day after school we visited the camp as usual. Everything seemed very different. As we neared the camp, we could see that the gates were wide open, the approach roads were empty; no tanks, no trucks, no jeeps, no men.

We rushed in to the first hut. Empty beds with nothing on them. Debris littered the floors—books, papers and odd coins. The silence was eerie as we ran from hut to hut.

The date was the 5th June, the significance of which became clear the following day. . . .'

Sheila Hansford *recalls the bombing in* **Southampton**

Air raid shelters and Barrage balloons

'When the war was at its height we slept all night in the air raid shelter. It smelt of damp and mildew, so too did the biscuits that were kept there for emergencies, in an old tin box!

One night we held our breath as a doodlebug putt-putted overhead. The sudden silence was a signal for me to put my fingers in my ears, as a silent doodlebug meant that it was falling out of the sky overhead. It landed with a direct hit on the house two doors away from us; the enormous explosion shook all of the windows out of our house and lifted the air raid shelter a few inches out of the ground. We thought that our end had come. Once the all clear sounded we crept back to the house in trepidation. Shattered glass lay everywhere and we spent several hours covering the draughty open spaces with boards.

After almost every raid we could look out of our front door and see an eerie orange glow lighting up the docks, which were the prime target. Even after a serious raid the buses always seemed to run (perhaps not always on time) and we travelled into the city to view the many ruined buildings. Wallpaper on partially collapsed walls hung in shreds, flapping sadly in the wind. Everywhere you looked, the staircases in these ruins were still intact, in lonely defiance of the havoc wreaked around them. My Gran used to hide us under the stairs if the raid was too severe to make a dash down the garden to the shelter. Everyone agreed that under the stairs was the safest place to hide.

One day in June 1944 we heard an enormous ear splitting sound overhead which continued to build and seemed as if it would go on forever. We rushed outside and looked up to see that the sky had almost turned black with all of the 'planes passing overhead, droning on out over the coast towards occupied France. We didn't know at the time, but this was D-Day, the invasion of Europe.

As a small child, I was very frightened of the barrage balloons because I was told that they were full of poisonous gases. One day, as I stepped out of the outside toilet door I looked up and saw the silver skin of a burst balloon floating gently down towards our house. Petrified, I slammed the toilet door shut and sat on the loo seat with my head in my hands, convinced that it would envelop and smother our house and we would all die of gas poisoning. Finally my Gran came out to look for me; she probably thought I was constipated! The silver skin had, of course, drifted out of sight on the breeze, with no harm done.

On one summer evening in 1945 the wireless proclaimed that the war was over. I leapt excitedly up and down on my bed as Gran came rushing up to collect me in my dressing gown and take me down to join the elated neighbours in the street. All I knew at the tender age of eight was that I would never be so frightened again.'

Dave Mitchell *spent his teenage years in* **London**

The Blackout

'During the blackouts, no lights were visible from the air and the police, wardens, firewatchers and other services were all aggressively vigilant. Motor vehicles and cycles had lamps with hoods over the top. Batteries were in short supply. I had an acetylene lamp for my bike. Water was allowed to drip through to the container of carbide, making the gas. One night, late in 1940 whilst cycling to central London, I was passing the site of the old Crystal Palace on Sydenham Hill. I gave my failing lamp a little more water and disturbed the tank. This sent up a ball of flame, which engendered many sharp and some quite rude requests to desist!

A few years later, I passed through the Straits of Gibraltar and the sight of the cities of North Africa all lit up seemed strange after so many years of darkness back at home.

I joined everything to do my bit. At the age of fifteen I was regularly on all night duty as a Firewatcher and as an Air Raid Warden. I was a sergeant in the ATC and a Police Messenger as well as a blood donor and a St Johns's Ambulance volunteer. At sixteen, employed as a junior clerk in a well known assurance company and living in their country premises, I was also in the Home Guard, the Auxiliary Fire Service and an Aircraft Spotter (duties on the roof of the main building!)'

Paul Brown also *recalls a familiar sound over* **London**
towards the end of the war

Doodlebug

'It was a 'busting out all over' June day. Away in the southeast a black dot appeared against the mid-day blue. Before long the glint of the sun on its wings and the unmistakable throb, throb of its engine gave it away—another 'doodlebug.' I called my mother, and the next door neighbours came out into the road too. We gazed up as it came over the school behind our homes not all that high above, strangely elegant and innocent. Immediately over our heads the engine stopped. It gently swooped on beyond our vision, behind the roofs of the houses opposite. After what seemed a surprisingly long time the explosion shattered the calm, sending a pillar of black smoke writhing up and up, while a window behind us cracked. I believe it fell on a factory causing a number of fatalities.

At that time we slept in the concrete air raid shelter out in the road. During earlier air raids my brother and I had usually slept under the stairs, with Mum anxiously watching over us and clenching her fists until the blood ran under the pressure of her nails on the palms of her hands. The shelter had three tiers of bunks on either side of the central passageway. I started off on the top bunk but fell off, so I was relegated to the bottom. Then I had to be rescued while sleepwalking down the street in my pyjamas. One morning we were awakened by an explosion that seemed very close at hand. Dad put on his ARP helmet, got on his bike and went off to investigate. Since early in '43 he had been minister of East Acton Baptist Church. The main church building had been bombed earlier in the war and stood with its roof open to the sky. We worshipped in the wooden church hall alongside. The latest flying bomb had landed on the cricket pitch next to the church buildings, close enough to shatter half of the hall into splinters.

June 1944 also saw my seventh birthday. I received my first cricket bat. In the afternoon Dad, Den and I went to the park to try it out; cricket was always a favourite with us. We hadn't been playing very long before the air raid siren began its discordant shrieking. We were not going to leave for that, but when 'planes began to criss-cross the sky and the ack-ack opened up we walked back home, the game unfinished. Another typical day, really.'

Christine Lloyd spent part of the war in *Malvern*

A little known water shortage

'As a result of the unexpected arrival in Malvern of the Research Establishments, there was a severe shortage of accommodation. A number of residents with spare rooms found themselves obliged to take in lodgers under the Government's billeting regulations. In return for a clean bed they were paid 5/- a week.

I moved to Malvern with the Research Establishments in 1942 and was allocated to an elderly lady who was very kind and considered my presence in the house to be her contribution to the war effort. Her housekeeper, however, was none too pleased, as she had to wash my sheets (not very often!) She was very deaf and consequently grumbled to herself loudly about my presence in the house.

I thought things had taken a turn for the better when she presented me with a hot water bottle but she immediately directed my attention to the water meter. This secret weapon was unknown to me and I was surprised to be told how carefully it had to be watched. I was not to wash at night or flush the lavatory. In the morning, the water from my hot water bottle was to serve for cleaning my teeth, washing myself and finally, using the small basin provided, as a means of flushing the toilet. Fortunately for me, bathing facilities were available, courtesy of the Ministry of Supply, at the Establishment.

Water was not the only item in short supply and I was pleased to be able to make myself several items of underwear from parachute material. However, the cami-knickers that I knitted from Chadwick's white mending cotton outshone these—the cotton cost one penny per card and required no coupons!'

Aitken Lawrie spent the war years in the **Middle East**

Middle Eastern Memories

'Before World War II, I had visited Egypt to see the Pyramids, had watched cavalry patrols clattering through Palestine and had stayed in a splendid hotel in Basra. So when I was posted to the 8th Indian Division in 1941 and rushed into Iraq to head off a possible German attack on the oilfields, I was delighted. It sounded much better than Burma and I would be able to see more of the Middle East.

I sailed from Bombay in an unescorted convoy on the 'Khadive Ismail', which the Shah of Persia had hired for his honeymoon cruise. I was appointed 'Officer in Charge of the Ship', so enjoyed the luxury of the pale blue honeymoon suite. There was a real threat from German submarines and smoking on deck after dark was strictly prohibited. Every morning I held summary court martials on men who had broken the rule and could sentence them to being lashed to the mast for so many hours a day—no joke in the Persian Gulf! My severity was justified when the Khadive Ismail was sunk on her next voyage, with the loss of all hands.

On landing at Basra the first thing we saw was a line of Negro soldiers having a shower. My Indian troops were shocked at their nakedness, but amused at their attempts at preserving their decency by tucking back their ample private parts between their legs!

We had a seven hundred mile drive to Mosul, mostly through trackless desert, which produced astonishing mirages of camels and palm trees and houses which disappeared when we got close. On the way we passed many interesting places. First of all was Ur of the Chaldees, where we scrambled up the Ziggurat. It seemed a dismal part of the world and I was not surprised that Abraham had left it and gone to look for the Promised Land.

Babylon was fascinating with the remains of The Hanging Gardens and the Tower of Babel carefully escavated and preserved. Kirkuk had the tombs of Daniel, Shadrach, Meshach and Abednego. Near the oil wells the ground was covered with small, licking flames, which may have given rise to the story of the 'burning, fiery furnace'.

Erbil is said to be the oldest continuously inhabited city in the world. It stands up eighty feet on its own debris and you can find coins of Alexander the Great just six feet below the surface. Next we saw the massive ruins of Nineveh, where two chariots could race abreast along its ramparts. Finally we came to Nabi Yunis and the tomb of Jonah. To prove it is the real thing, the jaws of the whale that swallowed him are hung up in the porch!

Mosul is a large cosmopolitan city. I had to set up my Officers' Mess just outside it and found that the cook I had hired in India, who claimed that he had spent WWI as a cook in Mesopotamia, had passed his time cooking boiled rice and knew nothing else. I found an English recipe book in the town and translated it in to Urdu, but he was still very restricted since the British rations comprised only tins of bully beef and dates. We had to manage with bully beef stew, bully beef fritters and bully beef curry!

We had hired a thousand Arab coolies to dig an anti-tank ditch. They were paid according to the hardness of the soil; the harder the soil, the more they were paid. I remember one oily headman assuring me that there was no need to measure any further since it was all solid rock; in other words 'We should be paid the maximum.' When it was obvious that it was quite untrue, he showed me a gold watch in his pocket. I was very shocked at this attempt at bribery, but he was quite unconcerned. I was even more shocked when he whispered in my ear 'Effendi, I have a very beautiful daughter'.

There were endless opportunities for skulduggery. Once I was told that a train would arrive from the base with fifty lorry loads of stores. But when it arrived, every one of the sealed wagons was completely empty.

Gurkhas guarded the main store dumps. They were promised ten rupees for every dead Arab caught thieving. This was quite successful until the Gurkhas realised that they could soon get rich by raiding nearby villages!

As usual the British authorities in India had underestimated the effects of the climate. The first winter we had a cold spell with thirty-four degrees of frost. The Division had been sent off in thin khaki uniforms and hundreds of men from the south of India died of pneumonia. Warm battle dress turned up in March when the weather was heating up again.

At last our work was done and the Germans never attacked the oil wells. I was sent to the Staff College in Haifa and enjoyed living in a proper house and having good meals. Apart from that I went about my spare time in plain clothes and talking German. I got to know many Jews and could sympathise with their point of view, living as they did below the high ground dominated by Syria and Jordan. But there was no interracial friction. Both Jews and Arabs told me that they wanted us to win the war and would do nothing to hinder our efforts. They lived in complete harmony in what was then Palestine.

A memorable weekend in 1946

After the war, I was appointed Military Advisor to the Indian Princes and as such had to meet them for discussions. I was delighted to be invited to Kapurthala, a small state in the Punjab. In 1857 the father of the present Maharajah had helped loyal troops to cross the Sutlej on their way to take part in the siege of Delhi. For this he had been created a Maharajah and granted the income from a distant territory. When he died his son was only two years old and he was brought up and educated under British supervision, with a large income piling up in the bank.

When he was sixteen he was told that he ought to have a palace. He asked to see pictures of various palaces and liked the look of Versailles. So a huge building, which was an exact copy of the central block of Versailles was erected in the Punjab in about 1900. The furnishings and décor were all 'a la Française', and the Maharajah thought of himself as the reincarnation of Louis XIV. Everyone had to speak French in the Palace.

The Palace at Kapurthala

Lots of important guests assembled for this weekend, including three other Maharajahs, who turned up with corteges of Rolls Royces and were greeted with guards of honour and the appropriate gun salutes. There were many officials and visitors of various nationalities. About forty of us sat down to meals at a long table with a flunkey behind each chair in antique French costume with powdered wigs and silk stockings. The food and drink and place settings were out of this world.

Each morning with our early tea we received a copy of the Hindustan Times, which had been ironed flat and stitched together and a programme of the day's events. These included such things as a State Ball, a concert by the State Orchestra, a flower show and a visit to the zoo. I remember being driven around the grounds in a carriage drawn by four zebras with two Maharajahs on the box. On the last evening there was a cinema show, which took place in what would have been the chapel in Versailles. Each guest had a comfortable armchair with a side table holding drinks, cigarettes and a bell-push.

I left by train in the special coach to which my boss, the Military Advisor in Chief was entitled. This was the ultimate in luxury, with comfortable sitting and dining rooms and six bedrooms and baths. The coach could be attached to suitable trains and dropped off at any station on the line. Next morning we stopped at Nabha and found that we were twenty yards off the red carpet, so the Guard of Honour had to fall out and push us along to the right spot.

My wife could not be with me on that visit, but later was asked to lunch with the Maharajah in his summer chateau in Mussoorie. When she admitted that she had not seen the latest Carmen Miranda film, he clapped his hands, had it brought back from its latest showing one hundred miles away and booked the whole cinema for her to see it. That was the way to do things!

In my job as Military Advisor to the Maharajah I met many of the military leaders and was drawn into discussions with Lord Wavell, Field Marshal Auchinleck and later Lord Mountbatten. I met and liked Nehru but disliked Jinnah. I strongly supported the Wavell plan for a gradual withdrawal, which would have avoided the horrors of Partition, but London overruled us.

When the great day arrived I went to a huge reception at the Viceroy's House, shook hands with Mountbatten, immaculate in naval uniform ablaze with medals, and with Lady Mountbatten, who was clearly sagging, and then strolled out into the sunset. I walked round the wonderful Mogul Garden which required three hundred malis to keep it in order and was really amazed that we were about to give all this away.

I met the Rajah of Faridkot, who invited me to take potluck at his Delhi Palace. There were just the two Ranis—his mother and his wife—and we ate off a silver service that had once belonged to King Charles I. The other half of this is in Buckingham Palace. They were all excellent Bridge players and we played a few rubbers before he had to go back to Viceroy's House, dressed in pale blue satin with a bejewelled turban and a ceremonial sword.

I watched him drive off in his Rolls Royce and then wandered rather sadly into the streets, which were full of friendly happy Indians. At midnight the Union Jack came down to the sound of the Last Post and the brand new flag of India was raised in its place. We all joined hands and sang the National Anthem.

For a few days everything shut down for a well-deserved holiday. Early one morning I was ordered to Amritsar in the Punjab. Major General Rees had asked for one hundred and fifty British officers to join the Punjab Boundary Force, which had been set up to maintain order, but he only got seven, of whom I was one. I found myself in charge of ten thousand square miles of bloody massacres with seven Indian army battalions to control them. However, without their British officers and the senior Indians who had done so well in Burma, they were of little use, taking sides and even assisting with the killings. The only troops I could rely on were Gurkhas and Madrassis, who had no men from the Punjab.

Two of the first instructions that emerged from Delhi after Independence had been declared were that the English language would be given up and also all British insignia. A few days later the first was revoked because English was the only language everyone could understand and the Bengal Sappers refused to give up their badge of the Prince of Wales' feathers of which they are still very proud.

I had volunteered to stay on for seven years and the Engineer in Chief, Major General Williams ordered me to Kirkee, near Poona, where a brand new School of Military Engineering was to be built. I was taken to the site and shown five thousand acres of black cotton soil, horrible marshy stuff with not a single tree or blade of grass. 'We need a School of Field Engineering very urgently', they told me, 'the first course starts in two weeks.' The timetable had been drawn up a year ahead, and the students nominated. I was determined that they would not be disappointed, and the course started on time with accommodation and classrooms in tents.

I was supposed to be there as an advisor only, but at once took full charge, and my orders were never challenged. I was shown the plans for the buildings, which were due to be built, but tore them up and produced new ones, which the contractor accepted without demur. Money was no object and I designed a magnificent building around two quadrangles, with ample classrooms, model rooms, a library and cinema. I am sure it was as good as any in the world. It went up quickly and we soon had four courses running continuously. I managed to recruit four majors from England to run the different departments of Fieldworks, Bridging, Tactics and Signals.

It was immediately apparent that there was not a single junior officer in the Indian Engineers. Rather doubtfully I advertised in local newspapers all over India for patriotic young men interested in a career in engineering and received an overwhelming response. They were of a very high standard and some of them still write to me as retired Colonels and Brigadiers.

It was also planned to build a very large Military Academy in Poona. A team of so-called experts under Dr Jha visited military academies all round the world and produced a layout based on their findings. These plans were to be handed to Nehru when he came down to lay the foundation stone. The day before this function General Williams came to stay with us and showed me the plans after dinner. We both agreed that they were obviously unworkable, being completely unsuitable for the conditions in India. There was only one thing to do. I went back to my office, broke a window and worked through the night to produce a new set of plans, which were duly handed over to Nehru next day.

I met Nehru on another occasion. It was a big dinner in the Poona Club. I have forgotten the reason for it. At that time India was strictly teetotal, but I was led in through a side door and given a large whisky and soda behind a screen. I found myself sitting next to Nehru and found him a sophisticated and amusing companion. After dinner the company was walking up and down on the lawn, as was the usual custom while listening to the band. The Bandmaster marched up to Nehru, saluted and asked what he would like as an encore.

Having had to sit through a long dinner on lukewarm lemonade, he came out at once with, 'Let's have Roll out the Barrel', which was a popular song in England at the time!'

Les King *attended to the wounded during the war in the* **Mediterranean**

Medics

'In 1942, having been called up to the Royal Army Medical Corps, I was posted to Ormskirk, where a new military hospital had been formed. After a few months, there were rumours of being posted overseas. Everyone getting 'jabs' (inoculation and vaccination) strengthened these. During the middle of October we were herded onto a train, and all carriage doors were locked. We had been given some sandwiches, which had to last most of the day. When we finally got off the train, we were on the dockside at Gourock, on the Clyde. After more sandwiches and tea, during which we had noted that a great number of Naval and Merchant ships were lying at anchor all around, we were 'fell in' ready to embark.

At the dockside, in grey and murky weather, was a small ship the size of a ferry. We thought that we were only bound for Ireland or somewhere fairly near. Some hopes! In the centre of the Firth waited a large grey troopship and to our despair that was to be our transport. An ex P & O liner named the 'Cathay'. It had been fitted with several types of anti-aircraft guns, plus on each side amidships, low down, was a six-inch gun. That night, on October the 23rd, we sailed in the middle of a large convoy out across the top of Ireland well into the middle of the Atlantic Ocean.

We sailed in this large convoy protected by the Royal Navy for almost three weeks. Apparently the route neared America before doubling back towards Gibraltar. The first three day's duties were carried out while suffering from sea-sickness. These included getting food from the galley and bringing it to the messdeck, which was just below the waterline. There were several regiments of infantry on board, including The Royal Scots and the Gordon Highlanders. We all slept, or tried to, in hammocks slung above the mess tables. There was not much fresh air and it was a relief to be allowed on deck for exercise during the daytime. It was an inspiring sight to see the many ships scattered all around us, occasionally being herded by some destroyer if they lagged behind or were out of place.

Sometimes there was boat drill, so that we became expert at donning the canvas and cork life belts, and running to our boat stations. This sometimes happened when there was either a submarine or aircraft scare, which increased as we neared Gibraltar. Dolphins and flying fish were something to look out for, if only to break the monotony. The vastness of the endless ocean and the sky, especially at night, was quite impressive. To watch the ship's bows slicing through the fluorescent water at night was also memorable. Sometimes the ship's crews would have to practice firing the guns, mainly the anti-aircraft; although the six-inch guns were tried once only, as the whole ship was shaken when they were fired.

On the 10th of November we dropped anchor in the Bay of Algiers where, after a few hours some of the troops were sent ashore to the town. After some sporadic firing was heard, we learnt that Algiers was in joint Anglo-American hands. Then into a deep-water dock to disembark more troops and transport/supplies. While there, Italian aircraft bombed us. Our company of medics was down in the messdeck at the time and heard the loud banging of shrapnel and pieces of dockside striking the ship's side. Apparently one of the lifeboats had been smashed, along with some soldiers. So we then knew that our visit was no longer a surprise (if it ever was) and to expect trouble. The whole object, of course, was the invasion of Algeria by the 1st Army, aiming to link up with the 8th Army in North Africa, further east.

That night and the next day, on the 11th, part of our convoy went further east another one hundred miles, while the rest ploughed on towards Malta. We found ourselves in the Bay of Bougie. Unfortunately, the Italian airforce also found us and it was not long before we were under a heavy bombing attack from twin-engine 'planes. Our ships put up a good barrage, which was heartening to watch especially the tracers when they found their targets. This went on all day and early evening, with ships getting damaged and sunk and several 'planes crashing into the sea and the surrounding hills above the town.

Our share of excitement (and fear) was getting chased and machine-gunned by a bomber as we slowly left our ship in a small landing craft. The sailor in charge bravely stood up and returned fire with a Bren gun; at last the 'plane sheared off, and we reached the docks in one piece. To take shelter for a short while we crawled underneath some of the French railway wagons.

There were about eighteen ships in the Bay, and at least half of them were sunk, including our troopship. We lost all of our kit, both personal and the tented hospital equipment. We had escaped in time, with only our large and small packs, plus water bottles.

When it was fairly safe, one of our NCOs led us into the town, about forty of us, searching for a suitable school building in which to base ourselves. Having found such a building we spread out on the cold tile floors of several classrooms, eventually trying to get a few hours sleep, which was almost impossible owing to the noise of bombs and guns. The night sky was lit up by constant flashes, as well as ships on fire. Early the next morning some water and biscuits were issued, and we set to with borrowed stretchers and some medical supplies from the local hospital to do what we could for the hundreds of casualties who had started to arrive by various means. A mixture of soldiers and sailors, most of them suffered from terrible burns. Many of them did not survive.

After about five days we met up with more of our unit members, the 69th BMH (British Military Hospital). Transport was found to convey us all five miles inland, to the middle of a Frenchman's large vineyard. We set up a hospital in the large brick and stone built stores and wine vat buildings. Always with us was the smell of wine, for many of the huge vats were full. The staff and patients slept on stretchers, with only a few inches between each man. Although there were a few more air raids on Bougie, at least we were never visited by the enemy.

After about six weeks, a new load of tents and equipment arrived. A large space had been cleared in the middle of the vineyard fields, which covered many hectares. Then we all set to and laid out a tented hospital large enough to take six hundred patients, being then termed a Field Base Hospital. Marquees were used for the wards, each holding twenty beds. Smaller square tents were used as offices, ward kitchens, a laboratory and the X-ray dept. Other large tents were used as stores and the operating theatre, all with canvas flooring sheets.

Soon ambulance convoys were arriving, with battle casualties including Italian and German soldiers. There was always a mixture of surgical and medical cases. Malaria was then quite common and we all had to take Mepacrin tablets, which were yellow and tasted bitter.

Once, during night duty, some chaps created a little diversion by driving some donkeys through the wards; these being owned by local Bedouin Arabs. This caused a certain amount of mayhem! These Arabs lived in small goatskin tents around the camp area, and sometimes managed to sneak into our camp. Some mornings, men would wake up to find that their tent had disappeared from over their heads!

While on embarkation leave before going to North Africa, I had met a girl named Doris in my hometown of Portslade. She lived in the next town, Southwick, both near Brighton. Several times I went to her home for tea (and a cuddle), but never got beyond the kissing stage. Her father was very deaf, which was convenient at times. We both said that we loved each other, and swore to be married when I returned from the war.

However, during 1943, while I was a patient in my own ward, suffering from bronchitis, I received a 'Dear John' letter from Doris who, having met someone else, broke off our affair. This was a depressing period, but after a few days I put it down to experience and carried on as usual.

A memorable occasion was when there came a plague of locusts. Imagine many acres of lush, green vines bearing many grapes, plus a lot of trees near the river. Then one day the sky gradually became dark, then darker still with a rustling droning sound all around. Within minutes the ground and all green plants were covered with a carpet of three-inch long locusts. Impossible to control, within three days every plant had been devoured, and to walk anywhere meant crushing and crunching one's way over thousands of voracious locusts. Eventually they were removed or otherwise disappeared.

Towards the end of the year, large Nissen huts replaced the tented wards, with each one holding forty patients, plus kitchen, treatment room and office. It was while working in one of these wards full of dysentery patients, that my turn came to catch it. Not surprising, with all the flies that were always with us. One of the sulphanilamide drugs was the cure then. A very weakening disease, taking quite a while to recover from.

To help recovery, I was given one week's leave. This was taken in a very small camp, consisting of three huts on a sandy shore of a bay a few miles along the coast, in an easterly direction. All that five of us could do was to swim, walk to a small village, or listen to six records (78s) played on a wind-up gramophone. I must say that those six records, all of Vera Lynn, kept me in touch with home, with all the sugary sentiments, as well as increasing the feeling of home-sickness! Since then Vera Lynn has represented those long years of alternate periods of hard work and boredom.

Early in 1944 we began preparing to move into another theatre of war—Italy. A regiment of the Sudanese Army began to take over our camp, conspicuous by their tall red fez.

So, during February we made our way to the Port of Bougie and embarked upon a hospital ship. After the 'Cathay' this was a comparatively small ship, painted all white with large red crosses on the sides, funnels and decks, being also lit up at night. We were a little apprehensive, as we had heard of several such ships being bombed and sunk, especially when at anchor near other troop and supply craft. Notable were the special swinging beds pivoted from a frame, made to counteract the sideways motion of the ship when at sea. However, we slept in normal bunks. Travelling in a small convoy, we sailed for about a week with no major incidents and arrived at the Port of Naples. This coincided with an eruption of Mount Vesuvius, which rises 4,200 feet above the Bay of Naples, on the east side. A most spectacular sight, with a huge pall of black and grey smoke pouring into the sky towards Africa. This was laced with fiery red glows, with a continuous thunderstorm producing much lightning just above the cone. White and red-hot lava was steadily rolling down the sides, obliterating several small villages perched on the mountainside. The black clouds had been seen while on our way, two days before.

While the centre of the city had many fine and wide roads, laced with the double tramway system, there were also many narrow and hilly streets filled with refuse and starving people, especially children it seemed. Most of us soon gave away our small ration of chocolate and sweets which had been issued, which meant that wherever we went we were followed by a crowd of begging children, and at times adults as well.

Major allied army landings had taken place at Salerno during 1943 and by this time the battlefronts were in the area of Cassino. After an overnight rest in a large building north of the town, early the next morning we were taken to the railway station. There we were herded into ordinary covered wagons, which also contained our hospital supplies. Some hours later, an American diesel loco was coupled up to our train, consisting of a coach for the officers, and about forty wagons. All that day and the next night we rolled and bucked along, with many stops and delays. Fortunately we could sit or lie on some of the tentage, for it seemed that our wagons had square wheels! Spectacular views of the still erupting Mount Vesuvius were had during the journey, especially at night. Aircraft dropped bombs around the train, but only minor track damage was done, causing further delays for repairs. After a seemingly endless journey, we discovered that the final destination was only about fifteen miles away, to the north of Vesuvius. A mile or so from the railhead, we settled into an already prepared campsite courtesy of the Royal Pioneer Corps. This was situated between the towns of Nola and Madalloni, with Caserta to the north. We were a forward Base General Hospital, the 69th BMH.

After some months, a small Leave Camp was opened at Salerno. This consisted of a group of wooden huts on the sandy beach, from which it was easy to swim. I had one week there, during which I foolishly went for a midnight swim. The moon was full, casting a romantic light on the calm water. As no one was about, no trunks were worn, which was a mistake. For 'lo and behold' a friendly jellyfish stung me on the scrotum! However, I recovered enough to visit the battered cinema in the town a few days later where could be seen the film 'Bernadette', starring Jennifer Jones.

It is a long time ago.'

George Senior joined the RAF in 1941

Parachutes and fortunate escapes

'I had been called up to join the army on the 1st September 1939, two days before the war started. I managed to transfer to the RAF two days before my 21st birthday, an altogether happier event. I began training as a pilot but failed because I could not land safely. My CO told me to get out of his sight in no uncertain terms. I became an air gunner, flying most of the time in Africa, Italy, Sardinia and Corsica. I recall the time that I inadvertently opened my parachute inside the aircraft. I was sitting on the packed 'chute when we hit an air pocket. I was thrown off of the parachute and then thudded back down, causing it to burst open; it spilled all over the place inside the aircraft. It is surprising how much room it takes up! It was also an expensive experience for me as there was an unwritten rule that you paid the packer 10/-, which was a lot of money from a sergeant's pay. Another similar incident happened when I tried to clear a gun stoppage. I caught the quick release of my 'Mae West' life jacket getting into the turret; it inflated and I was trapped. We were all quite bulky when we wore our flying jackets and life jackets too. After much fiddling the other gunner managed to deflate the life jacket and I crawled out.

On one operation my skipper had trouble with the engine. We hurtled down the runway three times and three times we had to stop abruptly at the end—very abruptly. We got up into the air at the fourth attempt, did a circuit of the airfield and came down again; the skipper refused to go on as he said the engine was faulty. We were given another aircraft and went off on patrol. Later we were signalled to go and search for the wreckage of an aircraft in the sea—the aircraft that we had left a few hours previously!

I was injured shortly after this. We were on a bombing mission when we had to turn back, still having our payload on board. As we landed, we hit a slit trench and damaged the aircraft; fortunately our bombs weren't primed. I suffered cuts to my face when a flying tin of Corned Beef that we carried as part of our emergency rations hit me! I imagined the headlines in my local newspaper, 'Local flyer invalided out of the RAF; details classified.'

Not long after this one of the other crew members had a very lucky escape. We returned from an op, breathing a sigh of relief that we were all still in one piece. As usual the bottom hatch was open in case we needed to bale out quickly. When I looked down to the other gunner he wasn't there, he had fallen out just as we landed. It is hard to believe that he was hardly bruised and after that incident he became known as 'The one who walked back!'

Later, when I was on a Liberator night bombing squadron flying over Sicily we encountered a lot of flak and the skipper told us to bale out. The rear gunner was on his last trip and told me to open the hatch and get ready to go but don't jump. He disappeared up to the front to try to persuade the skipper to fly on with us all on board. Fortunately, the heat died down, we escaped relatively unscathed and managed to fly back to base.

The scariest experiences were those in the Marauders when we flew at fifty feet above the ground. I was wounded when two

German ME109s off the south coast of France attacked us. I had part of my watch shot off; the strap and the base of the watch were still fastened to my wrist. The other gunner sorted me out and then said that his foot hurt. We found that he had a bullet in it and in the excitement didn't realise that it had happened. Despite the aircraft being badly damaged, the skill and determination of our skipper brought us back to base where we crash-landed due to extensive damage to the hydraulics.

Unfortunately, after we came back to England and I left the squadron, my skipper, our navigator and my fellow gunner were all killed when they crashed while returning from an op.

I had one more lucky escape when I was in a Sunderland Flying Boat squadron. I was a spare gunner and was detailed to fly but another gunner, a New Zealander, elected to go as he had one trip to do before he finished his tour. Unfortunately he was killed when they attacked a U-boat and the concussion from a depth charge damaged the tail turret and the Sunderland crash landed in the sea. By sheer luck the rest of the crew all survived.'

*George Green started work in **London** as the war broke out.*

GNATs and Nagasaki

'My first job was at Brown Brothers, Great Eastern Street for which I was paid 17/6d per week. To save money I often caught a 'Workman's' bus and got a return ticket for the price of a single. The snag here was that I arrived far too early for work and so spent my savings in the nearby café. I then moved to the iron shop at the Standard Telephones and Cables factory near Southgate. When it was my turn to be called up and I was leaving the factory, I was handed a slightly grubby sheet of paper, which read, 'A collection for our good sport George Green who has been called to the colours.' Several oily hands had signed to wish me luck and donations varied—3d, 6d, 1/-, even one 2/6d. I wrote a note to pin on the 'clocking in' clock, thanking my colleagues for £3-6-9d. I had never travelled farther than Southend but I was told to report to HMS Raleigh at Torpoint, Devon, for ten weeks of training. I met up with another lad, Brandon, who was going to the same place and we travelled down on the train together. A lady on the train informed us that we would like

Plymouth as there were about forty pubs along Union Street. What she omitted to add was that German bombs had already flattened the majority of them. We arrived at HMS Raleigh and Brandon was first up to the table to receive his number—369098. I followed and was given 369099. He got killed, I survived. I have often wondered what would have happened if I'd gone up first.

In training we received pay of £1-12-0d every two weeks. At the end of the ten weeks, five of us were sent to Thurso, the most northerly tip of Scotland and a good deal farther afield than Southend! From there, we were taken across to Scapa Flow to join a small destroyer, HMS Obdurate, engaged in the hazardous trips to and from Murmansk. There was never a dull moment and although I was not much more than a boy when I joined, I became a man overnight. The trips were full of action and apart from the enemy, we had the terrible weather to contend with. The conditions we endured bordered on the limits of human endurance. The cold was so intense that no amount of clothing could keep it out. Spray froze on masts, rigging and decks as it fell and it was a constant struggle to keep guns in working order. 'Chipping parties' were in constant action to prevent the ship from becoming top heavy due to the accumulations of ice.

The living quarters were often little better. Sometimes when you jumped out of your hammock you landed in water up to your ankles. You were cold, wet, tired, hungry, scared and sick. You were constantly being thrown about and sometimes you couldn't stand upright for days on end.

I don't know which was worse—summer or winter. The darkness of the winter nights, which lasted from mid afternoon until mid morning, helped to protect us from enemy aircraft and U-boats; but the cold was unbelievable. In summer, it was light almost around the clock and from the moment that we were first spotted by enemy aircraft we knew there would be little respite in the days to come. We lost many fine ships with tanks, guns, ammunition, grain and fuel—and hundreds of brave men.

I remember Chief Petty Officer Benham losing a foot in an accident whilst oiling at sea. Soon afterwards, our Doc, surgeon Maurice Hood was transferred over to a US merchant ship to carry out an operation on one of their crew. Their ship went up and we lost our Doc. Then there was Ordinary Seaman Eade who was washed overboard and lost.

In January 1944 a 'GNAT' (Gyroscopically Navigated Acoustic Torpedo) fired, I later discovered, by Lieutenant Commander Becker in U Boat U360 scored a direct hit on us. Although we were damaged we managed to limp on to Murmansk; we were very lucky not to have been targeted again. Anyone who went into those Arctic waters had only minutes to survive.

The following year I was sent to very different waters. Southend seemed just down the street in comparison. From Plymouth we went back to Scotland, to Glasgow where we boarded the Queen Elizabeth and crossed the Atlantic to New York. There, we boarded a train for Chicago, then another to San Francisco. We continued our journey on a US troopship, which transported us to New Guinea. We then tried to catch up with the only British warship that was operating in these waters, attached to the 7th Amphibious Task Force under Admiral Nimitz. We eventually met the ship, HMS Ariadne, in Manus and after a few trips, ended up in Sydney. By this time the European war was nearing its end and we were directed home, with various duties including escorting Crown Prince Olaf of Norway back to Oslo. We returned to the Pacific in 1945 and peace in the Pacific was declared whilst I was in Melbourne. The war for us may have been over but our duties were not. The fleet was required to transport troops to liberate the occupied territories and free the poor Prisoners of War and internees. We sailed for Japan on the 24th of August and arrived in Tokyo on the 4th September. The troops and supplies were put ashore and we returned to Sydney. The following week we set sail again for Japan, this time via Guam. We reached Tokyo on the 30th of October then sailed back down the coast to Nagasaki. We arrived here on Sunday the 4th of November and were allowed ashore only in organised parties. The second atomic bomb had devastated the city ten weeks earlier and the scene of devastation was quite unforgettable. There was nothing but rubble for as far as the eye could see with muddy puddles everywhere. Very few people were on the streets. One old Japanese gentleman plodded along on his wooden platform shoes. He had a pole across his shoulders with a bundle on each end; most likely his only possessions. A jeep full of laughing GIs appeared and drove straight towards the old man causing him to fall in to one of the puddles. They drove off, with renewed laughter. The old man slowly lifted himself up out of the water, pulling his sodden bundles up on to a dry pile of rocks. I did not feel sorry for him and had no guilt about those feelings. A little later we came across the remains of a tan coloured bridge. Imprinted upon it was the unmistakable shadow of a human form, which had been vapourised during the explosion.

Seeing Nagasaki, I had no emotion about it then and I have none to this day except that war is hell; I know, I've sampled it.'

Hellen Price *worked in* **India** *during the war.*

Memsahib beware

'At the start of World War Two, fifteen hundred women had responded to join the 'Massage Corps'. The Chartered Society of Massage and Medical Gymnastics negotiated conditions with the War Office. The title later changed to the 'Chartered Society of Physiotherapy' and that of the 'Massage Corps' to 'Physiotherapy Service'. By 1943 there was an urgent need for volunteers to go overseas; military hospitals now had Physiotherapy departments and 'rehabilitation' was 'in'. Members of the Physiotherapy Service were classified as 'Civilian Attached, Officer status' and came under the umbrella of the Red Cross. In practical terms this meant that if we were captured by the enemy we would be treated as military personnel. We wore a slightly adapted Red Cross officer's uniform, with HQ London shoulder tabs and 'Physiotherapy Service' on the sleeve. A uniform allowance was given and we proceeded to an approved tailoring establishment, in my case, Hector Powe in Edinburgh.

I volunteered for service in India and became one of about a dozen who served in the subcontinent. We set sail as part of a thirty-two strong convoy of ships from Greenock in June 1944. It took us five weeks to reach Bombay. I spent the next two years helping to set up the Rehabilitation Departments in Bareilly and Lucknow. One of my fondest memories is of lovely Gurkhas pointing out that my Urdu terms for parts of the body was 'soldier language' and not what Memsahibs should use!'

Joan Packham recalls the war in **Sheffield**

Tea and the WAAF

'Sheffield escaped a lot of the early bombing but when the enemy turned its attention to us it was horrendous. Several hundred people were killed in one night. Every one of the many tram routes had its casualties and all had tracks broken and blasted into surreal shapes. One night there was no public transport running so my father had to walk home after work from the other side of town. As he walked through the smouldering rubble he stopped in a shop doorway where a teenage girl was crouching down. He offered her a hand to get up and she fell dead at his feet. The trauma of that stayed with him for many years, not least because she was a similar age to me. But even amongst such horror there was occasion for laughter. One night, there were about seven people sharing our cellar. We hadn't anticipated the raid lasting from dusk to dawn so there came a time when we were all longing for a cup of tea. Another teenage girl and myself volunteered to make a pot of tea. We ran up to the kitchen between waves of bombers, put the kettle on, then ran back to the cellar. When it went quiet again, we rushed out and found the crockery. Back to the cellar. This went on for about an hour, backwards and forwards until we had made enough tea for everyone. We all finished up laughing hysterically.

When the All Clear was sounded my mother surfaced and went out to see what damage had been done. She returned soon afterwards with a family of four complete strangers who had been bombed out. They stayed with us for several weeks until the corporation erected hundreds of emergency pre-fabs to house the homeless. These little bungalows were meant to last ten years; many of them are still in use!

As soon as I was old enough I joined the WAAF and although it may seem awful to say it, from then on I enjoyed the war. It gave me my first taste of freedom from very strict parents and the opportunity to meet people from all over the country. When I qualified as a radar operator I was posted to 'B' Watch at Bempton and became a member of another sort of family. The same party of eight or so young people stayed together and worked together through every shift or 'watch'. We socialised together too and I soon realised that I was very naïve. I learnt a lot at that time and enjoyed every moment of the learning. A couple of incidents, in particular stand out in my memory. I won't go in to the details of how incoming 'planes were identified (or not) but if it was suspected that enemy planes were approaching it was our job to alert the Naval base at Humber. One blip we were tracking had been unidentified for some time and was then declared hostile so we hastily passed on the information. No doubt the barracks would be immediately put on full alert and the gunners at Action Stations. The threat got nearer and nearer and then someone high up decided that it was a false alarm and that what had been labelled Hostile 142 was now relabelled Friendly 142. We contacted the navy again and said 'relax, Humber. Hostile planes now re-identified Friendly.' Presumably the gunners were stood down and off to the NAAFI for a cuppa. However, a few moments later Humber contacted us and in an impeccable Oxford accent and a most courteous tone someone asked quietly 'Excuse me Bempton, are these friendly bombs?'

Another incident made quite an impression on me. I had been trained as a very junior assistant mechanic and as the rest of the watch went across the site to a primitive 'stand-by' set for an hour, it was my job to close down the transmitter and receiver for maintenance. I was just about to switch off when I saw an SOS signal flashing so I contacted the officer of the watch and asked for instructions. The old set had not yet picked it up so I was told to continue tracking it until it did. I had to watch it and plot it on a graph and then pass on the position to the 'ops' room. I continued to do this over and over again because it had not been picked up by anyone else on our station or those either side of us. It never was and I kept it under observation until it was over our coast and the echo was lost. At the end of the hour the watch returned, the day's maintenance was abandoned and everything returned to normal. About fifteen minutes later the officer in charge sent for me. She told me that someone with gold braid halfway up his sleeve had asked her to pass on his congratulations to the WAAF who had monitored the SOS and could I be told that the crippled 'plane had landed safely. I was as pleased as if my own brother had been one of the crew but I never ceased to marvel that someone in such an exalted position would pass on such a message to a very humble ACW 1.'

*Alan Caudle spent the last years of the war in **India***

Indian Steam nostalgia

'I joined the RAF in May 1944 as an aircrew volunteer but when the war in Europe came to an end, the need for aircrew diminished. So, after a series of remusterings, I finished up as a meteorologist and was sent to India in May 1945.

We were required to service Transport Command's then predominant air route, bringing back our troops for demob from the Japanese theatre of war and also to help train and expand the Royal Indian Air Force Met Service.

So after a long Dakota flight from Merryfield (near Taunton)— the only experience I have ever had of hay-box cooked meals, and to be my last in the UK for two and a half years—we arrived eventually in Poona. We made refuelling stops at Sardinia, Cyrenaica (now Libya), Palestine (now, of course, Israel), Habbaniya (Iraq), Bahrain and Karachi.

My first train journey was a relatively short one from Poona to Bombay, from where of all crazy things, I was posted back to Mauripur (Karachi)! (After a period of hospitalisation with malaria and dysentery which soon took hold of many others besides myself).

Thus began my steam railway journeying in this great sub-continent, on probably one of the world's largest rail networks over a given area. I had a Kodak 116 folding camera and always regret not having made better use of it.

When I arrived at RAF Worli (Bombay) it was the beginning of the monsoon season and it was not possible to travel by rail on the short route to Karachi via Ahmedahbad because of flood risk.

It was necessary to take the much longer route via Delhi and Lahore. I well remember a very uncomfortable night spent with a number of colleagues (and many of those unfortunates more used to it!) sleeping on Lahore station platform, waiting for our connection to Karachi.

The trains were very primitive and overcrowded with many 'hangers on'—on the roof and sides! We soon got used to the three-in-one 'window' protection designed to deal with the heat, the elements and privacy. It came as a shock to let them all down on arising from a rough night to be greeted by a band of determined locals—all doing their utmost to sell us an array of fearsome knives and kukris etc. Eventually at every stop, and there were many, we got used to fruit, drink and food sellers and the baksheesh wallahs that besieged us.

One of the more pleasant aspects of Indian rail travel in the mid '40s was to be able to get a meal in the restaurant of the larger stations while the train waited for you!

I believe first-class passengers could actually order their meal in advance at a preceding station or via an official on the train—all done by inter-station telegraphy.

Troops were not permitted such luxury. One interesting feature that we did have, though on some of the second-class carriages was the presence of a very large wooden-bound, tank-lined icebox from which a variety of bottled drinks could be obtained if you were lucky.

Towards the end of 1946, I was allowed to take all my accumulated leave in one slice. Instead of going to the hill station of Srinagar in the foothills of the Himalayas which most servicemen from Karachi did, I decided to go south and take a much longer journey to Ootacamund (Ootty), in the Nilgiri Hills. I had a good friend stationed at RAF Bangalore and we had synchronised our leave. This is still the longest railway journey I have ever undertaken on my own—but you are never on your own for long in India! It took me a week each way to get there and back and I'm sure could never be matched in terms of experience by any of the luxury tours being offered to today's world travellers.

Setting out from Karachi, it was necessary to change at the first stop, Hyderabad, the capital of Sind province, which is predominantly desert country. At Hyderabad I boarded a train of the Jodhpur State Railway, on which I recall the well-maintained carriages, especially the beautifully appointed miniature restaurant car with its aisle between single and double tables.

Jodhpur itself was an irresistible tourist attraction. However, I was en route to Ahmedahbad for an exciting—one could say frightening—change in the middle of the night to a Bombay, Baroda and Central India (BBC!) train at the other end of a very long single platform. This was a real nightmare! All main rail stations in India are crowded, whether by day or night, and my absolute concern was to keep the closest eye on the coolie/porter who was conveying on his head all my leave possessions in my tin trunk through what seemed to be an everlasting chanting throng.

Unfortunately I had no opportunity to take a look at Baroda on this part of the journey to Bombay, where it was necessary to change terminals by taxi, another 'interesting' experience. From here I travelled by Great Indian Peninsular (GIP) train to Nagpur; then on to Bangalore, where I resided unofficially at RAF Bangalore, having met up with my friend Eric.

We travelled to Mysore, which had a pleasant 'Garden city' atmosphere. Among our sightseeing we particularly enjoyed visiting the Maharajah's elephant stables where the film Elephant Boy starring Sabu was made, and climbing the 1,000 steps to the summit of Chamundi Hill (3,484ft) without meeting the resident Black Panther. On the way up we did meet Nandi—the huge Hindu sacred bull hewn out of a single boulder nearly four hundred years ago.

There is a temple on the summit and the Maharajah's summer palace, with a fine view across to the Nilgiri Hills, a hundred miles away.

For our tortuous journey to 'Ooty' which has been described as a quasi-European mountain township, we took an ancient semi-open sided, well overladen (inside and out) bus, through tea and coffee plantations and circuitous mountain roads to our leave destination.

Our base was a comfortable chalet owned by a Swiss lady who mothered us pleasantly. Walking and trying our hand at horse riding and canoeing were our main occupations. It was a very enjoyable and restful stay.

Pakistan had not been born then but was on the path to its formation. I well recall the ever widening band of sweat around my middle through my khakis, as a member of the guard of honour when Lord Mountbatten took over from Lord Wavell as the last Viceroy on March 22, 1947. He held this post until August 13th of that year when India received her independence and Pakistan was formed. Lord Mountbatten then stayed on to become Governor General of India. I stayed on too, though only until the end of the year when I returned to the UK; my memorable years in India indelibly etched inside of me.'

Tony Reedman *lived in* **Birmingham** *during the war*

My surprise day out

'What if there's an air raid, dad?' I asked, bothered it might ruin my day out.

'We'll go into one of London's underground rail shelters, but don't worry, jerry's not bombing much since Monty's thrashed Rommel in North Africa.'

Trust lousy old Birmingham to not have 'Undergrounds', I thought to myself. Just some old basements, ground level brick shelters, and corrugated steel Anderson shelters buried in the small gardens of most houses in our street.

I remember how exciting it was when war was declared and our shelter was delivered. Then the first air raid! Mum and dad panicked us out of the house down into it. Mum got frightened when dad went back to turn off the gaslight and shut the front door we'd left open in our dash. That was two years back, and since then, I'd got used to the crump of bombs and the 'ack-ack'. Anyway, I wasn't going to be killed because I was 'going to grow up,' join the army and free my brother Gordon who had been captured at Tobruk, and was now a prisoner of war in Italy.

Besides, Mrs Allen and son Barry who lived two houses up had their house blown up. It collapsed over their shelter, but they were rescued ok. We were living at number 4 Myrtle Grove, Leonard Road, Handsworth then, and we were bombed a lot. Dad told mum and me that if our house was hit, we would come through ok as well—unless the water main broke and drowned us! That happened to the old Harriet sisters, they went down into their cellar because they were frightened of spiders in the shelter. They lived in the next grove to us, and the bomb didn't explode it just collapsed their house on top of them. We did not know about it until they started screaming at the cellar grating as the water rose.

In eleven months I would be fourteen and ready to start work like a man, yet I still held onto my dad's hand as we threaded our way through servicemen packing the platform of Birmingham's New Street station. Dad stopped in front of two soldiers sharing a cigarette butt.

'Here you are son, here's twopence halfpenny, get yourself five 'Woodies' out of the machine there.' He slipped the coins into the youngest soldier's hand. 'You're a good 'un pop,' the young one grinned, slapping him on the back happily. 'Not 'arf,' the other agreed. 'I reckon we'd have had to have gone on the 'earhole' if you hadn't come by.'

'I know what it's like being out of fags. I was in the first lot. I've known lads crawl across no mans land and get the fags out of dead men's pockets.' Dad looked down frowning. Suddenly he burst out 'Come on Tony, let's see if we can squeeze into the waiting room, Ta rah lads.'

Dad steered me gently through the door. The room was thick with tobacco smoke and overflowing with men and women of all three services. Kitbags, rifles, gas masks, and steel helmets were lumped around them. The lucky ones were sprawled asleep on the tabletops and benches, the rest huddled against each other on the floor. An ATS girl was the first to notice me.

'Do you want somebody sonny? One of these 'orrible blokes your dad, or one of us pretty girls your mum?' she asked cheekily.

There were a few drowsy chuckles.

'My, er, dad's, um, taking me to London on the Grimsby fish train.' I stammered, and dad came through the blackout curtain, laying a protective hand on my shoulder. 'It's ok, I thought there may have been some room. There's a cold wind cutting along the platform for a lad in short trousers, 'specially at half three in the morning,' Dad said.

''Ere, come on, squeeze in 'ere dad and sit the boy on your lap,' a friendly sailor invited.

Talking that had hushed when we entered began again, and I heard a 'bloody'.

'Cut yer language,' an angry voice snapped. 'there's a kid in here!'

'It's that landlubber of a soldier 'as swore,' the sailor next to my dad whispered self-righteously. 'Still, from the look of 'im I'm glad he's on our side!'

I must have fallen asleep, for the next thing I knew, I was being shoved out of the doorway. Along the dimly lit platform, servicemen were milling towards a train clanking slowly to a halt. Amongst them, tall soldiers in red caps and armbands lettered MP, bawled for them to board the train in an orderly fashion. Dad steered me towards an open door and we scrambled into the corridor.

'Nay more room up this way,' grunted the soldier in front of us struggling with his kit, 'and now the corridor's full behind you. 'Meck the best o' it here.' He sat down on his kit bag, propping his rifle against the door of the adjacent full compartment. We made ourselves comfortable sitting on the floor, and after what seemed a lifetime, the train jerked, 'clackity clacking' slowly away. I cheered inwardly. I was off to London where the cinema newsreels showed The Prime Minister two fingering the Huns as he inspected the bomb damage done by the blitz.

I squinted through the window blind. Dozens of servicemen were crowding anxiously round the redcaps, who were writing in their notebooks.

'Shut the blind, else jerry might see us,' my dad said sharply. 'Anyhow, what's so interesting?'

I had started explaining what had been going on as we left the platform, when the Scottish soldier broke in.

'Weel if yon 'laddies' dinna get back to their barracks because the train was full, their Officers can check the truth of it with the Rail Transport Officer, once the MPs have teken their names.'

That said, he closed his eyes and dropped off to sleep, and it wasn't long before I did the same. It was a restless sleep, I felt my dad pull me in close as people moved up and down the corridor. Some going to the toilet, others to get on and off the train. In one of my restless dreams, Churchill was on a platform giving service-men a puff on his cigar, before they jumped into a rushing river where the rails would normally be.

'Come on Tony, wake up!' my dad shouted. 'We're there. London. Euston. It's quarter to six.'

Drowsily I got up and followed my dad on to the platform. There was a vacant end place on a nearby bench, where three RAF men were laughing and joking.

'Go and sit there and wake yourself up properly while I go and see if Smiths have got the papers yet.'

He disappeared in the crowd and I wondered how long he would be. After a while, I felt thirsty and fished out of my school satchel our Tizer bottle of cold tea. Unscrewing the top, I took a long swig.

'Crikey we got a real little boozer here,' one of the airman laughed. 'What you got in the bottle sonny? Black and Tan?'

I did not know what Black and Tan was and I thought he must have been referring to its colour.

'My mum makes it strong and sweet,' I replied. 'Because dad gets condensed milk from 'under the counter' at the works canteen.' I wondered whether I should have said that, and quickly added, 'You see, he's on special war work.'

'Ain't we all!' chuckled the airman, who I knew was an air gunner because of the AG and half wing on his tunic. Then he winked at his companions and went on. 'What sort of special war work's he on then?'

I struggled for an answer that would impress them. 'It's secret.' I came up with triumphantly hoping that would be good enough for them to stop questioning me.

Just then, there was a commotion along the platform where my dad had gone. People, mostly servicemen, were shouting, jumping, and waving their arms in the air. Some of them were doing little jigs. Then I saw my dad running towards me, waving his Daily Express in the air.

'They've surrendered, Italy has surrendered Tony. Gordon could be free soon.' For a second I had a nasty thought that the war would be over before I grew up. By this time, dad had reached me and the three airmen were crowding round him reading the headlines.

'Would you believe it, Wednesday the 8th of September 1943,' the airman with the handlebar moustache exclaimed. 'My son's first birthday falling on the day Italy surrenders: What damned good luck.'

'It will be better luck if Germany surrenders on his second,' said my Dad optimistically. 'Come on Tony lets see if we can find somewhere to eat in the warm.'

There was a restaurant not far from Euston station, just opening for breakfasts. We had some fried dried egg and fried bread. I wanted to drink some more of the cold tea, but dad made me drink a glass of hot milk he charmed out of a charmless counter assistant. I judged it was a good time to ask what my surprise was.

'Wait and see,' he smiled. 'Now come on, we've got a bus to catch.'

Workers were moving by now, and there was a long queue at the bus stop. I had visions of a long wait. However the buses came along every few minutes and we pushed our way upstairs to the top deck at my insistence. I wanted to see as much of London as possible, and as luck had it, we did get a seat right at the front. I expected to see lots of war damage but didn't; I reckoned Birmingham's was worse! Anyway, everyone on the streets seemed very cheerful for all the bombing they were supposed to have had. It was popular at the time to blame some news information on propaganda. I did just that. Buses did not have their destination indicators showing since war began so I still did not know where I was going. After twenty minutes, I began pestering dad about it. The conductor called out the names of the stops, which meant little to me until approaching one, dad caught hold of my hand and led me down on to the bus platform.

'Regents Park, anybody for Regents Park?'

'Yes please mate.' Dad said to the conductor, who yanked on his bell rope and the bus ground to a halt.

'Is this all we're coming to, a park?' I cried, with a rush of un-grateful anger.

'Something wrong with parks?' my dad countered.

'*Parks* only have grass and swings in them.' I gritted, adding grudgingly that 'some parks do have lakes with boats on I sup-pose.'

No sooner had I vented my anger on dad about 'lousy old parks' than my eyes lit on ZOO. The park had a zoo! The sign said ZOO: my surprise from dad. Regents Park Zoo! Yippee, I had never been to a zoo; Birmingham didn't have one. Just a rotten old 'pets cor-ner' with a couple of monkeys and a few rabbits on the top floor of Lewis's. I wanted to see and know about Elephants, Camels, Rhino, and were there *Lions and Tigers*? Dad said because of the war and the difficulty of getting food for them there might not be too many animals there. Moreover, perhaps they didn't keep too many fierce ones in case they escaped if a bomb hit the zoo. I had to be satisfied with that, although I kept hoping that there would be at least *one* lion or tiger.

Dad paid and we were in the zoo. Straightaway, I looked for a keeper, and saw one by an animal pen. Without even asking dad I ran across to him.

'Could you-I mean, excuse me sir, are there any lions here?' I asked breathlessly.

'Your name isn't Albert by any chance?' He asked solemnly, ''Cause if it is . . . No we ain't got no lions.'

The keeper looked down at me with a serious face, although his blue eyes twinkled as he glanced across at dad.

'No, I'm called Tony,' I said desperately 'and I've never seen a real live lion. If I'm Tony, and not Albert, can I see one?'

My dad came up smiling. The keeper ruffled my hair, and pointed. 'Sonny, follow the road right to the bottom and there's a lion more famous than Tarzan's.'

Dad found it hard to keep up with me as I raced down the road towards the lion's cage.

We passed two police officers going the same way and a car pulling up alongside the cage. Around the semi-circular cage were about twenty people of both sexes. Excitedly, I edged my way to the front. I stared in awe. There he was swaggering round his cage, his magnificent head, and mane swinging back and forth. Here was my first real live lion, truly the King of Beasts! Vaguely I recollected from the wireless that this fearsome animal represented Britain and Churchill had warned Hitler not to 'tweak the lion's tail.'

Unexpectedly the lion pushed his backside up to the bars and sprayed 'pee' over some of us. Squeals of disgust and laughter as we all jumped back, many bumping into the car.

'Steady on down there please,' a voice shouted from above. On the roof of the car a man with a cine camera mounted on a tripod glared angrily down on us. Someone in the group voiced the opinion that he was there to film the lion. Another questioned why the camera operator was focusing down the road then? I made my way over to dad who had gone to look at a plaque fixed on the brickwork below the cage bars. 'The lion's called Rota, Tony,' he read aloud, 'and it was presented to Mr Churchill by a Mr Thomson. How about that!'

Dad had barely finished reading this when things started to happen! The policemen began shepherding all of us towards an area behind the car. That brought about a bit of good-natured grumbling and questions, which the smiling policemen ignored. Dad and I were being jostled into the middle when a woman cried excitedly. 'It's Winnie, Gord luv us it's Churchill hisself.'

Dad quickly hoisted me onto his shoulders: Was I really seeing Britain's greatest man coming down the road? There was no mistaking him with his bowler hat and cigar. Winston Churchill, flanked either side by a plain clothed bodyguard. The party stopped briefly and one of his bodyguards adjusted his body tape.

The crowd were cheering, shouting patriotic slogans with some 'Good old Winnie's'. In addition, 'that's finished the Spaghetti Bashers', and 'Adolf's in for it now'.

By now the great man's party had reached Rota's cage. A zoo official supervised keepers fixing a large flank of raw meat on to a long pole. One of them opened a small gate in the cage while another helped Winston push the pole of meat in. Rota dived on it, sunk his great fangs into it, and ripped it off the pole, dragging it to the far end of the cage. The scene could have been stage-managed. He stood on the meat, lifted his great head, and roared triumphantly. Its symbolism was not lost on us. We cheered loudly, long after Winston's car had disappeared from sight.

'Winston Churchill feeds his Lion Rota the day Italy surrendered.' were the commentator's opening words on the next edition of Pathe's News. A few of my school friends were with me at the 'News Theatre'.

'I seen him there, I've seen Winnie!' I boasted proudly.'

*Frank Waghorn recalls his journey home from **The Far East***

Home at last

'At Bangkok there were thousands of troops and we were to discover that the Japs had surrendered on August 15th 1945 the day we had arrived at the last camp. As it was now the 18th August, we realised that we had endured three days longer than most. Several Yanks seemed to be in charge of this huge compound and the Red Cross were there in numbers. For reasons best known to the Command, the Japs were put in charge of us, retaining their rifles. I suppose there was some logic in this—if we had the guns we would have shot the lot. What a difference though. They now bowed to us and were helpful in every way. Never trust a Jap, I thought at the time.

However, we were free at last, though in very bad health. We still could not believe that we really were free. We were welcomed by the Yanks, with the tannoy system blaring out the good news of our release; at last we knew it was true. We still only had the clothing of make shift loincloths, though everything had been thought of for our release. We were soon issued with army tropical kit. Many of the POWs had been moved to various hospitals with dysentery, beriberi, tropical ulcers and amputees, some on the point of dying. Of those of us who were left, few weighed over seven stone. There were marquees equipped with real beds, a luxury indeed, but first we were waited upon with our first proper food for three and a half years; a bowl of soup and a soft bread roll.

In the morning we were thoroughly examined, I was given medication for malaria and beriberi, my weight being just under seven stone. I was at this base for a week, being fed with food every two hours; very scanty portions as it was vital that we had the correct vitamins for a slow build up of strength. A doctor saw us each day. Eventually we were put aboard army trucks, driven by Japs and taken to Bangkok airport where several Dakota planes were lined up. Each 'plane took twenty people sitting on the floor, ten each side. Even then our ordeal was not over. The Canadian crew told us that the planes had taken a real battering during the war and they were all slightly worst for wear. There were no parachutes for us. But we didn't feel too hard done by—there were no parachutes for the crew either! In our state of health the flight was looked forward to with a mixture of excitement, trepidation and fear!

Eventually we got airborne and in no time at all we were high above the clouds. Soon I noticed that several chaps had passed out with blood oozing from their noses and ears. Not long afterwards I must have suffered the same fate. We arrived at Rangoon airport where ambulances took us to hospital; we knew nothing of this until waking in our hospital beds. Every care and attention was lavished on us but we were still on the same strict diet of protein food—little and often. After a few days the beriberi was much better and the malaria bout had completely gone, but I was still not allowed out of bed. Being frustrated, I disobeyed orders and got dressed, went outside to find that sheer devastation greeted me. As I later found out, Rangoon had been captured and then recaptured several times. The little way I went, I did not see anything of the town. Feeling very tired I went back to the hospital and was severely reprimanded and sent back to bed. After a few more days I was allowed to walk about in the hospital—my weight was now 7st 10lb. As I was getting stronger I volunteered to look after the amputees who were soon to be sent home. The next day a lorry arrived with more volunteers and off to the docks we went. What a sight to see a ship which although small in comparison to the great liner going out at the time, was my salvation to get me back home. The ship was the 'Boisveign' a Dutch cargo ship with a wonderful Dutch captain who shook hands with all of us and treated us like heroes.

The next surprise was to find we had been given the wrong information. The ship had been fitted out as a hospital ship with doctors, nurses and auxiliary medical staff; all we had to do was sit back and enjoy a wonderful trip back home. Well looked after, complete comfort and good food—what a change in our circumstances!

Soon we were on our way, blue sky and calm waters. The captain estimated that we would be routed to Southampton, which pleased me as this was nearer home than Liverpool. The food on board was excellent; a wider variety than in hospital but still little and often. We had also been issued with a further set of kit. Life was now a bed of roses, so different from our plight a month before. Our first stop was Kandy in Ceylon. All the ships in the harbour hooted their horns in greeting. What a sight this was to see after being used to nothing but jungle. We were not allowed to leave the ship. However, a contingent of Wrens came aboard and told us about the many restrictions and the rationing which was going on in the UK. An amazing coincidence happened here. One of the Wrens was my sister-in-law! She was an officer on Lord Mountbatten's staff stationed in Kandy. I was hardly recognisable to her, being four stone lighter in weight than when she had last seen me. I was also speaking pigeon English, yellow in complexion and probably slightly deranged. I was more like a zombie than the chap who had left the UK several years previously. However, once she realised who I was, we had a long chat and I learned that all was well at home.

After refuelling etc, we were off again. I was to be home before my sister-in-law who would be in Ceylon for some time, she informed me. On board ship I visited the hospital; it was wonderful to see the cheerful faces of our comrades, some with amputated arms, some with amputated legs, several with both amputated. It made us feel how lucky some of us were.

We were now in the Red Sea, which was quite eerie with the water so calm, at the start of the Suez Canal. Here the captain was ordered to stop for a while until the canal was clear, as it was very narrow. He was furious as he was attempting to be the first ship back to England. He must have broken all the rules and certainly smashed the speed limit through to the other end of the canal at the Port of Suez.

Arriving at Suez, those of us that were able disembarked where we were greeted by the British Red Cross. Again we were told of shortages back home. We were given a variety of goods, such as toothpaste and soap, enough to fill half a kit bag; the rest was filled with more clothing. After embarking once again we were told that the captain had been severely reprimanded and suffered a heavy fine for his action through the Suez canal. He said he would do it again, as his job was to get home as quickly as possible and that was what he was going to do. What a man! We also found out at this point that our destination was Liverpool not Southampton, so our journey would last a day or so longer!

I now had two large kit bags full of clothing and various goodies that were still in short supply in the UK. Soon, we were in the Bay of Biscay, the last lap before Liverpool and after three months at sea, this was the only time I had slight seasickness. I was lucky—my sickness was very mild and soon cleared, whereas most of my fellow travellers had a terrible time. They were ill, very ill!

As we entered the Mersey, a thick English fog came down and we had to weigh anchor a short distance from the docks that we could not see. The captain kept us informed of the situation, the next message being that we would lay off of the berth for about twenty-four hours due to the thick fog. Utter dismay for all of us! So near and yet so far! Eventually the fog lifted; at last we were in Liverpool. Soon we were disembarking, carrying our kitbags and pushing through the throng of people who were waiting to see if their loved ones were amongst the returning prisoners. Home at last!'

*Jack Ramsey from **Suffolk** served the army
in very salubrious surroundings*

Two wheels in the West Country

'I joined the RASC Waterborne Fleet which operated harbour launches, landing craft, high speed launches, etc. I did my training at Golden Hill Fort on the Isle of Wight, which was a very pleasant location. After qualifying as a coxswain, however, my first posting put the Isle of Wight firmly in the second division. I was sent to Venice, where I operated my own harbour launch, with three crewmembers, for over a year. After this I moved to Port Said, in Egypt to serve on landing craft. So my service years enabled me to see parts of the world that I would probably not have seen otherwise (certainly not in those days). Let's face it, to be skipper of your own boat in Venice of all places must have been one of the best postings in the army!

On my return to Civvy street, things were not quite so rosy. Low paid jobs in factories and a two up, two down country cottage with outside toilet. I had an eight mile cycle ride to work each day. By this time I had married and within a year we moved to live in the town. I joined the Territorials; the money came in very handy and soon I was doing quite a few weekends and summer camps. The extra money enabled me to buy an old side valve motorbike and sidecar. One summer weekend we borrowed a tent (which leaked), half a dozen blankets, one primus stove and two maps. With a mixture of hope and apprehension, we set off to tour Devon and Cornwall. The old bike never missed a beat and we had no trouble until we arrived at Stonehenge, en route to Devon. We had a quick look round at the monument, then back to the bike to find a flat tyre. I pumped it up with a foot pump and carried on until the air went down and I stopped to pump it up again. This was repeated several times until we arrived at a wayside campsite, in a picturesque setting by a lake. We stopped here, got out the primus, erected the tent and my wife, who was hugely enjoying the whole experience, cooked a delicious meal. The evening was very hot and we paddled in the lake to cool down. We strolled back to the tent and I pumped up the tyre, hoping that it would stay up until morning or I would have to mend it. Morning came, so did bacon and eggs and the tyre was still up so we carried on. We had a lovely week in the West Country and all too soon it was time to set off home. The tyre had stayed up!

On the return journey we stopped at a small campsite in the pouring rain. We put the tent up in double quick time, enjoyed a simple meal then went to bed. The next morning we were woken by the smell of frying bacon coming from the only other tent on the site. The two men who were organising breakfast were very friendly (as everyone was in those days) and we chatted away before starting to cook our own breakfast. One of the men remarked that they would get Grandma out, upon which they dragged a trestle table out of the large Ridge tent. The equally large sleeping bag, which was laid out on the table, began to wriggle and Grandma's head appeared from one end. We were astonished but the men assured us that she always travelled with them like that on their camping weekends. Grandma, a lady of few words, nodded in agreement. About an hour later their motorcycle combination, a table strapped to the roof of the sidecar, went merrily on its way. With a cheery wave from Grandma inside the sidecar and a shouted 'Goodbye' from the two men, they set off to wherever they were headed, never to be seen by us again.

We arrived home later that day. The following morning the tyre was flat, the first time since the day at Stonehenge, twelve days previously, that it had let us down!'

Joan Barnes in *Nottingham recalls living in London Road*

The Transport House

'On London Road a local widow ran a 'Transport House'. This was a large house that provided lodgings for lorry drivers. They didn't need to book and slept several to a room in cheap, basic accommodation. There were lorries parked everywhere. The owner's husband had been killed in the Second World War and the Transport House was her only source of income. She seemed to do all right though and brought up her two children—one she spoilt and the other she did her best to ignore.

We lived in a street off London Road and every year the whole neighbourhood got together to hold a bonfire in the local square on November 5th. All the neighbours paid in to a fund for fireworks and food. Chairs were brought out from the houses and one old lady had her piano brought out to the square so that she could accompany the singing. It was great fun. One year though, a terrible accident happened. A boy who was wearing tight trousers had three crackers in his back pocket. A nine-year-old girl crept up behind him and set light to them. He couldn't get his tight trousers off and was badly burned on his back, bottom and legs—he was in hospital until after Christmas. I can still hear him screaming . . .'

Don Hoskins *'mispent' his youth in* **London**

Addiction

'I have to concede that from an early age I was addicted: in my case the addiction was to cinema. It probably started when I was taken to the pictures for the first time and saw what I think must have been one of the old Laurel and Hardy two reelers. This I thought was the funniest thing I had ever seen and I have not changed my opinion since. I was well placed to feed my addiction as it was about two minutes walk to the cinema opposite Brockley Station, known in various incarnations as the Palladium, the Giraldo and the New Palladium. The Giraldo was known as the fleapit. It was really basic. The power plant was a gas engine that throbbed away with a continuous put-put-put. This could be heard inside as a gently pulsing background to all the programmes. The seats were rickety and torn and occasionally a few rows, more than usually dilapidated, were roped off. The management's main selling point seemed to be the length of the programmes. There was the feature film, the supporting film, a newsreel, trailers for coming attractions and sometimes 'The March of Time' or a two reeler comedy. Usually there was also a serial.

The serials were either Westerns, tales of the American Civil War, or the US Marines on inter-planetary warfare with, I think, Flash Gordon. They went on forever and I suspect that instalments were not necessarily shown consecutively, but no one complained. Programmes were subject to unscheduled breaks when numbers flashed on the screen in rapid succession, to the cheers of the audience. Sometimes the emergency exit doors flew open as enterprising local youths sought free admission, or the usher ejected some patron who declined to comply even with his easy-going standards of deportment.

My cinema going was interrupted when the Giraldo lived up to its reputation. I reported a number of red spots on my chest to my mother. Aghast she said, 'You've brought home a flea. It's that Giraldo. You'll go there no more.'

I had a vision of walking up Brockley Road arm in arm with the flea prior to introducing him to the family. But I realised that it was a serious matter and merely protested that the insect could have come from anywhere and it could have happened to anyone. This did me no good. I was comprehensively cleansed and forbidden to return to the Giraldo on pain of dire consequences. As ever in our easy-going family, I observed the ban for a time and then slipped back into my previous habits. Fortunately after this incident the fleas seemed to confine their attention to other patrons.'

Mike Fountain recalls his early introduction to soccer

Designer Boots

'At Primary school we didn't have the chance to play with a proper football, so it was quite a shock when I went to Grammar school to find that we had to attend on Saturday mornings for games. The teams were pinned up on the noticeboard in the cloakroom and at first I would hope that my name wasn't featured on the team sheets. I was fortunate that I lived close to school and didn't have to catch a bus or train from one of the far flung 'outposts'. My Dad was in the army at the time and my mother was unable to buy football boots of my size, due to post war shortages. So, during the first term I had to play football wearing a pair of ex-WAAF (Women's Auxiliary Air Force) black shoes which had been kindly provided by mum's friend's sister-in-law—very embarrassing!'

*Frank Mileham grew up on an Army camp in **Dorset***

Getting an education

'I lived at Bovington Camp after the war where my father, a regular soldier, was posted. In order to get to school, I left home just after 6am and walked the two miles to the nearest railway station, at Wool. I caught a train to Wareham, then another to Swanage. School was about three-quarters of a mile from the station, which meant another healthy walk. So I (and all of my fellow pupils who lived in outlying areas) had plenty of exercise before I started my lessons. Then we repeated the journey in the evening to return home. A long day!'

Norma Benney *saw one far-reaching after-effect of the War
in her home country of* **New Zealand**

Six pints of beer and a good cry

'My father had an evening job cleaning the local cinema and we
always studied the type of film that was showing. Sad films always
brought a harvest of dropped, tear sodden handkerchiefs. In the
days before 'Kleenex' these were precious. Father brought them
home and mother boiled them all up in an old soup pot; the ironing took hours! One day my father brought home several combs.
Mother attempted to clean them up in the same way with disastrous results—when she tipped the water out she found several
small round melted plastic globules in the bottom of the pot.

The licensing laws for pubs in New Zealand were particularly
severe. Closing time was 6pm. Men would go in at 5pm after work
and order six or more pints of beer and line them up on the bar or
at the table. They swilled them straight down one after another as
fast as they could. Not everyone was able to last the pace though.
Suddenly assailed with gallons of cold beer, some stomachs heaved
and men vomited in the pub doorways or under lampposts. The
'Drunk's Tram' was, of course, the first one to leave the city after
6pm and the inside was a sorry sight with the occasional fight and
frequent vomiting. Soldiers returning from the war, who had experienced the more liberal drinking regimes in Europe, continually
told all who would listen that the NZ licensing laws were coun-
terproductive. It took several years before licensing hours were
extended and the 'Drunk's Tram' became a thing of the past.'

Rosemary Moore *worked as a tailor in* **Bournemouth**

Under the canopy and break the glass

'I come from a practical family, a back to basics, hands-on family.
My grandfather was the local wheelwright and my grandmother
could turn her hand to anything. She could knit, sew, cook, crochet, wallpaper, paint; all the necessary things in her day and
age to make a home for her ten children. My mother was a dress-

maker and my father was a journeyman tailor, brought up in the sweatshops of London's East End. I remember being got up in the middle of the night, aged about four, to be fitted for a coat and hat so that it could be ready for the next day to go on holiday to visit my grandparents.

When I left school it was therefore a natural thing to follow them in to the same trade. My mother took me to Robert Old and Madame Campbell's tailoring business in Westover Road, Bournemouth and I gained a coveted place as an apprentice. When I first began I earned 17/6d per week and my bus fare was 17/10d! Mr Old was a very small man but we were all in awe of him. We also showed great respect to his son who was known by his Christian name of 'Mr Bertram.'

Mr Gabriel, the cutter and fitter and the head of the workroom was a Jewish gentleman who also ran a dance band in his spare time and was known as Monty Gay. He was the only person in the workroom to be allowed to the fitting rooms on the floor below and the showroom on the ground floor was completely out of bounds to us. We reached our third floor workroom by a steep iron staircase at the back of the building and were not to be seen by the clients.

We were about fifteen people in all. There was Mr Cooper, who must have been at least seventy but could still hop up on to the waist high cutting table to sit there cross-legged working on his trouser making, much of it still being done by hand. Tony, the swarthy Italian, who sang arias from the operas as he worked. Maria, who sang little Irish ditties with her beautiful red hair down to her waist and green eyes; a typical Irish Miss. In the dressmaking department, Helga was about to 'go under the canopy and break the glass' with her wealthy Jewish gentleman friend.

All of us on summer days with the windows open, enjoyed the band playing opposite in the Pleasure Gardens twice a day. All days seemed sunny then as the war had just ended.

The workroom was multi-national and this is where I learned one of the most important lessons in my life—that all people have equal status in life and are entitled to the same respect, even as I made the tea and learned how to keep my machine in running order.

Until you had run a machine needle through your finger and faced it with equanimity you were not considered a full member of the team. I remember being asked on my first day by the cutter and fitter 'Where is your thimble?' I answered in my innocence 'I don't wear one.' His answer was immediate—'You do now.' I have never been able to work without a thimble since.'

Sue Anderson went away to Boarding School in 1948

No trousers allowed

'When I first went away to school, trousers for girls were unheard of. Even the boys wore shorts for their first two years. In the summer of my first year I went off one Saturday with one of my friends, who was a daygirl, to ride ponies. Our ride was marvellous and we stayed out longer than we had anticipated. Consequently, I turned up for tea back at school still wearing my jodhpurs. I can still see the amazement on the housemaster's face as I walked in. He would have made me go and change except that there was no time. I was used to wearing riding clothes all the time at home and had never considered that they would be forbidden.

In my third year, trousers suddenly became fashionable and I went back to school after the summer holidays with a pair in my suitcase. We eventually managed to gain permission to wear our trousers after school, after several weeks of discussions!'

Ann Parker grew up near *Poole*

Schools and hospitals

'When I was four, we moved to Parkstone where my mother opened a guesthouse and my father left the Army to join the Post Office. I used to go back to Frampton for holidays and it was during one of these that I became extremely ill and was taken to the Children's Hospital where streptococcal septicaemia was diagnosed. The symptoms are the same as rheumatic fever and so are the side effects apparently. These days, antibiotics would be pumped into me and I would go home quite soon, but in those days things were different. I stayed in for eleven months and then they took my tonsils out in case they caused it!

Life in hospital was very different then from now. I was six years old and spent the first three months on my back in a cot at first and then in a small bed. I was not allowed to sit up even to eat. When I did sit up and attempt to get out of bed I could not walk I was so weak. We did not have regular education, although I have vague memories of a little. Parents were not allowed to visit when they chose. I had two visits a week, whether that was all my parents could manage or all they were allowed I never found out. I had toys and made friends, including a girl who was crippled with polio, with whom I stayed in touch until she died about three years later. The food was pretty dreadful and I remember being very sick after one meal with spinach in it. I think the staff must have been very cross because I have a dread of being sick anywhere anytime, unlike my children who take it as a matter of course! I've hated spinach ever since.

I left hospital and returned home to discover that in the year I had been in, my parents had moved to Poole in a bigger guesthouse beside the Park. My mother was also pregnant, although I didn't realise it. In those days no one discussed the facts of life and so I had no idea. I was sent to stay with friends soon after my arrival at home and when I got back there was a baby in my doll's cot. I was most upset and it took me a long time to get used to the idea.

I must have been about nine when I contracted yellow jaundice 'from the toilet seat at school', my mother muttered darkly. That meant I had to be in a constant temperature for a fortnight, no leaving the room, which was kept like a hot house and no visitors, it was believed to be highly contagious. I was off school for about twelve weeks, back to the trusty books and radio. Since then I have been a very healthy person!

By now it must have been around 1948 and I was at junior school. My parents sent me to the private school next door to where I lived and I was late most days! Discipline was strict. I got black marks regularly because I couldn't do my plaits tidily. I was well ahead with reading and writing, but well behind with maths (still am!). I remember quite clearly being made to sit on a wicker type chair for hours in my little school skirt, so that the sticks bit into my bottom, or you had to stand in the corner while they told you what you had done wrong. It was horrible and I was very unhappy there.

Occasionally, if my parents were going out for the night or they had so many guests they needed my room, I boarded, and on one such occasion I stayed over a weekend, which meant going to church on Sunday. During the service I felt dreadfully sick and

I tried to tell the teacher that I needed to go out. She kept telling me to be quiet until the inevitable happened and I was very sick everywhere! When we got back I wanted to go home, but not only would they not let me, they wouldn't tell my parents that I had been sick. My parents were so angry that they took me away and sent me to the local primary school. I say local; it was a bus ride away. I loved it and thrived there. I remember we had a bus strike and we had to walk to school, about a couple of miles, but I did it. There were three other children who lived in my area and one of the staff had a motorbike and sidecar. Most evenings he gave us a lift home, and we took it in turns to ride on the back of the bike, it was a much sought after position!

Often, a boy who lived near me and I used to walk home to save our bus fares. One Mothering Sunday I used the money that I'd saved to buy a little posy for my mother. It felt really good to think I'd earned that posy for her! Mind, I also recall that with having no brothers I was curious about the male body and he was in the situation of having no sisters so we crept into the bushes and had a look at each other's 'different bits'—imagine what the modern world would make of that!'

Donald White grew up in *Newcastle*

Skinny dipping

'We lived in a nice suburb of the city and I had a fairly comfortable, unremarkable, middle-class upbringing, at least by the standards of the post-war period. One incident though gave me a very serious lesson in life. A group of us went on a day-trip to Seaburn, which is on the coast between Newcastle and Sunderland. It was a lovely sunny day and we stripped off our clothes and ran down the beach and into the sea. I don't suppose that Seaburn has the least polluted water in Britain washing on to its beach but we didn't think about that at the time. We even took turns to jump off of the big metal sewage pipe that ran out from the beach. It was a lovely day, an escape from the day-to-day routine and we all returned to our home in high spirits. Soon afterwards several people became ill, including one of the friends with whom I had enjoyed the waters of Seaburn. The illness turned out to be Polio. I had very mixed emotions; sadness and concern for my friend and relief that I had escaped with my own health intact. I've never taken my health for granted since.'

George Parish was born in Newcastle

A great solo adventure

'Sometime around the end of 1948 (when I was twelve years of age) I and a friend had childish ideas about stories we had heard regarding kids who could go to South Africa or Australia. Here, kids could ride horses to school and do all sorts of other exciting things. My friend, without the knowledge of his parents, had already made inquiries in Newcastle-upon-Tyne about a place with the title 'Fairbridge Farm School' where there were large photographs of kids clearing land and burning blackboys (grass trees) and what appeared to us, as having a good time. On the second visit, he invited me along. We walked to town to the place in question in Newcastle, and spoke to a person about South Africa and Australia, not having a clue about what we were doing. We left our names and addresses there.

About a month later, a lady came to our house and told me that I had been selected to go to Australia. I never ever got to find out how it all happened like it did, but I assume they must have been to see my parents who must have agreed to what was about to happen. My friend, for whatever reason, didn't get selected. Why my parents gave permission for a thirteen-year-old boy to travel to the other side of the world, only they would know.

I recall that at about 10 or 11 o'clock at night in June of 1949, instead of getting ready for bed, my mother dressed me and took me with my belongings to the Newcastle-on-Tyne railway station. Here, I said a tearful goodbye to my equally tearful mother and boarded a night train to Birmingham where I joined twelve mostly orphaned kids (although I wasn't one), ranging in age from four to thirteen years old at the Middlemore Homes (Birmingham). We stayed here for about five days followed by a reception at Australia House in London, which was attended by the Duke of Gloucester. There I met Lord and Lady Glendyne who took me under their wing as Godparents. I might add that this was very appreciated by me, with the earlier years of my life in Australia being a very lonely time. (They continued to correspond with me right up until Lord Glendyne's death in 1968.)

George meets the Duke of Gloucester

We were then transported to Tilbury Docks and boarded the P & O liner Otranto for Australia through the Fairbridge Farm scheme. Our chaperone was a Miss Coles. As we left Tilbury I cried as I thought of my family back in Newcastle and wondered why I was travelling to the other side of the world alone. While we were well looked after, I was at times seasick and just about the entire time very homesick (which lasted for three years).

It was about 5 or 6am on August 9th 1949, that someone told us that the Australian mainland was in sight and that we would be docking in Fremantle around ten or eleven o'clock in the morning. Of course, we were all very excited—had breakfast and then stood on deck watching the land draw closer.

On arrival, we were ushered through customs and then confronted by a very large lady by the name of Miss Middleton ('Middy', as she became known to us). Middy was employed by the Fairbridge Farm Society as our Cottage Mother and after bundling us into a small bus with Fairbridge Farm written on its side, we set off for the country town of Pinjarra, about fifty miles south.

The trip took about two and a half hours as we stopped here and there—but I saw my first orange groves and real oranges growing on trees. We passed through a town called Armadale, before following the Darling Ranges south to about five miles north of Pinjarra where we were confronted by a sign saying Fairbridge Farm School. We turned off the highway onto a gravel road that seemed to go into deep bush and head toward the big hills in the background. After travelling two to three miles, we entered the Fairbridge compound. I always remember the blackboy (or grass tree) that was at the entrance (and is still there today). We travelled along what I discovered later to be the main thoroughfare through the compound which was lined by at first double-story wooden buildings and then single story wooden bungalow buildings—all had names on the outside, such as 'Shakespeare,' 'Darwin,' 'Raleigh,' 'Livingstone' etc. We stopped at a single story building by the name of 'Hudson' and that is what was to become my home for the next two and a half years.

The Farm School consisted of about twenty family buildings, a Principal's residence, Church, Hospital, Main Hall, sports fields, vegetable gardens, orchard and the main farm area where there were pigs, chooks (poultry houses), cows, sheep, etc. The total area, I think, would have been about three thousand acres. I had never been near a farming environment in my life, so to see pigs, horses, cows and bulls was a bit awe inspiring.

After disembarking from our bus outside of 'Hudson' Cottage we entered through the back door. Each cottage housed ten children. The cottage consisted of a large bathroom-cum-wash house, a dining room, a large dormitory, which had ten beds in it, and the Cottage Mother's quarters which consisted of bedroom and veranda. As we became used to our environment we each had chores allotted, such as cleaning, housework etc. My main job was chopping wood using a terrible axe with a pipe handle. We didn't do any cooking as we ate our evening meal in the Main Hall. We only had to get our own breakfast.

The big boys, such as myself, had to go to the farm area and get our first taste of animals, milking cows etc. I always remember that the flame trees were in full bloom (bright red) with the green '28' parrots ('28' is the local name for the parrots) flying around them.

After a few days we were told we would be going to school in Pinjarra which was about eight miles away, and so to be ready for the following Monday. Prior to going to school, we discovered that we were (that is, our party of thirteen kids) the second party to leave England after the war and that the first party had arrived some six months before us. They were allotted 'Darwin' Cottage and numbered ten—so there was twenty-three children in Fairbridge at that particular time. Of this twenty-three, about ten of us were of the age to go to the Pinjarra School. The younger ones were taught at Fairbridge. (Perhaps I should explain here that the earlier parties to Fairbridge Farm occurred years before the 2nd World War and most of the residents of that time had left the Farm School for work reasons etc, leaving just a few at Fairbridge to help run the place.)

Going to Pinjarra School was where my initiation into the Australian way of life began. We travelled in an old Chev Ute (a Chevrolet Utility vehicle—a 'Pick-up' truck) with a canopy on the back, over a dusty pot-holed gravel road to reach the highway, which was half gravel, half bitumen before Pinjarra. We generally arrived covered in dust and not looking the best. We had already heard from the first party about how we would be greeted and it wasn't long before I was in deep trouble with my teacher and the headmaster for fighting. I had no idea what a 'pommy bastard' was, but that was what we were branded. Of course, I had to learn to counter that in my own way, and in time we earned our place in the school, becoming just as bad as the local kids with our bad language. During my school period at Fairbridge, I attempted to run away and hide in the bush, awaiting an opportunity to stow away on a boat, so I thought. For that little episode I received eighteen cuts (caning) in one day—six from the teacher, six from the headmaster and six from the Fairbridge Principal.

On two other occasions, I ran away and hid in the Fairbridge orchard and ate oranges for two days. Another time, I ran away and hid in the vegetable gardens (which were very big) and lived on vegetables. On one particular occasion, I received the hiding of my life from the then Principal, Mr Healy. I, along with another boy, had been playing hockey and returned back to our cottage to be confronted by the Cottage Mother. At that time, some sort of argument had developed between Harry (the other boy) and the Cottage Mother (who hadn't been with us very long)—mind you, we didn't like her very much. Harry, after voicing his opinions, ran out the back door with her chasing him—he turned and threw his hockey stick along the floor and caught her on the shins. With that, we both took off shouting profusely, and hid in the orchard. After a cold night (or half a night) I said, 'I'm going back.' Harry said, 'I'm not.' I went back and the next day was confronted by Mr Healy who brandished a thick leather strap about 2ft long, half-inch thick—this strap was so thick it didn't even bend when held out. He pushed me down over one of the beds in the cottage dormitory and commenced to beat me—(he was in a rage). After my beating, I was black and blue from my neck to almost my knees. Never to be forgotten.'

Postscript

I am still living in Western Australia and following my schooldays, I built a successful career and have a wonderful family. I first saw my parents again after ten years of being away, a meeting which I approached with a mixture of excitement and disappointment. Excitement because I was going home and disappointment because childhood ideas of the past may not be the same as ideas as seen when an adult. I felt my father was a very hard man and only looked for the material things in life. My mother, I feel, was sorry for what had occurred with my leaving as a child but had probably gone along with my father when the decision was made. I never asked why they had sent me away and they never offered any explanations. To put it in a nutshell, times were hard after the Second World War. It may not have seemed such a bad thing (to them) for me to go to Australia—perhaps for a better future there—or perhaps it might have been 'one less mouth to feed'. I don't know.

1940s Discoveries/Developments

- Genes are made from DNA
- The Microwave Oven
- The Transistor
- The Computer
- The Electronic Calculator
- Rocket Propulsion
- The Magnetic Tape Recorder
- The Polaroid Camera
- The Hologram
- Bar Codes
- The Atomic Bomb
- The Biro

1940s Firsts

- Non Stop Flight around the World
- Organic Farming
- Tupperware
- Electric Guitar—The Les Paul
- Prefab Houses
- The Music Singles Chart (in the USA)
- Oxfam Shop
- The United Nations
- Murray Mints
- The 11+ Exam
- The Morris Minor
- The Launderette
- The Bikini
- TV Commercial (in the USA)

1940s Anniversaries

- 50th of the first Automobiles to be manufactured in Britain (1895)
- 50th of the start of the Boer War (1899)
- 50th of the Bra (1893)
- 50th of the Dow Jones Share Index (1896)
- 100th of The Factory Act, limiting women and children to a 58 hour working week (1847)
- 100th of the Potato Famine in Ireland (1845)
- 100th of the launch of the first propeller driven ship, the Napoleon (1842)
- 100th of the publication of Karl Marx's Communist Manifesto (1848)
- 100th of the issue of the first Penny Black Stamp (1840)
- 100th of the Telegram (1844)
- 200th of the first public rendition of Rule Britannia (1740)

The Future

In 1940, at the beginning of the decade, it would be:

- 10 years before the first Kidney Transplant in the USA
- 12 years before Queen Elizabeth ascended to the Throne
- 21 years before Betting Shops became legal in Britain
- 26 years before England won Football's World Cup
- 31 years before Decimal Currency was introduced in Britain
- 32 years before Britain joined the EEC
- 33 years before VAT was introduced in Britain
- 39 years before Margaret Thatcher became Britain's first woman Prime Minister
- 43 years before the development of 'Virtual Reality'

The 1950s

The world at large—the historical context

As the decade began, the Second World War was fresh in people's minds and rationing remained a fact of life; fresh fruit was still a rarity. For many people looking back, the 1950s seems to be the decade during which 'black and white gave way to colour.' Fashion, furniture and photography all looked much brighter at the end of the decade than they had at the beginning.

In industry, the traditional primary industries of coal mining and shipbuilding were in decline. However, unemployment levels were low, due to the increased production of consumer goods—cars and household appliances in particular. The former was given a massive boost by the ending of petrol rationing in May 1950. Employment opportunities in the service industries also grew to the point that vacancies remained unfilled. Immigration was encouraged, to help solve this problem and whilst the new arrivals were welcomed by many, the first signs of racial intolerance among the indigenous British population began to emerge.

Escaping from Austerity
The 1950s saw a housing boom. Areas flattened during the war were rebuilt, many with blocks of flats replacing the back to back terraced housing which had proudly housed successive generations. New towns were also developed and Crawley, Bracknell, Harlow and Hemel Hempstead all began to develop their own sense of community as the decade progressed. Inside the home, Formica was the last word in style and old wooden furniture was often covered with Formica 'to give it a new lease of life.' Panelled doors were covered with hardboard and fireplaces were ripped out or boxed in—electric heaters or central heating making them redundant.

In the High Street, the self-service store appeared. Almost 10,000 of these appeared during the decade, most being refurbished grocery stores. Although not universally popular, these new style shops changed the face of food retailing forever.

The first official Retail Prices Index (RPI) began in 1956. This updated the 1947 list of items used to monitor price changes and included brown bread, quick-frozen peas, tinned fruit, ice cream, washing machines, television sets, second hand cars and NHS prescription charges.

In May 1951, The Festival of Britain opened. This had been planned since 1945 and was held to commemorate the 100th anniversary of the Great Exhibition of 1851. It was also intended to lift the spirits of the British people who were still suffering in many ways from the after-effects of World War II.

The Festival was a national event with celebrations in many towns and cities throughout Britain. In London, the Festival was held on two sites, both of which had been extensively bomb damaged during the war—the South Bank Exhibition near Waterloo and the Festival Pleasure Gardens at Battersea. Almost eight million people visited the Exhibition during the summer of 1951.

Many Britons decided to start a new life abroad. Tens of thousands took advantage of assisted passages to English speaking countries that had formerly been part of the Empire. Canada, South Africa and New Zealand were all popular. Australia, with its £10 subsidised passage was the most popular destination.

Politics

The Labour Party was victorious in the election of 1950 and remained in power, but with a reduced majority. Clement Attlee's government had an overall majority of five seats. Winston Churchill returned to government at the age of seventy-seven after the election of October 1951 when his Conservative Party was elected with another narrow majority. Socialist 'infighting' was blamed for Labour's defeat. Churchill led the government until his resignation in 1955 when Sir Anthony Eden succeeded him. Eden immediately called for a General Election in which his party was victorious with a much-enlarged majority.

Hugh Gaitskell, a party moderate, was elected leader of the opposition Labour Party and vowed to bring stability to the divided party.

Sir Anthony Eden's tenure as Prime Minister lasted for less than two years. He retired, due to ill health, in January 1957 following the Suez crisis. Harold Macmillan became Conservative Prime Minister and his party remained in power after the election of

Visiting the Festival of Britain

1959, mainly because the electorate endorsed Macmillan's slogan 'You've never had it so good.'

The Royal Family

George VI died of cancer in February 1952 and was succeeded by his eldest daughter who became Queen Elizabeth II. The Duke of Windsor (formerly King Edward VIII) was invited to the funeral but not to the palace afterwards. The Queen and her daughters closed ranks around the monarchy, marginalising the man who they saw as being responsible for King George's premature death. The former king was now living in France with his wife, for whom he had abdicated his throne sixteen years previously.

Queen Elizabeth was crowned in Westminster Abbey and watched by millions live on television, the first major televised event broadcast live by the BBC.

George VI's wife became a widow at the age of fifty-one. She refused to be known as the Dowager Queen so took the title 'Queen Elizabeth the Queen Mother.' She also refused to leave Buckingham Palace to move to Clarence House, calling it 'a horrid little house.' She grieved for many years until shaken out of her mourning by Winston Churchill. She returned to public life and immediately became immensely popular with the Queen's subjects around the world.

Princess Margaret, the Queen's sister began a serious relationship with Group Captain Peter Townsend, a popular and likeable man. Talk of marriage was soon quashed however, because he was a divorcé. Both the Church and the government disapproved of the relationship and pressure was put on Margaret to end it, which she reluctantly agreed to do.

In October 1957, the Queen met US President Eisenhower in the White House, the first British monarch to step inside this symbol of US Independence. The year marked the 350th anniversary of the British settlement in Virginia.

Overall, the members of the Royal Family were extremely popular with their subjects throughout the decade, both at home and throughout the Commonwealth.

The Coronation

Sport

The FA Cup Final of 1953 saw a fairy tale ending with the veteran Stanley Matthew's Blackpool coming from behind to beat Bolton Wanderers 4-3; the winning goal coming in the last minute of the game.

On the 29th May 1953, Edmund Hilary and his guide, Sherpa Tenzing became the first people to stand on the summit of Mount Everest, 29,028 feet above sea level. News of this came through in the same week as Queen Elizabeth's coronation, a double cause for celebration.

Twenty-five-year old Roger Bannister became the first person to run a mile in less than 4 minutes. His record-breaking run of 3 minutes 59.4 seconds took place in 1954, on a track at Oxford.

In the Grand National of 1956, the Queen Mother's horse Devon Lock stumbled and fell only yards from the winning post whilst in the lead. E.S.B. went on to win the race.

In May 1956, Surrey cricketer Jim Laker took all ten Australian wickets for 88 runs in a match at the Oval.

Tragedy struck in February 1958 when the 'plane carrying the successful Manchester United football team, the 'Busby Babes,' as they were known, crashed on take off at Munich airport. Twenty-three people died including eight of the players. Manager Matt Busby survived the crash and went on to rebuild the team in the following years.

Entertainment

During the decade, television ownership grew rapidly, despite the screen being 12" wide or less and with programmes shown in glorious black and white. By the end of the decade almost two thirds of households in the UK owned a TV.

The most popular form of home entertainment, though was still the radio. The BBC had three radio channels; the Home Service, the Light Programme and the Third Programme. Pop music was actively discouraged! Pop music was played though, on the famous Radio Luxembourg—'208 metres on the medium wave.' This was a commercial radio station that broadcast in the evenings, apparently from the continent, though this was never really clear.

Children only knew the BBC radio programmes. They listened to Children's Hour every day. Larry the Lamb in Toytown, with the grumpy Mr Growser was a firm favourite. Later the programme transferred to TV and became an equally popular puppet show (complete with strings).

The Goon Show was a favourite with adults. Peter Sellers, Harry Secombe, Spike Milligan and Michael Bentine starred and featured the incredibly idiotic characters of Eccles, Bluebottle and Neddy Seagoon.

Until 1956, the BBC was the only TV channel available. ITV began broadcasting that year and its popular programming was soon stealing the BBC's audience in increasing numbers. Prior to the arrival of ITV, the BBC ceased broadcasting between 6pm and 7pm

An Ekcots 10" black and white TV

to allow parents to put their children to bed. This was known as the Toddlers' Truce. ITV however continued to broadcast throughout the early evening and the BBC soon followed suit.

Blue Peter was first shown in 1958, presented by Leila Williams and Christopher Trace.

TV's increased popularity had a negative effect on cinema audiences. Attendance slumped by almost a third during the course of the decade and many cinemas were forced to close their doors.

A contest that was destined to become an international institution was first held in May 1956. The first Eurovision Song Contest was won by the host nation, Switzerland.

The 1950s was the decade that invented the 'Teenager.' Youth found its identity, particularly in the areas of music and fashion, with blue jeans becoming the 'must have' look. In 1955, 'Rock 'n Roll' burst into life. At last young people had a type of music that was their own; the first music that was produced for youth, by youth. Of course, the older generation hated it—it was decadent. Boys were called Teddy Boys (after the Edwardian style clothes that they wore), with slicked back hair, large drape jackets and crepe soles shoes. Their girlfriends kept their hair long often in a ponytail. They wore pretty blouses, very full skirts, tight at the waist with billowing petticoats.

The first big star was Bill Haley, backed by the Comets. He had a huge hit with 'Rock around the Clock' but Rock 'n Roll really took off when the twenty-one year old Elvis Presley burst on to the scene with his first hit, 'Heartbreak Hotel'. The boy from Memphis, Tennessee soon gained the nickname Elvis the Pelvis, due to the suggestive manner in which he gyrated his hips when he sang and this helped his record sales to rise in to the millions.

The most popular British stars were Tommy Steele and Cliff Richard. Some of the new stars were very young. Paul Anka was fifteen when his hit 'Diana' stayed in the charts for several weeks. Brenda Lee was only twelve! The young idols sang about young people's issues—first love, breaking up, cars and having fun. In this decade, for the first time, youth found their own identity rather than being adult apprentices, waiting to grow up. They had their own cults, their own personalities.

One day in 1952 a new craze began when a Mr Adamski took a photograph of a 'Flying Saucer.' The photograph launched the phenomenon of the UFO, the Unidentified Flying Object. Adamski claimed that the object was about 10 metres by 6 metres, 'with underhanging globes.' The UFO 'industry' began and developed in to a worldwide obsession.

For most people, the annual holiday was a fortnight at the British seaside and the 1950s was the heyday of this form of relaxation. The 1948 'Holiday with Pay' Act had ensured that most workers could afford a holiday. Northerners flocked to Blackpool, particularly factory workers who took the same two weeks every year when their employer or town took their 'Wakes Weeks.' Friends met year after year on holiday but had little or no contact in between. Northerners went to Blackpool and Morecambe, Midlanders went to 'Skeggie,' Londoners caught the train to Margate, Clacton, Southend or Brighton and Southerners headed west to Torquay and the small fishing villages of Cornwall. Money was often tight and boarding houses or campsites at one shilling a night were common. Camping in the rain was no fun and the boarding house was often little better, as guests were not allowed to remain in their rooms during the day.

The Holiday Camp also flourished at this time, with Butlins leading the way.

Kite-flying, crabbing, sand castles and shell collecting all joined swimming as integral parts of the child's holiday. Punch and Judy shows were featured on all major beaches, as were communal games—cricket and volleyball.

The most popular small car was the 'Moggie,' the Morris Minor. This had been on sale since 1948 but was now more affordable than ever. By the end of the decade, nearly a million owners were enjoying the freedom of the open road in their favourite 'Moggie.' Another unique automotive feature of the decade was the Three Wheeler car. The Messerschmitt Tiger was compared to a 'plane's cockpit, while the first models of the Heinkel didn't have reverse gear and if they were parked straight against a wall, had to be pushed out. At the other end of the auto scale, the increasing prosperity enjoyed by the rich led to some incredible examples of decadence; Lord and Lady Docker were driven around London in their gold plated Daimler! At the end of the decade, Alec Issogonis unveiled the Mini, a revolutionary car that was both roomy and stylish. He achieved this increased internal space by mounting the engine sideways, a design first.

Political Tension

In 1950, Communist North Korea invaded the South and the Korean War followed. United Nations troops were committed to supporting the non-communist South. The Chinese entered the war in support of the North Koreans and the war raged until 1953 when a cease-fire was agreed.

In Eastern Europe, citizens of the communist satellite states rose up against their oppressors. East Germans demonstrated against Soviet domination in 1953 and three years later, the Poles and Hungarians followed the same route. All were ruthlessly suppressed by Russian troops within weeks. In Russia, Joseph

Stalin died in 1953, to be succeeded by Nikita Krushchev who had a slightly more positive view of the decadent West than his predecessor.

Many colonial countries were keen to gain independence and this led to violent uprisings around the globe. Algerians rose up against the French colonists and a guerrilla war carried on through most of the decade. The French were even less inclined to leave when oil was discovered under Algerian soil.

The Mau Mau uprising in Kenya was a violent struggle against British colonialism. White farmers were terrorised and many killed before the uprising was quashed. Jomo Kenyatta, accused of being the Mau Mau leader was imprisoned for seven years.

In Cuba, rebels Fidel Castro and Che Guevara led a rebellion against the corrupt Batista regime. They succeeded in overthrowing the government in 1959 and a communist regime was introduced, led by Castro. Assets of companies were nationalised and wealthy families fled abroad.

In 1956, the Egyptians nationalised the Suez Canal, leading to the 'Suez Crisis.' Soon afterwards, Israel invaded Egypt and Britain and France sent troops, ostensibly to restore order but actually to protect their interests and regain control over the canal. Pressure applied by the United Nations forced the British and French troops to withdraw and Prime Minister Anthony Eden resigned the following January on the grounds of ill health.

In China, Chairman Mao introduced the first of his 'Five-year plans' designed to ensure that factories and collective farms produced enough output to meet their high targets. These targets were met but the goods were often of poor quality. In 1958, Mao announced The Great Leap Forward and peasants were encouraged to set up small steel furnaces in their back yards to process household utensils into raw steel. Once again, the result was a very poor quality product that was often useless. Worse, the peasants focus on their mini steel plants had diverted them from their fields and famine followed. Millions of Chinese died in the latter years of the decade.

Decade developments

On the scientific front, Cambridge molecular biologist Francis Crick and American James Watson made the greatest breakthrough of the decade. In 1953, they announced that they had identified the molecular structure of deoxyribonucleic acid, or DNA—the genetic blueprint of life.

In 1956 the first nuclear power station opened at Calder Hall, in Cumbria. Nuclear power produced a new sustainable source of mass-produced fuel that was seen as the way forward for the future, producing very cheap electricity without using up the country's limited reserves of coal.

Christopher Cockerall patented the Hovercraft in 1955 and launched the first full-scale version in 1959, which was produced at a factory in Cowes on the Isle of Wight.

The first kidney transplant was successfully carried out in the USA giving hope to thousands of people suffering from kidney disorders.

Antarctica was declared a 'preserve for scientific research' after all countries with territorial claims on the continent agreed to forgo them. Free access was agreed for scientists of all nations but military bases were explicitly banned.

Italy, France, Belgium, West Germany, Holland and Luxembourg signed the Treaty of Rome in 1957, which brought the European Economic Community (EEC) in to existence.

The Russians won the 'Space race' by successfully launching a satellite, called Sputnik, in 1957. The US was the first to successfully send animals in to orbit and return them to Earth. Two monkeys, Able and Baker, survived the flight with no serious ill effects.

Prices
Some approximate prices from the 1950s:

- Loaf of bread: 4d
- 1lb of bacon: 4/6d
- Pint of milk: 1½d
- Pint of beer: 1/8d
- 1lb of potatoes: 1/1d
- 20 cigarettes: 4/-
- Flight from London to Paris: £10
- Skilled worker's weekly wage: £11
- Average price of a house: £2,100

Closer to Home—
Personal Memories of the 1950s

The 1950s are remembered as a decade of change, the 'bridge' between post war austerity and the 'Swinging 60s.' Many of the personal memories in this chapter reflect these changes. Some, however, particularly the lovely recollections of life in rural Ireland from Anna Murphy, show that change happened at a much slower pace in some areas.

Brenda Hall *moved to* ***Arbroath*** *in the 1950s*

Orange boxes and holiday makers

'My husband was a Leading Airman in the Fleet Air Arm. When he was stationed in Arbroath there were no married quarters available so we moved in to a local flat. This was an attic flat in a three-storey sandstone tenement. It comprised a living room with a stove in a cupboard and a bedroom, which was just large enough to take a double bed. There was no bathroom. Light for the bedroom was from a skylight above the bed. I often worried about the possibility of fire because there was no way out of the flat except for the stairs at the end of the corridor.

We had to share a toilet with the tenant who lived across the landing. She was not too particular who saw her in the 'smallest room' and would leave the door open during occupancy.

As there were no bathrooms in the tenements, I used to go to the public bathhouse with my friend, another Navy wife who lived in the ground floor flat. We were both pregnant at the time and found it very difficult to negotiate the turnstiles at the entrance to the bathhouse.

The bathrooms seemed huge. All the walls were covered in white tiles with big pipes going up them and across the ceilings.

There was a strong smell of pine in the rooms. It was bliss to have unlimited hot water and to get a good long soak.

Our laundry was done in a building behind the tenements. It had a copper in a brick surround, under which a fire was built to heat the water. All tenants were given their own day on which to use the facilities and woe betide anyone who used the lines on the drying green when it wasn't their day.

After the birth of my baby, the district nurse said that the attic flat was unsuitable for us as the stairs up to it were unstable. My friend and her husband had vacated the ground floor flat and after much persuasion the landlady agreed that we could have it. This flat was little better than the other but it did have a rack for drying clothes. This was on pulleys on the ceiling and I found it very handy for the terry towelling nappies, which seemed to take over our lives.

To get to the toilet we were supposed to go out of the front door, into the street and down the alley between the buildings. This was hard work. We put an orange box beneath the bedroom window at the rear of the flat and took the short cut to the toilet by using it to climb through the window; not very elegant but very effective.

A couple of months later, in June, we found out why the landlady had been reluctant to let us have the flat. People trying the door and peering in through the window interrupted our evening meal. She had let our flat as a holiday home to some people in Glasgow. We refused to budge so the poor holidaymakers had to move in with the landlady in her second floor flat!'

*Ronnie Barnes in **Lincolnshire** was a regular holidaymaker*

Holidays in Butlins

'We went to Butlins every year and visited three different camps during the '50s; they were all run along the same lines. I thought that it was marvellous. There was always plenty to do, three meals a day and I didn't have to spend all of my time with my parents. The Redcoats looked after us and always seemed to have time for everyone. There was live entertainment every night for parents and children were safe in their chalets, watched over by the members of the chalet patrol.

Irene and Jeff Tomley on honeymoon at Butlins, Skegness

In the morning we were all woken up by the jolly announcer, whose bouncy enthusiasm was broadcast around the camp over the loudspeakers. 'Good morning, good morning, good morning it's another lovely day.'

Rain ran down the windows.

'When it's raining, it's still fine at Butlins . . .'

The whole family enjoyed themselves and it was a sad day when we had to return home. New friendships were forged and several of these were resumed in following years as we all booked to return at the same time as each other.'

Malcolm Batt *visited his grandmother in* ***London*** *at the time of the Queen's coronation*

The coronation but no bath

'I was taken to see the decorations along the Mall and the surrounding areas. My grandmother rented her house and sublet the upstairs to another family. They had a television and we went upstairs to watch the coronation on the little black and white screen. The following day we went 'into town' and were fortunate enough to see the Queen drive past in an open car.

Grandmother's house had led a grander life in earlier times and she still referred to the kitchen as the 'scullery' and another room as the 'pantry.' This still had a cast iron range but by then all the cooking was done on a gas stove in the scullery. Hot water was provided for the scullery sink via an Ascot water heater, which must have been a real luxury when it was first installed. We all washed there as the family upstairs had exclusive rights to the bathroom. No bath, no shower, not even a cold one!'

Bob Hunt *in* ***Lincolnshire*** *recalls the days before central heating*

Frost patterns

'I remember waking up on cold winter mornings, lying under the bedclothes and seeing my warm breath coming out of my mouth as water vapour. The room was so cold that frost patterns built up on the inside of the window panes during the night. I would lie in bed building myself up to leap out of bed, pull on my cold dressing-gown, run downstairs to the bathroom and turn on the hot tap to run a bath and warm up the room at the same time.

We spent most of our time in the Living room. It was heated with a coal fire and was the hottest room in the house. On Sundays, though we went in to the Front room. It was the only day of the week that we used this room except on very rare occasions when we had visitors. It was a cold room because it hadn't been heated all week and it would take until about teatime before it warmed up. The thing was though, we still ate our meals in the Living room, all seated at the table. Because we had a fire in the Front room, mum used to turn a one bar electric fire on in the Living room, 'to take the chill off.' Well, the one bar didn't make much difference and I can remember Sundays as being the day that I never got warm!

Home delivery was widely available and on Tuesdays, the fresh fish van called at our house. Silver Ling was usually on the menu for tea in the evening. On Fridays the 'Esso Blue' van called to top up the heating oil in the morning while the baker's van delivered fresh baked bread in the afternoon, ready for the weekend.

At Christmas, we went to my Grandparents house on the other side of the county. This was a serious and infrequent journey for the old Vauxhall car and dad religiously checked the oil, water and tyre pressures before setting out on the seventy-two mile round trip. Mum always made sure that we had a supply of 'barley sugar' sweets for the journey, to help travel sickness.

My grandparents lived in a small village. They would entertain a significant percentage of the family and invariably we would have venison and pheasant for Christmas dinner, provided by one of the local farmers; it was probably poached. This would be followed by a very rich Christmas pudding stuffed full of silver sixpences. A real Christmas Tree always stood in the corner of the room and it would be decorated with tinsel, coloured baubles and real wax candles. The latter were lit during the evening and odd branches of the tree invariably caught fire and briefly flared up before being 'pinched out' by my grandfather's thumb and forefinger. My grandparents never had a television (or a telephone) so entertainment was home made. I remember one Christmas, Uncle Jim, his jet black hair slicked back with an excess of Brylcreem, demonstrated the sound of a cow shitting in a field. He achieved this by holding a pack of cards behind his back and dropping the cards on the wooden floor, ten at a time (try it, it's quite effective).

Occasionally, mum took us to the cinema, or 'pictures,' as we knew it. At the end of the film, the National Anthem was played and everyone stood up in silence. They waited for this to end before filing out of the cinema. How times have changed!

Another thing that sticks in my mind is that my best friend's grandfather had a wooden leg. He'd lost the original in the First World War. Looking back, I can recall seeing a number of older people with limbs missing and it never occurred to me that this was the result of a war which had taken place forty years previously.'

Anna Murphy *was born in* **Ireland***, the youngest
of a family of four, two sisters and a brother*

Growing up in rural Ireland

'My father was a farmer and farmed a small mountain farm. It was situated one mile from the main road. A river ran all along one side of the farm and the family crossed over the river by means of a bridge, which was made of wooden planks or sleepers, as they were called at the time. There were no sides on the bridge, and when the flood was high this made it very frightening to cross for the planks became very slippery. My mother was a full-time housewife and farm help, for farming was a very busy lifestyle.

Early in the morning the cows would be milked by hand and the milk would be cooled in the dairy in a cement tank. Some of the milk went to the creamery in either ten-gallon or eight-gallon tanks. My father carried the eight-gallon cans of milk on his back to the main road. At the end of the lane there was a creamery stand built for the convenience of the lorry drivers; they were able to load the cans with ease from a certain level. The milk would have to be very clean and the cans had to be washed with great care. If the milk was unclean the creamery would send a report to the farmer, it usually read 'pips and grains.' As a result the price would be greatly reduced. Some of the milk was stored in a crock. The crocks were brown with a gold band on the upper part, the inside of the crocks were very well glazed. Their bottoms were narrow which made them easy to empty. The crock was filled to the top with milk and covered with a white cloth, and in about a week the milk would be churned and butter made. The churn was made of wood and held together with six hoops, which were made of straps of iron riveted to hold the churn together. It also had a wooden lid with a handle, and a hole in the lid to let the stave move up and down, thus churning and so the butter was made. It was important to keep the churn very clean. When ready the butter was placed in a small bowl and salted. There were many wooden items that were used to make the butter. The main wooden stand could be held underneath and the water was all squeezed out from the butter with a flat wooden spatula. It was patted into shape and finally it was decorated with another wooden implement with designs; the butter was always well presented.

There was always a plentiful supply of fresh milk kept for the family's own use. Everything had to be kept very clean and salt played a big part. It took all the buttermilk to make home baked bread for the family. The flour to bake the bread could be bought in four stone bags or packs. Flour baking soda and buttermilk was mixed in small yellow crockery bowls. Sometimes there would be fruit added or treacle to bake a variety. There was also pan bread baked and it was usually fried for breakfast with eggs and bacon or sausages. Some families used lard for frying, but bacon in the '50s was very greasy and the pan would be full of grease; bread would be dipped in it and toasted until it was golden brown.

The bread was cooked in heavy black pots with flat bottoms that were sometimes called ovens. The dough was placed in the ovens and the lid was fitted. On the top of the lid, coals were placed, bright red coals from the hottest part of the fire, this helped the bread to rise and brown.

The fireplace was about eight-foot wide and the fire was placed in the centre usually on a slightly higher stone. The back of the fireplace could get very sticky with the cooking and the steam often made the dry soot from the top of the chimney fall down. It was very important not to remove the lids of the pot on the fire or the soot would drop into the food and it would become useless. The crock was secured from one end and hooks hung on the pots. The crock was made from cast iron, as were the hooks. Farming clothes and rough coats were often dried on the crock. There was no other means of cooking except the fire.

The big black pots that boiled on the fire were very heavy, and usually a family had four to five of these of different sizes. The small pots were called skillet pots and porridge was made in these for the morning. Also custard or rice could be cooked in the small skillet (rice was eaten when potatoes were off-season). The flat-bottomed pots were used for making bread and cooking meat and stews. When apples were in good supply there were apple cakes made. There was one large pot kept full of boiling water and this sat beside the fire. This water was used to wash dishes and clothes, it had a large heavy lid and it was useful to heat plates and utensils for cooking. The big pots were also used for cooking potatoes and usually held about three buckets full. One would be boiled mid-day when dinner would be made and another would be boiled at night. I recall winter nights when the big pot of potatoes was boiled, and then there would be some toasted on the hot coals and eaten with salt and pepper and plenty of fresh milk.

All of our bed sheets were made of flour packs. Four of the flour packs made a single bed sheet, and six to eight made a double bed sheet, depending on the size of the bed. The flour packs had red and blue print on one side, so it was a hard job to remove this. With boiling and bleaching this was removed, then they were sewn together and hemmed, making a cool cotton sheet. The pack itself with no alterations made a pillowcase and no sewing was necessary. Some of the pillowcases were torn up for bandages for minor accidents. The blankets then were surplus army blankets, and there were also heavy quilts, which the countrywomen made. The beds themselves were wooden all the way round, a complete wooden enclosure and this left them very private for usually all the family slept in the one room for warmth. There would be two enclosures and each would be bigger than a giant double-bed and could be closed off. In the main bedroom area there could be a large bed and often a cot for a baby or a cradle. The bedroom would have a fireplace with a small grate; it was seldom used unless one of the family was sick. The insides of the enclosures were papered all the way round and the front and doors were varnished wood which was also right around the bedroom walls half way up. The top of the wall was papered. The ceiling was also wood, grooved and varnished. The enclosures came to about two feet from the floor; below this a valance made from white material hung to the floor.

The dwelling house was thatched with a bed of straw. This kept it warm and cosy, but my parents always feared wind and storm. Sparks could go on the thatch from the wide fireplace and set the thatch alight. High wind could blow the thatch, after a dry spell and let the rain soak through, and in turn run down the walls of the dwelling. Certain men were good thatchers and were sought after. Sometimes the roof did not need a full thatch and the thatcher would just patch or darn the weak areas. But, if it was a good corn year and straw was well harvested, the farmer often put on a full thatch. If this was done and well thatched it would last many years.

The hen house was close to the dwelling house and the roosters in the flock would awaken everyone up very early in the morning. The hens were a very big part of my family's livelihood, and part of my spare-time work. In springtime batches of chicks were bought—one hundred or two hundred at a time. They would be put in a brooder, which was made of wood and had several compartments. The sleeping compartment had a wooden floor with a lamp in the centre. In the first week of the little chicks' lives there was a small piece of blanket spread to keep the chicks warm. The next compartment had wire flooring and water drinker in the centre. The feed was placed in the outside compartment in a narrow trough, and the chicks would feed through wire spaces. I loved and enjoyed this part of the work. My mother home hatched chicks by setting a hen on a dozen eggs for three weeks. These chicks in my eyes were nicer than the hatchery chicks. They were all different colours, and as they got bigger their feathers were tipped with beautiful colours of greens, blues and reds. Sometimes most of the flock would turn out to be cockerels, and they would be fed for the table. When I was growing up there was a lot of soup made especially in the winter months. The free-range cockerels were very good for soup and also for roasting. By late summer the pullets or young hens would start to lay eggs. Their eggs would be much smaller than the eggs from the older flock. If the demand was good the smaller eggs were never noticed and were sold at the same price. It varied from year to year and mostly the family used some of the eggs for table use. The hens laid their eggs in creels, which were hung around the hen house and bedded with straw. From time to time the hens would need to be culled, due to overweight or illness. They were usually bought by the fowlman, as he was called and he travelled from farm to farm in a van, with the back of the van divided into cages. He gave a reasonable price and it was thought they were often used for human consumption.

Our family kept a donkey, as did nearly every farming family and the donkey worked hard. It had a wooden straddle, pad-ded on both sides to protect the donkey's back. The donkey did several useful jobs, like drawing turf in wet years, and was light on its feet, which was particularly useful when horses and carts were unable to travel. It was also used to bring potatoes from the potato pit, take eggs to the shop and bring back flour, hen feed and oil. There was also a small wooden cart for the donkey, which increased its workload. A good donkey was very valuable but some were hard to work with and were stubborn. I recall get-ting rides on the donkey, it was agreeable on some of the days, but other days it was moody and disagreeable, and would unseat its rider. There was also a horse kept. This was a strong working horse and he was well cared for. In the spring and summer the horse would be fed with oats unlike the donkey. When father had his main meal, there was a nose bag put on the horse, if this was not done someone would have to hold a bucket very high, for the horse would have all its tackle on. Our father joined with a neigh-bouring farmer, as did all the farmers. There were certain pairs of horses that worked well together. If they didn't get on they would try to bite each other and would not work in harmony, making the farmer's job impossible. In spring the pairs of horses would plough one acre in a day, with a farmer having to walk after them all day and guide them. The horses had names like Bob or Dick and it was by their name that the farmer guided them. In March they would plough fields for potatoes and corn. When dry, the ground would be harrowed roughly and prepared for planting the corn. Then the farmers either bought new fresh corn or they would have saved some from the previous year. It had to be best quality corn. The farmers sowed this by hand or 'fiddle,' which moved a bow round to sow the corn evenly. The fiddle was difficult to work, and mostly the farmers preferred to sow by hand. The field was marked in sections so that the sowing would not overlap. Grass seed was also sown in the field to grow the following year. Then the ground had to be harrowed to complete the job. The seed would grow from April to September getting green first and then yellow and golden.

The corn was used to feed the hens and cattle. It was cut in September with a scythe and a man generally cut about an acre a day. I recall one year the corn was almost ripe and there came a storm at night and the crop was flattened. It was very difficult to cut so two men helped with the work, one had to hold a rod, pulling the flattened corn upright so that it could be cut easily. Men and helpers were always plentiful and in good weather the family all came out to save the corn. I would hold the rod, this was tiring work and the stubble was hard to walk on. The corn, which was about three feet high was tied in sheaves. These were tied individually and stood in 'stooks' of fours or sixes. Crows and birds of all sizes ate the seed, and it was important to get it scythed to protect the seed. When dry it was carted in close to the dwelling house to be stacked; convenient for when the thresher came on its round. The farmers all got together to stack the corn and they would go from one farm to another. Then the corn stack would be thatched to protect it from the weather and left to be threshed.

I started school at four years old to save a teacher, for pupil numbers had decreased. The school was two miles away and I had to walk there. I recall my first weeks at the school with mixed emotions. The journey to school was rough and hazardous, I recall father carrying me on his shoulders over the wet, rushy fields to the uneven stony lane. This led to the road, which was stoned, but was easier to walk on than the lane. I started school in September; it was a small three-teacher school in the country. A high wall separated the boys and girls. The front of the school was all windows for there was no lighting. There were two lady teachers and the head master. The teachers travelled to school on bicycles. On my first day at school I was given a small box of bricks and a piece of slate and chalk. The school desk seated two pupils so I sat with Mora and made friends. The school was cold for there was no heating and many days the children kept their coats on. The blackboard on a wooden easel stood at the top of the room. The teacher would write down various lessons. There were three sections of pupils in the first room. The bigger pupils used to stand around the blackboard, and the teacher would use her chalk and duster. She had a ruler to encourage the children to pay attention. She also had a cane with a rounded head. The teacher did not use it very often unless someone was very bad. She often used the head of cane to bring a pupil forward if they were fidgeting or fooling around.

Generally the teacher was very nice and helpful. There was a cooker at the top of the classroom beside the small kitchen, but it was never used. The small kitchen had a few shelves, a primus stove and a sink type hand basin. The floor was tiled and the walls were damp and cold. The kitchen was hardly ever used as the teachers brought flasks and sandwiches. They would often go for a walk at break time, and on the good days they would allow pupils to play longer. The boys were allowed to play football in a local field. They would walk very slowly on their way back and break time would be extended. The master had a bell and it would ring and echo over the countryside, but if the game was at an exciting stage they would pretend not to hear it.

In summer the boys would be able to leave school to help in the bog or on the farm. The girls also could go home early if their mother was sick or there was a small baby in the family. So the work on the farm came first and in busy periods school hours became flexible. After school hours when the teachers went home, the children would play games on the road. Often fights and boxing took place with the boys getting bloody noses and black eyes. Parents and teachers ignored this—it was all part of growing up. There was no traffic on the road at the time except two men with hackney cars, and it was quite safe to play in the road.

The hackney cars would be hired for special occasions, like for instance they might bring a family to a funeral, or to visit someone in hospital or indeed to a wedding. An illness had to be very serious for someone to go into hospital. Most babies were born at home and too many mothers died in childbirth. There was no immunisation for polio or tetanus and many people suffered from tuberculosis and died young. A local boy suffered from polio and was lame, with his legs strapped. Families were able to cope with minor ailments with different remedies and potions. I recall getting some mixture in the springtime, sulphur was the main ingredient and it was supposed to clear your blood. At the end of every week children were given a laxative. There was always a bottle of milk of magnesia kept in the house and it covered a multitude of ailments. Germoline was the one and only cream that was used for cuts and rashes. Dettol played a big part as an antiseptic. There was orange juice and cod liver oil left in the school to be administered to the children. There was always a bottle of whiskey kept in the farmhouse and a cup of hot punch cured all colds and chills. This was also used when children had measles to bring out the spots.

Our father always went to the country shop when any of the family was sick and he would bring home Arrowroot biscuits. The country shop was just a room in a family house that sold groceries and small items. They also sold oil and if you bought your weekly goods there, they would give you a big bag of sweets at no extra cost. The sweets were not wrapped then but were weighed from jars in white bags. A family would have a passbook and each week they would get a similar list. Most of the goods came in large amounts and had to be weighed. This was a time consuming business but customers didn't mind, for the local shops were meeting places and there was very little other social life.

Men would get together to play cards, or pitch pennies or make poteen. The women would get together to crochet and knit, some made patchwork quilts.

Tea came to the shops in tea chests lined with tin foil and was weighed. When the chests were empty the shopkeeper would give them to their customers and they made very useful storage boxes.

In summer ice cream was cut from a large block into cones and slices. Cigarettes were sold in singles; tobacco came in plugs and had to be cut and teased for pipe smoking.

I recall the strong smell of herrings in winter; they were sold from a barrel and were salted. Country people thought that they prevented colds and flu. Apart from these items that had to be bought, the country people were mainly self-sufficient.

Our father's clothes were rough and sturdy and these were bought from the second-hand shop. These clothes were worn for a long time, and were patched and darned many times. Pullovers and socks were knitted and the wool was sold in the Post Office, as well as shirts and underwear. Shirts had detachable collars and could be bleached and starched. Some farmers never wore socks but wrapped a meal bag square around their feet. Father would also wear a bag apron, as would mother if doing farm work. For special occasions they would get a suit made by a tailor. Their shoes would be made by the cobbler and would be repaired several times.

The women, if money was plentiful, hardly ever bought a coat on its own, but would buy hats, gloves and shoes all together and these would be worn for many years. Some of the countrywomen were good dressmakers and did this for a living. Most women made lace of some sort. Some made coarse lace, like table centres and napkins while others made fine lace. Gloves were made of fine lace and hankies were edged and cornered with fine lace. A few women made fine lace dresses and blouses. Lace buyers would buy the items and wash and bleach them and send them off abroad, mostly to America.'

Jules Evans in **Hertfordshire** *remembers freedom to play without fear*

Dens and Rawhide

'Immediately after the war, cheap housing was hastily erected to accommodate new families, and those who had lost their homes during bombing raids. After a short spell in my grandmother's, already overcrowded house, my parents and myself moved into one of the new 'steel houses' on an estate in Luton—like all ex-soldiers, my father was on the priority list for housing. Before enlisting he had worked as a car salesman and he had resumed his career after the war. Many cars still resembled horse drawn carriages, but incorporated the new benefits of petrol engines. They were mostly only purchased by the 'well off'. However, because he was 'in the trade' my father had the use of a company vehicle from Dickinson Adams in Luton, which was where he worked, so as a family we had the luxury of car travel and trips to the countryside, or Bournemouth. When I grew older, I remember him bringing home Sunbeam Rapiers, Ford Anglias, Zodiacs and Zephyrs, Humbers, Hillmans and smart liveried Rovers. I never knew which make of car we'd have from week to week. Sometimes, if Dad happened to see me walking home from school, and stopped to offer me a lift—driving yet another new car—I had to be quite certain it was him before jumping in.

Slowly, the world began settling down—though it could never be the same again! New factories and housing sprang up, and food supplies and clothing became more readily available. After the trauma of war, people wanted to laugh again, and were anxious to re-build shattered lives by living as well as possible and enjoying it. Everyone wanted to jettison pre-war caution and thrift, forget the terrors of war and build for the future.

These feelings were manifest everywhere, and in everything. The pace was increasing and change was the order of the day. New goods, new music and new clothes made of innovative materials appeared in the shops. People, especially young ones, wanted fun. Luton was, and still is, a large industrial town traditionally known for its hat making, Vauxhall cars, and a football team nicknamed, 'The Hatters'—once a league force to be reckoned with. Greenline buses, with conductors aboard, thundered through busy streets lined with furniture shops, department stores, cafes and pubs, and through these streets my mother hauled me by the hand as we went on shopping trips or to visit her numerous sisters. Wondering what to cook my father for tea, she would often pause to admire the latest furnishing fabrics and household items displayed in the windows of Blundells. Twin-tub washing machines, Hoovers and electric food mixers were the very height of labour saving luxury when not all houses had telephones, or even indoor lavatories!

Clinging to my mother's hand, I trotted beside her, chattering nineteen to the dozen and tripping over kerbstones that seemed monumental to a plump legged four-year old, busy gazing, wide-eyed, at the world.

My parents noted with dismay that I was picking up unsavoury habits and copying very poor speech from other children in our street. To combat what they viewed as my obvious early decline, they sent me to a small private school which was owned and supervised by the kind, woolly cardiganned, and string-pearled, Miss Barber, together with her stern, waspish, claret frocked friend, Miss Pedder.

I was four and a half when I started to attend Miss Barber's and my very few memories of it are probably due to the lack of attention I gave my lessons! However, I clearly remember my terror of Miss Pedder, the art classes where I painted blue budgerigars and the music lessons in which we sang words from two small cloth bound books, which I still own. Lastly, I remember mother making me a May Day dress of sky blue crepe paper decorated with fake forget-me-nots. The maypole dance was watched by doting mothers and grandmothers; the local press took photographs. Considering that my father worked all hours to sell as many cars as possible so that he could afford to send me to private school, perhaps I should have rewarded him by turning out to be a genius. Becoming Prime Minister perhaps, or at least, a school prefect. Alas, my school performance was merely adequate. However, I did learn to speak correctly, that swearing was considered naughty, and that there were rude games that 'nice' little girls didn't play. Though I'm blowed if I can remember what they were!

I attended Miss Barber's school until I was nine, and then something happened that changed my life forever.

I mentioned, earlier that we were lucky to have the use of a car and once, while out for a drive in the country, my parents stopped to admire the new houses, which were being built. We'd already moved from the steel house into a new two-bedroom bungalow in Luton, but they liked these smart new semi-detached houses and before long we were getting out of the car to look around. The houses were opposite lush green fields, and at the top of the road was a dense private wood. Nearby, in a bungalow garden, a pair of large white geese roamed. I think we were among the first to move on to the new development because scaffolding remained on many of the houses, and when it rained the bulldozers and lorries turned our unmade road into a quagmire.

Harpenden was only a few miles from Luton, but in terms of the different landscape, I might have been taken to another planet! In the '50s, Hertfordshire was full of fields, punctuated by quiet villages and towns that only ever 'bustled' on market days. Farmers grew wheat and barley, fruit and vegetables, and raised cows and sheep. Although only nine years old, I fell in love with this rural idyll and was, to coin a phrase, as happy as a pig in muck.

My personal, most important comparison with today is that when I was young there was less fear. Soon after moving to the countryside, I had discovered that my new surroundings made a brilliant theme park where friends and I could amuse ourselves for hours. We climbed trees, rambled woodland paths, and made secret dens under huge oaks. Cowboy films were popular viewing on the new televisions that everyone had started to acquire, and us kids would charge out next day to re-enact an exciting episode of 'Rawhide', or 'Wagon Train', right down to the last blood-curdling yell. Round and round we raced on imaginary horses; being shot time after time, but still heroically managing to gallop on until at last a painful death by Indian arrows, which we played out in full with loud groaning, and rolling around in pretended agonised, glory. Nike trainers and designer jeans were still in the future, so we wore canvas plimsolls, and any old clothing to play in. We must have got filthy but we were far too busy having glorious fun to worry. Fun was possible because we weren't afraid. Children walked quiet lanes home from school untroubled by molesters. Today, anxious mothers line up in cars to ferry their children home. I was allowed to wander miles from home because my parents knew I loved the fields and the animals that I was impatient to learn about. True, I was often with friends and always accompanied by our dog, but the thought of being attacked, raped, murdered, or mugged never entered my head! Of course, murder happened, but when it did, it was horrifying and the newspapers really went to town. It was discussed in shocked amazement for weeks!'

Jill Gane in Surrey had a dream

The summerhouse

'When I was about five years old I looked out of the landing window of our house, over the garden of the house next door to the garden beyond that. I saw a large revolving summerhouse, painted green and white. That summerhouse became my dream playhouse. I had a large family of dolls and teddy bears. There was Pamela, whose eyes opened and closed and was dressed in a lovely red coat and bonnet with fur trimmed collar. I also had a squashy rubber baby doll called Sylvia who was dressed in a flimsy pink dress. Topsy was a black doll, who wore a colourful flouncy red and white dress and you can guess the identity of Teddy and Golly.

In my mind I visualised the summerhouse furnished with miniature tables and chairs, rugs and curtains, an ideal place to hold dolls' tea parties. I had it all planned out. Imagine my surprise when I was told that we were moving house; not very far, just two doors down the road to the bungalow with the summerhouse! I was amazed and bewildered—for quite a long time I thought that my dreaming and wishing had somehow made it happen. Perhaps it did!

The move itself was quite funny. For days beforehand we had access to the bungalow and my father made a path from the back of our garden, round the bottom of our neighbour's garden and in to the wilderness that at that time surrounded the bungalow. Along this path, in procession, went my mother, grandmother (who also lived with us) and I carrying clothes baskets full of china and bedding, followed by my father pushing the wheelbarrow which was full of books. This saved some money for us as the removal men didn't have to pack these items. They were probably glad of this as the rest of the furniture must have caused them enough of a headache. Amongst other things there was a walnut bedroom suite with a huge wardrobe, which had very striking woodgrain that looked to me like the faces of lions and tigers. My own bed had a carved oak headboard and footboard that was very heavy. I also had a huge oak desk inscribed with the words 'the pen is mightier than the sword', which my parents had bought at auction for £4-10s. In the dining room there was a very large heavy ornate oak dining table with bulbous legs and six matching chairs plus a massive sideboard carved with decorations of fruit and flowers. So the removal men had plenty to worry about. They decided it wasn't worth lifting the heavy piano in and out of the van so they put it on a trolley and wheeled it down the road—a delicate operation as the road wasn't made up and it was full of ruts and potholes.

So we moved in to the bungalow and I couldn't wait to take over the summerhouse. But, of course, it didn't quite live up to my dreams. It was very old and warped and the mechanism which made it revolve was rusty from years of neglect. It could be moved but it needed a hefty push and made such an agonising grating noise that we didn't do it very often. Inside, it was very cobwebby and the floor was uneven but there was an unexpected surprise in one of the cupboards—a box of huge exotic seashells, which were soon added to the toybox.

I did eventually have dolls' tea parties and real ones too with friends, but the summerhouse never quite lived up to the play-house of my imagination. An early lesson in the difference between dreams and reality, I suppose.'

Hilary Nellist found one of her old school exercise books whilst sorting through her mother's belongings. An English homework exercise brings back memories of a simpler life in the country . . .

Mushrooming

'The next morning I awoke much earlier than usual to hear a goods train steaming past, grey smoke drifted over the end of our garden. I awoke with a start thinking it was the '7-20,' my time signal for getting up. I peered at my clock and was surprised to find that it was only the 'Five o' clock Goods'. My window faced east and a pale yellow light told me that dawn would soon be breaking. Suddenly everything seemed calm and still and I decided it would be a good morning for mushrooming.

I put on my rubber boots and brown raincoat and crept out. As I walked past the meadow where the two carthorses grazed and out across the fields I left behind me a dark trail in the dewy grass. The blackberry bushes were covered with dew-dripping cobwebs. I saw some dark shapes pass an open gateway. I realised these were only cows and my fears left me until a startled rabbit ran from near my feet. The only mushroom I found had been nibbled and was also full of maggots. Although I was unsuccessful in my mission I thoroughly enjoyed the unusual experience of rising to capture the beauty of the early morning as Wordsworth did and which he describes in his sonnet 'Upon Westminster Bridge'.'

*R Healey moved from London to **Kent** where he grew up*

Jamboree bags and Mick Jagger

'I was born in north London but when I was still a young boy my parents decided to leave the smog and shift south-eastwards to a half built estate of largish detached houses on the edge of Forestry Commission land between Bexley and Dartford. My father, a naval officer, was away from home for months at a time and it was a lonely life for my mother with just myself and my two brothers for company. Of course, she made friends with other young mothers, notably the lady opposite in whose front room I discovered years later, the young Mick Jagger had rehearsed with her eldest son in a rock band that later became The Rolling Stones. Nevertheless, my mother's social life was seriously restricted by our lack of a car. With the nearest buses nearly a mile and a half away, I remember long walks with my mother wheeling my brother in a pram to Bexley for the doctor, dentist, butcher, library and post office. Nor did we have a 'phone for several years, though there was a TV, which a grateful employer had given my mother back in 1951.

Yes, I was very much part of the TV generation, but the nearby woods and building plots offered so much more excitement. I remember some sort of nudist colony on scrubland on the edge of our estate, before the land was developed. Then there were the piles of bricks that my friends and I made into miniature houses and dens. I remember too with some pain, being caught stealing vegetables from a garden that adjoined the woods and the humiliation of being marched to my parents by the irate gardener. I can still feel his fingers pinching my ears. There were dragonflies in the woods and mysterious 'Dene holes' that appeared to reach the centre of the Earth.

Looking back, I am amazed how my mother managed. For five years the nearest shop was a sort of white-painted cottage called 'The Tuck Shop' which lay up an unmade track a good fifteen-minute walk away. I can't remember whether it sold groceries, but it certainly supplied us with Jubblies, Jamboree Bags and Sherbet Dips. Later, when the smart new shopping parade arrived I graduated to Everlasting Strips, red Liquorice Laces and Big Chief lollies. The parade also brought us the excitement of visiting our first supermarket—a Spar. I seem to recall that this experience coincided with my encounter with TV adverts that were the talk of the playground but a mystery to me until we got our own two channel set.

School was over a mile and a half away. With no car there was nothing for it but to walk the whole distance along the suburban streets in all weathers. I sometimes met up with schoolfellows along the way, but before the days of 'school runs', getting a lift from a dad on his way to work was a very occasional but much appreciated treat. I can recall the journey quite clearly. I'd pass the telephone box, then The Tuck Shop, then further on I'd try not to look at the boy with his frightening leg irons (polio, explained my mum), who lived on the route. Then, closer to the school, we'd pass the corner sweet shop where, one wonderful hot afternoon ice cream and lollies were given away to passers-by when the freezer broke down. Then, it was up the hill, past the semi-forbidden place where we would stay behind after school to knock down conkers with huge sticks. Then the school—Maypole County Primary. I did well here, but cannot remember a single lesson. But I do remember what we did at break time. In the mornings we would be let out on to Dartford Heath, where I would pretend to be a tube train with trees and bushes as stations. I later actually drew a plan of this railway system and wrote an account of it for 'composition'. At lunch break we would impel our Dinky racing cars across the playground asphalt pretending to be Stirling Moss. Or we might make tanks out of cotton reels, bits of candles, a pencil and a rubber band. Most astonishingly, I remember lunchtime recitals with Mr Tagell at the piano tinkling his way through Schubert's Trout Quintet. On the odd evening too, Mt T would rehearse us recorder players, somewhat more difficult for him than playing Schubert.

Looking back I am amazed at the naivety of our teachers. Opposite the school was one of the largest mental hospitals in England—and patients would regularly wander through the unlocked gates in to the playground and offer sweets to the children. I remember Mrs Chambers, the headmistress warning us at assembly not to talk to these strangers.

I later discovered that Mick Jagger and Keith Richards had attended my school a few years previously—I wonder what they made of the place . . .'

Rosemary Reavell grew up in Hampshire

Travelling libraries and sidecars

'It was about 1950, before I started school, that my parents moved to Hartley Wintney, a village in Hampshire. The first person to speak to them there was an old man who said 'av oo seen them thar armets?' It took ages for them to work out that he was talking about ants! Our cottage was very small with just four rooms, two bedrooms, living room and kitchen. The toilets were at the bottom of the garden. Bath nights were fun—the tin bath in front of the living room fire, the draughts kept out by the clothes on the wooden clothes-horse. My brother Stephen was born here in 1952.

Further down our lane and past a farm was a small wood with bluebells and primroses and then the little River Hart where the celandines grew. In summer my brother and I would paddle or fish for sticklebacks with jam jars. In the autumn my family and I would cross the little wooden bridge over the river and make our way up the hill to the forest and gather chestnuts. To a young child it was a forest but perhaps it was only a large wood. I loved picking blackberries and hazelnuts from the hedgerows and we also picked the dandelions for my mother, so she could make dandelion wine. She also made chutneys and jams and was a super cook. Rabbit or pigeon pie, treacle tarts, spotted dick, dumplings with treacle, and rolypoly puddings were favourites. I remember the ration books that my mother had to use for shopping and little bottles of orange juice, which I think were free from the Government! The fresh butter from the dairy was 'patted' into a golden yellow block while you waited.

Church was very important to my family. I went to Sunday school, getting a little stamp stuck in my attendance book then later in the day the whole family went to Church. I loved Harvest Festival, the church decorated with fruit, vegetables, flowers and sheaves of wheat. Mothering Sunday was nice too, the children receiving a posy of violets to give to their mothers.

Pre television we would listen to the wireless. I loved Storytime in the afternoon, when the lady would say, 'Are you sitting comfortably? Then I shall begin.' Each week my mother would read us the story about the Robin family from a magazine.

In 1953 there was a party for the children on Hunts Common to celebrate Princess Elizabeth succeeding to the throne. Lots of sandwiches, little cakes, jellies, balloons and paper streamers. Some time in the same year my mother, pushing Stephen in the pram and myself riding a tricycle, went to Odiham. There I stood with lots of other children waving a little Union Jack as the Queen went past. My parents bought a television, one of the first in the village and our little front room was packed with people watching the Coronation. On the TV we also watched Sooty and Sweep, Muffin the Mule and Dixon of Dock Green. On Sunday nights after tea there was Sunday Night at the London Palladium, which we all watched while munching a Penguin bar—a special treat.

I went to Hartley Wintney Junior School and my first teacher's name was Miss Hedges. I didn't like going to school in the winter, my legs, feet and ears ached from the cold winds. My gloves were attached to either end of some tape, draped around my neck and through the sleeves of my coat but I still managed to lose them! My mother sat up till the early hours of the morning knitting cardigans and jumpers.

Mum also made all of my dresses, one of which I tore on the first day of wearing it, by climbing out of the front room window instead of using the door! Normally my mother would sit me on her bike and push me to and from school but on a few occasions the district nurse would take me to school in her car, the first car I had ever been in, I thought that was very exciting.

I recall going by bus to the cinema, possibly in Aldershot, to see Bambi and also to Reading to see a Christmas pantomime and Father Christmas. Then there was the time when the house shook and windows were broken as a 'plane broke the sound barrier for the first time. I remember watching the aircraft as it flew over.

Sometimes we would travel by train to Birmingham to spend Christmas with my aunt, uncle and cousin. I loved the clickety clack of the wheels, the countryside going past and what wonderful pictures there were on the walls of the carriage, showing lovely holiday destinations.

The Travelling Library was wonderful too, lots of lovely books. One was about Amelia Jane and I remember that one particularly as it had a lovely smell to it. I eagerly look forward to my weekly copy of the Childrens' Newspaper. What lovely stories there were in that, all about other children and nature articles. Tiptoes, The Kitten, Winnie-the-Pooh, Noddy and Big Ears and Rupert the Bear were also favourite stories.

Sometimes we would have a holiday at the seaside, my father taking us down on his motorbike and sidecar. We stayed at guesthouses in Bognor or a caravan at Selsey or Hayling Island. We always took plenty of indoor games as it usually rained. Cards, snakes and ladders, dominoes or colouring-in kept us amused.

In the late '50s we moved to Sutton, in Surrey. My father got his first car—a Morris Minor van, it seemed so luxurious after the motorbike and sidecar. I joined the Brownies and later 'flew up' to the Girl Guides and went on camps. It usually rained and we got used to eating half-cooked sausages when the wood was too wet. Being the youngest I was made to sleep near the tent entrance and would often get wet. I also had roller skates and spent nearly all of the school holidays with them strapped on, even on the bus! I was a bookworm and read all the Secret Seven adventures and any book I could get my hands on, even struggling through a Charles Dickens book.

Saturday mornings my brother and I went to the cinema, Zorro was a great favourite. I enjoyed the movie 'The Parent Trap' with Hayley Mills and 'The Adventures of Robin Hood' starring Richard Greene. We also enjoyed the music of the Australian Shirley Abicair who I think played a 'zither'. Frank Ifield, another Australian was also a favourite.'

*Martin Phippard lives in **Wiltshire**. He admits to falling some way short of being an Olympic medal prospect*

Extra time

'I was always terrible at any sport, having absolutely no interest and even less inclination. I also suffered a total lack of talent, but that's beside the point. To me, sport simply had no point and I would go to great lengths to avoid it.

As a result of this petulance and my obvious reluctance to run quickly, leap over things or catch or kick differing types of ball, I recall that I was nearly always on 'ground maintenance duties'. This punishment involved the painting of white lines, rolling the cricket pitch, etc which coincided neatly with my lunch hour. The sports master meted out these 'duties' and it seemed that my name was always at the top of his list.

So while all of my fellow students were eating lunch, chatting up girlfriends or simply lazing away the time, I was on a permanent round of painting, rolling and sweating. And dim as I was, I think even I appreciated the irony of the situation whereby I spent more time on the wretched sports field than many of our very best athletes.

I was twelve years old, possibly thirteen, certainly a child by the standards of the 1950s and yet another glorious summer day found me toiling at the front end of that familiar instrument of torture, the school roller. It was, in our day, a huge affair modified by dint of a large steel frame in and around which about eight fellow prisoners could fit in order to grace it with motion. I had used it so often I had assumed a certain status with the more regular offenders. I was also familiar enough with its operation to realise that when you were on duty with a bunch of fellow sports-haters, one could inflict fairly serious damage to the hallowed cricket pitch by executing ninety degree turns which left a satisfyingly deep cut in the turf. This, as you will realise, was one of the very few forms of protest to which one could resort and if discovered I think would have almost certainly resulted in public execution.

Anyway, the bell was ringing, our punishment was over for another day and on a whim I decided it might be interesting to discover approximately how fast eight skinny teen-age boys could propel the dreaded roller en route to its parking spot behind the school canteen. I think we had reached about 25mph (seemed like it anyway) when one of the party, John Hardy, slipped and fell. I can still feel the horror, astonishment and euphoria as John disappeared wordlessly out of sight beneath the roller and emerged a second or two later not flat or dead but apparently unscathed! Kids were undoubtedly tough in those days.

To be honest, the rest is a bit hazy. I was immediately identified as the ringleader having apparently shouted 'The charge of the Light Brigade' just before the incident and was hustled up to the Headmaster's office to await sentence. John, meanwhile, was whistled off to see the nurse and it is a great credit to him that he was OK then and is apparently OK all these years later never having displayed any unnatural tendencies to grow very tall or thin. The roller, abandoned the instant John fell, continued at some speed, eventually demolishing about fifty yards of wooden fence and gouging out large tufts of grass as it went. It was, as you can imagine, a talking point for days to come and we were all extremely fortunate that no serious harm was done.

For the record, I still feel bad about it but it was, after all, an accident. I still treat all sport with contempt—actually that's not quite true, I just don't notice it goes on—and I continued lunch-time roller duties for years as punishment, though always with a Prefect supervising after the incident. It took ninety week's pocket money (earned from my pre-school paper round) to pay for the repairs to the fence!'

Edward Young *started school at the age of four in* ***Hampshire***

The best years of my young life

'I attended a small Church of England school and on the whole, I'm sure I received a good education. I managed to pass the 11+ so it can't have been too bad. There are a number of incidents that stick in my mind. We all had free school milk, in 1/3 pint bottles. I was not fond of milk but was made to drink it 'because it was good for me.' One of my friends, who was equally averse to milk brought flavoured straws to school. These had chocolate or strawberry fla-vouring impregnated on the inside of them and made the drink quite palatable. My mother wouldn't buy these for me so I had to put up with the standard flavour. After not many days of feeling sick but not daring to complain I quietly drank my milk one morn-ing then regurgitated it all over the girl who sat next to me in our shared double desk. She cried, I managed to hold back my own tears. It was the last time that I drank school milk.

We learnt our 'times' tables by rote. At the end of the lesson we all stood up and were asked questions. A correct answer meant we could sit down, so there was a powerful incentive to learn and not be left standing to have questions continually bombarding you until you got one right. This approach to learning certainly encouraged us to pay attention and to try hard to remember our tables. However, looking back it must have been truly terrifying to the slower learners in the class. Some of them may have been scarred for life by the experience.

All lessons were written on a blackboard using coloured chalks. By the end of the day, one of the masters in particular had multi-coloured clothes, due to the fact that he had a habit of leaning against the blackboard. One of the other teachers had a nervous affliction and continually rubbed his thumb and forefinger across his forehead. By the end of the school day, this was usually multi-coloured too!

The headmaster, who shall remain nameless, was particularly severe on anyone who he considered was not paying due attention to his pearls of wisdom. He started off by shouting at the offender. If the indiscipline continued, a big wooden blackboard duster would be hurled through the air towards the head of the poor unfortunate child. I once saw him throw a large bunch of keys at a child; imagine if that happened today!'

Learning one of the 3Rs—note the totals!

Ann Parker had moved to Hampshire when she sat her 11+ exam

The 11+ and Dick Barton

'In those days only certain people sat the 11+, but I don't remember feeling any pressure from my parents to do well. There was an expectation I think but as far as I was concerned my day at the Grammar school where I sat in a big hall with what seemed like hundreds of others, was simply an opportunity to get home early because it was much closer than my junior school. We sat several tests. Intelligence tests, where you had to do strange things like moving flags around on paper so that they matched, working out which was next in a sequence, picking the odd one out and so on. Then the Maths, which everyone knew I would do very badly. I had been in the bottom of the bottom group. Finally we took the English tests, which were fine. If you did well enough you got a letter to say that you were in and that was that. Unfortunately, my Maths was, as expected, a total disaster, and my Intelligence tests were middling, but my English was excellent so I had to go for interview to show that I was a serious and academic sort of child. At this point there was a certain amount of pressure from my mother not to let her down, not because she wanted me to go to the Grammar school but because she wanted the way I behaved to reflect well on her. The Head mistress and I discussed the film of Lorna Doone and compared it to the book, which I preferred. I have to say I felt no sense that it was an important interview, she put me at my ease and we just sat and chatted. At one point she asked me what my favourite subject was at school and for some strange reason I said 'Needlework.' I say strange reason because I hated it then and I hate it now and always have done. My mother was so angry when we got out fearing that I had proved I was not an academic and would be sent to the dreaded Henry Harbin Secondary Modern which everybody knew was 'a bit rough' and not good enough for those of us with pretensions! However, her worst fears were not realised and I started at Parkstone Girls Grammar school in September 1952.

Events from Primary school that I remember were the death of George VI and the implications for Princess Elizabeth. We all had to go and stand in the playground to be told, standing in silence. It was cold, I recall. Having always been a great reader I was struck, even then, by the similarities between the Princess's accession and that of the first Elizabeth. In those days too, we always had Ascension Day off school. On Good Friday everything was shut. I used to be sent to Sunday school, like most of my contemporaries, although my parents didn't go to church. We didn't have TV so most of us read or listened to the Radio. Yes, I'm still an Archers fan! There was Valentine Dyall, 'The Man in Black' and excellent radio plays. Later, I graduated to 'Dick Barton, Special Agent' and 'Journey into Space.'

I remember when sweets came off ration, in 1951 I think. My mother gave me an extra penny so that I could sample the delights from the corner shop on my way to school. After that I had to walk to or from school if I wanted sweets. Before that my father used to buy my younger sister and I (my older sister had left home by then) our week's ration on a Friday night. Mine were all gone by Sunday but my sister used to eke hers out over the week.

I remember those days as happy on the whole, in my case, punctuated with injections from the doctor on a regular basis to keep my septicaemia at bay, I suppose. I used to come out in rashes and

1950s fashion

that meant I had to take baths in gentian violet, from which I used to emerge all purple. Because my illness had left me with a heart murmur my mother used to send me to bed very early, long before my friends and when I complained she used to say 'But you're not like other children' and I hated that. It wasn't until I went away to another Boarding school that I lived a 100% normal life in regard to other children.

Fashion wise it was the time of the full skirt, worn down to the lower calves, as exemplified by Princess Margaret, highlighting slim waists and hips. How I wanted one but never got it. In those days your mother chose your clothes. My mother had an account at Beales in Bournemouth so every so often she would make me wear my best clothes and we would sally forth to Bournemouth, a very posh place in those days, and go to Beales where we bought 'sensible' clothes. The disappointment was always softened by tea out, with ice cream as a special treat!'

Joan Stacey *grew up in* Dorset

Late for surgery

'When I was twelve years old, I had to attend the plastic surgery out patients' clinic at the Royal Victoria hospital in Boscombe. My mother did not drive so we went by public transport, which was quite an adventure! It was winter and the ferry service between Shell Bay and Sandbanks was suspended because the boat had gone on its annual holiday to have an overhaul. We left Swanage by bus and travelled to Shell Bay. Here, we boarded a small boat to cross the mouth of Poole Harbour to Sandbanks. Another bus took us to the centre of Bournemouth, where we boarded a cheerful yellow double-decker bus, which was powered by overhead electrical cables. This delivered us to the hospital, several hours after we had first set off from home. We waited with everyone else and were eventually told that the visiting surgeon had been delayed with the morning's operations at Odstock hospital in Salisbury. It was a very long wait, time to do my homework twice over! We were finally seen by the surgeon, then set off in the dark to make the return journey!'

Nigel Withers in Dublin still has the occasional flash back to his youthful visits to the dentist

Pedal power

'Our dentist's name was Mr Lamb, I think, but he certainly wasn't gentle! Sitting in the waiting room you could hear the drone of the drill as the poor unfortunate in the dentist's chair was having his teeth attended to. Apprehensively, I would go in to Mr Lamb's surgery and sit in the big brown leather chair, which tilted back slightly. The main worry was the drill. There were no local anaesthetic injections when you had a filling; just straight in with the whirring instrument of torture. By today's standards the drill was very slow and extremely noisy. I think it was electric but I also have a vague memory of a pedal powered drill. It wasn't very efficient and the noise as the drill bit in to the tooth enamel was almost as bad as the inevitable stab of pain as Mr Lamb apologised for hitting another nerve.

The room smelt of the anaesthetic gas that was used to knock people out when they had teeth removed. I had several teeth removed as a child, always under gas rather than a cocaine injection. The gas mask was held over your face and you breathed in as normal. Except that breathing normally was impossible as you were always on the edge of panicking before you drifted off to sleep. Instantly (or so it seemed) you awoke with a bleeding mouth and a handkerchief soaking up the blood. Mum would take me home to sleep off the after-effects tucked up on the sofa feeling sorry for myself.

The majority of older people including my dad but not my mum, had full sets of dentures. As a young boy, I expected to have dentures as I grew older. At night, dad kept his dentures in an old water filled teacup on the bathroom windowsill. It always frightened my younger sister who thought that the teeth were laughing at her.

There was no fluoridation of water or fluoride toothpastes at that time which have had such a marked effect on reducing tooth decay in more recent years. We used tooth powder which came in a round tin and tasted like pumice powder, which is probably what it was!'

John Phillips lived in *London*

Not for Sale

'Like a lot of kids at the time, I had a passion for autograph hunting. My particular favourites were the cricketers and footballers of the time. Touring cricket Test teams often stayed at the Piccadilly Hotel in London and we regularly waited outside for the appearance of the teams. Most of them were very good and patiently signed our books. One year the South Africans toured and I managed to hide myself on their team bus. They found me, of course, but let me stay on until we arrived at The Oval and the whole team gave me their autographs.

I lived near The Oval and this was my regular haunt. Jim Laker signed my book so many times that he knew me by name. We travelled home on the tube together several times and shared my sweets!

One day a grey-haired older man waited with us to get a particular player's autograph. He showed me his old leather bound autograph book, which included the prized signature of the great W.G.Grace. 'I've been offered £25 for that signature,' he told me solemnly, 'but I'll never sell it.'

In winter we watched Charlton Athletic and waited for the footballers to arrive, both the home players and the visitors. There was no football on TV at the time so we didn't recognise many of the star names. Football was very different then. Most of the players had working class backgrounds and almost all of the spectators would class themselves in the same way. As we waited outside of the Charlton ground one Saturday a chauffeur driven Daimler pulled up and a young, pinstripe suited gentleman emerged. We thought he was probably the visiting manager and were pleased when he signed our books. When the two teams ran out on to the pitch before the game we were astonished to see that our pinstriped gent was wearing a Charlton Athletic strip! I think his name was Stubbs and he became a regular first team player, travelling to away games in his chauffeur driven Daimler rather than the team coach!'

Maurice Maxwell in **Devon** *recollects his brother's hobby*

Ostrich eggs

'What would now be considered unacceptable by almost everyone was a popular pastime for children brought up in the country. My older brother David had a fantastic bird's egg collection. He had over 100 different eggs all laid out on cotton wool in a chest of drawers. Some he'd inherited from one of our uncles, some he'd swapped with his friends but most he'd collected himself. In those days, nobody really cared about conservation but he never took more than one egg from each nest. He used to go to the cliffs in Spring and clamber down the rocks to collect gull's eggs. Once he took our mum's washing line and used that to lower himself down over the cliff edge. He must have been mad! He once showed me an egg that he told me belonged to an ostrich. It was twenty years before I realised that it was actually a goose's egg!'

Len Smith *grew up in* **Derbyshire**

The school milk run

'As a boy, I lived at Ambergate and attended the local school that backed on to the main railway line between Derby and Manchester. Most of us were very keen train spotters in those days. At 1-15pm and 1-30pm every day, two express trains passed through. However, as our lessons started at 1pm it was officially impossible to see the trains and collect their numbers. Officially impossible but not actually impossible. One of the school duties was to wash the school milk bottles and we would always volunteer for this duty, which we carried out after lessons resumed at 1pm. Two of us washed the bottles while a third boy would sneak out of the door, over the back wall and down the road to a convenient bridge to wait for the two trains. Mission accomplished, he would return with the details of the engines and we all returned to class. This went on for a long time and strangely enough we were never reported or found out. Somebody must have seen us and thought it strange as we were a small community where everyone knew each other's families. The headmaster was a very strict disciplinarian and we would have been in real trouble, had we been rumbled!

Holidays at the time usually meant a trip to London to visit my grandparents. This was an ideal opportunity to 'spot' trains and I spent a lot of time on the main London stations. On one particular homeward journey, I grabbed my usual seat, notebook in hand, facing forward with a good view of the oncoming line. Two off duty drivers sat opposite me. As the minutes passed we got into conversation and the discussion got round to the fact that I was writing with my left hand and ought to be learning to write with my right. My father went along with this and they all suggested that I should write down the number of the next train number that I saw with my 'wrong' hand. This would not have been so bad, except that we were approaching Camden shed where I knew we would see several engines together. The next loco that I saw was standing on the turntable as we approached the depot. By the time I'd written the number down with my right hand, in barely discernible handwriting, I had missed all of the other engines in the shed. To say that I wasn't well pleased was an understatement and I was in a really bad mood all of the way home. The badly written number stood out on the page of my notebook, which I kept for a long time afterwards. It always reminded me of that day.'

Pete Jary has early memories of industrial relations in the North East

Union troubles

'In the summer of 1950 I was six months short of my fifth birthday. The railways had been recently nationalised and the industry was in turmoil with strike after strike. One day, I was in a field having a picnic with my mother, a young friend and his mother. It was a hot day and we were sitting at the foot of a railway embankment on the Newcastle to Sunderland line. An engine was waiting at a signal and the driver and fireman were hanging out of the cab, trying to keep a little cooler from both the heat of the steam boiler and the warmth of the sunny summer's day. Apparently, I wandered up the field to the engine and shouted up to the crew, 'Are you having a tea bwake or are you on stwike?' At which point the crew fell about laughing! The thing was, I was serious—even at 4½ years old!'

Ron Hak *grew up in the* **North West**

Main line or Dublo?

'At last Saturday morning arrived. Duffel bag gathered complete with butties for the day and all necessary notepad, pens, pencils and ABC book. Out the door I'd go with a wave to mum and off to meet my mates from neighbouring houses. The adventure had begun. Decisions about where to go had been made earlier in the week and dad had got me the privilege ticket as requested. He was a shunter on the railways and was able to get me such lucrative tickets. Now the first decision with my mates—do we wait for the bus to get to Hunts Cross station or do we 'leggit.' The 81D bus was always unreliable and infrequent, so we usually 'legged it' all the way from Speke to Hunts Cross. The only pleasure during this physical exersion on the way was the bridge over the Liverpool—London main line at Woodend Avenue, and even that could prove to be very annoying. Usually we would be about a hundred yards away when there would be a cloud of smoke and steam billowing up from the cutting at great speed as something important stormed by in either direction, the best we would usually see would be the last coach racing away into the distance. Anyway, mustn't wait, we had a train to catch at Hunts Cross. We just had time to get the inevitable bottle of Tizer from the sweet shop at the nearby shops. Hunts Cross station always seemed impressive so long ago with its four platforms, despite being just a suburban station. Our destination, in all its grime and glory, was Warrington Bank Quay station.

On arrival, we would find a space on the loading bay dock amongst all the other regulars and the day proper would begin. I think you would have to queue up here for twenty-four hours in order to be the first one to arrive, always it seemed to be teeming with spotters. We never had to wait long before the excitement started. Trains came and went here every few minutes, from the continual procession of the London—Scottish expresses to the regular interruption of the local engine to and from Newton-le-Willows.

This train seemed to have the knack of leaving or arriving right in front of us just in time to obscure the passing of some non-stop express hurtling through. Then the fun would start as everyone tried to determine what it was. There would nearly always be two or three numbers that someone would swear to that he clearly saw. Such was the frequency of trains here, that it was not unusual for a freight to be trundling through obscuring everything as two expresses would pass by in the background. None of this would have been a problem if we had gone and stayed on the platform, but with the number of spotters around, often getting close to a hundred or so, spotters were quickly ejected from any such luxury as sitting on a station platform trolley. This was all part of the fun and excitement of the place.

Something regularly upset us at 'Bank Quay.' Always, it seemed, just as we got our 'butties' out at about 1pm, the smell from the soap works at the back of the station suddenly pervaded the air. Did the workers watch for us to start eating and then eject what seemed a great load of soap powder into the air? Such was Bank Quay!

Edge Hill, the ultimate local shed, was always worth a visit but there was always the challenge of getting through a long tunnel under the tracks from the houses in Taunton St into the shed area. There was nearly always some enginemen coming or going; most of them never bothered us, but you could never be sure. Once past this obstacle however and paradise lay before you. Engine upon engine in quiet ranks left and right and as far as the eye could see, or so it seemed to someone in short trousers. Once into this vast area, it was rare to be spotted and thrown out, so the access tunnel challenge was always worth it. Even now I can smell that strangely thick addictive cancerous smoke rolling round the shed like a fifties smog and the occasional whiff of strange smelling steam escaping from some pipe work somewhere.

Over on the far side from the shed across the yards was the strangely named Pighue Lane, which ran along the border of the railway property. It was here that the remarkable Meccano factory existed. I wonder how much inspiration was gleaned from Edge Hill yards in the creation of Hornby Dublo model railways? My father once told me that before the Second World War when he used to live nearby, it was possible to go round the back of the factory and find enough thrown out scrap/faulty pieces to assemble, with a little bit of work, your own model railway for free!'

Mr Lucas *has had a lifelong interest in the railways in* **London**

A bucket of steam

'I started working on the railways when I left school. My first job was as a trainee signal boy and my main duty was to sort the guards' journals. In those days, the guard on the train was required to keep a log of the train's performance—time in the station, time out of the station, minutes late or early, etc. The guard also recorded the 'load' of the train—number of carriages, weight and so on. This was all written up in to the journals, which I kept in order. The guard was also responsible for watching the signals, as a back up to the driver. There was a periscope at the back of the train that the guard used to look up the track and watch for the oncoming signals. If the driver missed a signal, the guard was able to drop a handle and stop the train. This very rarely happened. The guards, though, paid particular attention to their periscopes in 'pea-souper' fogs when visibility was down to a few yards. More usually, if the guard wanted to attract the driver's attention he would gently apply the brake so that the driver knew that something was up, without worrying the passengers.

After about eighteen months I transferred to Hampton Court junction as a signal boy. This was the only signal box on the southern region that had central heating! It was an experimental installation with four radiators and hot water, all run from a solid fuel boiler. The drivers that stopped in the winter often joked with us, 'The signalmen in other boxes are all wearing overcoats; you lot are in your shirtsleeves!'

I applied to be transferred to Waterloo station as a signal boy but was turned down because I wasn't able to get there by 6am in the morning. So I was given a job as a 'relief boy,' which was 'the' job for training as a general railwayman. This was a better move for me, made even better when they told me that I'd be working at Waterloo and my first job there was in the signal box!

There were 309 levers in that signal box. During the day four signalmen, two boys and a yard inspector manned it. At night, this was reduced to two signalmen.

When the wind blew every single pane of glass banged and rattled; it was terribly draughty. One pane had a perfect round hole in it, the result of a German air raid during the war.

The signalbox had heating installed by this time and the radiators were too hot to touch. But hot air rises and the heat all rose up in to the high roof space leaving us shivering down below. If a bulb blew, I had to climb up an enormous pair of stepladders to change it. It was very warm up there and I could have stayed all day on my precarious perch!

At eighteen, I became a leading porter and moved to Egham. The station had to be open at 5am and we had to attend every train. In addition to passengers, parcels and letters, there were other items to handle. 'Passenger Luggage in Advance' or PLA was popular with people who were going on holiday. The luggage would arrive, usually two days before it was required, to be sent on ahead of the passengers. This cost 2/6d if the passengers brought it in and it was collected at the other end. It cost 5/- if the passengers brought it in but it had to be delivered to an address at the other end and 6/- if it was collected and delivered. PLA had special labels and was given priority, in the same way as livestock. Livestock included pigeons. There were 'pigeon special' trains, usually on a Friday night, that carried the birds hundreds of miles away from their lofts where they would be released, to race home against the clock. Individual baskets of pigeons also arrived at a station and the birds were released by the porters. We used to carry the basket down the end of the platform and release the birds, noting the time, which we enclosed with the basket and returned it to its owner.

Some time later, I worked at Clapham Junction. A new trainee boy started working with us and one of the signalmen asked him to clean the signal box windows.

'What with?' asked the boy

'Use steam,' the signalman joked, 'get a bucket and go down to that tank engine over there and fill it with steam.'

Trying not to laugh, we watched as the boy carried the bucket down to the tank engine. We saw him talking to the driver then coming back empty handed.

'He says he can't fill the bucket because I haven't got a lid.'

We barely restrained ourselves as we gave him a makeshift lid. The boy walked back to the engine, the driver opened a valve and held the bucket over it to collect some steam and put the lid on. The boy returned with his bucket of steam. He opened the lid and the smallest puff of steam escaped from the otherwise empty bucket.

By this time the boy had cottoned on that he had been stitched up and joined in with our laughter!'

This R White's Lemonade delivery lorry was made by Albion with a coach-built wooden cab

Valerie Cushing grew up in Sussex

The Pips

'Early in 1952, at the age of twelve, I recorded the death of King George VI in my diary. I described him as 'someone who was very important.' Queen Elizabeth II came to the throne and she became an icon for me. I was inspired by the whole Coronation and the painting of the Queen by Pietro Annigoni. In this painting her Majesty wore no crown or tiara and was dressed in a long dark robe. There was another portrait of her wearing her full regalia in Westminster Abbey, which made a lasting impression. Painstakingly I copied the portrait using pencils and worked hard on every detail.

Our family holiday in 1953, the year of the Coronation, was spent at Sunshine Holiday Camp on Hayling Island. This was our first experience of life in such a camp. We slept in small chalets and ate 'en masse' in a large dining room. Campers were put into two competitive teams called the 'Reds' and the 'Blues.' Each team was given a chant for various victories at games and competitions. We were in the 'Reds' and our chant ran as follows '2 4 6 8—who do we appreciate?—R E D S—Reds!' For the 'Blues' the chant ran like this—'Ra Ra Ra—here's good news,—there's only one team, and that's the Blues!'

Each evening the campers would gather in the bar and a man at the piano would lead the bawdy singing. The favourite was 'Green grow the rushes O' accompanied by what I recognise now as rude hand gestures whenever the words 'Two two' came into play. Innocent and naïve as we were, we all enjoyed ourselves and a good time was had by all.

I played my part in the netball team and was pleased and proud to score lots of goals. Young women took part in the beauty contest and paraded in their swimming costumes up and down at the side of the pool. Young men used to display their strength by lying on the ground and lifting up heavy bars and dumb-bells with their muscular arms.

When we arrived home we turned on the radiogram and saw smoke coming out from underneath the base. What a homecoming—the radiogram was as important to us as television is today. We had to pay a visit to our friendly neighbours so that we could hear the service of the Coronation on their radio. When we heard the sound of the music my father said that the hairs on the back of his neck 'prickled.' We went and saw the whole state occasion at the cinema (in colour) and there were dozens of pictures in newspapers, magazines and souvenir books. The young Queen in all her fine regalia was a real figurehead for the nation entering a new Elizabethan age and there was a lot of hope and expectation for a bright future in the years following the end of the war. The Queen with Prince Philip travelled around the Commonwealth countries in the Royal Yacht Britannia and when they sailed up the Thames they passed under Tower Bridge to meet crowds of people welcoming them home. The Royal family was very popular then as a young couple with small children. People could identify with them. I was very impressed and inspired by the Queen's sense of duty and service and the vow she made at her Coronation.

1955 was my last year at school and this meant constant revision for Ordinary Level Examinations. I took eight subjects—English Language, Maths, History, Art, French, General Science, Cookery and English Literature. I failed one and that was Cookery, much to my amusement.

At lunchtime we used to sit on the hard ground with our backs to the wall and our legs stretched out so that we could get a nice tan. Skirts had to be a certain length and each term we had to kneel in front of the teacher so that she could make sure that the skirt hem just grazed the floor. That summer there was a partial eclipse of the sun and we viewed this through photographic negatives. The eclipse came and the light could be described as eerie.

School days were coming to an end and I couldn't wait to be free of study so that I could go out and earn some money for myself. I longed to have some nice clothes and had no wish to go on to the VI form to study for A levels—places were reserved for the brightest in any case.

My father came along to a careers evening and spoke about my future with the Maths teacher. Since Maths was my strongest subject, it was thought that I should try getting a job working in the bank or (something that appealed to me far more), make an application for a job working at the Royal Greenwich Observatory which had recently moved from Greenwich to Herstmonceux in Sussex. I was invited to attend an interview at the bank but I told them that I was really interested in working at the Observatory. They did not take offence at this and offered me a job.

Later on, together with a close friend, I went to the Observatory for the all important interview. The work place was idyllic. Herstmonceux Castle had been bought by the Ministry of Defence and the large rooms had been converted into sections for the Meridian Department, the Solar Department, the Chronometer Department, living accommodation for the Astronomer Royal and the staff dining room. I sat on one side of a long impressive table facing five people who questioned me about my knowledge. Since I was in the throes of study I was able to answer quickly about subjects such as trigonometry and physics. The second interview took place in some temporary huts that were placed in the area in front of the bridge that spanned the moat. This was the Nautical Department and we had to examine columns of figures concerning the movement of the stars. It reminded me of the logarithms at school. The fact that I failed Cookery did not go against me and I was offered a job as a Scientific Assistant in the Meridian

Department. My friend was also offered the same kind of work. I was thrilled.

We worked together as a team in the Meridian Department and sat on opposite sides of a large desk. Mr Smith was head of the department, a large portly gentleman who wheezed a great deal as he talked and rather lumbered along. Mr Adams was our immediate superior and gave us our tasks, which involved working out mathematical problems with the aid of a 'Grunsbriga' calculating machine. The machine had tiny levers in grooves, which were pulled down to reveal numbers in a window. A handle at the side was used to produce the answer to a multiplication or division problem. Mr Adams suffered from an over-active thyroid gland and was always moving about even when sitting next to us to explain something. We were given an amazing amount of freedom to work together. For example, every morning we walked up to the 'Photographic Zenith Tube' (P.Z.T.) and collected the photographic plates which we then developed in the dark room. During the previous night the stars had progressed across the heavens and the plates had recorded their images as they did so. Four photographs of each star were taken and they appeared as black spots; sometimes very well defined if the weather had been clear of cloud. Each day we would sit at the 'Zeiss' machine and while one took measurements of the images the other recorded. Then came the task of working out all the mathematical gymnastics to eventually arrive at the time to the nearest one hundredth of a milli-second. This information was given to the Chronometer Department and hence the Greenwich 'Pips' were heard daily on the radio.'

Kathy Munson left school in **Highbury**

From the Office to Goonhilly

'My friends and I stayed on at school to do a business course in the sixth form. We left there in 1957 to work in a solicitor's office in New Court, Carey Street, opposite the Law Courts, as assistant book-keepers. We worked in a room with the accountant, the book-keeper, a clerk/typist and an office boy.

Articled clerks and department managers would come into the room to be paid by the clerk/typist over the very high counter, for any disbursements e.g., searches in Somerset House, which had been incurred on behalf of their clients.

Often they would pass the time of day with us, but we were not allowed to reply—by order of the book-keeper. In fact we were not allowed to speak to each other in the room unless it was important—and then we had to address each other formally as in 'Miss Bianchi' or 'Miss West.' The office boy was called by his first name, which demonstrated his lowly position.

As assistant book-keepers, we typed entries from foolscap sheets of disbursements into unwieldy, thick elongated ledgers with heavy covers. These were added up on a machine that was turned with a handle and the totals checked by an old retired soldier in the outer office (with a permanent dewdrop on the end of his nose).

The typewriters were the open pre-war type whose keys I was often having to untangle. Each year they were taken away for servicing by a gentleman who always said, with genuine surprise, 'I don't know how they've lasted another year.'

The room—high ceilings, large windows—was draughty and very cold in winter, as the sun never shone on that side (we were

The efficient secretary

in a quadrangle). We had a small coal fire which had to be kept going by one of us in rotation. Woe betide you if you were so busy you lapsed in putting on more coal or poking it and the fire went out because it took forever to get going and that meant staying late to get your work done (with no overtime pay).

To use a toilet we had to take toilet paper and a key, walk down stairs to the ground floor, across the quadrangle and down steps to a basement toilet. On one occasion when this was being 'done up,' we had to carry our paper surreptitiously down the road to a toilet in Lincoln's Inn Fields.

We sat on dining room chairs at huge desks that sloped at an odd angle. Coffee wasn't heard of but we had a cup of tea morning and afternoon while we were working—no breaks. Rotation again to make it for the six of us plus two or three of the solicitors.

We were issued with half a pint of milk per day and a small amount of tea. We didn't dare ask for more of these items and it was very difficult to stretch it. I remember one occasion when I had sixteen cups to make one afternoon and an impossible amount of milk. Thinking 'well it just can't be done and I'm too busy to go and ask another tea club,' the bookkeeper came up, brushed me aside and said 'she would do it and I wasn't really trying.' Well, with the help of 1" of cigarette ash that fell into a cup (she always had a cigarette in her mouth with ash dropping all around her—even though the accountant had just had his lung removed), she made the sixteen cups and I took them round on the tray. Not the strongest cups of tea that I've ever seen!

It was interesting to see how the gloomy '50s moved towards the brighter '60s while I worked in that office. Upstairs in the divorce department, females were not allowed to type out anything to do with divorce cases. In conveyancing, though, a zany young secretary would come to work in a mini skirt and a straw hat with long blond pigtails dangling down over her shoulders.

These changes were also brought home to me when, at the turn of the decade, I went touring with my husband in the West Country. One evening we enquired at a B&B for a room. It was a small farmhouse with no electricity—we went to bed like Wee Willie Winkies, with a small candle each. Waking up in the morning I noticed two things. In the room, our water for washing was contained in a jug and basin; straight from the well and freezing cold. Looking out of the window across the field I saw the biggest possible contrast—the Goonhilly Down Scanner! It was certainly a time of change!'

Brenda Allen began work in the 1950s

Speedway

'I started work in 1952 and my first job was in the cheque office at the Co-op. We would sort the little cheques into pigeonholes, which was fine until someone opened the window and they would all blow out. Luckily, that soon changed when the early punch card machines were installed in the office.

My weekly wage was 37/6d (less than £2). My mother took 30/- for my keep and my train fares totalled 2/6d for the week. The other five shillings funded my weekly treat—Birmingham speedway at Perry Barr. The 5/- paid for my fares each way, my entrance money and a programme!'

John Dymock was demobbed in 1950 and trained as a nurse

Out of bounds

'After my interview, Matron showed me around the nurses' home. She was quite clear when she said, 'If you are caught with one foot on that staircase (pointing to the stairway to the female staff rooms) it will be instant dismissal.' The fact that female nurses had to pass the male rooms to reach the dining room didn't seem to matter; they could easily have visited our rooms without any suspicions being raised!

In the dining room, one sat at the table allocated for your year. If that was full, you had to ask permission to sit at a senior table. At breakfast time, Night Sister came in ten minutes before 'on duty' time at 7-30am and called the register. If we arrived as she was calling the register, we were required to wait at the door. If we missed her altogether, it resulted in a visit to her office to explain ourselves!

One could have a late pass once a week. Apart from this, curfew was at 10-30pm. Those with ground floor rooms climbed in the window of their own room, others arranged to use the same method then creep upstairs. A favourite trick was to put a bowl of water under the window for the unfortunate late returnee to step in to. I recall one evening when we had been to a ball my partner's evening dress was too large to allow her to climb through the window. With a smile and a sigh she stood outside the window and took her dress off, passed it through the window then followed closely behind.

I worked for a time at a chest hospital in Warwick. Here, each ward had special mortuary linen, which had been lovingly embroidered by past patients. These had beautiful satin embroidery of lilies, etc and were used when a patient passed away. Sometimes, a patient would say, 'I've got a beautiful pillow case, all embroidery.' It was quickly changed, with no explanation given or perhaps a quick-witted nurse would explain that this was Matron's linen which had been misplaced.'

Irene Howes and her older sister lived in **Doncaster**

Busted

'My older sister Joan was not blessed with a large bust and was very conscious of her appearance. In her teens she usually wore padded bras, joking that 'What the Lord's forgotten, you pad with cotton!'

Women's underwear took a leap forward in 1952 when a blow-up bra was launched, called the Tres Secrete. This was inflated by blowing in to a narrow tube, like a drinking straw and my older sister excitedly bought one of these as soon as they were available. She wore it several times and I don't think she ever had any problems, though it was rumoured that some of these bras developed an unhappy habit of deflating themselves when they weren't supposed to!'

Barbara Rodgers *has a memorable claim to fame*

Fan club reminiscences

'In March 1956, my friend Ann and I had tickets to see a singer called Slim Whitman at the London Palladium. He was touring Britain for the first time since taking the record chart by storm with 'Rose Marie,' 'Indian Love Call' and 'Tumbling Tumbleweeds.' His records were heard constantly on the radio and were played in coffee bar juke boxes everywhere. We sat in the Royal Circle waiting expectantly through the other acts—the theatre was packed to capacity and the atmosphere was one of excited anticipation. Slim strode on the stage to tumultuous applause. His voice live was as strong and melodic as it was on his records and the crowd loved him. We learnt later from Slim's tour manager that this had been quite an ordeal for the singer—back home on the country and western circuit there were no large theatres and here he was topping the number one variety theatre in the world.

After the show the scene around the stage door was chaotic. We all waited expectantly then, out of the stage door stepped Slim himself. He was genuinely interested in his fans and signed autographs for everyone, staying until we were all satisfied. Ann and I saw Slim several times during the course of the next two weeks, travelling all over Britain—he always made time to talk to his fans, us amongst them. During the second week, Ann suggested that we set up the Slim Whitman Fan Club. I said I would help and Slim agreed. That's how it all started; easy—but little did we know how much it would change our lives! Slim's manager, Charles King, wasn't happy about us—'You don't even know the girls,' he remonstrated but the great man didn't listen—he is a pretty good judge of character! What we lacked in experience, we made up for with enthusiasm and for the next four years we dedicated ourselves to promoting Slim Whitman and his music—we were just eighteen years old. After Slim returned to the US in 1956, Ann and I worked hard to get the Fan Club going. We advertised in various music magazines, organised photos, badges and a quarterly magazine. One of the things that sticks in my mind is sending out that magazine. Every three months we sat down and addressed hundreds of envelopes by hand—even in 1956 there must have been a better way!

Slim returned to the UK the following year and we attended concerts throughout the country. He was particularly homesick on this tour as his son Byron had been born in January of that year. By this time we had devised a uniform and wore straight black skirts and imitation white leather jackets. We look back today and laugh but at the time we thought it looked good to dress in Slim's colours.

Slim seemed quite impressed with the work that we did with the club—he had seen a lot of club members all over the country wearing their badges when he met them at the various stage doors after his shows. We even won over Charles King who by this time had become great friends with us.

The Fan Club continued until 1960 when we decided that it was time for us to pick up our 'other' lives and live a little before we became too old and decrepit! Great years, which we will never forget'.

Jane Cook *grew up on the outskirts of* ***St Albans***

Without knobs on

'One of my early memories is of being wheeled along in my pram. This was a fashionable model of the time with very small wheels and a large false bottom below the mattress. I am sure that I can remember my mother regularly putting an empty one gallon Tate and Lyle syrup can in to this false bottom before we set off for the village shop (she denies this still). Three spinster sisters ran the shop and they topped up the can with something before my mother replaced it in its secret compartment. I presume that it contained something that was still rationed after the war and was only available on the Black Market. They also sold pieces of sugar, which they hacked off of a large block using something that resembled a small ice pick.

The only material or fabric that my mother seemed to be able to get hold of was Harris Tweed. She made me a pair of dungarees out of this coarse material and wearing them was purgatory!

The butter ration for my parents and myself was ½ lb one week and ¼ lb the next. I asked mother to 'make my bread and butter as oozing with butter as possible,' knowing that this would be partially possible one week but impossible the next—without a fridge, butter wouldn't keep.

Rationing was still in force at the beginning of the '50s

My family's house was built after the war on a large patch of land that had been a practice ground for the Home Guard. The garden was full of trenches and there was a large ammunition store at the end. This was supposed to have been demolished but was pressed in to service as our garden shed, to good effect. We grew all of our own vegetables on this land which helped a lot, particularly whilst rationing was still in force in the early years of the '50s.

My father worked for Marconi and he and some of his colleagues had a bet to see who could build a TV set first. Their objective was to see the Festival of Britain. I don't know if any of them succeeded but I do recall that our set was working at the time of the Queen's Coronation in 1953. It was never actually finished though. Our baker built an enormous wooden cabinet to house the set, with its 12" black and white screen but you had to reach inside this to turn the set on—the knobs were never fitted!'

Trudy Lazarus *had an enterprising father*

Cleaning up

'After his wartime 'Black Market' days my father resumed his legitimate career running the shoe business. During the 1920s, a two-tone men's shoe called a Correspondent shoe had been extremely fashionable. When these fell from favour, father's business found itself with many pairs of these unwanted shoes. They were stacked high at the back of the storeroom and gently gathered dust until the 1950s. Suddenly, these shoes became the height of fashion once again, mainly among the increasing numbers of black immigrants from the Caribbean. Father's shop had the widest range of stock in the local area and he made a killing!'

Linda Migro *emigrated to **Australia** with her parents and brother Raymond. Her mother kept a diary of the voyage. The extracts from this which follow, as well as giving a graphic account of the voyage, highlight how outlooks on life have changed since the 1950s*

MV Fairsea—Tuesday morning December 10, 1957
'My dearest Mum and Dad,

We are just settling down into our new routine but it takes a bit of getting used to. We had a reasonable journey to London but it was very wet and blowy. The train left Waterloo at nine minutes past one but we didn't arrive at Southampton until after 3pm, so we didn't leave those shores until 5.15pm. There was such chaos and muddle with the luggage too, but it was soon sorted out. In the meantime as soon as we got on board we were shown to our cabins and then found our way to the dining room for tea. We were then given our regular table numbers and given the choice of first or second lunch and dinners. Raymond has to go with the little ones but Linda comes with us. I want to tell you everything that has happened since Saturday so I shall make this letter like 'Mrs Dale's Diary.' But before I start I must tell you that we went to see our vicar on Wednesday and he said to get in touch with the

Port Padre in Southampton. Well, while we were sorting out our luggage he came up to us—he'd waited by our luggage so that he'd know us. He wished us God speed and told us there was a Church of England Padre on board going out to the 'Bush' and he will be conducting communion services.

Now to start my diary:
Saturday evening:
We took Raymond to have his dinner at 5.30pm then had a wander around until our dinner at 8pm. Just before then the boat started to make itself felt because we were in the channel and it was very rough. We had taken our seasick pills but Linda started to turn colour. We went into dinner but soon I had to dash to the toilet with her twice. As soon as dinner was over we all went to our cabins and got into bed. I don't think I slept all night. Linda kept on being sick and so were a good many more. There are twelve bunks in our cabin and a cot, and the majority of them were pretty groggy—the children as well. It got rougher and rougher but apart from being scared stiff at first I was all right.

Sunday:
Reg got up next morning all bright and breezy but he had to go back to his bunk. Raymond had been seasick too. So all Sunday we stayed in our cabins. I was all right lying down but as soon as I put my feet on deck I felt dizzy and awful. The cabin steward brought us some meat rolls and cheese—no drinks because it's the worst thing to take and the thing you want most because the seasick tablets give you a raging thirst and you feel you can't quench it. At about 11.20am it was announced that we were leaving the English Channel. That brought us out into the Atlantic Ocean. The seas were mountainous and were washing over the deck. What with the smell of the diesel oil and the rock and roll of the boat the best place was in bed believe me. By Sunday evening, only about 550 people went in to dinner. By the way dears, there are 1500 people on board (loads of children including babies) and it's an all Italian crew that can only speak broken English. It's Italian cooking too which is not to our taste and there's a terrific amount of waste at every meal. I suppose they cook in oil and it spoils the taste of everything. The soup is always nice though and I expect in a while we shall get used to everything. When we got to the Bay of Biscay

it was pretty awful. We lay in our bunks and one minute we felt as if we were lying on our heads, the next we were sliding down in our beds. It was a relief when morning came and it was a wee bit calmer. The cases were sliding back and forth in the cabins and at one particular heavy swell all the dishes and food went sliding off the dining tables onto the floor with a terrific clatter.

Monday:
Reg and I felt better and actually went down to breakfast. We got the children up afterwards and took them on deck. Linda was still under the weather and didn't eat a thing. She's not much better today because last night they speeded up the vessel and we've got to get used to the vibrations of the diesel engines. Now that we're in calmer waters things are being organised better. Last night there was a film show—two performances. It was a new film not yet re-leased in London called 'The Seven Thunders,' about two British escaped prisoners of war in France and the Germans, of course. It was very good entertainment.

Tuesday:
We have passed Cape St Vincent, the southern most tip of Portugal. In a few hours time we should be going through the Straits of Gibraltar and into the Mediterranean and then we can really begin to enjoy ourselves. It is certainly an experience we shan't forget in a hurry. We had a nice lunch today—the meat was actually recog-nisable as beef and very tasty. We had soup first of course—they always serve tasty soup before each meal. Reg and Ray had their hair cut this morning—2/6d each. Reg had a shampoo as well. The shop on board is German and pretty expensive. We have to do our own bit of washing and lines are rigged on deck. They sell Persil and pegs and we have to manage as best we can. It's not bad though and we share the cabin with quite decent people. Our cabin steward is very nice too.

Wednesday:
It is disappointing today because it's raining and the sea is quite choppy and not blue at all. The boat is swaying a bit but we're tough sailors by this time and aren't bothered by it. The worst part is the vibration all the time. Somebody said the engines are too power-

ful and something will be done about it when we reach Port Said, but we shall see. I took Linda to have her hair cut today; it needs washing now. The barber didn't know where to start on it!

Thursday:
We learnt this morning that the clocks go on thirty minutes every night from now on because we have to gain ten hours before we reach Australia. They're also talking about arranging things for the children—a bit of instruction probably about what to expect at their new schools. Tonight there is a possibility of arranging darts games. It would be nice to have a game again. The children are being good at present—I hope they keep it up. We have to hand all our mail to the Purser's office in the morning ready for posting at Port Said because although we are staying there the whole day we shan't be going ashore. So now my dears, I'm going to close this letter and carry on tomorrow with a new one. God bless you both and our love to all our family and yourselves, from ever loving

Pegs, Reg, Linda and Raymond xxxxxxxx

SECOND LETTER—SAME ADDRESS

My dearest Mum and Dad,
I have not written anything since last Thursday so now I must collect my thoughts and get up to date. The seas were a bit choppy on Thursday and so the boat did a rock and roll and sent a good many people back to their cabins. Linda wasn't very good and I had to go back to my bunk to keep her company. Reg stayed up and watched the pictures but there weren't many there. On Friday it was better and the sun shone. We spent most of the day up on deck. It really is a lovely life and I shall be sorry to get to the end of our journey. We've both bought ourselves some shorts at the shop on board so we're just waiting for the opportunity to wear them.

Sunday:
I went to communion at 8am and then went on to breakfast. After lunch there was a film show for the children from 2-3pm and a Sunday school afterwards. In the evening we went to the pictures and saw 'High Tide at Noon.' A very good show again. There was great excitement this morning because we were due in Port Said

early. So we were up on deck at 6am. It was just beginning to get light—the moon was still up and there was the beginning of a lovely sunrise.

We could see the lights of the town in the distance. After we had stopped, small boats full of Arabs and their wares soon surrounded us. It was a wonderful sight. They call up to the passengers and we bargain over the side of the boat. If you want anything, they throw a rope up for you to catch and fixed to this rope is a small basket, which brings up the article and you then send the money back down in it.

The noise is terrific but it has to be seen to be believed. Linda had a pair of all leather slippers for 6/- and Raymond had a camel for 4/6d. He's going to keep it as a souvenir. I was lucky to get a smashing pair of white leather sandals, which fit me like a glove. He was asking £2 for them but we got them for 25/- plus three cigarettes. I've never had such comfortable shoes and they look smart and dressy. I wish you could see me today in my very short shorts and red and white blouse. I don't feel a bit like thirty-six years old.

I'm looking forward to the first letter I get from you, dear Mum and Dad. I do hope you're keeping well and not having too much bad weather. It's difficult to realise it's still December. One of the Egyptians on board yesterday gave a conjuring show, he was excellent and made quite a bit of money by passing his fez (hat) around.

It was most interesting sailing up the Suez Canal and very hot. We left Port Said at 10.30am and then had to tie up in the Canal to let a convoy come through towards Port Said before we could go on. That took quite a few hours and it was pretty hot. It's cooler today because we are on the move and there's more breeze. We've seen a few porpoises and one flying fish. We have also passed Mount Sinai. Linda has been in the swimming pool this morning; it is the first time it has been filled. We have made friends with a family from Northern Ireland by the name of Mulligan. Mary and her two little girls are in my cabin and her husband and son are in Reg's cabin. Funnily enough we were given the same table number for our meals, so we see quite a lot of each other. They are very nice people and are going to Perth. We hope to see something of each other—it will be nice to keep in touch. There was dancing up on deck last night. It was a warm evening and everyone enjoyed themselves. There are still pictures every night as well as various other games and concerts. I went and had a chat with the C of E Padre on board yesterday afternoon. The port Padre at Southampton has given him our name. He's going out to the 'Bush' for five years. He has only been ordained three years; before that he was working in the docks. I went to communion this morning—there were only two of us—the other girl was from my cabin. She's a fully qualified state registered nurse going to Sydney. She's a very nice girl too also from Northern Ireland. We are in the Red Sea now, and it's quite hot although there is a breeze blowing at present. I did some washing this morning—it soon dried. Now I have to choose a good opportunity to iron. The clocks go on another thirty minutes tonight. We shall be worn out in the morning again. But we can always laze about and have a nap anytime we feel like it. It's hard to realise it will be Xmas Day a week today! I bet it will be bedlam on board but I'm sure everyone will enjoy themselves immensely.

We have to hand all letters and cards to the Purser's office in the morning for posting at Aden. So I'll close now and continue in my next letter our journey to Australia.

All my love as always dears, from Pegs, Reg, Lin and Ray xxx

THIRD LETTER—SAME ADDRESS

Christmas Day (somewhere near the Equator)
My dearest Mum and Dad,

The last time I wrote to you was before we reached Aden. So now I shall carry on with from where I left off. We were late arriving at Aden—it was 5.45pm. The children and I stayed on board while Reg went ashore. I just didn't fancy it somehow because we had to go in a motor-launch. Reg wasn't away too long—he said I hadn't missed much. There were terrible smells there and beggars were everywhere. He saw families curled up on the side of the road sleeping—it was dreadful. Goats were roaming around everywhere and did they smell! He bought Raymond an aeroplane, Linda had a nice evening bag and me a pearl necklace, bracelet and earrings. We left at 1am on the 21st and since then we've seen nothing but sea and flying fish. It's very hot too. We had a rolling time on Sunday—there was a lot of wind about making the sea choppy. Everybody was fed up with the trip. Linda wasn't too grand and she felt sick again and she had a rotten cold, so Reg took her to the doctor. The first thing she was asked was whether she had been to the toilet. Well it seems she hadn't been for three or four days. So they gave her an enema, a couple of tablets and sent her to bed. I'm happy to say she has been as right as rain since. They certainly are good on board. We've not done very much these last couple of days—we've all been too lazy. Yesterday afternoon all the children had to line up for a present from Father Christmas. They were good things too, given by the officers and crew. Linda had a toy hospital set that she was very happy with and Raymond had a rifle, which suited him a treat.

Last night Reg came with me to the communion service at quarter to twelve. We are now about four hours ahead of you. It is half past ten here so you'll be asleep in your bed I expect as it is only 6.30am. It's difficult to realise it's Xmas Day and I am sitting here in my sundress! I wonder what sort of weather you are having—remember the snow last Christmas?

Well dears, Christmas is over once more and now I'm going to tell you about our day. We went to breakfast as usual and then went on deck and took some snaps. When we went to lunch at midday, we each found a present on our plate. It was very unexpected and everyone was delighted. The men had tiepins or cuff link sets in boxes. Reg had cuff links with a heart, club, diamond and spade on. He doesn't wear any ever but they'll be a souvenir. Linda had a smashing powder compact with water lilies painted on the lid. I had a fan lipstick mirror—the mirror in the shape of a fan is fixed to the holder and it's all in gold colour. For lunch we had lovely soup then cold ham, pilchards, mixed pickles and lettuce. After that came the turkey, roast potatoes, peas and applesauce—delicious. Then we had real Christmas pudding with rum sauce over it—I had two helpings I'm afraid! There were two bottles of Italian wine on each table, also nuts. Then we were given an orange each before we left.

Later, at 4-30pm, there was the 'crossing the line' ceremony with King Neptune and his followers making people eat raw eggs and spaghetti and all sorts of things and then ducking them. So we actually crossed the equator on Xmas afternoon. We all had a certificate to show we had done so. After dinner at eight o'clock we were all given a Xmas Day menu as a souvenir. There was a dance later with streamers and lovely hats and everyone enjoyed themselves although it was so hot. The crew has certainly gone to every length to make sure we have a wonderful time.

It is now January 2nd and we've only one more day to go dears! We arrive tomorrow night but won't go ashore until Saturday morning. I want to take this opportunity of wishing you all the very best for 1958 dear Mum and Dad. I think of you a great deal. I shall be sending you some photos after we have settled down at Eileen's. I bet she is excited now. Our nominators have to come on board to claim us before we are allowed ashore.

We've had a rough few days again since we left Aden. The old boat was rolling plenty and making people seasick once more. We didn't feel very happy about it. In fact one night we all slept on the deck because it didn't seem so bad as being down in our cabins. There has been a cool wind blowing for a few days—the cardigans have been brought into use again. It's quite unusual because it is usually very hot. We had a good jolly evening on New Year's Eve with a grand fancy dress parade. Yesterday lunchtime was a lovely surprise—we had Xmas dinner all over again with plum pudding and nuts and wine. It was lovely.

There's to be a concert tomorrow night given by some of the passengers—it is supposed to be pretty good. There was a darts competition held and Reg entered for it. Believe it or not he won but he has not received his prize yet. We've been told it is an eight-day chiming clock. I hope it is because we've never had a decent one. It might be a sign that we're going to get on in our new home—I do hope so!

I will post this letter when we reach Australia and the postmark will tell you that we've arrived safely won't it? So cheerio once more and God Bless you all with our love as always! From Peg, Reg, Linda and Raymond xxxxxx'

Ken Davis *lived in* Ross-on-Wye

Bananas and bandsmen

'I grew up in Ross-on-Wye and started my first job at the age of twelve, whilst still at school. I worked at the local barber's shop as a 'Lather Lad.' My job was to lather up the faces of the customers before the barber himself came along to apply the cutthroat blade. When I left school I joined the army as a bandboy. After three years I decided to purchase my discharge and try my luck in Australia. As I was an ex-serviceman, my passage was free. I landed in Fremantle, not knowing what I was going to do and was accosted by a man who was looking for someone to work in his shop in a small town called Pingelly. I accepted his offer and travelled with him back to his hardware store. Arriving at Pingelly was like going back in time. There were old Model T type cars on the road and a stone water trough outside of the shop. I almost expected cowboys on horseback to ride into town, hitch up their horses and have a shoot-out in the street!

Next door to the shop was a delicatessen. In the early months I went in to that deli almost every day to buy a banana—something I hadn't seen in Britain since before the war. At tea break I used to take five or six biscuits rather than one, like everyone else. Again, I had hardly eaten any biscuits for a number of years.

I lived in what was called a 'sleepout.' This was not much more than a corrugated iron shed set up on the back porch. I shared it with another lad who was a bank-teller.

After about four months I was driving a Ford Pilot with some friends along a gravel road (almost all of the roads were gravel) and had an accident. We all ended up in hospital but none were seriously injured. One fellow had to stay in for several days though. The hospital was in a place called Narrogen and I went back to visit my friend only to find that I wasn't allowed in, as visiting hours hadn't started. To while away a few hours, I went over to the local showground and listened to the Narrogen Band playing. As they finished, I clapped. I was the only person that clapped and the bandleader came over to see me. As we talked the local Mayoress appeared and joined us. She listened as I told her that I could play various musical instruments and she asked me where I worked. To cut a long story short, her husband owned the local hardware store and wrote to me several days later, offering me a job. So I moved to Narrogen, to a new job and joined the band.

Within three years I was the bandmaster and had married the boss's daughter, none of which would have happened if we hadn't had that car accident!'

Jim Heron *recalls his days of National Service*

The 'Colours'—1958 to 1960

'I left school in 1956 at the age of fifteen and went straight into work as a warehouse boy in a general drapery business in Glasgow city centre. Jobs were 'ten a penny.' Unemployment was very low. Enjoying life as a teenager—then at eighteen years of age, the bombshell! A brown paper envelope marked OHMS (On Her Majesty's Service) was waiting for me as I arrived home from work one evening. Mother was petrified; she knew about National Service (NS). I had not given it a thought even though my brother, three years older, had failed his NS medical. With enthusiasm I opened the envelope and read the (straight to the point) details. I was given a date, one month ahead, for my medical.

Passing my medical, A1+, whatever that meant, they asked me if I wished an early call-up. 'Yes' was my reply, now excited at the prospect of fighting for my Queen and Country. Two months later, another envelope arrived giving details of my train warrants and place of arrival for basic Army training. At my medical they had given me a choice—Army, Navy or Airforce. I chose the Army, requesting the Scots Guards, The Armoured Regiment or the Scots Greys. The place of arrival was Portsmouth, Hillsea Barracks, home of the Royal Ordnance Corps! So much for choices. I even heard of plumbers in civilian life being called up to the Army Catering Corps.

National Service, consisting of two years with 'The Colours,' would mean that I would not be home again for good, until I was in my early twenties. Most of my peers, doing well at school, were deferred, and would not be called to the Colours until they had finished their university education, So, excited as I was to discuss my forthcoming two year adventure, my peers did not seem interested.

Off I went at the beginning of July 1958, by steam train to London and then on to Portsmouth. It really was an adventure, not having been out of Scotland before. Father, mother and elder brother saw me off at Glasgow Central rail station. Mother was tearful, father and brother took it as 'just another day,' I thought. My then girlfriend, stated that she would stay home—knitting—until my return! (Some hope).

Whilst working in the Glasgow textile warehouse, a small private firm, I was earning £5 per week (quite good money in the 1950s, at my age). How would I manage on £1-30s a week—army pay for a National Serviceman? Government legislation at the time was that the firm you worked for had to keep your job open, for at least six months, on your return from service. So a bit of security was there, although at the age of eighteen this was not a major issue.

During the rail journey south, various boys of all shapes and sizes boarded the train at Carlisle, Crewe, Birmingham etc, all trying to appear grown up and not speaking to each other. As we left London for Portsmouth it was clear that we were all heading for the Royal Army Ordnance Corps, Hillsea Barracks. We began to chat: 'The army won't change me—they won't cut my hair—my girlfriend is going to wait for me—two years won't be a long time'—etc etc. We all came down to earth with a bang when we stepped off the train at Portsmouth Station. A rather tall mean looking drill sergeant was standing on the platform, bawling and shouting at the top of his voice. Some, rather, most of the words he used I did not know, but they were not very nice and my mother would not have liked it!

We were all, about forty of us, bundled into a three-ton truck and driven through Portsmouth to the barracks. More shouting and swearing greeted us as we were shunted from the barber's shop (so much for 'They won't cut my hair'), dentist chair, to shower room, to the uniform, equipment and bedding store. Then it was up to our respective barrack rooms, lights out 10pm. Quietness descended but not much sleep.

I admit that there was a tear in my eye as I telephoned home from the bleak barrack surroundings. Not really homesick, just bewilderment and a bit frightened as to what lay ahead. What lay ahead was six weeks of foot slogging, running about and continuous shouting from the instructors. Four weeks into training, I found out that after 'passing out parade' in two weeks time, I would probably be posted to some other grim barracks/camp, in the UK where I would be handing out uniforms and ordnance to army units. I could not do this for two years, even though I would get leave home to Glasgow now and again.

On completion of my National Service I thought that maybe I could get into the Glasgow Police if I had been in the Royal Military Police. So I applied, not knowing that, if successful, I would start all over again with my training. Successful I was, off I went with a rail warrant in hand to the Royal Military Police depot and training establishment in Woking, Surrey. The shouting and cursing started all over again, this time, seventeen weeks of it! I was with a good set of chaps, from all walks of life and from all parts of the UK. The depot, Inkerman barracks, just outside of Woking, had been a women's prison until 1876! It was a freezing cold building. Twenty boys in the one large room with only one wood burning fire. Still, enjoyable it was. Time passed quickly. Arms training, military law, marching, vehicle training, close combat fighting, was the order of most days.

The pass-out parade was memorable. Parents and relatives were there (not mine, the cost of the rail transport preventing them from coming) all dressed up, enjoying their day out. Next morning, the 'posting notice' was delivered. I was off to Cyprus. What made this exciting was that the Eoka terrorists were seemingly attacking the British trying to gain self-determination and union with Greece. To me, a young lad of eighteen, it sounded great, just the thing to fill in the remainder of my two years!

We sailed to the Middle East on the troopship 'Dunera,' (now a schools cruise ship) a calm, uneventful voyage, sailing through the Bay of Biscay without much of the celebrated seasickness. On deck, every day, (a twelve day trip), we kept fit by running round and round the ship, weapons training and as we neared Cyprus, filling in our Will, to be sent to our parents.

'Active service' meant that we would land near Famagusta fully equipped, armed to the teeth, ready for anything. Quite an experience. We went straight to 51 Infantry Brigade H.Q. and were shown to our tents. Four in a tent, one locker each, and a pole in the centre of the tent with the one and only mirror available. A briefing next morning, then into the routine of foot and mobile patrols.

Over the next few weeks and months we had a few nasty experiences, separating the Greek from the Turks, being bombed, shot at, spat at, etc. Whilst on patrols I used to wonder what my peers would be doing at home in Glasgow—going to work, football matches, the cinema etc. All the normal things my pals would get up to. I thought, 'Do they think of me?' I doubted it. We could write home but the letters had to be opened at the Army Post Office and censored, in case we were giving away information that was 'not allowed.'

I enjoyed my two years abroad, receiving only one injury on duty, a fight in a bar in downtown Famagusta! It was exciting, frightening at times, but great friends were made. We all relied on each other, and as such, became very close. Cyprus gained its independence early in 1960, when things calmed down. We sailed back to Southampton on the Dunera. This time it was a very rough voyage, seasickness the order of the day.

Back home was difficult for the first six months. Back to my wee room at home, with no excitement and nobody really wanting to hear of my experiences. It took nearly a year before I got the experience out of my system and settled down. Back to my job in Glasgow.

I would not have missed my National Service for anything. A great learning experience.'

David Taylor joined the RAF, leaving his home in **Lincolnshire**

Earwigs and The Bomb

'The warm, humid summer preceding the time of this tale encouraged the egg laying and subsequent hatching in north Lincolnshire of a plague of millions of earwigs in the early autumn of 1950. I had just completed my Radio Apprentice training at RAF Cranwell and my first posting was to RAF Hemswell—this station was not exempt from the earwig infestation. Smokers found the creatures in their boxes of matches; the pungency of raw tobacco evidently deterred them from penetrating cigarette packets. In the billet blocks, they seemed to be everywhere except the ablutions, congregating in clothes, bedding, towels, shoes and socks. Before going to bed at night it was advisable to search between the sheets for any potential insect bedfellows. It was not unknown for whimsical roommates to collect earwigs in an empty matchbox the contents of which might be discharged in to the shoes or bedding of an unsuspecting victim.

The recently introduced wax-paper wrapped loaves of sliced bread were not immune to the little pests entering through any gap in the wrapping and simultaneously securing moisture warmth and nourishment! I never heard of anyone who actually ate an earwig but I'm sure that some of us did—I may have even done it myself and remain unaware to this day of the added protein in my diet!

Towards the end of the decade, in the autumn of 1958, prior to the international moratorium on the testing of atomic weapons in the earth's atmosphere, Operation Grapple Z was to be the last in the UK series of above ground weapon tests. This took place from the base on Christmas Island, in the South Pacific. A flight of four Vickers 'Valiant' bombers were detached from RAF Wittering to Christmas Island, one of which carried the atomic bomb which was to be used in the test. A few days later, at dawn, those of us stationed on Christmas Island were transported to the harbour in three-ton trucks and embarked on to landing craft that immediately put to sea. The intention was that the vessels would stand off, two miles out as the 'Valiant' took off with the bomb, in case of any accident. We could rapidly move farther away from danger if anything went wrong. Fortunately, nothing of that nature occurred and we soon returned to the harbour where we disembarked to view the event with a mixture of fear and excitement.

There were areas on the beach, marked by numbered display boards and bounded by hurdles, in to which each group of servicemen was ordered to assemble while the final preparations were made and from where we could watch the aftermath of the ensuing test.

The morning was still and warm and the atmosphere, as ever at that latitude, was sticky and heavy with humidity. Our nerves were taut as we waited to move to our allotted section on the beach to witness the blinding flash and distinctive cloud rising in to the upper atmosphere. The Beachmaster, a Naval Officer stood on an elevated platform and addressed us through a loudhailer. As we formed up, he broadcast the instruction 'All personnel are to proceed to their allotted pens.' Pens? This was just the trigger that was needed to break the tension. As soon as the words were out of his mouth, someone broke the tangibly charged silence by bleating like a sheep. 'Baa-baa, baa-baa.' Within next to no time the sense of humour of the assembled British servicemen triumphed as we all took up bleating. Some five thousand male voices resounded over the sands breaking the previously still tropical morning, 'Baa-baa, baa-baa,' followed by excited but rather nervous laughter.

The tension was immediately defused and even the Beachmaster had the grace to join in the laughter.'

*Aitken Lawrie continued his army career
and returned to the* **Middle East**

Treachery and Treason

'Those were exciting times. I had been posted to be a military attache in Afghanistan, was all packed up and ready to sail to Karachi. I was not happy about it with three children at school in England, but they said that there was no one else who could speak Pushtu and Persian. But after Glubb Pasha had been summarily dismissed from Jordan, the War Office realised that they had no direct military link with that country. 'Can you speak Arabic?' they said, and flew me off to Amman a few days before the start of the Suez operation.

Glubb Pasha had spent his whole career building up the Jordan army and was passionately devoted to King Abdullah. But after the old King had been assassinated and his son had abdicated, the young and inexperienced Hussein succeeded to the throne. He relied on Ali Abu Nuwar to advise him, who turned out to be a traitor and a communist. Glubb had about twenty British officers and needed more to keep the army efficient. In order to attract them he built new quarters for them and an Officers' Club. He also advised King Hussein that it was tactically unsound to maintain a large part of his army on the West Bank, where they could be easily cut off. Ali Abu Nuwar persuaded Hussein that both of these ideas proved that Glubb was not acting in the interests of Jordan, and he was sent packing. I was ordered not to contact Glubb before I left England but kept in touch with him later through the diplomatic bag and he was always most helpful.

Soon after I arrived Britain and Israel attacked Egypt. I was asked to dinner with Ali Abu Nuwar and found him on first acquaintance to be friendly and intelligent. He took me up onto the roof of his house and pointed out a man in the garden standing by a wireless set. Ali Abu Nuwar told me that he had four thousand desperate men armed with knives waiting for his signal to cross over into Israel at its narrowest point and kill every Jew they met—men, women and children. They had been turned out of their homes by the Israelis and would stick at nothing. I don't know why he asked my advice, but it took me an hour to persuade him not to go ahead with his plan.

Next day the Egyptian military attaché in Amman was blown to pieces when he opened a parcel in his office. Suspicion fell on me, and there were two abortive attempts on my life. For the rest of my time in Jordan I was provided with an armed guard around the clock.

I decided to inspect my parish and drove over to the West Bank. We passed refugee camps holding half a million displaced Palestinians, who were being fed by the United Nations. I began to realise the bitterness they felt when my driver pointed out his old village a few hundred yards inside the border with Israel. The Jews had occupied his ancestral home after an unprovoked attack and had killed his wife and children.

The next step was when Ali Abu Nuwar persuaded the communist Prime Minister, Suleiman Nabulsi, who had come to power after a General Election, to abrogate the Anglo-Jordan treaty, under which we maintained a garrison at Aqaba. Hussein was now on his own, and Ali Abu Nuwar sent an officer to see him with a document of Abdication which the King was invited to sign.

Luckily the orderly who accompanied the officer was loyal to the King and shot his officer dead. Now the fat was in the fire. Hussein showed his spirit by arresting Ali Abu Nuwar and taking the government into his own hands, but, instead of having him shot for treason, he allowed him to take his staff car and drive to Egypt with his family. Later when I asked Hussein why he had been so lenient, his reply was that Nuwar came from a powerful tribe, who would all have been alienated if Nuwar had been shot. This was a fate, which he well deserved, as I realised when I was shown a flag lying in his desk, which he had intended to fly on his car when he had become Head of State.

Towards the end of the year, when things had quietened down, my wife and the other Embassy ladies were allowed to fly out. I remember a big celebration party when I accidentally knocked over a screen, which fell on a marble floor with an almighty crash. Everyone threw themselves on the ground thinking it was a bomb.

In 1958, the Kings of Jordan and Iraq decided to unite their kingdoms with the capital alternating between Amman and Baghdad. After a week of festivities in Amman the Iraqi party went off, leaving a brigade of troops outside Amman who were to take part in joint manoeuvres. The British ambassador went off on leave.

A few days later I was awoken by the telephone at 6am. 'Please come round to Army HQ at once.' I heard that communists had assassinated the entire Iraqi Royal family and there were plans to repeat the outrage in Jordan. What could be done to foil them? King Hussein hesitated to ask England for help, since his communist government had just abrogated the Anglo-Jordan Treaty. I promised to do my best for him and sent a telegram to London explaining the situation.

The town was very unsettled. My wife turned up to keep an appointment with the hairdresser, but was sent away. 'Sitti, it is not safe for you in town today. You had better go home.' Bombs were going off here and there. The British Library was blown up at the time we often went there. All our servants made excuses and went home leaving my wife alone with a small baby. Then all the lights in town went out.

When my wife phoned to ask what she should do, I told her to go round the house looking for a bomb in a cupboard or under the stairs. If it was ticking to throw it out of the window. Luckily she found nothing and went to bed in the dark.

I was up all night making arrangements for the hoped-for arrival of British troops. I heard later that Macmillan had called a cabinet meeting at 10pm and at midnight orders were issued for the Parachute brigade, who were in Cyprus, to fly to Amman. I had to fix up barracks for them and ordered the bakers to produce a thousand extra loaves of bread.

I came home in the early morning and heard an announcement from the BBC that British troops were not going to fly to Jordan. There had been problems about overflying Israel. However, when I looked out of the window I saw a long line of aeroplanes coming in to land. King Hussein was safe.

Later King Hussein asked me to recommend a Royal Engineers officer to train his Sappers. Major Gardiner was glad to accept the job and brought out his family. The King fell in love with his daughter Toni and made her his Queen. Now she is the highly respected Queen Mother and her son Abdullah is on the throne of Jordan.

So my telegram had far-reaching results.'

The Jordanian Army

Chris Darlington *worked in a local shop after leaving school*

The Captain

'The Captain came in to the shop every few weeks. I remember the first time that he appeared. He stood there in his flat cap and long overcoat holding a ladies leather shopping bag. Suddenly, he shouted at the top of his voice, 'Emergency, Emergency, I need to use the 'phone.'

I presumed that there had been an accident of some sort, perhaps a serious car accident. I handed him the 'phone.

His face lit up as if he had seen an angel. 'This is the Captain speaking,' he shouted in to the 'phone. 'Open the bridge immediately, the fleet's coming through.'

I was amazed.

The Captain finished barking out his orders, put the 'phone down, turned to me and ordered two dozen blue suits. He asked me to charge them to his account.

I humoured him by handing him one of the shop's carrier bags. He walked out of the shop quite happily with his new bag after saving his invisible fleet.

Apparently, it was a tragic story. The Captain had indeed commanded a submarine during World War II. His vessel had been hit by enemy fire and had sunk. He survived the ordeal in body but his mind had never recovered and still, a decade later, he imagined himself in charge of the fleet.

The effect of war on the mental state of servicemen who fought in the First World War has been well documented. Less has been written about the Captain and his brave comrades who fought in the second great conflict.'

Bobby Shaw, *who grew up in* **Leicestershire**, *recalls his summer holidays on the south coast*

Old friends

'Every year we went on holiday to the same village in Hampshire. Not only did we go to the same village, we stayed at the same farm. And not only did we stay on the same farm, we even hired the same caravan for the same two weeks in July. My parents were nothing if not predictable!

The caravan in question looked like a cross between a Gypsy caravan and a large beach hut. It was static and as far as I can remember showed no signs of ever having had any wheels. So perhaps it was actually a large shed (which we would call a 'chalet' today) which was passed off as a caravan to encourage families like ours to stay there and enjoy the local facilities. These included two single iron bedsteads with mattresses that made marvellous trampolines for active ten-year-olds, another single bed at right angles to the others and a well preserved Victorian washstand. Outside, about thirty yards away next to the hedge stood a small shed that contained the Elsan toilet. This had a very distinctive smell of toilet chemicals, which I can still remember now. It was not as bad as it sounds and had one very distinct benefit. There were so many cracks between the planks that made up the side of the shed that it was possible, if not compulsory, to admire the sea view whilst sitting on the 'throne'!

The water supply came from a cold tap up at the farm. Hot water was optional—if we boiled it in the kettle.

One advantage of going to the same place on holiday every year was that we got to know the local children. More than that, we also became firm friends with the French exchange students who stayed with the local families. One of these, Martine, visited Hampshire almost as regularly as us and we enjoyed playing rounders and cricket with her three years in a row!'

The Caravan being delivered

Welshman **Rhys Ab Elis** *spent his early years in* **London**

Button 'A' and that wallpaper

'My first day at school was a traumatic, tearful experience. Five of my classmates wet themselves as they were equally overcome with emotion. School did gradually improve, though my first steps in learning to write were given an unnecessary dent when my poorly constructed letter 'm' was seized upon by the teacher. She demonstrated this on the blackboard as a lesson to the class in how <u>not</u> to write the letter 'm.' How to humiliate a small child . . .

Throughout my childhood we lived in north London at number 30 in a gaslit street whose name must remain anonymous. Next door, at number 28 lived Mr Elliot and Mrs Mitchell. He was a puny, shrivelled little man and she was large and rather domineering—rather like the sort of couple often portrayed in the Bamforth comic postcards! Questions to my mother as to why our neighbours had different surnames elicited evasive responses; in the 1950s 'living in sin' was simply not discussed. Eventually they moved away to be replaced by the Plummers, whose teenage son had a guitar and thus evoked a certain envy. They also went for holidays to interesting places like Bulgaria while we ended up in Sheerness-on-Sea, or similar.

The neighbours on the other side, at number 32 were the O'Learys; a very elderly wheelchair bound mother looked after by her middle aged, bachelor son. I was liable to be sent there on Sundays for afternoon tea, to make conversation with these two. It would be fair to say that I didn't look forward to these visits but at least it got me out from under my parents' feet for an hour or so.

Being dragged around the local shops by my mother cannot be considered one of my favourite memories, though some places do stand out. The nearest Co-op was about a mile away and we walked there regularly. When rationing ended, there was a large poster in the Co-op window, which showed a woman throwing her ration book away. A more colourful memory is that of a shop in Palmers Green called Grouts, a haberdashers. To describe it as old fashioned would be somewhat understated. Many of their goods were priced in farthings (they continued to price in farthings until Decimal Day). Grouts also had one of those marvellous overhead pulley systems with pots attached to transfer cash from the tills to the back office; a great attraction for a young boy.

The local 'phone box was of the 'Press Button A, Press Button B' type and on the rare occasions that we needed to make a 'phone call, the operator connected the number (and for all we knew, probably listened in too!). This was replaced in the early 1960s with a coin operated upgrade.

One year we went on holiday to Leigh-on-Sea. We stayed in a B&B and the landlady was a particularly joyless person. The room was equally joyless with the wallpaper being fixed to the walls with drawing pins! Our next holiday found us in Sheerness-on-Sea and we took the 'cheap' route to get there. We took the trolleybus to Haringey where we caught a special excursion train that ran to Southend. Here we walked to the pier and boarded the paddlesteamer 'Medway Queen' in which we crossed the Thames Estuary to Sheerness. It seemed to take ages to get there.

We returned to the same place the following year but took a different route due to the fact that the steamer pier at Sheerness had been condemned as unfit to use. We took a train from Victoria to Sittingbourne and changed for Sheerness. There were two trains on this little branch line, one painted red and one painted green and they contained three vintage coaches. Each had a 'birdcage' raised roof over the guard's compartment to allow the guard to look along the roof of the train. Our train crossed over to the Isle of Sheppey on the old Kingsferry Bridge, a massive bascule structure, with a lot of echoey rumbling.

Sheerness in those days was a depressing place (at least it seemed that way to me) with a pebbly beach—more like an industrial town than a seaside resort.

The holidays were largely forgettable. I can recall one incident that makes me smile every time I see the scene repeated. My parents were staring into the window of an Estate Agent reviewing the house prices. The cheapest yellow brick Victorian terrace house cost £580. There were several for sale at just over £600. And still we remarked on how expensive they were!'

Colin Foe grew up in Blackpool

Visitors to Blackpool

'In the 1950s, Blackpool had reached the pinnacle of its notoriety as the foremost seaside resort in Britain. In all respects it was a boomtown with a thriving vibrant community. Many people had escaped the wartime blitz in the cities to make a new life in the town and they worked hard to achieve success, which many of them accomplished.

My father was a well-regarded ladies hairdresser and we owned a shop in Dixon Road, not far from the old North Station. The main holiday for the mill town folk and the factory worker was a few days in Blackpool. The average wage earner just could not afford the kind of holiday that most people take for granted these days and the thought of a holiday in such exotic places as the 'Costas' was just a pipe dream.

In those days Dixon road was a busy shopping area and I well remember my father opening the shop early in the morning to accommodate the local landladies who wanted their hair to look neat and tidy for the prospective hordes of guests spilling out of North Station. And pour they did! As an eleven-year-old I remember the countless visitors from the mill towns of Wigan, Bolton and Rochdale frantically trying to keep their children in tow as they pushed their luggage trolleys along the platform. The occasional suitcase fell on to the ground and a number of my friends would be waiting like vultures to accost the unsuspecting holidaymaker with offers to transport the luggage in old prams or makeshift trolleys—all for a bob (5p)! I envied my pals who seemed to be making quite a killing with their 'almost legal' trade and dodging the Bobbies on the Beat became an enjoyable pastime. My parents never allowed me to participate in such a vulgar profession although my desire abated as quickly as it appeared. Who wanted to be a barrow boy anyway? Many kids apparently, in those heady days when we had so many freedoms that are now sadly denied to children today.

My father was quite well known and it wasn't long before some of the acts appearing in the town's theatres became clients. The pianist Winifred Atwell was very pleasant and gave my dad and his staff complimentary tickets to see her show at the Opera House. Max Bygraves and Lionel Blair also came in for a trim and a chat.

Sometimes mum and dad would take me to a show and I well remember splitting my sides at the antics of the late great Max Wall or listening to Joseph Locke singing 'Goodbye' replete in a Foreign Legionnaire's uniform!

In those days, summers seemed to go on forever. Did they really, or is it all in my imagination? Crime was minimal and a petty thief would make headlines. But we had our wide-boys and spivs and many a fortune was accumulated through shady dealing. Some of these characters were actually quite good-hearted and only out to make a fast buck as quickly as they could. Blackpool was a microcosm of the wider world.

Summers were spent with my pals and we'd usually go to the local park or go swimming at the Olympic size Derby Baths, sadly no more. Sometimes we'd go to the morning cartoon at the beautiful Palace Varieties which was a theatre and a cinema. One and sixpence (7.5p) to watch the cartoons! The Palace was one of the finest theatres in England, let alone Blackpool and it was a sad day when it was destroyed, making way for the new 'consumer society' in the form of a supermarket.'

Stuart Way *from* **Lancashire** *spent his wedding night in a Boarding House in Blackpool*

The Honeymoon

'Margaret and I were married in Burnley on a lovely day in June. We had a reception at a local hotel then caught the train to Blackpool, leaving behind the urban grime which was part of our daily lives, arriving in the early evening. We found the Boarding House without difficulty, hung our clothes up in the huge dark wooden wardrobes that stood either side of a matching dressing-table in our 'honeymoon suite—bathroom down the hall.' We went straight back out to make the most of the warm Blackpool summer evening. Our shoes came off, I rolled my trousers up and we raced hand and hand along the beach and in to the shallow water, splashing each other playfully. It was a wonderful feeling. We were in love, married and on holiday. Margaret stood on the sand looking towards Blackpool Tower, took a deep breath and said 'Smell the air Stuart; the salty sea air with not a hint of coaldust anywhere!'

We dined in style on traditional Fish and Chips with mushy peas, bread and butter and a pot of tea. After that we went to a pub on the seafront for a drink before returning to our 'honeymoon suite.' It was a nervous time for both of us, as we knew that tonight would be the first time that we would 'do it' together. Our love life to date had consisted of nervous fumblings on parents' sofas, ever aware that someone might walk in to the room.

With increasing excitement, we returned to our Boarding House and were met by the landlady, Mrs Newsome. She was a sweet old lady, not a bit like the bossy landladies for which Blackpool was famous. She was sweet but she insisted that we come into the lounge and meet some of the other guests. We were introduced as 'Mr and Mrs Way, the honeymoon couple' and knowing glances and winks went around the room between the other holidaymakers. We had to sit and make small talk for another half hour before we were able to make our excuses and go up to our room. We ran laughing up the stairs knowing that we were being talked about back in the residents' lounge.

I won't go into the details of the wedding night except to say that the bed squeaked. It squeaked again in the morning, as did the bed in the room above us. Disappointingly for me, their bed's squeaks lasted longer than our bed's squeaks. I felt that I needed more practice and managed to get some in during the course of our week in Blackpool!

We had to be on parade early for breakfast at 8-30am prompt and we washed, dressed and generally got ourselves ready for the day in record time to arrive in the dining room at exactly 8-30. We walked through the door on the morning after our wedding night and immediately received a round of good-natured applause and cheers from some of the other (younger) residents. It was very embarrassing but everyone was very friendly and it certainly broke the ice with our fellow guests!'

Jessie Weekes lived in Kent

Eastenders

'One of my memories is of the kids from London who came to visit us. 'Anuvver world.' they used to say when they saw the cornfields and the cows being milked. Most of them had no idea that milk came from an animal. They also thought that the night was 'too dark and too quiet'. At Hop picking time we had whole families of Eastenders coming to us to take a working holiday. They turned up in their lorries with everything including the kitchen sink and lived together in wooden huts. About a hundred thousand people came to Kent to pick hops every year; it was an annual ritual for many of them. They generally cooked outdoors, making the most of their short time away from the smoke and noise of London. In the evening they chatted non-stop when they relaxed but hardly said a word while they were working. The hop fields were very quiet even though they were full of people working their way along the rows of ripe hops. I was sad at the end of the harvest when everyone left to go back to the city. Then, it seemed quiet to me.'

Enjoying the sun and the company

Pam Malekin lived by the sea in **Sussex**

Day Trippers

'My parents ran a beach cafe in what was commonly called the Arches, virtually on Brighton beach. It was very hard work so all the family pitched in, in those glorious summers we used to have (or am I wearing my rose coloured glasses!). The weekends were the busiest because of the day-trippers from London. They started arriving at about ten o'clock in their shiny Sunday best and headed straight down Queens Road to the seafront, just in time for all the men to go into the pubs and the women and kids to the beach where they rented deck chairs for the day. The kids took off to stare with great excitement at the wide expanse of blue water (it was certainly different from the murky Thames!). At two o'clock when the pubs shut, a lot of 'merry men' found their families and then they descended on the cafe for fish and chips, egg and chips or roast of the week, followed by jelly and ice cream or apple pie and ice cream.

Then, en masse, they found their deckchairs. Dad snoozed, the kids ran around getting sick on candyfloss and ice cream and mums settled for the 5/- tea trays (2/6d refund when returned to us). At about five o'clock there was a mass removal of socks and shoes, trousers were rolled up, skirts raised slightly and paddling began. By five past five, many a kid was getting a clip round the ear for splashing his dad. At six o'clock the pubs re-opened. Mum and dad went inside, came back out with crisps and lemonade for the kids, then left them to their own devices! Ten o'clock was closing time. Everyone was rounded up, heads counted and hot dogs bought at O'Hagens (the best in England!) and they all merrily sang their way back to the station to catch the last train. They all reckoned they'd had a bloomin' marvellous time and so they had!'

Stephanie Campion *now lives in Paris but during the '50s she spent her summers on the* **Isle of Wight**

The Box Brownie

'Just after the war, my grandfather, a photographer from Manchester, set up shop in Sandown, Isle of Wight, in the days when most people did not own a camera. He ran an all-inclusive service for the holidaymakers of camera hire (a Box Brownie) with 12-exposure spool film already loaded, then developing and printing of the customers' holiday snaps. During my school holidays in the 1950s I used to help in the shop: loading the films into the cameras on Saturdays, unjamming the cameras brought back by the ham-fisted during the week, unloading the films for developing and taking the money and the customers' details.

I was too young to be allowed into the film-developing darkroom—one false move and you've ruined the customers' holiday souvenirs! But I did help with developing the photos in their chemical bath—quite a skilled job when you've got several in there at once, each having to be fished out individually and 'fixed' at the right moment. Then I would spread the wet photos out on the metal face of the drying machines, and come back later to collect them, stamp them on the back with the particular customer's reference number, and batch them for collection in the shop. Very important not to mix up the different customers' films, and there were hundreds of them. And very tempting to spend time marvelling at the peculiar things people photograph!'

Graham Whyte *had an adventure in 1951*

Le Mannequin Pis

'It was the summer of 1951 and my last term in school. John and I were good friends and coincidentally we were both adopted. We lived in Birmingham about 3 miles apart.

We both had a desire for adventure and decided that in the summer holidays at the end of the final term we would have a holiday together. After many hours we decided that a Youth Hostelling holiday in Europe would be within our budget - if we went on our bikes. John was the more studious of the two of us, and he did the booking of the ferry tickets from Dover to Ostende in Belgium.

It was in August we set off for a two-week cycling/Youth Hostelling tour of Belgium and Holland. We had planned on an average day's cycling of 50-60 miles. Having cycled down to Dover with a stop off at a hostel on the way down we boarded the ferry for a night crossing to Ostende. Arriving at about 6.30am, we were hungry and tired as we had little or no sleep on the mattresses in the communal area on the boat. On disembarking we walked the streets of Ostende to find something to eat but nowhere was to open before around eight o'clock so we decided to go and get our heads down on the beach until the people of Ostende started to stir.

On our first day we cycled to Brugge a very historical town with beautiful architecture. On the second day we then cycled to Ghent and spent the night at the local hostel to get a good night's sleep before a long day the next day as we had to make Brussels in one hit. On arrival in Brussels we were overawed by the grandeur of the buildings, the superb architecture and the church spires. John and I were standing on a bridge contemplating whether we should stay for an extra day when a bespectacled gentleman of generous proportions waddled up to us and in broken English asked if we were on holiday and where we came from. He gave us ideas of places we should visit and stressed that we must go and see 'Le Mannequin Pis' the boy on the bridge who is peeing into the river. The story goes that a man, many years ago lost his young son and that when he found him he would erect a statue in memory of how he found him - the rest is self-explanatory.

Then the bespectacled man said that he worked at the bibliotecque and he would like us to come for tea and cake at 3.30 that afternoon as he wanted to hear about England which he had visited before the war. So after a few whispered words between us we decided the Belgian was genuine and we accepted and had a very nice time.

The next day we mounted our bicycles and made our way to Leuven and after one night at this hostel we cycled on to Liege, from memory this was a very industrialised area and leaves me with no lasting memories. Then we had to go northwards the next day and cycle to Maastricht - not knowing that the whole of Britain would eventually know the name of this city well for the Maastricht Treaty.

My memories of the following two days are rather hazy, as the place we were aiming for was Arnheim, which we had heard so much about - the troops who parachuted in during the war a few years previously. We both liked Arnheim, there were pine forests and the area was hilly which was a change from the flatlands of Holland.

After Arnheim we decided we were well rested and that we should make the concerted effort to cycle all the way to Amsterdam in one hit. It was a long way something in the order of one hundred miles. Next we were to cycle an easy ride to the coast to Loisdeunem a small resort with the flattest beach I ever remember seeing.

The rest of our holiday was on very flat land, the roads being lined with trees and the villages, with their cobbled streets, were a hazard for bicycles and I ended up with a buckled rear wheel. On the edge of the river we found a small cycle repair shop and the owner said that if we could wait for a few minutes he would straighten the wheel. We were absolutely fascinated to watch him as with a small spanner he systematically tightened spokes crisscrossing from side to side until the rim miraculously came back to its original shape and the man only asked two Guilders which was around five shillings, I was so pleased that I gave him four Guilders and we went on our way.

Next day we cycled onto The Hague, then onto Dordrecht, Vlissingen (Flushing to the British) and ultimately back to Ostende.

What a wonderful adventure. This sort of holiday was probably very rare for two young lads to embark on during the post war years of the 1950s, and we were rightly very proud of our achievement.'

1950s Discoveries/Developments

- The structure of DNA
- Fibre Optics
- The Contraceptive Pill
- The Silicon Chip
- The Photocopier
- Electronic Integrated circuits
- The Carphone
- The Rotary Engine
- The Video Recorder
- The Hovercraft
- The Mini Car
- The Atomic Powered Submarine
- Velcro

1950s Firsts

- The first Kidney Transplant was performed in the USA
- Sainsbury's first Self Service Store
- Postcodes
- Wimpy Restaurants
- Tea Bags
- 33prm Gramophone Record
- The British Standards 'Kite Mark'
- Britain's first Motorway
- Britain's first Nuclear Power Station
- Premium Bonds
- The Pop Music 'Hit Parade'
- Commercial Jet Flights
- The Four-Minute Mile
- Commercial Television in Britain
- Life Peers
- Sponsored Walks
- Britain's first TV Commercial (for Gibbs SR Toothpaste)
- Disneyland in California
- Mattel's Barbie Doll
- Directory Enquiries
- Successful Ascent of Mount Everest
- Eurovision Song Contest
- An Airliner Flight over the North Pole
- The Duke of Edinburgh Awards

1950s Anniversaries

- 50th of the opening of Britain's first Cinema (1901)
- 50th of the Wright Brothers' first Flight (1903)
- 50th of Britain's first Beauty Contest (1908)
- 50th of the Nobel Prize (1901)
- 50th of the first Boy Scouts Camp (1907)
- 100th of the publication of 'The Origin of the Species' (1859)
- 100th of the Postcard (1859)
- 100th of Britain's first Free Lending Library (1852)
- 100th of the introduction of the Victoria Cross (1854)

The Future

In 1950, at the beginning of the decade, it would be:

- 11 years before Yuri Gagarin became the first man to travel in space
- 12 years before the death of Marilyn Monroe
- 16 years before the introduction of the Barclaycard
- 20 years before the introduction of the £20 note
- 21 years before e mail appeared
- 21 years before the launch of The Campaign for Real Ale (CAMRA)
- 24 years before the opening of Britain's first McDonald's restaurant
- 52 years before the Euro replaced the national currencies of most EU member countries

The 1960s

The world at large—the historical context

The decade of the 1960s is remembered for its fashion excess, sexual liberation and the success of British pop music around the world. The 'Swinging Sixties' was probably the seminal decade of the century, from the point of view of changing people's outlook on their own lives. 'Youth,' which had arrived in the previous decade, finally found its identity and developed a world of its own in which to live. 'I hope I die before I get old,' sung by The Who, was the motto of many teenagers. Women looked forward to an era of equality and emancipation. Men, too, enjoyed the more liberal outlook on life. In the world before AIDS, it seemed a paradise waiting to be explored and enjoyed.

The Royal Family

During the decade, the Royal Family continued to be held in high esteem by the majority of their subjects, at home and in the wider Commonwealth. Their public appearances and tours were widely reported but their private lives remained firmly hidden behind closed doors for much of the decade.

In 1960, the Queen's sister Princess Margaret married commoner Anthony Armstrong-Jones. In the same year, the monarch's second son, Prince Andrew was born. The Queen's third and last son, Prince Edward was born in March 1964.

The Duchess of Windsor refused to curtsey before the Queen Mother when she and her husband visited London in 1967 to attend the unveiling of a plaque in memory of Queen Mary, the Duke's mother. This was the first time that she had attended a function with other members of the Royal Family since the abdication in 1936. The Duchess allegedly blamed the Queen Mother for her husband's ostracism by the Royal Family. The Queen Mother had made it plain that she felt that her husband, George VI had died prematurely as a result of his unexpected elevation to the throne, following Edward VIII's abdication.

At the end of the decade as economic conditions worsened, the Royal Family offered to give up the Royal Yacht Britannia as an example to the nation of cost cutting. This gesture was refused by the Labour Government but not disclosed to the public until official papers were released, thirty years later.

In July 1969, twenty-year-old Prince Charles was invested as the Prince of Wales at a ceremony in Caernarvon Castle. In the same year a TV documentary, Royal Family, gave the public the first ever view of the private life of the Royals—possibly not a good idea as events later proved.

Politics

The decade opened with the continuation of the Conservative government that had been in power throughout the '50s. The government's popularity was waning however, largely due to pay restraint and the famous Orpington by-election of 1962 saw a large government majority overturned by the Liberals. A cabinet reshuffle followed as Macmillan sought to reinvigorate his government.

In 1963, Harold Wilson was elected leader of the Labour Party. Shortly afterwards, the 'Profumo Affair' rocked the Tory government and the wider political establishment. Secretary of State for War, John Profumo was forced to resign after he misled the House of Commons about his relationship with Christine Keeler. She was also linked with various Russian diplomats, presumed to be spies. Macmillan's government was fatally wounded and the Prime Minister resigned during the Tory Party conference at Blackpool in October. Macmillan was succeeded by The Earl of Home. He renounced his peerage in order to take up the position and Sir Alec Douglas-Home became leader in October 1963.

Despite the new Tory leadership, the Labour Party won the election of 1964 after thirteen years of Conservative rule. Harold Wilson became Prime Minister with a slender majority of four seats. He was the first party leader to understand the importance of the media in shaping an image rather than merely reporting the news and used this to his advantage. Wilson promised to position Britain at the forefront of world development and spoke of 'The white heat of a technological revolution.'

Sir Winston Churchill died in 1965. The whole nation mourned before, during and after the state funeral that was accorded him in honour of the magnificent service that he had given his country, especially during the war years. A great leader had passed away.

Edward Heath was elected to lead the Conservative Party in July 1965. For the first time in British history, grammar school educated men rather than public school 'Patricians' led both main political parties. Once again, the change in Tory leadership could not stop the Labour Party from triumphing in the election of 1966, this time with a substantial Labour majority of ninety-six seats.

The following year, Liberal Leader Jo Grimond resigned to be succeeded by Eton educated Jeremy Thorpe.

The financial crisis deepened, leading to the devaluation of sterling in November 1967. Prime Minister Harold Wilson explained that 'This does not mean that the pound in your pocket, here in Britain, has been devalued.'

In 1968, Tory Enoch Powell made his famous 'Rivers of blood' speech on the perils of immigration. This led to an increase in racial tension and the isolation of Powell within his party.

The Labour Party continued to govern the country until the end of the decade, confidently expecting to win the next election in 1970.

World Politics

North Vietnamese communist troops invaded South Vietnam in 1963. The US and Australia, fearing the spread of communism sent troops to assist the South Vietnamese. Thus began the long desperate war in Vietnam, which continued until the middle of the following decade and cost over 58,000 US and Australian lives and many more Vietnamese soldiers and civilians.

Several African countries gained independence from colonial rule. Nigeria, Congo, Gabon, Zaire, Northern Rhodesia (now Zambia) and Kenya all set up their own governments. In Southern Rhodesia (now Zimbabwe) the white Rhodesians demanded independence but refused Britain's request to share power with the black Africans. In 1965 Southern Rhodesia, led by Ian Smith made a Unilateral Declaration of Independence (UDI) from Britain and continued in this manner into the next decade. In South Africa, the African National Congress (ANC) fought against the white government's apartheid policies. The ANC's leader, Nelson Mandela was sentenced to life imprisonment in 1964 for 'political offences.'

In 1962, the US discovered Soviet missile bases on the island of Cuba. US President Kennedy ordered a naval blockade and for several days nuclear war seemed inevitable. Finally, Soviet President Kruschev backed down. The 'hotline' between the USA and the Soviet Union was set up soon after this to ensure that the world would not be brought to the brink of war through misunderstanding or lack of negotiation.

The following year, Kennedy was assassinated while on a visit to Dallas in Texas. Five years later his brother Bobby was also shot.

The Civil Rights movement in the USA had surfaced in the 1950s, as black Americans campaigned for equal rights. In the 1960s, Martin Luther King, a Baptist minister and charismatic leader, picked up the baton. His famous 'I have a dream' speech focussed world opinion on the injustices against the black population particularly in the southern states of the USA. He was awarded the Nobel Peace Prize in 1964. Four years later, in Memphis, he was assassinated for his beliefs.

In China, Mao launched the Cultural Revolution. Young people denounced their elders and neighbours were wary of discussing anything controversial with each other. Intellectuals, teachers and anyone on the wrong end of a grudge were 're-educated' as peasants. Places of culture and historical significance were ruthlessly destroyed. Millions were killed in the upheavals.

The Israelis were victorious in the Six-Day War of 1967. The Sinai desert and Jordan's West Bank became Israeli territory, causing upheaval for the indigenous Arabs. The Palestine Liberation Organisation was formed in the decade, led by Yasser Arafat, to fight for the rights of the Palestinians who had been denied citizenship following the birth of Israel after the Second World War.

In Sri Lanka, Mrs Bandaranaike became the first woman in the world to be elected Prime Minister of her country in 1960.

In 1967, Aborigines in Australia were granted the right to vote, though they were still considered second class citizens by many white Australians.

Berlin had been divided between the communist East and the capitalist West since the end of World War II, symbolising the split throughout Europe as a whole. In 1961, the border was closed and Soviet and East German troops built the Berlin Wall. This prevented East Berliners from escaping to the West; border guards shot those who tried to scale the wall.

Russian tanks rolled into Czechoslovakia in August 1968, bringing to an end the 'Prague Spring' of demonstrations against communist rule. Hundreds were killed in demonstrations against the continued imposition of the communist doctrine.

Decade Developments

'Convenience' began to establish itself as a term to describe anything that was quick and easy. Frozen foods, sliced bread, packet meals, even instant mashed potato offered a convenient alternative to cooking with basic ingredients. Canned soft drinks and ice-lollies provided refreshment 'on the move.' The growing number of supermarkets that stocked every type of food under one roof was also very convenient for shoppers in a hurry.

Recent additions to the Retail Price Index list also reflected this move towards convenience—sliced bread, potato crisps and fish fingers made their debut. Other new entrants included sherry, the electric cooker, the girdle, gloss paint, thick knit sweaters, nylon panties, the motor scooter and a man's wrist watch.

During the decade the middle classes discovered the garden as a place for entertaining. Patios became fashionable with sliding doors leading out from the house replacing the old fashioned wooden French windows. Plant nurseries benefited from this move and repositioned themselves as 'Garden Centres'. Houseplants, too, increased in popularity.

Immigration to Britain increased dramatically during the '60s with over half a million Asians and West Indians setting up home in the UK. Racial tension grew in many of Britain's cities and it seemed that confrontation was inevitable. The immigrants also brought their culture with them and 'going for a curry' after the pub at the weekend increased in popularity.

In 1967, South African Dr Christiaan Barnard carried out the first human heart transplant. The patient lived for eighteen days after the operation.

The human egg was fertilised in a test tube for the first time by gynaecologist Patrick Steptoe, following a successful trial using rabbits.

Travel

Transport went through a major change during the decade. Road building was intensified with motorways cutting lengthy concrete ribbons through open countryside and long stretches of 'A' roads were widened in to dual carriageways. At the same time, the Beeching report recommended widescale closure of loss making railway lines. Almost 25% of Britain's rail network and over two thousand stations were closed.

Steam trains were gradually replaced by diesels and electric powered engines during the '60s

Intercontinental travel also saw a major change as the speed of the jet aircraft encouraged many travellers to forsake the slower yet more opulent cruise liners. Concorde, the first commercial supersonic aircraft, made its first flight in 1969 but did not go into commercial service until 1976.

The 'Space Race' continued in the '60s. The Soviets won the next round when Yuri Gagarin became the first man in space in 1961. Three weeks later, US astronaut Alan Shepard repeated the feat. A Soviet cosmonaut also became the first man to walk in space when Colonel Alexei Leonov stepped outside of his spacecraft for about ten minutes in 1965.

The USA won the big prize, the race to the Moon, when Neil Armstrong and Buzz Aldrin became the first men to step on to the surface of the Moon in July 1969.

Sport

Tottenham Hotspur won the FA Cup and the league championship in 1961. Two years later they beat Athletico Madrid 5-1 to become the first British winners of the European Cup Winners' Cup. Celtic won the European Cup in 1967. Manchester United won the same trophy in 1968.

Arguably the most memorable British sporting event of the decade was the Soccer World Cup of 1966. England, led by Bobby Moore beat West Germany 4-2 in the final to claim the title of football's World Champions.

Francis Chichester became the first man to sail single-handedly around the world in his yacht Gypsy Moth IV. He was knighted during the voyage.

On the cricket field, the West Indians became the side to beat. Led by Gary Sobers and a strike bowling force of Wes Hall and Charlie Griffiths, they were formidable opponents.

Britain produced four world motor racing champions. Jim Clark, Graham Hill, John Surtees and Jackie Stewart all won the Formula One world championship. Jim Clark was later killed in a crash during the German Grand Prix of 1968. The previous year Donald Campbell had also died while attempting to break his own world water speed record on Coniston Water in the Lake District.

The Olympic Games in Rome, in 1960 produced a new heavyweight boxing gold medallist—Cassius Clay. In 1964, the Games were held in Tokyo. Britain won both the men and women's Long Jump events with Lynn Davies and Mary Rand collecting gold medals. The Games of 1968, in Mexico, became a focus for 'Black Power' as several US athletes gave the clenched fist salute at medal ceremonies. Less controversially, Bob Beamon's victorious long jump increased the world record by almost two feet!

Entertainment

The first James Bond movie, Dr No was released in the summer of 1962. Cinema audiences discovered a relatively unknown actor called Sean Connery in the title role. Ursula Andress, who was nominally covered by 'that' bikini as she emerged from the surf in one of the most memorable scenes in cinema history, supported him. A legend was born. Other major films of the '60s included Lawrence of Arabia, Dr Zhivago, Midnight Cowboy, Alfie, The Sound of Music, Mary Poppins and 2001: A Space Odyssey. However, the popularity of the cinema continued to decline, as more families became television owners. Cinema audiences fell by over 50% during the decade and a similar percentage of Britain's cinemas were forced to close their doors as a result.

Television popularity was driven by favourites such as Coronation Street, launched in 1960, Crossroads, Dr Who (fighting the Daleks), The Magic Roundabout, That Was The Week That Was, The Avengers, Z Cars, Dr Kildare and many more. Juke Box Jury, hosted by David Jacobs, Ready Steady Go and Top of the Pops ensured that pop music received its fair share of airtime. Notable dramas included Cathy Come Home and the Forsyte Saga. BBC2 arrived in 1964 with 625 lines replacing the old 405 lines, giving a sharper black and white picture. This was as good as it got until 1967, when fans of Fred and Joe Davis could finally see which snooker balls they were potting—colour TV had arrived!

Whitsun weekend in 1965 saw the first major confrontation between Mods and Rockers in Brighton. Mods wore Parka coats, rode Lambretta or Vespa scooters and followed the music of the Small Faces and the Who. Leather wearing Rockers, or 'Greasers' rode large British motor cycles, most notably the Norton 650 and Triumph Bonneville. Large groups of both Mods and Rockers regularly visited the resorts on the coasts during the '60s and early '70s, particularly Brighton, Hastings, Southend, Margate and Clacton all of which were within easy reach of London. Confrontation was commonplace though most weekends passed off without too much unrest.

The dance craze of the early years of the decade was The Twist. This was popularised by Chubby Checker's song 'Let's Twist Again' which stayed in the charts for over six months in 1961. The Twist was the first popular dance that could be performed without a partner.

The Daquiri, particularly the strawberry variety was very popular. This Bacardi based cocktail was the drink of choice for John F Kennedy, helping it to gain widespread appeal. Babycham was also popular with young women. The car for the rich man was the E-Type Jaguar, launched in 1961 and British made, in Coventry.

The Swinging Sixties

The '60s was the decade of the mini skirt and the mini car, both often appearing in psychedelic colours or paisley patterns. The Beatles burst on to the music scene in the early years of the decade closely followed by the Rolling Stones, the Who, the Small Faces, the Kinks, the Hollies, the Searchers and a host of others. British music was on top of the world. At home, the Pirate Radio ships, moored just outside of British territorial waters, played non-stop pop music. These were closed down in 1967 and many of the DJs moved to the newly created BBC Radio 1. London fashion too, was in great demand, centred in Soho's Carnaby Street and Chelsea's Kings Road. Men as well as women wore bright colours and flamboyant designs. Hipsters, mini skirts and kipper ties were worn with panache. Kaftans and Cuban Heels also featured in many wardrobes but weren't necessarily brought out together. Women began wearing front fastening jeans, previously only worn by men. Tights also replaced stockings and suspenders as the most appropriate hosiery to wear under a mini skirt!

The hippy movement grew in the latter years of the decade. Educated people (in the main) 'dropped out' of society and sought an alternative lifestyle, usually helped by hallucinatory drugs such as LSD. 'Protesting' was also a factor in many young people's lives. Protest marches against the war in Vietnam, Atomic weapons (Ban the Bomb) and University fees regularly made news headlines.

Huge Pop Festivals were held in the latter years of the decade, the most famous of which at Woodstock in New York State attracted over half a million people. Tamla Motown music, performed by black groups and centred in Detroit (motor town) also became popular around the world with young people of all races.

The contraceptive pill became available to British women in the early years of the decade. This, more than anything else, paved the way for the 'sexual revolution' that took place during the '60s. Women no longer feared pregnancy and for the first time they were in control—they took the Pill, not their man.

1960's fashion

Closer to Home—
Personal Memories of the 1960s

In the 1960s, the pace of change began to increase and many people, particularly the young, sought either to change the world, or change their own world, for the better. Several of the memories in this chapter highlight this move towards betterment. This is particularly obvious in the recollections relating to emigration. Moving from a cold country with mixed opportunities to a sunny land where jobs were freely available was a dream realised for many thousands of families at this time

*Roger Montgomery, in **Gloucester** passed his 11+ exam and went to the Grammar School*

School torture

'I have many memories of school. In the first year, when we were eleven or twelve years old, we had to complete a cross-country run every week. The course was about two miles long and crossed fields and dirt tracks. It was quite steep in places. The first week, we were taken around the course by the gym master. He ran in the front accompanied by the slowest boy in the class, a lad who was well overweight and had flat feet (we'll call him James). We jogged around steadily until James began to lag at which point the gym master smacked him across his bottom with a slipper. This went on all the way around the course until we returned to school, damp, muddy and completely exhausted. I think that was James's only run around the course—he arranged for his parents to write to school and excuse him from games on the grounds of ill health. Incidentally, he's a barrister now. I hope that the gym master doesn't find himself in the same court!

We had a French master, who shall remain nameless in case his ghost comes back to haunt me. He was one of the most feared masters in the school. His favourite torture, which he seemed to hand out for anything from staring out of the window to forgetting irregular verb endings, was to wind a clump of the poor unfortunate's hair around his index finger and yank it upwards until the boy's feet left the floor. Believe me that can be very painful.

Each of my grandparents had enormous numbers of brothers and sisters—thirty-five across the four families—so I had many surviving great-aunts and uncles. Several of the great-aunts, who by this time were in their 60s and 70s, lived together in twos or lived alone. None of them had ever married. I was in my 20s before I realised that the generation of men that they would have grown up with had been decimated in World War One and there just weren't enough men for the women left behind. My great-aunts and thousands of other women of a similar age were resigned to a barren life with no children of their own. When I think about it now, I wish that I'd understood this when my great-aunts were still around to talk about it.'

*James Knowles in **Lancashire** also passed the 11+ exam*

Don't tell Dad

'When I was young (about nine or ten) I was an 'Ensign of the Knights of the Road' and very proud too! In order to gain this high accolade, I had to pass a cycling test, like an advanced cycling proficiency test. I remember wobbling around cones in the school playground and racing from one end to the other then stopping without skidding or falling off. I think that there was a theory test too, related to road safety. I passed and received my certificate and badge, which, had I not lost them somewhere along the way, I could probably have sold on 'ebay' today to a collector of that sort of thing. The same could be said for my Blue Peter badge, which I won in a competition and which has also mysteriously vanished. And thinking about it, my collection of red plastic soldiers that I rescued from the waxy insides of packets of Kellogg's Cornflakes might have been worth something too. Oh, the folly of youth!

As a reward for passing the 11+, my parents promised to buy me a new bicycle. One Saturday, I went off into town with my mum to the bike shop. I really wanted a racing bike; my mum really didn't want to pay that much. In the end, we bought a blue racing bike with five speed derailleur gears and a racing saddle, which cost a magnificent £27. This compared to about £10 for the type of bicycle that my mum had in mind. As we left the shop I was smiling, she was worried. 'Don't tell your dad how much it cost, will you.' I never did.

In 1969, I went on holiday with a friend to South Wales. We travelled down in his mini car, licence number AMO 567, which I later bought from him (and, of course, didn't keep the number plate which today would be very collectible!) We stayed with his aunt near Merthyr Tydfil and had a great time in the valleys and in Cardiff trying to chat up the local girls and drinking too much. The holiday sticks in my mind though, not for the fun but for one of the saddest sights that I have ever seen. We stayed not far from the village of Aberfan. Three years earlier, a coal tip had collapsed causing a massive mudslide and burying the local school. Over a hundred of the children and teachers were killed. The huge black scar on the side of the tip was still plainly visible, running down the length of the hill towards the village. It was a really haunting sight.'

Peter Wright recalls school dinners in Suffolk

Satisfactory

'At school we sat on tables of eight—three down each side and one at each end. I can still smell the cabbage and mince, semolina with jam and and chocolate cornflake pudding (which was actually delicious!). We couldn't leave the table until we'd finished. If you didn't finish by the end of the lunch break, you had to go back after school. I remember one girl sitting with pork fat in her mouth for about twenty minutes before bursting in to tears and spitting it out.

We all received a report at the end of each school year, of course. Most teachers tried to add comments that were helpful or summed up the overall performance. The PE teacher, however, wrote 'Satisfactory' on every member of the class except one. This was a boy who was gloriously overweight. His report elicited the observation: 'Tries hard but lacks co-ordination.' Harsh, but true.

My elder brother was a teenager in the '50s and wore 'winkle-picker' shoes. These were very tight with pointed toes and he still has deformed toes today as a result. I spent my impressionable teenage years in the '60s and the fashion was for wider 'chisel toe' shoes and as a result, the need to be like my friends and follow the fashion actually helped my feet to develop!

Like all of my friends, as I got older I took up smoking. We smoked Piccadilly, Embassy and No 6 unless we were feeling rich, in which case it was Benson and Hedges, Rothmans and the occasional packet of Dunhill's. It was very easy to buy cigarettes—there were dispensing machines in the streets. Vandalism was not such a problem then.

The cult of the TV chef is not a new phenomenon. I remember watching a middle aged married couple called Fanny and Johnny Cradock. Balding, moustachioed Johnny got the wrong end of Fanny's tongue almost every week for some minor misdemeanour in the kitchen and nobody commented on their names!'

Nick Williams wrapped up warm in Devon

Sledges and Arnold

'On Boxing Day evening of 1962, I looked out of the back door and saw a snowstorm in progress; very exciting for a ten-year-old boy who lived in the countryside near the coast and who rarely saw snow. I kept looking out every half-hour or so until I went to bed and the snow was blowing against the back door, forming a drift about a foot deep. Very satisfactory. When I woke up the next morning I couldn't believe my eyes. I looked out of the bedroom window to see—not a lot. Everything was covered in massive amounts of snow. The fence was covered, the coal-house was covered and every plant in the garden was buried under at least three feet of snow. Dad opened the back door and the snowdrift came almost up to the top of the doorframe. The world seemed to be covered in a very thick blanket of snow. The buses couldn't run, the water pipes were frozen and the post didn't arrive. Who cares! Out with the sledge and up the hill. It was a child's paradise for days.

Slowly things returned to normal although it was very cold at night. Then we had another big snowfall, which, on top of the ice, was extremely dangerous. School was closed because everything was frozen up and we spent most of January outside either helping to grit paths, clear ice or sledging down hills. I had never seen so many snowmen! More snow fell in February and the cold spell lasted right through until the middle of March, something I had not known before and have not experienced since. A magical time to be a child but not so great for those with responsibilities in the world.

I had my appendix out when I was eight years old. I had a pain in my side and was taken to the doctor who had me admitted to the local cottage hospital. The next day, the surgeon came to examine me. He pushed his fingers under my right rib cage and asked me if it hurt. I remember being frightened of the operation and told him that it didn't hurt, even though the pain was excruciating. He asked me if I wanted 'bandages or plaster.' I thought he meant plaster of paris, so opted for bandages. A few hours later I came round from the anaesthetic to find my middle swathed in bandages. I stayed like this for six days until the bandages were replaced by a large sticking plaster. Ten days after the operation I left hospital—a week and a half of medical supervision following a minor operation! The NHS was still alive and thriving in the '60s!

I collected stamps when I was young, as did most of my friends. We all had our stamp albums with blank pages headed with the names of countries around the world—some well known and some very obscure. I'm sure my knowledge of world geography was helped enormously by my stamp collecting. When I didn't know where a country was, I looked it up in an atlas. Magazines and newspapers had adverts for stamps. 'Bumper Lucky Dip selection of 100 stamps from around the world' was a typical headline designed to attract the attention of many an excited young stamp collector. I can't remember how much these cost but they weren't very expensive and large parts of my 1/- a week pocket money was spent in this way. There was great excitement when the post arrived and my latest 'Bumper Lucky Dip' collection was tipped out on to the table and sorted in to countries and 'swaps.' The stamps were fixed in to the album using gummed paper stamp hinges so that the stamp could be taken out again without causing any damage.

I went to my first scout camp when I was eleven in 1964. We went to a place called Lapford in North Devon. Three scout troops travelled down together, with all of the tents and assorted gear, in the back of something resembling a removals van (it probably was a removals van). We sat on kitbags and tents and sang songs about the scout leaders. '. . . and there was Robin, Robin, trying to get his nob in, in the stores, in the stores, in the quartermaster's stores . . .' We pitched our tents and built a wooden bridge across the river. Very exciting. In the evening I tasted something that I had never eaten before—baked beans. We didn't eat these at home; we were a traditional meat and two veg family. The baked beans were mixed with minced beef and onions in an enormous pot on a campfire. Eaten with hunks of bread, it was tasty at the time but I'm not sure that I'd rush back for seconds now.

In 1967, the BBC launched Radio 1, 2, 3 and 4. Radio 2 had previously been called the Light programme, Radio 3 had been the Third programme and Radio 4 was the Home service. Radio 1 was new and was the BBC's answer to Pirate Radio. I remember the first day of Radio 1. Tony Blackburn played the first record—Flowers in the Rain, by The Move. He also had a dog called Arnold, I think, which barked (well, a tape barked) when Tony spoke to it. Simple pleasures!'

*Jimmy Haskins from **Leicester** recalls becoming a vegetarian*

A funny handshake

'My mum used to take me shopping with her and we would visit most of the local shopkeepers—the butcher, the baker, the greengrocer, the fishmonger, the iron merchant—they all had their own shops in those days; you didn't get everything from a supermarket. One day, when I was about eight years old, we went to the butchers, 'L.F. Norman and Sons—purveyors of quality meat and provisions.' Les Norman was the owner of the shop and my mum called him 'Mr Norman.' We walked in to the shop and Mr Norman stood behind his counter, his blood stained, blue and white striped apron covering an ample belly. He smiled as we walked in. 'Hello Mrs Haskins, how are you this fine June day? What can we do for you?' I can't remember if he winked at mum, but he might have.

Mum looked at me, 'Say hello to Mr Norman and shake hands, Jimmy'.

I held out my hand and Mr Norman stretched his arm out towards me. Just as his hand was about to meet mine a pig's trotter appeared from out of his sleeve and I shook the cold, pink, clammy, dead cloven hoof. I screamed and ran out of the shop sobbing. It was actually quite frightening for a little boy. I didn't eat meat for a month or so afterwards—it was my 'vegetarian' period, the one and only.'

*Keith Warner, in **Somerset** remembers*
his favourite confectionery bar

It was Bliss

'Cadbury's Bliss had a biscuit base with runny toffee, four almond halves (I think) and whipped cream. The whole bar was covered in chocolate. It was a sort of 'Walnut Whip bar.' I wonder what happened to that?

We always had an open fire at weekends and mum made toast by holding thick slices of bread against the glowing embers using an extending toasting fork. After both sides were crispy brown she handed the first slice to dad who smothered it in Beef Dripping. This seemed quite normal to me at the time but I can't imagine eating it now.

Before we went to bed, dad had a cup of cocoa and mum, my sister and myself all had cups of Ovaltine, all made with milk boiled in a saucepan over a single gas ring in the kitchen.

In bed, I used to listen to Radio Luxembourg in glorious mono sound—'208 metres on the medium wave.' I had a 'Benkson' transistor radio with an earpiece, which cost about £5—many weeks of pocket money!'

Anne Hilton lived in *Northern England*

Andy Pandy and twin tubs

'I grew up in the 1960s, when television was black and white and only had two channels. 'Watch with Mother' was on every lunchtime. Monday was Picture Book, Tuesday was Andy Pandy and Wednesday saw Bill and Ben eluding the gardener. The highlight of the week, Thursday, gave us Rag, Tag and Bobtail who seemed very lifelike at the time, even if they were only in black and white. The week was rounded off with The Woodentops, on Friday, complete with Spotty Dog. On Tuesdays, Wednesdays and Fridays we pretended that we couldn't see the strings; on Thursdays we imagined that there wasn't really anyone working the hand puppets behind the wobbly woodland set. I still remember making stand-up house fronts with garden fences out of sheets of paper. Also, after Watch with Mother is my first memory of hearing the News—'Russian tanks rolling into Czechoslovakia.'

My grandparents, with whom I often stayed, lived in a mining village (which as a child I referred to as the country, because we had to travel on a bus past some fields to get to it (we were town-dwellers). Their house was a step back in time. The old copper still stood in the corner of the kitchen although I do not remember it being used—Grandma had a modern washing machine: a tub with an electric agitator and electric-powered mangle! Instead of a cooker she had a cooking range with pans simmering on the open fire which powered the oven beside it. This was also relatively modern, being enamelled, rather than needing to be black-leaded regularly like the one in her neighbour's house. Sewing was done on a treadle-operated Singer Sewing Machine. By contrast my mum had a gas cooker which we lit with a battery powered hot wire, a twin tub and an electric sewing machine.

On holidays (always by the sea, and always reached by coach or train as we had no car) we used to wear rucked nylon swimming costumes which clung terribly when wet and had to be peeled off, leaving a criss-cross pattern on the skin. Also we had rubber beach shoes which squelched when we walked, but did protect our feet from sharp pebbles and, best of all, we could paddle in them.'

Jan Balsdon *from* **Cumbria** *recalls her first job*
in the Building Society

The tea lady and computers

'I grew up in Whitehaven in Cumbria. I'm afraid moving to the South from Cumbria was a really big cultural shock—different school curriculum, different uniform and everybody spoke differently from my thick north country accent!!!

After leaving Grammar School I went to the local Technical College and from thence to my first full time job in the Halifax Building Society. Our original office was an old office opposite the Barclays Bank complex by the railway station. We then moved into new offices opposite the bus station. It was sheer luxury!

We didn't have electronic typewriters just the original 'bash bang' manual models. All mortgage payments were processed using an old Burroughs Accounting Machine but the piece of office equipment that I found most fascinating was the boss's automatic cigarette lighter shaped like an apple!

The women staff all wore what I presume to be the forerunners of corporate dress; sludgy olive green overalls—very fetching!

The changes in the modern office environment since the 1960s have been absolutely staggering (to me). Then, we had old-fashioned manual typewriters, hand delivered letters to local firms and the tea lady.

Now, our run of the mill office has computers, which facilitate speed typing, e-mails, and spell check as par for the course. Fax machines, telephones with call-back facilities and image scanning are taken for granted. I still find it brilliant that I can e-mail friends staying in a New York hotel, or order my husband's favourite cheese from a farm in Vermont over the internet.'

A state of the art calculator

Helene Lanska trained as a Ballerina

No applause

'In the early 1960s something happened which had been almost impossible to imagine in previous years. It was something very new and a great novelty—ballet on the television!

No audience, no real stage. The camera was the audience, the TV studio was the stage. It was very frustrating; so different, so un-friendly. The camera, that little monster, could pick you up or leave you anywhere at any time. All the shots were discussed between the choreographer and the producer. It seemed that nobody paid any attention to my fellow dancers and me. The studio manager kept everyone informed of what was going on, but there was a lot of waiting—a LOT of waiting. Waiting, doing nothing and getting tired of doing nothing. This new medium appeared indifferent and so cold at first. Just think—no applause at the end of a performance, no curtain calls.

But soon the dancers started thinking. 'Tonight,' we reasoned, 'millions of people will see the ballet—many for the first time. People who would never have gone to see a ballet performance in the theatre.'

This new medium wasn't so bad after all!

On the 12th March 1963 the ballet Marguerite and Armand opened at the Royal Opera House in London with Margot Fonteyn and Rudolf Nureyev. The Queen Mother and Princess Margaret were in the Royal box. I was also in the audience. The ballet was received with what I describe as euphoria. Hand-clapping, feet-stomping, cheers and flowers raining on to the stage. The audience was delirious. But that triumph in London was nothing compared to that in New York. After the first performance, more than 10,000 flowers were collected from the stage.

Marguerite and Armand, the ballet created by Frederic Ashton for Fonteyn and Nureyev was unique. No one else has ever danced it.'

*Brenda Hall moved with her husband to the Royal Naval Air Station in **Lossiemouth** in the North of Scotland*

Fishing and Religion

'We lived in a rented bothy on Commerce Street, just up the hill from the harbour and the fish processing sheds. At this time there was a thriving fishing community at Lossiemouth and the harbour was full of boats. My favourite time was late evening when the boats returned, their masthead lights producing a string of red and green dots over the sea. In the early morning we would hear the sound of the men's boots clumping down the street as they made their way to the boats and the start of their day at sea.

Most of the East Coast fisherfolk belonged to a religious sect which, if I remember rightly, was called 'The Closed Brethren.' Their headman lived in the USA but made the occasional visit to Scotland. It was difficult to get to know the fisherfolk, even though we lived amongst them.

When the men were at sea they broadcast prayers and Bible readings to each other on their ships' radios. Our introduction to their strict religious principles came one Sunday when we took our little daughter to the park to play. All of the swings were padlocked so that they couldn't be used to break the Sabbath.

While we lived in Lossiemouth, our landlady died. We planned to attend her funeral, as a mark of respect but were told not to go. On the day of the funeral the cortege came down the length of Commerce Street with all the mourners following on foot. To my surprise, they were all men.'

Footnote
On a sentimental return visit to Lossiemouth in 2001, it was both disappointing and dispiriting to find not a fishing boat in sight; only a 'Museum of Fishing' on the quay.

Pat Brookes *recalls coming of age*

Football and Politics

'Looking back now I realise that the 1960s was a decade of discovery. For me, among other things, it was it was an era of hair, football, politics and girls.

Having been a schoolboy in the '50s short hair was the norm. I can remember going to the barbers (not men's hairdresser) with my father and sitting in a barber's chair alongside him and hearing him say 'a short back and sides for me—and the same for the nipper.' Once I had left school (school also expected pupils to wear their hair short at the back and sides) things changed. It was a gradual process at first, but once I got going my head of hair really showed what it could do. I went quickly from early Beatle, to Rolling Stone (Mick Jagger of course), to what my mother described as the 'disciple' look—long hair with beard. I eventually settled on what I now call my early 'New Romantic' look—clean-shaven with long hair tied at the back with a bow of velvet ribbon. Worn with a blue Denim shirt, plum coloured waistcoat, skin-tight jeans and pixie boots I really was something!!!

In the early '60s not only did my father take me to the hairdressers he also took me to watch English League football. Living halfway between Southampton and Portsmouth we watched the Saints, recently promoted to Division 2, one week and Pompey, recently demoted to Division 2 the next. When the two teams played each other I well remember the 'informed discussions' on the terraces by opposing fans on the merits of each team. In particular there was heated debate about which team had the better right-winger (now referred to as right-wing forward I believe)—Terry Paine for Saints and Peter Harris for Pompey. They were both great wingers but it depended on whether you were a 'blue' or 'red and white stripe' as to which was the better.

The '60s also meant 1966 and the year the England football team won the World Cup. My father knew Alf Ramsey who had been a Saints player in the early '50s. When Mr Ramsey, as I was allowed to address him, finished playing, he became manager of Ipswich Town Football Club, a team he led to Division 1 championship success. On the back of this he was appointed the England football manager for the 1966 World Cup competition held in England. The friendship between Mr Ramsey and my father resulted in tickets for both my father and I being made available for both of us to watch England's games live right through to the final. Everything went well as we travelled to every game and saw the English team win through to the final at Wembley. World Cup Final day arrived—England v West Germany—and my father and I travelled with some of his (and Mr Ramsey's) friends to Wembley. Under the twin towers of that hallowed (now gone) stadium my father handed me my ticket explaining that there was not enough tickets for everyone to sit in the stands and therefore I would have to watch the game standing up in the North End of the ground. It was only when the two teams walked out on to the pitch that I realised that all around me were cheering for the West German team. Thanks dad, I was at the end of the stadium with all the West German supporters! Still all's well that ends well and it meant I was there at the 'they think it's all over—well it is now' final when the English football team won the World Cup.

I think both my parents voted Conservative, but I can never be sure because voting was between them and the ballot box and never discussed with anyone else. When I first got interested in politics it was early in the 1960s and I decided to rebel against family tradition and become a Liberal. This meant joining the Young Liberals, buying and reading the Manchester Guardian (the only Liberal daily newspaper) and thinking radical thoughts. The leader of the Liberal Party at the time was a chap called Jo Grimond, who looked and sounded like everyone's favourite uncle. After a year or so, and as my hair grew, my radical thinking persuaded me that I needed to move on. I veered to the 'right' and joined the Young Conservatives who seemed to have a large number of attractive young ladies in their ranks. This meant buying and reading the Daily Express (one of the many Conservative daily papers) and thinking about and chatting up girls—a lot! The leader of the Conservative Party at the time was a chap called Sir Alec Douglas-Home who looked and sounded like everyone's upper-crust grandfather. After a little while I decided that my political path, along with my long hair and beard etc, should lead to the left. This meant buying and reading the Daily Worker (the only left wing daily paper at the time). I then spent the rest of the decade supporting CND in Britain, campaigning against South African

Anti-apartheid, raising my clenched left hand in the air in support of Ho Chi Minh and Ernesto 'Che' Guevara among others at various demonstrations and chatting up girls. I never did join the Young Socialists, whose leader was Labour Prime Minister Harold Wilson who didn't look like anyone's favourite relative.

It was in the 1960s that I 'really' discovered girls. Like every generation before (and I am sure since) my generation believed that they had 'invented' sex. Bearing in mind how 'free' sex was we were very lucky. We were the first generation to have the advantages of the 'pill' and unlike today's youngsters we did not have to think about AIDS.'

The introduction of the Mark 1 Ford Cortina began a dynasty
which lasted for twenty years

Mike McGall also caught the football bug in **Southampton**

The Saints!

'Following England's famous victory in the 1966 World Cup, I attended my first professional football match the following November. My godfather took me to see Southampton play Manchester United at the 'Dell.' I was thirteen years old and I remember being struck as we walked in by the intensity of the light from the floodlights at each corner of the ground. Southampton favourites Terry Paine and Jimmy Melia were overshadowed by the fame of the visiting team—Bobby Charlton, George Best, Dennis Law, Nobby Stiles, Pat Crerand, Alex Stepney; a fabulous array of talent. Bobby Charlton scored after ninety seconds; a marvellous introduction to football and I was hooked. Manchester United won 2-1 on the day but I've followed the fortunes of Southampton ever since.'

Aitken Lawrie *continued his memorable army career*

Prime Ministers and Handkerchiefs

Ghana 1966
'Early one morning the 'phone rang. It was the High Commissioner. 'Harold Wilson will be landing in fifteen minutes. Can you meet him?' This was right out of the blue. The Prime Minister was on his way home after the failure of talks about the future of Rhodesia, and suddenly decided to stop off in Accra without realising the effect of a different time zone.

There was a big party with him and I took them all into the VIP lounge at the airport and found a supply of champagne. He wanted to meet the High Commissioner and President N'krumah. While we waited, it developed into a party and I sent for my wife to chat to them.

N'krumah was pleasant to talk to, but difficult to deal with. He was known as Osagyefo, the Redeemer, and saw himself as Head of the Organisation of African Unity, in which there was no place for white Rhodesia. After a heated discussion in an inner room, he burst out, declaring that he was breaking off relations with Britain.

The party broke up. On the way back to the 'plane I was told to walk between Wilson and a hostile crowd that had gathered, but nothing was thrown at us.

Soon afterwards the High Commissioner and all the diplomats departed, leaving me to deal with the Ghanaian Army. Saying goodbye, I asked for some guidance. 'Get rid of N'krumah' was whispered in my ear.

He had many enemies in Ghana, but at first none of them was willing to stick his neck out. I heard that Lord Mountbatten, then Chief of Defence Staff, was due to visit Nigeria, and asked him to call in at Accra. N'krumah at once invited him to make use of his country house in the hills. This was a fabulous place, with a heliport, swimming pool and all mod cons, including two grand pianos but it had never been used. A helicopter was put at my disposal and I went round the town with my wife buying bedding, cutlery, dishes, etc for Mountbatten and his party, which included his daughter and son-in-law, David Hicks.

When they arrived we were invited to join the party for dinner. I found myself alone with Mountbatten and took the opportunity to mention that the last time we had met was in India in 1947. He was convinced that the action he took there was all for the best.

N'krumah wanted Mountbatten to meet the communist mayor of Kumasi, but I sabotaged this and took him to lunch with the Ashantehene, descended from the old hereditary rulers of Ghana. He reminded Mountbatten that HMS Kumasi was the only destroyer of its class to come through WWII unscathed and attributed this to the magic monkey's paw, which he had presented to the captain. He would like to present another monkey's paw to the present HMS Kumasi. This was right up Mountbatten's street and he sent an immediate signal to HMS Kumasi in Hong Kong to report to Takoradi. In due course I was able to take the Ashantehene down to Takoradi dressed in his ceremonial robes to carry out the presentation.

I got Mountbatten to suggest to N'krumah that his armed forces should be reorganised in the way that had been set up in Britain. I knew that this would lead to trouble, since N'krumah would have to dismiss his senior generals, who had served the British faithfully.

Not long after, when N'krumah was on a visit to China, two pro-British brigades marched on the capital. I was woken by bursts of firing and went out to see what was happening. They were attacking N'krumah's residence, which was defended by Russian guards. The main road was under fire, but when I drove up, they recognised my car and stopped shooting to let me through.

The town was already in turmoil. N'krumah's statue had been pulled down and the mob was shouting 'We want the British' and 'Gold Coast come back' but the British government was not interested.

Pro-British General Arthur Ankarah took over as Head of State. I called on him to offer my congratulations and found him in a neat blue suit with a white handkerchief in his top pocket. When I asked him how he had folded it so that it showed four corners in a line, he tapped his nose, saying 'state secret, old boy.'

Next morning a big black car drove up to my house and an ADC jumped out carrying a large cardboard box. When I opened it I found it contained an envelope with four cards on which the four corners of a white handkerchief had been stitched. I still find it useful!'

Rosemary Reavell *moved on during the decade*

A new life

'In the early 1960s we moved to Redhill, in Surrey. What a lovely home. There were fruit trees in the garden and the railway line ran past the bottom of the garden. My father now worked at Walton-on-the-Hill in an antique shop, restoring and French polishing furniture. I went to Earlswood Secondary School, where my music teacher actually smoked in the classroom but I still loved music and joined the choir. The Science master was a relation of a famous musician and he was very strict, especially with the boys, while the Maths teacher threw blackboard rubbers at those misbehaving. One year we had a student teacher assigned to teach us Biology. He had terrible acne and some of the girls gave him a rotten time by asking very intimate questions and the poor young man would blush and stammer.

I left school in 1963 and found work. Part of my first wage was spent on a real Edam cheese, with its waxy red skin, I thought that was great.

I worked with some lovely people, including a lady called June who later went on to manage the narrowest hotel in England, an interesting claim to fame. There was excitement too when I found out that I was walking to work past the house of one of the Great Train Robbers.

Family holidays took us further afield now we had a car. Cornwall, the Isle of Wight or Wales where we stayed on a farm, always with pencils and sketch book in hand, for I loved to draw. Harlech Castle, the stone walls or the mountains made super subjects. We had lots of 'I Spy' books to take on the journey.

My friend Delyse and I became members of a 'gang.' There was John and Tony Fenton and Derek Newton who I remember. They tried to teach me how to ride a motorbike, in a field covered in ice and snow. One of the lads sat behind me on the bike while someone else showed me how to change gears etc. I let the clutch out slowly but one of them had left the throttle wide open! The bike leapt into the air, my passenger fell off and I, hanging on for grim death, went hurtling across a bumpy and slippery field, straight for the river! I did manage to turn away at the last minute though.

It was a very innocent gang I suppose, listening to the latest single records, Radio Luxembourg and going to the 'fleapit' to see the horror movies. We took a coach trip to Blackpool where we saw Lawrence of Arabia on the new 'wide screen.' Delyse and I 'cut a single record' in a booth on the pier at Blackpool, which I still have, along with all of my other old singles. Friday or Saturday night would be dancing and listening to a live rock band in Redhill. The Hollies, Freddie and the Dreamers, Manfred Mann, Heinz and I think we even saw the Dave Clarke Five there. Sometimes we would catch the train to Brighton, just to get a hamburger. We would listen to the Pirate stations on little transistor radios and my bedroom wall was covered with pictures of The Beatles, Gerry and the Pacemakers and other great rock stars. Top of the Pops was a must for TV viewing.

In 1964 my grandfather emigrated to Australia, to join his son, his daughter and their families. Then something terrible happened—my parents decided to emigrate to Australia, too. My father had had enough of the cold weather. I didn't want to go. I had lots of friends and a good job. We were not £10 Poms though, my father had to pay full fare for all of us. So I was a reluctant passenger when we emigrated at the end of April 1965, sailing from Portsmouth on the Fairstar. I was not a very good sailor. However I soon made new friends, particularly a lovely guy called Dave. We travelled through the Mediterranean and the Suez Canal, stopping at Port Said. There had been gunfights and bombs set off there not many days before we arrived and soldiers were still patrolling the streets. I thought it was very exciting. I believe they stopped the shipping through the Suez Canal not long afterwards.

Late on the night of May 31st we docked at Fremantle Harbour, Western Australia. It was pouring with rain (come to sunny Western Australia!) and we waited ages to get through Customs before finally meeting our relatives who had come to welcome us. We stayed with my aunt, uncle and three cousins for a while until my parents got their own house in Medina. Dad and I found work and I started to settle down. There were Stomps (dances) to go to, concerts at the Capitol Theatre in Perth. There we saw Billy Thorpe and the Aztecs, Ray Brown and The Whispers, all Australian rock stars that we never heard of back in the UK. We were introduced to the game of Aussie Rules (Footy) which I thought was far more exciting than soccer and went to the Speedway on Friday nights; it was a great time for me. After many outings and barbecues I gradually grew to love Australia and its people. One of those people became my husband in 1967 and we still live in Perth to this day.'

*Pam Malekin was a teenager in **Brighton** in the early '60s*

Leaving home

'My memories of the '60s in Brighton were of having a ball in the summer with all the visitors to the town and being able to walk home late at night with no worry at all. Maybe it is my 'rose coloured glasses' again but people seemed to be nicer and cared much more. All I can say is that I had a fabulous teenagerhood growing up with the magic of the Beatles and Brighton. Even the Mods and Rockers' 'wars' were fun and I can remember one shopkeeper being so fed up with them all outside her seafront cafe that she got a huge bucket of water and chucked it over them. We all fell about laughing at the mod who went mad because she had ruined his hairstyle and wet his Lambretta!

The main haunts of teenagers in the '60s were the ubiquitous coffee bars. They were great because everyone had their own 'turf' and for a cup of coffee or coke (the drinking kind) you could chat or dance all evening. The jukeboxes were our bibles and if an 'outsider' came in and put on something that wasn't 'Top Ten' the place just went silent 'til they slunk out.

In 1966, my husband, Mike and myself emigrated to Australia. I think that we were some of the last '£10 Poms.' We were two, young naive twenty-two year olds and I actually turned twenty-two the day we landed in Fremantle, near Perth.

I suppose the main reason that we decided to go was that there was really nothing for us then. Jobs weren't easy to come by especially for Mike who had given up a secure government job to go contracting and that 'fell in a heap' after six months so he was getting quite disheartened. I was working for my brother at the time and Mike came to see me. We discussed life in general and my brother suddenly turned round, slapped a £1 note down on the desk and said 'Get yourselves up to London and Australia House and get yourselves a new start.' Mike looked at me, I nodded and six months later we were on our way to Oz! (note that all it cost to get from Brighton to London in '65 was £1 return). The reason we chose Perth was that another brother was considering emigrating and had really gone into all the pros and cons and had come up with Perth. Also, a brother-in-law flew for Freddie Laker's airline at the time and he reckoned that it was the best place in Australia for immigrants.

It was really easy to emigrate then, especially for young couples without children. In fact, we applied in the August and we could have sailed in October. I wanted a last Christmas with my Mum so we put off about four sailing dates until we left in March '66. The medical we had to have was a complete farce. We went to see an elderly doctor who must have been old when Queen Victoria was on the throne. He waved a stethoscope around us both, Michael had to do the 'cough' and that was it! We could have been a couple of raging psychopaths and riddled with goodness knows what but at least we knew Michael could 'cough!' Don't ask me what the old fella looked like as we couldn't see him for the cigarette smoke in his room!'

Joe Lunn *left* **Yorkshire.** *He also travelled to the other side of the world*

It's a long way from Yorkshire

'In 1956 I married my childhood sweetheart, Diana Bulmer in the small village of Rothwell in Yorkshire. We both had dreams of emigrating to Oz, but our enquiries revealed we were too poor to go. The cost was £20 plus £8 for health injections, money we didn't have.

The idea was shelved until 1967 when we befriended a Leeds couple whilst on holiday. They had emigrated to Melbourne in the late 1940s. Our conversations were all about Australia and though we were still rather poor, £28 was now possible. So we went for it. Our meeting with the Melbournites was in May, we contacted Australia House on our return from holiday and on 8th October that same year we were disembarking from the liner Fairsea, in Fremantle.

I was born in Rothwell, the youngest son of a family of ten children. Our family had resided in the area for hundreds of years. My wife, also from the village, was the oldest girl from a family of nine and her family had a similar heritage. No one from either family had been far from Yorkshire, except for military duty, so the thought of a family member emigrating was big news indeed. We had children of our own by this time, three boys; Denys, who was eleven, Gary nine and Steven seven, when we made our way to Southampton to embark on our adventure. The ship looked very small for the six-week journey to Oz, it was from memory 35,000 tons.

We were all excited at the prospect of a cruise to a new country, but the excitement didn't last long. All male migrants had to share a cabin, which was well below the water level. Mothers and children were in a separate cabin also in the bowels of the ship; all migrant cabins were 4 berth with bunk beds.

Our enthusiasm waned even more when everyone was seasick. I smile now about an announcement that came from the ship's tannoy system. 'Please do not visit the medical officer, as he and all his staff are seasick.'

A few days before arriving in Fremantle, all migrants were asked to write a short story as to why they had chosen Australia as a preferred destination. At this time, South Africa, America, Canada and New Zealand were also all in the race for migrants. My story was chosen as the best and was printed in the West Australian daily newspaper. It began like this:

'I feel like a modern day Captain Cook. I have been sent by my family to find out what Australia is all about and if the report I send home is good you can expect a big invasion from my village.' And so on. . . .

As we walked down the gangplank at Fremantle, business people were holding up placards:
DRIVER WANTED ring xxxxxx
PAINTERS REQUIRED xxxxxx
Jobs were on offer even on the dockside.

We were put on a bus and taken to a migrant hostel called Graylands, where we would be allowed to stay for a maximum of six months. I remember turning to my wife and saying, 'Di, I feel great and know we are going to be happy here.'

35 years later I still feel good.'

Getting acquainted with the local wildlife

Bob Hollings *spent his teenage years in* **Somerset**

The requisite furry thing . . .

'I worked for a British Motor Corporation distributor in Taunton. After getting cheap lessons and passing my driving test in an old Austin A30 that I bought from my supervisor for the purpose, I went back to riding two-wheelers for the convenience, low cost and sheer pleasure of riding them. I had owned three different motorbikes prior to this.

I kept the car just long enough to go and see Bob Dylan and Jimi Hendrix live at the Isle of Wight Rock Festival in 1969. It was so rusty I was told it would not pass another MOT test, but I found someone who wanted it just until the existing certificate expired, and he paid me more than enough to buy a second-hand 150cc Vespa Sportique. I joined a local youth club, had a Parka jacket and the requisite additional mirrors, lights, and furry thing on my scooter. At weekends we sometimes rode down to Torquay to ride around the town and camp overnight. I could just as easily have chosen to be a Rocker and our group never caused any real trouble, we just enjoyed harmless anarchy. One night a shout of 'Greasers!' (our name for 'rockers') caused fifteen scooters and their owners (including myself of course) to disappear from the Torquay cafe car park in a matter of seconds!'

The Highway Code

Steve Shields *lived in* ***Saltburn*** *and also recalls his 'scootering' days*

A quiet country lane

'In the late '60s I worked at a local dairy and started work at 5am. I had a Lambretta SX200 with all the chrome at the time and one morning it 'clapped out' on me as I was riding to work. I stopped by the side of the road and took off one of the side panels to see if I could see the source of the problem. As I looked at the electrics,

I heard a dull thudding noise that sounded like thunder. I looked up and saw a black shape in the distance. But it wasn't in the sky. It was in the lane coming towards me—the South Shields Chapter of the Hell's Angels!

I was terrified as they approached me, then started riding around the scooter and me, saying things like 'lend us your mirror' and 'let's do 'im.' This went on for a few minutes before the leader dismounted and walked across to me.

'What's your problem?' he asked quite casually.

I told him what had happened, pointing towards the exposed engine and trying not to visibly shake. I did start shaking when he pulled out the biggest knife I'd ever seen. He waved it past me, knelt down by the side of the scooter and reached for the HT lead. He pulled it out, trimmed the end and replaced it.

'Now try' he said

It started first time.

He asked me where I was going and I didn't know what to expect when he suggested that the Hell's Angels should follow me to the dairy in case I 'clapped out' again. But join me they did; some in front and some behind. When we arrived at the dairy I thought something would happen, but it didn't. They roared off down the road with the leader waving and smiling. Not the way that I would choose to start every day!

A few weeks later I was riding to Sunderland with a mate on the back, to see Gino Washington and the Ram Jam Band. I wasn't really concentrating hard enough when we approached a staggered crossroads and overtook an Austin Cambridge 'Home James' taxi. Needless to say, as we overtook, the taxi turned right and we hit it side on. You weren't required by law to wear a helmet then and my mate on the back didn't have one. He flew past me when we hit the taxi as if he'd been fired from a cannon, holding his hands and arms around his exposed head. He hit the road quite hard and broke his leg but his head was fine. I hit the ground headfirst but luckily was wearing a helmet and got away with heavy bruising.

We picked ourselves up, dusted ourselves down and sorted things out with the taxi driver, who was quite understanding after he overcame his shock. I pushed the damaged bike in to the back streets of Sunderland with my mate following on behind complaining about his leg which, at the time, he didn't realise was broken. I parked the bike in a quiet place and we were just about to leave to go and find help when a black Mark II Police Jaguar appeared. My mate and I smiled in agony as the car slowed down and surveyed the damage. We expected them to stop but they didn't, just looked closely and drove off. I don't suppose that they wanted to get involved and have to fill out all of the paperwork.'

Ray Oldam grew up on the Isle of Man and recalls June 1967 and what many followers of motorcycle racing still believe was the greatest race ever run

The Diamond Senior

'Every year in June, the Isle of Man is taken over for two weeks by the TT races, and the thousands who come to watch. Living on the Isle of Man was generally pretty dull when you were 10 and 9 years old—except for race fortnight, when suddenly our little Island was a different world. The colour, the noise, the excitement of the racing, and the teams and spectators from all the different countries changed it totally. Our dad had taken my brother and myself to watch a race two years earlier, and we had become immediately hooked.

We would ride our push bikes down to the Bay Hotel, a couple of miles from our house, where the Yamaha and MV teams were based, and would often hang around there for hours just to get close to the machinery and famous riders. Best of all, we got to know some of the mechanics, though none of them spoke more than a few words of English. Two of MV's mechanics were Vittorio and Rugerrio. Sometimes they would take a machine out for testing on the road, which looped around the headland. We would follow on our pushbikes, sit down on the pavement, and cheer and clap as they came past, still in their overalls and of course no crash helmet either. All totally illegal, but they certainly seemed to enjoy this part of the job!

We thought Yamaha's Japanese mechanics were like people from another planet—they looked very different, they had really strange writing, and they sat on the floor to eat very odd food from little bowls using sticks.

Occasionally we would see some of the famous riders, Phil Read and Bill Ivy rode for Yamaha, and Giacomo Agostini rode the Italian MV machines, so they would often be calling by the garages. One day Bill Ivy drove up with a familiar passenger in his American sports car, I recognised him straight away—this was Honda's English rider Mike Hailwood. They stood chatting and joking outside Yamaha's garages, and we very timidly approached for autographs. My brother's pushbike had a carrier above the back wheel, and just as he turned to pedal off again, Hailwood picked up the back of the bike with one hand. He was balancing it and a furiously pedalling, confused nine-year old was going absolutely nowhere, as Ivy and all the Japanese mechanics burst out laughing. My brother was not impressed, which only made it more funny. Hailwood calmed him down by promising not to do it again, and offered a reluctantly accepted handshake.

Race Day
On Friday we saw Hailwood and Agostini again, this time on the last day of racing in the Diamond Jubilee 60th Anniversary TT. By Monday the Island would be back to its dull normality, but everyone there knew today's 500cc Senior race would be an epic.

We joined the many people walking through our village and up the hill towards Signpost Corner. All the traffic, mostly motorcycles, was heading in the same direction. Dad was at work, and mum wasn't interested in the racing at all, but they were happy to let us wander off to watch on our own, and they probably wouldn't have been able to stop us anyway! As we passed rows of motorcycles parked either side of the road we began to realise we had set off a bit too late to get our usual spot—it was ages before the racing started but the banks around Signpost Corner were already packed with spectators. We settled for a long walk through cow pasture and nettles and eventually found a gap on the entrance to 'Bedstead', the next corner.

We were less than a mile across the fields from the start and grandstand at Glencrutchery Road. Above the chattering of spectators and the many radios tuned in to the commentary, you could hear the machines being warmed up as the minutes ticked away before the start. These were mostly the rumbling four-stroke Manx Nortons and Mathless G-50s, old designs from the last decade. Then a different, high-pitched sound began, almost drowning out the others, followed by another even higher note. The Honda and MV were easy to recognise, and stopped conversation, as spectators nodded or pointed in the direction of the start.

Once team-mates with MV Agusta, Hailwood and Agostini were now battling for the 500cc World Championship, but not only were crucial points at stake, this was the TT—and winning here was almost as important as winning the Championship itself.

The two men were good friends off the racetrack, although very different. Hailwood, at 27 was older, and more experienced. A tall, athletic-looking man, Hailwood was immensely popular with the crowds, famous for his unstoppable determination and cheerful but modest character. Hailwood now had the immense resources of Honda behind him, a team of white-gloved Japanese mechanics and engineers and the fearsome Honda 'four'. The 'four' had a frightening reputation—Honda had built the most powerful engine by far, and the machine had unheard-of acceleration and top speed. However, it had appalling handling, it twitched and jumped wildly with any change of power or direction. Other riders told Hailwood they couldn't understand how he stayed on it. Interviewed a couple of days before the race he had said 'That thing (the Honda) is going to be the death of me.'

Agostini was the young, good-looking and rather brash Italian who had come from obscurity in the last 2 years to be chosen by Count Domenico Agusta to bring his dream of an Italian world champion riding his MV machines. MV was a sideline from the main Agusta business of helicopters, but for Agusta winning was a matter of national pride. The new 'three' had been developed to replace MV's ageing 'four' and after a year of development, though slower than the Honda, it had exceptionally good handling, a real confidence boost for the rider on the dangerous Isle of Man circuit.

The Flag Drops

A klaxon sounded to signal the final two minutes before the start, and gradually the engines stopped, to be replaced by the commentary echoing around the fields. Shortly afterwards the first pair of machines cracked into life. Ten seconds later Hailwood was in the next two, Agostini in the pair thirty seconds after Hailwood, and so on. Eventually, the entire field of nearly 100 machines had poured in their pairs down Bray Hill at 130 to 140 mph, between stone walls and houses right next to the road. There were no massed starts at the TT, accidents on Bray Hill were usually fatal anyway, so they would only increase the risks still further.

The commentary followed Hailwood and Agostini around the circuit, and shortly the grandstand area went silent. In the distance we could hear the machines working their way around the 37 ¾ mile circuit as the sound drifted through the valleys now and then. Hailwood was flinging the Honda around, fighting the machine to keep it on the road. He was setting an incredible pace, but Agostini was closing the gap. They had now left the fields and villages of the western edge of the Island and were climbing the 1500ft onto the 'Mountain' section; sequences of fast corners lined with yellow concrete posts and fencing. The circuit went around 'The Verandah' where the road was cut into the side of Snaefel, the Island's highest mountain, winding around the heather-covered mountains.

A few minutes later they were plunging down the steep hills off the mountain section, back to open fields and rounding the slow corner at Creg-ny-Baa. We could hear them now, gradually coming closer. Then a flash as sun caught a windscreen, a screaming howl as the silver Honda flew towards us. Hailwood backed off the throttle and shifted on the seat, banking the machine steeply into the corner as it wriggled and bucked beneath him, then an explosion of noise as he shot past inches below our feet, his left shoulder almost touching the grass bank. The power screamed back on again and the engine note jumped and fell as the back wheel of the Honda bounced off the bumps, before disappearing towards The Nook and Governor's Bridge.

Twenty seconds later Agostini's MV rushed into view, using every inch of the road, banked smoothly into the corner, and another burst of noise. I held on to the fence post next to me, it felt almost like I was about to be swept off. Then a steady stream of Nortons and Matchlesses rumbling past as the rest of the field came through. Hailwood's first lap had been an average of 107.4 mph. Agostini's was even faster, 108.4 mph, close to the record, from a standing start!

An Unexpected Handicap and an Unlucky Break
Hailwood began to fight back, closing with a lap of 108.8 mph, but started to slow on the next circuit. As they pulled into the pits to re-fuel, Hailwood shouted to the Honda mechanics for a hammer, then began beating the handlebar furiously. Out on the circuit, the

twistgrip had worked loose and was coming off, and he was now hammering it back into place. Agostini made a faultless pit stop and Hailwood's hard-won seconds had all been lost as he set back off again, and now he had a huge problem to deal with. Over the next 2 laps the throttle was constantly working loose, and starting to come off. Somehow, Hailwood was managing to jam it back onto the handlebar each time, and still close the gap on Agostini. 'That thing will be the death of me!'

By now, the commentary was telling us of frightening moments Hailwood was having at different parts of the circuit as he struggled with the Honda. If the throttle came off at the wrong time the Honda would slam into a wall, fence, grass bank or trees at over 140 mph. All around the circuit Hailwood was being cheered on, but there was concern too. Some people next to us were arguing whether he should stop. Agostini was 3 seconds ahead now.

On the fifth lap Hailwood rushed past and the seconds ticked by, now he was pulling away from Agostini again. More seconds, then the gap had to be too long—where was Agostini? The MV was famous for reliability—unlike the Honda, they seemed rarely ever to break down. He was riding at the absolute limit, but with less experience than Hailwood, could he have misjudged a corner on the mountain section?

The word came through on the commentary—'Agostini is 'touring' (coasting with a dead engine) from Keppel Gate.' The drive chain on the MV had snapped, and Agostini's race was over. Back at the grandstand, the engineer from British chain maker, Renold, apparently went white with the news, then a minute later was jumping around in the pits shouting 'It wasn't one of ours!' MV used an Italian make—Regina Extra.

Victory and Despair

Hailwood got a signal from one of his crew on his last lap, it read 'AGO OUT!' Thinking it was a bad joke, he flew on, still fighting the Honda and its wayward throttle, until a second signal from the Honda crew confirmed it at the halfway point. As he swept through the corners on his way up the Mountain, through a sea of waving programmes and cheering crowds, the race was his.

Meanwhile, the other riders were going through, when in between their passing we heard a different, rippling sound. It gradually got closer, before Agostini's silent MV rolled into view,

Giacomo Agostini competing in the famous Isle of Man TT race of 1967

coasting on the pavement to applause from the crowd. Agostini nodded back, but he looked shattered, today was his birthday, only the celebrations would be very different to what he imagined just twenty minutes earlier.

As Hailwood completed his last lap, Agostini pushed the stricken MV along Glencrutchery Road to the grandstand, where the crowd rose from their seats. We could hear the applause from Bedstead Corner. A mechanic took the machine as Agostini, now in tears, was consoled by the others. Sportsmen weren't able to show quite the same level of emotion back in the 1960s in the way they do now. 'Bloody Ago's cryin'—he's cryin'!' laughed one of the spectators on our bank, but he quickly looked embarrassed at a few sharp looks from others nearby.

Hailwood crossed the line to a thundering welcome. He had pushed the lap record to nearly 109mph, a record which would stand for another nine years, on a machine which could have killed him at any moment. This was a fantastic achievement, but Hailwood always considered it a hollow victory. A few minutes later he was talking to Agostini. 'It wasn't your fault—and I am very sorry—you would have won and there was nothing I could have done about it.'

That evening, the birthday party was cancelled. After the prize giving, Hailwood took Agostini for a drink instead.'

Mrs A Hardy recalls her teenage years in the **North East**

Kitten heels and Lux

'As a teenager in the '60s I was very influenced by TV adverts and the clothes that my idols wore—we were the first generation to be affected like this, I suppose. We wore short mini skirts, kitten heeled shoes with pointed toes, white trench coats, black flares and 'Beatle' jumpers (polo necks). At the age of seventeen, I entered a competition called 'Girl 2000.' We were required to design clothes that we thought would be worn by teenagers in the year 2000. I went in leathers, others dressed in tin foil and plastic. Little did we know that fashion by the year 2000 would have gone full circle and girls would once again be wearing mini shirts and kitten heels!

Make-up was mainly white eye shadow and black mascara with Kohl pencil under the eyes. False eyelashes and false nails were also very popular. Jewellery was big and ceramic. Twiggy brought out her own brand of foundation cream, which I bought. I also used Lux soap after seeing the adverts on TV.

On Saturday nights we visited the Rink in Sunderland to see our favourite groups. Later, I worked at the Locarno Nightclub and saw the groups for free! The Who, Denzil Washington, The Animals, Donovan, Marc Bolan, Marmalade and lots more all gave us fantastic entertainment.'

Jules Evans recalls her teenage years

Frothy coffee and Juke Boxes

'In 1963, when I was sixteen, I think my parents felt relieved that, unlike some of my friends, I was still more in love with horses than with boys. Much to the disgust of the older generation, Harpenden's first Expresso coffee bar opened that year and was viewed with as much suspicion as most other American trends. However, I was certainly not beyond visiting the new cafe to drink 'frothy' coffee and gossip with girlfriends.

Wearing heavy black eye make-up and bouffant hair that required energetic back-combing and lots of hair-spray to keep it styled, mini skirts, and pointed-toe shoes, popularised by singers like Lulu and Cilla Black, we compared pearlised nail varnish, and American pop stars. The British model, Twiggy, was a rising star and new female role model. We all coveted her slim, boyish figure and pale make-up. If Twiggy wore it, then we all rushed to buy a look-alike outfit from Dorothy Perkins or Richard Shops. We queued for hours at our village hall to see young bands like Georgie Fame and the Blue Flames and Eric Burdon and the Animals. I still have a letter written in 1966 by a friend holidaying in Torquay, telling me she had been to see a little known band called The Who and they'd all smashed their instruments to bits as a finale to the concert! Of course, The Who went on to become internationally famous and they weren't the only band to smash up instruments and hotel rooms. Our parents saw this as deplorable behaviour and wondered where it would all end. As teenagers, we loved the loud juke box in our 'fab' coffee bar and readily fed our cash in to listen to Cliff Richard singing 'The Young Ones' and Adam Faith, softly crooning, 'What do you Want.'

What did we want? As the post war new generation, we seemed to have everything. The world had become vastly different in just sixteen years. We had contraceptive pills, rock and roll, freedom to work and to travel. Girls were starting to seize an independence undreamed of by their mothers. By the time I was nineteen, women were realising that maybe they could have it all—homes, husbands, children, cars, and aspire to management positions within lucrative careers. Scores of new books and women's magazines suggested that women must take advantage of these opportunities, or be seen to give way to old-fashioned male dominance. Women questioned why they were staying at home to look after the kids when their husbands were gaining success and mental stimulation at work. Surely, women were equal? And if they were equal, they must have equal opportunities!'

Liz Rosenberg grew up in Wales

A balanced approach

'In 1960, I took my 'O' levels, left boarding school and went to the local Technical High school. I did Pure and Applied Maths where I was one of two girls in a class of twenty-three boys! We used to go out on a Friday night in a big group, often to the local Repertory Theatre, where it cost 1/3d to get in. Then it went up to 1/6d. They were concession prices for students. Then we all used to go to a local coffee shop and sit there and talk etc. We didn't really just go out as boyfriend and girlfriend but just as a big group.

I had pictures of Elvis Presley and John F. Kennedy on my bedroom wall; I was so shocked when JFK was assassinated.

I got a part-time job in the school holidays working at a local café—I remember being so proud of my first pay! I think I gave some to mum for board and bought an EP (extended play) record by Cliff Richard. I started washing dishes and cleaning tables then progressed to making coffees etc, then finally I was allowed to take orders and speak to the customers and take their money.

I wasn't so much a Beatles fan but more Cliff Richard and Adam Faith. I also liked Bob Dylan and protest singers like Joan Baez and Pete Seeger. I went to see Bob Dylan at the Royal Albert Hall; I sat up in the gods. We also had records by Tom Lehrer, which my parents had bought. I think his irreverent way of looking at things was a great influence on my life.

My father was a great believer in having a balance so in the '60s we used to get the People newspaper as well as the Sunday Express and Sunday Times. I remember the very straitlaced teachers at the boarding school being horrified when I brought back a copy of the People after a weekend visit from my parents.

I used to listen to the radio a lot, especially Europe No 1, the pirate radio stations, and the BBC. Comedies such as The Goon Show, Round the Horne and Beyond our Ken were favourites. I used to listen when I was supposed to be doing my homework. As a family we used to play Canasta and Scrabble, also Monopoly. I think we did more things like that together than a lot of families do now. My parents also taught me to do cryptic crosswords from quite a young age, and there was always some friendly rivalry as to who would get the answer first.

I was never very interested in fashion but I remember my best friend at school starching her petticoats to make them stand out. Also there was the backcombing of the hair to make that stand out too. My hair was always very fine and never wanted to stand out. At university I thought I was very daring as I dyed my hair black. Everyone in those days wanted long straight hair. I remember the girls who had curly hair ironing it straight on an ironing board, with brown paper between the hair and the iron! I went to University College, Cardiff (Neil Kinnock was also a student at the same time, but I don't remember him). I was a member of the Folk Club and although I don't have a good singing voice (in fact it's terrible) I used to enjoy singing along in the choruses. When you have a few hundred people singing along one out of key person doesn't matter so much!'

*Lyn Welsh began work in **London** in the '60s*

Kissing Wayne Fontana

'I started work in 1965 in an office that had an adding machine with buttons 1 to 5. So, say you needed 9, you'd tap out 3+6 or 4+5 etc to make up larger numbers. It was a museum piece! We also had a Gestetner duplicating machine, the forerunner of the photocopier. A notice or letter was typed out as a stencil then put on to a roller which was turned using a handle like a hurdy-gurdy to copy the document. Multiple copies were made in this way. Your hands would get covered in the inky mess. If a mistake was made on the stencil you used a pink obliterating ink—bright pink like nail varnish—to paint over the error.

Just prior to starting work, I regularly attended a youth club with a lad called Ted Beckham; we used to play records together during recreation hour. Ted later went on to father a rather famous footballer called David.

I blush with embarrassment when I think of how I was madly in love with various pop stars. The boyfriend I had at the time was OK so long as when I kissed him I imagined I was snogging Wayne Fontana or one of the Beatles.

I wore make-up by Miners, Outdoor Girl or Yardleys; nobody else would do. The most popular lipstick colour was 'Iced Pink' by Outdoor Girl.'

Jane Cooke recalls long lost days

Love in a cold war

'As a teenager through most of the '60s, I followed the hippy life-style. I'm sure this was triggered by the assassination of President Kennedy. It was the time of the Cold War and my friends and I had the feeling that he was all that stood between us and oblivion. This feeling was particularly strong after the Cuban Missile crisis—we felt that we were all going to be 'nuked.' The assassination in 1963 led to the 'Laissez Faire' generation, people who lived for the moment, enjoyed life and hoped for peace.

In 1967 (I think) I attended a forerunner of the great Rock festivals that developed towards the end of the decade. On August Bank Holiday, Woburn Abbey hosted what was billed as 'The greatest hippy Love In'. If I could do anything, I'd love to relive those days!'

*Christine Moulié who grew up in **Paris** was a dedicated follower of fashion*

Trousers and meditation

'In the '60s our world changed drastically. Amazingly, we were able to cope with the changes that were all around us—fashion, language, politics, lifestyle, philosophy, music and much more. According to some 'experts,' the 1950s represented 'a period of apathy.' The 1960s certainly began with a total rejection of the outlook from the preceding decade. It was easy to see the change in the quality of life. Young people left their rural communities for the big cities where they dedicated themselves to 'living for the moment!'

'Don't trust anyone over 30' was the 1960s catchphrase. I believed it at the time—youth is a formidable asset.

Women tried to look like Nancy Sinatra, wearing mini skirts and white knee boots (plastic, of course). The slender look was fashionable, led by Twiggy, Mia Farrow and Jean Shrimpton. Loads of eye make-up was compulsory. Some girls were wearing two sets of eyelashes, one on top of the other!

In 1967, the trouser suit went public and was worn by women everywhere. My godfather, Jacques, declared that the Grand Couturiers like Dior, Nina Ricci, Balmain or Landin should be ashamed to design 'silly pants' for women. I firmly pointed out that the trouser suit was accepted internationally. Designers were using a wonderful range of feminine colours and florals and the creations looked very chic when worn with the correct accessories. I also thought that they could adapt themselves to a larger range of figures than the mini skirt. Jacques and I had long discussions on the subject! I loved the fashion of 1967. Every type of trouser was in vogue—casual slacks, hareem bloomers, bermudas, space age jump-suits, pyjamas and more. My favourite was the Yves St Laurent female version of the dinner jacket—Le Smocking—in black velvet. I really went crazy for it! Le Smocking was born in the St Laurent Couture Salon at the Rue Spontini in Paris on the Right Bank. It was soon on sale in his Ready to Wear Boutique across the Seine on the Left Bank, the famous Rive Gauche; its success was immediate. The French singer Françoise Hardy also contributed to its fame.

The Left Bank Boutique had a fantastic atmosphere. I remember the ambience; it was as relaxed as the prices. It was very different from the Couture Salon. The clothes were the same to look at but they didn't have the mega perfection that an army of seamstresses and fitters can give them. The Rive Gauche Boutique, in the Quartier Latin, had a Coca-Cola machine installed against the bright red walls and there were tables and chairs in the courtyard.

Clients were pretty women in mini skirts, coloured tights and hairpieces. Long-bobbed guitar-playing boys were also seen.

Enthusiastic buyers included Margot Fonteyn, Catherine Deneuve, Marianne Faithfull, Anita Pallenberg and Julie Christie.

In England, the Maharishi Mahesh yogi revealed a surprising line in meditation, a mantra based technique backed by some form of simplified Hindu philosophy. The technique was called T.M.—Transcendental Meditation. T.M. became a craze, a must for some! I remember the Maharishi. He giggled a lot and clutched flowers; he could easily get on your nerves. He held a seminar at the London Hilton hotel, followed by a weekend retreat in Bangor, North Wales. What a weekend! The Beatles and their wives with Mick Jagger and Marianne Faithfull accompanied the guru, together with his three hundred students. I was one of them.

There was a special train from London to Bangor. The fans and the Press were out in full strength. What a sight! Flowers, music and noise all over the place, a real circus. In the confusion, Cynthia Lennon was left behind on the platform!

While we were in Bangor, the Press broke the tragic news to the Beatles that Brian Epstein had died. It was an enormous shock, but the Maharishi's advice was 'Be happy.'

Massive media coverage guaranteed the guru a solid reputation. Many disciples followed him to his Indian retreat at Rishibesh—but there, the T.M. craze began to fade away. Life at the meditation camp was not to everyone's liking. It was far too hot. The food was far too spicy. There were flies all over the camp. The Beatles, Mia Farrow and Donovan booked for three months. Ringo and Maureen Starr left after a few days. Paul McCartney and Jane Asher were always moaning. John Lennon and George Harrison managed to stay on but obviously felt uneasy. The ambience was not right; in fact there was no ambience at all! Later, John Lennon said that the Maharishi's technique was 'coloured water.' In Bangor, Mick Jagger had already condemned the guru as 'a fraud.'

I too, left the camp, bored to death and disillusioned. I couldn't get out fast enough. I went to the Lebanon and to Egypt to study archaeology. I found Rameses far more interesting than the guru!

I also realised that the Maharishi was, above all, an avid businessman. I learned that he had formed a company called The Age of Enlightenment Co and was making rather a lot of money. Soon afterwards, John Lennon wrote the song Sexy Sadie, which included the line . . . 'who made a fool of everyone.' I wonder who was in his mind when he wrote those words?'

Karen Denny-Morley *lives in* Hampshire

Holidays

'For several summers during the 1960s our family drove down to the south of France. The start of our journey involved driving on to a 'plane (through the nose) at Southampton airport—my mother tells me that it was a Bristol freighter operated by Silver City Airways. It took three quarters of an hour to cross the channel and land in France and cost about £4 each way for the car and passengers. I suppose that is quite expensive compared to modern day prices. It was certainly an exciting start to the holiday.

We travelled down to St Tropez in our Ford Cortina, waving and honking the horn when we saw another British car. St Tropez was in its 'Brigitte Bardot' heyday and we were very lucky to have been able to experience the atmosphere of the town and the beaches at that time. We made friends with families from several nationalities. I remember one year when we left to return home a German family wished us 'Guten Fahrt.' We thought that this was very rude and had a fit of the giggles, much to my father's annoyance

Another year in the late '60s we holidayed in northern Spain, staying in Tossa de Mar. We stayed in one of the town's two hotels and we were the only English family there—back then it was not much more then a peaceful Spanish fishing village.'

The 'front loading' Silver City Bristol freighter

1960s Discoveries/Developments

- The Laser
- North Sea Oil
- The Hawker Harrier Vertical Take Off Aircraft
- The Police 'Identikit' Picture
- Dolby Noise Reduction System
- Concorde
- The Internet
- The Computer Mouse

- Liquid Crystal Displays
- Electronic Wristwatch
- Heart Pacemaker
- Nonstick Saucepan
- Felt-tip Pen
- Live Satellite TV
- Kevlar
- The Contraceptive Pill

1960s Firsts

- The first man (and woman) in Space
- The first man on the Moon
- Telstar, Britain's first Telecommunications Satellite
- Human Heart Transplant
- The Forth Road Bridge
- Legal Abortions
- Betting Shops
- Automatic Cash Dispenser
- Mothercare
- Colour Television
- Purpose built Supermarket
- One Day Cricket
- Club 18-30
- Cheese and Onion Crisps
- The world's first female Prime Minister
- The basis of Britain's Motorway Network
- The Dartford Tunnel
- Automated Public Telephone Boxes
- Embassy Cigarettes

- Coco Pops cereals
- Radio 1,2,3 and 4
- The Amex Card
- The Barclaycard
- Private Eye Magazine
- Which Magazine
- Amnesty International
- The Newspaper Colour Supplement
- The Boeing 747
- BBC2
- Pampers Disposable Nappies
- Instant Mash Potato
- Fairy Washing Up Liquid
- The Baby Buggy
- Starting Stalls on a British racecourse
- Plastic Carrier Bags, in Sweden
- Motorway Service Station
- The Parking Ticket
- The Breathalyser
- Top of the Pops was first broadcast

1960s Anniversaries

- 50th of the Crossword Puzzle (1913)
- 50th of the sinking of the Titanic (1912)
- 50th of the first Tank Battle (1916)
- 50th of the introduction of Escalators on the London Underground (1911)
- 50th of the first regular Air Service between London and Paris (1919)
- 50th of the distinctive wavy Coca Cola bottle (1916)
- 50th of the Moving Assembly Line for Ford car production (1914)
- 50th of the murder of Czar Nicholas II and his family (1918)
- 50th of the invention of Stainless Steel (1913)
- 50th of women gaining the vote in Britain (1918)
- 100th of the Internal Combustion Engine (1867)
- 100th of the Unification of Italy (1862)
- 100th of Sainsburys (1869)
- 100th of the Football Association (1863)
- 100th of the Suez Canal (1869)

The Future

In 1960, at the beginning of the decade, it would be:

- 10 years before the voting age in Britain was reduced to 18 years old
- 13 years before Britain joined the Common Market
- 16 years before Concorde made its maiden commercial flight
- 19 years before the appearance of 'Bar Code Scanning' in Britain's supermarkets
- 21 years before the launch of the Personal Computer
- 22 years before the appearance of 'Next' (formerly Hepworths)
- 41 years before The World Trade Centre in New York was destroyed by terrorists, killing almost 3,000 people

'I Remember When I Was Young Too'

The book that you have now finished reading (assuming that you didn't start at the end) and which hopefully you have enjoyed, is the first in a series of books relating to personal reminiscences. The follow up volume will include more personal memories similar to those that you have read but will also feature a number of intriguing stories that lie behind specific photos. The next volume will also include the decades of the 1970s and 1980s.

If you have any memories that you would like to share with the rest of us, particularly those that relate to treasured family photos, please contact the author in any one of the following ways:

Telephone: 02380 812753
E mail: rob@intheforest.freeserve.co.uk
Website: www.wheniwasyoung.co.uk
Post: 4 Barleycorn Walk, Cadnam, Hants, SO40 2LY

I look forward to reading your memories.

Rob Horlock

Acknowledgements and Thanks

The following individuals and organisations have generously contributed to this book. Copyright of individual's specific memories remain with that individual. I would like to express my sincere thanks to all of those people who took the time and trouble to help me with this project. If I have missed anyone, or 'misspetl' any names, please accept my apologies for the oversight.

1920s
Daisy Woods, Eileen Kelly, Emily Day, George Appelbe, Joan Barnes, Mary Cross, Nellie Lucas, Joan Packham, John Rouse, Doreen Stonebridge, Dot Pentelow, Eileen Oldridge, Bert Triggs, Leslie Solomon, Hellen Price, G Hubert-White, David Chapman, Jean Hooper, Vera Wildig, William Moxham, Les Kennard, John Rice

1930s
Denys Harvey, Edward Foxwell, Frank Salter, Fred Bishop, Jane Woods, Muriel Stirling, Nancy Hornsby, Barry Brown, Joe North, Gil Haines, John Lucas, Colin Holloway, George Green, Basil Marcuson, Gordon Barlow, Pearl Burton, Ruth Sheridan, Deana Whine, Jack Ramsey, Brenda Hall, Enid Pratt, Pierre Rinfret, Arthur Featherstone, George Appelbe, Eileen Kelly, Joyce Wood, Eric Pringle, Stephen Wright, Gwen Hatchard, John Garland, Aitken Lawrie, A E Thomas, Alastair Dunn, Dave Mitchell, Dorothy Hornby, Geoff Saunders, Jean Hooper, Edna Schofield

1940s
Mike Guy, Sheila Hansford, Ken Hansford, Gil Haines, John Dymock, Joan Barnes, Arthur Featherstone, Sue Anderson, Barbara Staton, Charles de Carteret, Mike Fountain, Mrs Self, Tony Reedman, Stan Shurey, Frank Mileham, Les Shergold, George Senior, John Parsons, Betty Longden, Don Hoskins, Gordon Carter, Jack Ramsey, F Spencer, Keith Levoir, Trudy Lazarus, Frank Waghorn, Norma Benney, Brenda Hall, Joan Donnelly, Derick Johnson, Eric Pringle, John Parsons, Heather Copeman, Jeff Jacobs, George Parish, Paul Brown, Aitken Lawrie, John Lucas, George Green, Alan Caudle, Brenda Allen, Horace Gamble, Dave Mitchell, Les King, Liz

Rosenberg, Peter Denzil Edwards, Eileen Wills, David Lowe, Roy Kenny, Joan Horlock, Christine Lloyd, Brian King, Barry Deighton, Rosemary Moore, Mrs Kennard

1950s

David Taylor, Hilary Nellist, Kathy Munson, Edward Young, Rhys Ab Elis, Stephanie Campion, R Healey, Brenda Hall, Malcolm Batt, Colin Foe, Ann Parker, John Dymock, Trudy Lazarus, John Phillips, Gill Gane, Jane Cook, Joan Stacey, Ron Hak, Mr Lucas, Rosemary Reavell, Aitken Lawrie, Brenda Allen, Pam Malekin, Valerie Cushing, Jim Heron, Linda Migro, Pete Jary, Chris Darlington, Ken Davis, Graham Whyte, Jules Evans, Len Smith, Barbara Rodgers,

1960s

Christine Moulie, James Knowles, Jimmy Haskins, Keith Warner, Mike McGall, Roger Montgomery, Jan Balsdon, Helene Lanska, Lyn Welsh, Brenda Hall, Bob Hollings, Steve Shields, Anne Hilton, Ray Oldam, Jane Cooke, Bobby Shaw, Rosemary Reavell, Joe Lunn, Aitken Lawrie, Pam Malekin, Karen Denny-Morley, Mr A Clarke, Liz Rosenberg, Pat Brookes, Mrs A Hardy, Jules Evans, Peter Wright, Nick Williams

Other content

The historical events which form the backdrop to the time covered in this book are obviously in the public domain. However, a number of organisations and individuals have helped me to add colour and context to the bare facts, as well as helping me to gather together the personal contributions. I am particularly grateful to these:

Nestle UK, The Bass Museum, Hampshire County Council, The Oldie, Mensa, The Jewish Chronicle, Choice, The Times Literary Supplement, Cadbury Schweppes, Writer's News, Washington Post, Coors Brewers, Speedscene, Scootering, Steam World, The West Australian, Subiaco Times, The Office for National Statistics, The Open University, Brighton Evening Argus, Perth DPS, Tenby Observer, Westmorland Gazette, 6PR Radio, Nottingham Evening Post, Guernsey Weekly Press, Malvern Gazette, The Swan, Dickie Riding, Yours, The Royal British Legion, Best of British, Revival, Irish World, Frank and Colin at Tandem Design, Judy Gamble, Liz Press, Western Daily Press, General Motors (Vauxhall), J Sainsbury, Judy Palaferro, The People's Friend, Southampton Library Service, The Ford Motor Company, Hampshire Record Office, National Federation of Women's Institutes, The Western Mail, Navy News,

Margaret Whitlock, The Brockenian, Charles Bird, Mrs E Salomon, Mrs E Miller, Margaret Price, June Clarkson, Lincolnshire Life, Sue Standing, South Wales Argus, The Royal Air Forces Association, Mr P Lawes, Keith Brown, Jean Mortimer, Madge Messenger, B Wardle, Iris Smith, Ken Le Lievre, Nick Oliver, Ian Banks, Tony Aylwin, Mary Calcraft, Bill Griffin, Norma Jacobs, Elizabeth O'Hara

Photographic images

The following organisations and individuals kindly gave me permission to use their photographic images. All copyright and trademarks remain with the original owners. I am very grateful to them all.

Cuban Matchbox cover—Thomas Gladysz—The Louise Brooks Society;

Fullers Sparta Crystal Set, Ferranti Nova Radio, Ekcots 10" Black and White TV—Steve Harris—www. vintageradio.co.uk;

Decorative Biscuit Tins, Actors and Actresses montage—Photos copyright Tracy Dolphin;

Cadbury's chocolates—all copyright and trade mark materials have been reproduced with the permission of Cadbury Ltd;

The Car Yard—Trevor and Jo Beer;

Sainsbury's Chelmsford branch, Sausage production and East Grinstead branch—all copyright and trade mark materials have been reproduced with the kind permission of J Sainsbury Ltd;

Golly brooch—www. gollycorner.co.uk;

To and from Europe—David Levine—www. travelbrochuregraphics.com;

Film Weekly—Karen Morley;

Multicultural Young Ladies, the Festival of Britain—Enid Pratt;

Hop Vines—Arthur Featherstone;

Isaiah Oldbury staff—Gordon Barlow;

Despatch Rider, Dennis Kelly—Eileen Kelly;

The Palace at Karpurthala, the Jordanian Army—Aitken Lawrie;

George and the Duke of Gloucester—George Parish;

Butlins—Frank Tomley;

The Caravan—Bobby Shaw;

Steam Engine—Ron Hak;

Ford Cortina—Stephen Braggs—www. fiftiesandsixties.co.uk;

Agostini—Ray Oldam;

Bristol aircraft—Wyn Denny-Morley;

The Worthington's Bottle Car, Brewery Posters and Prices, Bill Sticker and the R White's Delivery Lorry—all featured with the kind permission of Coors Brewers/Bass Museum. All copyright and trademarks remain the property of Coors Brewers Ltd with the exception of the R.White's trademark, which belongs to Britvic Soft Drinks Ltd

Last but not Least

A special thank you goes to the following people:

My wife Karen, who encouraged me and patiently allowed me to work on the book for hours on end.

My sister-in-law Sally, who gave up her time to proof-read my initial manuscript

Nick Howells who also proofread the manuscript and offered much sound advice and corrected some factual errors

Charlotte Brookes, my other proof reader, who also noticed some grammatical inconsistencies

Mandy Pink, Mandy's sister, Sally (again) and Liz Barnes who all helped to type this manuscript.

Charles King, who gave me invaluable advice when editing the manuscript

My sister Susan, who searched through the family photographic archives (several old cardboard boxes!) to provide a number of the images featured in this book